NBA Coaches Playbook

Techniques, Tactics, and Teaching Points

National Basketball Coaches Association

Giorgio Gandolfi, Editor

Human Kinetics

Library of Congress Cataloging-in-Publication Data

NBA coaches playbook : techniques, tactics, and teaching points /
National Basketball Coaches Association ; Giorgio Gandolfi, editor.
     p. cm.
  Includes index.
  ISBN-13: 978-0-7360-6355-5 (soft cover)
  ISBN-10: 0-7360-6355-2 (soft cover)
  1. Basketball--Shooting. 2. Basketball--Offense. 3. Basketball--Coaching.
I. Gandolfi, Giorgio. II. National Basketball Coaches Association.
  GV889.N342 2009
  796.323'2--dc22

                                    2008022558

ISBN-10: 0-7360-6355-2
ISBN-13: 978-0-7360-6355-5

Developmental Editor: Leigh Keylock
Assistant Editor: Laura Podeschi
Copyeditor: John Wentworth
Proofreader: Anne Rogers
Indexer: Betty Frizzéll
Graphic Designer: Fred Starbird
Graphic Artist: Tara Welsch
Cover Designer: Keith Blomberg
Photographer (cover): Jason Allen
Photographer (interior): Mino Boiocchi, unless otherwise noted
Photo Asset Manager: Laura Fitch
Photo Office Assistant: Jason Allen
Art Manager: Kelly Hendren
Associate Art Manager: Alan L. Wilborn
Illustrator: Lineworks, Inc.
Printer: Sheridan Books

Human Kinetics books are available at special discounts for bulk purchase. Special editions or book excerpts can also be created to specification. For details, contact the Special Sales Manager at Human Kinetics.

Printed in the United States of America   10 9 8 7 6 5 4 3 2 1

Human Kinetics
Web site: www.HumanKinetics.com

United States: Human Kinetics
P.O. Box 5076
Champaign, IL 61825-5076
800-747-4457
e-mail: humank@hkusa.com

Canada: Human Kinetics
475 Devonshire Road Unit 100
Windsor, ON N8Y 2L5
800-465-7301 (in Canada only)
e-mail: info@hkcanada.com

Europe: Human Kinetics
107 Bradford Road
Stanningley
Leeds LS28 6AT, United Kingdom
+44 (0) 113 255 5665
e-mail: hk@hkeurope.com

Australia: Human Kinetics
57A Price Avenue
Lower Mitcham, South Australia 5062
08 8372 0999
e-mail: info@hkaustralia.com

New Zealand: Human Kinetics
Division of Sports Distributors NZ Ltd.
P.O. Box 300 226 Albany
North Shore City
Auckland
0064 9 448 1207
e-mail: info@humankinetics.co.nz

NBA Coaches Playbook

Techniques, Tactics, and Teaching Points

Contents

National Basketball Association

David J. Stern
Commissioner

Welcome to the *NBA Coaches Playbook,* developed by the National Basketball Coaches Association (NBCA) in conjunction with the NBA. In the pages that follow, you will have access to the knowledge of many of the best and brightest basketball coaching minds in the world.

Our NBA coaches and those at the top level of the sport internationally are the great teachers and strategists of the game and are the key components in facilitating the extraordinary individual and team performances we witness throughout the season.

NBA Coaches Playbook is a treasure trove of basketball instruction and insight and is sure to be a frequently referenced manual on every coach's bookshelf.

Each person who contributed time and effort to this book deserves our gratitude. The NBCA should also be acknowledged for donating its share of the proceeds to NBA Coaches Care, a ticket purchase program for disadvantaged youth, operated in cooperation with the Boys and Girls Clubs of America.

I encourage you to take advantage of this great opportunity to tap into the experience and wisdom presented in such a clear and useful manner. I can assure you that at various points of the NBA seasons ahead, you will be glad you did.

David J. Stern
NBA Commissioner

Foreword

Basketball has been a big part of my life. Coaching the sport for 33 seasons at the high school, college, and professional levels; conducting clinics all over the world; and serving as a color analyst on TV broadcasts since 1982 have fueled my enthusiasm for the game through the years.

When I'm conducting a clinic or doing a telecast, I try to share that passion and appreciation of basketball. It's not simply a matter of one group of talented athletes playing a game against another. Rather, it's a wonderfully strategic game that requires exceptional discipline, competitiveness, skill, spatial awareness, quickness, tactical understanding, and strategic execution by one cohesive quintet of players to outperform the opposition.

When I present the game, whether to a group of coaches in a high school gym or on the air in front of millions of viewers, I never underestimate the knowledge of the audience. Instead, I try to challenge their basketball IQ with some of the knowledge I've gained about the game since first playing it as a youngster in Elizabeth, New Jersey.

People learn from being challenged. And that's exactly what will happen if you read and think about the material in *NBA Coaches Playbook*. This outstanding basketball resource contains a wealth of insight and instruction about the game that any serious coach, player, and even fan will find both fascinating and instructive.

I'm especially impressed that each of the coaches who contribute to this book presents his basketball knowledge on that part of the game for which he is considered the expert. I also find it extraordinary that the coaches, due to their diverse backgrounds and various ages, provide an insightful, well-rounded perspective on the game.

Those of you who coach or play the sport will find a treasure of technical and tactical teaching elements from the pros that will add immeasurably to your approach to the game. I encourage you to accept the challenge to learn the concepts and actions presented in the following pages so that you may improve your coaching and playing skills. This is a rare opportunity—the equivalent of 21 world-class basketball clinic sessions—to advance your understanding of the game and make you and your team more effective the next time you step on the court.

Hubie Brown
Two-time NBA Coach of the Year (1978, 2004)
Basketball Hall of Fame member (2005)

Acknowledgments

Even though I am from a soccer-mad country, I have always been fascinated by basketball in the United States, a remote paradise for a basketball fan located on the other side of the ocean. I started to correspond with several college coaches. These generous coaches included Bob Zuffelato, former head coach of Boston College and now with the Toronto Raptors as a scout; Chuck Daly, head coach at the University of Pennsylvania, who went on to win two consecutive NBA titles with the Detroit Pistons and was the (only) Dream Team coach, guiding the team to a gold medal–winning performance at the 1992 Olympic Games in Barcelona; and the mythical Lou Carnesecca, the Hall of Fame coach of St. John's University.

Soon after, I started to write about American basketball for Italian publications and I regularly made trips to the United States, where I covered many regular-season NBA games, NBA All-Star games, and the NBA Finals. From coast to coast, I met dozens of coaches and players over the years. In short, the U.S. and NBA arenas became my second home.

I also started to coach a local team in Cremona, Italy, my northern Italian city on the banks of the Po River, and I became more intimately involved with the beauty of this game. It is from my immersion in the details of the game's fundamentals and the defensive and offensive alignments that the *NBA Coaches Playbook* was born.

So many people have given of their time, experience, and wisdom in helping create this book that it is not possible to name all of them. I do wish to thank all those known and anonymous who have contributed ideas and information. I would like to extend a high five to Jack Ramsay, Hubie Brown, Paul Westhead, Del Harris, Jimmy Lynam, Lionel Hollins, Don Casey, Gary Vitti, Julius Erving, Pat Williams, Brian McIntyre, Terry Lyons, and Mike Bantom. These and many other supportive people introduced me to the fascinating world of the NBA and helped shape the ideas for the book.

I would also like to acknowledge Gerald Couzens, a former Princeton University player and writer, who opened his home to me in New York. We later collaborated on other books about NBA basketball that were published in the United States and Italy. *NBA Coaches Playbook* has been a long time in coming. Michael Goldberg, executive director of the National Basketball Coaches Association, believed in this project right from the start, shared his expertise and advice in many areas, and was my biggest fan throughout the entire process. High fives are also in order for the NBA head and assistant coaches, who wrote the chapters of this book. They carved time out of their busy days to answer questions and countless e-mails. I would also like to thank David Stern, whom I met before he became NBA commissioner and then the man behind the global success of the NBA.

In the book business, you can have a project in your mind, but you need to find people who believe and trust in your vision and help turn an idea into a book. In addition to Michael Goldberg, I must thank Ted Miller, vice president of special acquisitions at Human Kinetics, who enthusiastically supported my book concept. He is a great fan of the game and he shared many of his ideas and offered countless suggestions. I also thank Leigh Keylock, developmental editor, and Laura Podeschi, assistant editor at Human Kinetics, for their enthusiasm, hard work, and patience. Thanks also to Mino Boiocchi, the gifted photographer, and the players who posed for the photographs: Quad Lollis, J.R. Reynolds, Damien Ryan, Corey Albano, and Junior N'Guessan.

NBA Coaches Playbook is, above all, a resource book, and it couldn't have been written without the help of all the coaches, players, and executives from around the world whose thoughts are embodied in this book. I am indebted, too, to Patrick Baumann, FIBA secretary general, and Zoran Radovic, FIBA director of basketball development.

Many thanks to my team at the Cantelli Editore in Bologna: Filippo Mazzoni, Corrado De Belvis, Mirco Melloni, Gastone Marchesi, Donato Viglione, and Lisa Cavallini. They helped me over the years as I put the book together. My thanks also to three other basketball nuts like me: Achille Saulle, Dario Adami, and Michele Talamazzi. A special dedication and infinite thanks to Ornella, my very precious "assistant coach," the best possible.

About the NBCA

Founded in 1976, the **National Basketball Coaches Association** membership is a who's who in coaching: Every coach in the league is a member. Through the Celtics-Lakers rivalry in the 1980s, the 1992 Team USA Dream Team, and the unparalleled skill and marketing power of Michael Jordan through the 1990s, the National Basketball Association has become the world's most famous sports league over the past 25 years. Its coaches represent the top instructors and game technicians in the sport. They have mastered not only how to coach the world's top athletes but how to strategize and scheme against other world-class athletes and coaches as well.

ABOUT THE EDITOR

Giorgio Gandolfi is editor in chief of FIBA *Assist* magazine, the primary magazine of the International Basketball Federation (FIBA). Gandolfi has served as a European consultant for the NBCA and has been a member of the Italian Basketball Federation Coaches Association since 1974. He has authored one book with the NBCA (*NBA Coaches Handbook*) and two editions of the book with the National Basketball Players Association (*Hoops: The Official National Basketball Players Association Guide to Playing Basketball*).

About the Contributors

Kareem Abdul-Jabbar

Kareem Abdul-Jabbar is a special assistant coach working with post players for the Los Angeles Lakers. Abdul-Jabbar started his coaching career as a volunteer assistant for Alchesay High School on the Apache Indian Reservation in Whiteriver, Arizona. He later became an assistant coach for the Los Angeles Clippers and head coach of the Oklahoma Storm of the United States Basketball League. Before coaching, Abdul-Jabbar established himself as one of the best college and professional basketball players of all time. Known as Lew Alcindor before his conversion to Islam in 1971, he claimed NCAA titles and first team All-American honors in each of his three college seasons at UCLA. In the NBA for 20 years with the Milwaukee Bucks and Los Angeles Lakers, he won six Most Valuable Player awards and six NBA titles and set several statistical records. Abdul-Jabbar was elected to the Naismith Basketball Hall of Fame in 1995.

John Bach

John Bach is one of the most revered assistant coaches ever to work in the NBA. Bach attained his first head coaching job at the age of 26 at his alma mater, Fordham University, where he remained for 18 years. He went on to Penn State University for 10 seasons and was an assistant coach of the U.S. basketball team that competed in the 1972 Olympics. Bach started his NBA career as an assistant coach for Golden State, then became the Warriors' head coach in 1983. His first of two assistant coaching stints with the Chicago Bulls began in 1986, and he won three NBA titles during his 12 seasons as architect of the Bulls' defensive attack. Bach also served as an assistant coach for the Charlotte Hornets, Detroit Pistons, and Washington Wizards.

Pete Carril

Steve Yeater/NBAE/Getty Images

Pete Carril was a legendary coach in the college ranks who moved on to the NBA later in his career. Carril started his coaching career with a total of 12 seasons at the high school level in Pennsylvania, then became head coach at Lehigh University for one season until 1967, when he accepted the job at Princeton University. His Ivy League team would win two-thirds of its games for the next 30 years running the renowned Princeton offense, based on sound passing and screening fundamentals and backdoor cuts. Inducted into the Naismith Basketball Hall of Fame in 1997, Carril served as an assistant coach for the Sacramento Kings for nine seasons and as a volunteer assistant with the Washington Wizards before retiring in 2007.

Rich Dalatri

Steve Freeman/NBAE/Getty Images

Rich Dalatri is an assistant coach responsible for strength, conditioning, and flexibility programs for the New Jersey Nets. Dalatri began this, his second, stint with the Nets in 1997-98, having served in a similar capacity from 1987 to 1992 when he became the first full-time strength and conditioning coach in the NBA. In addition to his duties with the Nets, Dalatri has spent extensive time in the off-season speaking and conducting basketball camps and basketball clinics throughout Europe. He has also worked for the Cleveland Cavaliers, in the Italian Professional League, and with the Italian men's national team.

Mike D'Antoni

Barry Gossage/NBAE/Getty Images

Mike D'Antoni is head coach of the New York Knicks and has more than 30 years of professional coaching and playing experience in the NBA and in Europe. D'Antoni started his coaching career in Italy as head coach of Phillips Milan, where he won the Korac Cup and was twice voted Coach of the Year. He went on to coach Benetton Treviso, where he won one Italian title, one Cup of Italy, and one Cup of Euro. In 1997 he was hired by the Denver Nuggets, for whom he became director of player personnel and then head coach. After a stint as assistant coach for the Portland Trail Blazers and a return to Treviso, where he won another Italian title, D'Antoni became head coach of the Phoenix Suns and was named NBA Coach of the Year in 2005.

Mike Dunleavy

Noah Graham/NBAE/Getty Images

Mike Dunleavy is currently head coach of the Los Angeles Clippers and is among the top nine NBA coaches of all time in number of wins. Dunleavy got into coaching after an 11-year career as an NBA player, first as an assistant with the Milwaukee Bucks in 1986. His first head coaching opportunity came with the Los Angeles Lakers in 1990-91, and he led them to the NBA Finals. After one more season with the Lakers, he returned to Milwaukee as the Bucks' vice president of basketball operations and head coach. In 1997, Dunleavy moved to Portland, and while with the Trail Blazers he was named NBA Coach of the Year (1999). He became the head coach of the Los Angeles Clippers in 2001 and guided the club to its best season ever in 2005-6.

Steve Babineau/NBAE/Getty Images

Kevin Eastman

Kevin Eastman is an assistant coach in charge of player development for the Boston Celtics. Eastman amassed more than 20 years of coaching experience at the collegiate level, including five seasons (1994-99) as head coach at Washington State University. He also was head coach at the University of North Carolina at Wilmington and Belmont Abbey College and an assistant at the University of Tulsa, Virginia Commonwealth University, Colorado State University, and the University of Richmond, his alma mater. Eastman works Nike basketball camps during summers and has owned and operated Kevin Eastman Basketball Camps since 1999.

Jeffrey Bottari/NBAE/Getty Images

Jim Eyen

A veteran NBA assistant coach, Jim Eyen currently works for the Los Angeles Clippers under Mike Dunleavy. Eyen began his career as a Clippers assistant in 1988, then served in the same role for the Los Angeles Lakers for three seasons. From there he moved on to assistant coaching jobs in Milwaukee and Portland before returning to the Clippers in 2003, when Dunleavy asked him to become lead assistant. Before joining the Clippers in 1988, Eyen served as an assistant at his alma mater, the University of California at Santa Barbara, after joining the coaching ranks as an assistant at Santa Barbara City College in 1979.

NBAE/Getty Images

Lawrence Frank

Lawrence Frank was named head coach of the New Jersey Nets in 2004 after having spent three seasons with the club as an assistant. Frank began his NBA coaching career in record-setting style by going 13-0, which set a new NBA mark for the most consecutive wins by a first-time head coach. Before joining the Nets, he was an assistant coach for the Vancouver Grizzlies. Frank's basketball career started at Indiana University, where he spent four seasons as a manager for the Hoosiers under head coach Bob Knight. He then got assistant coaching jobs at Marquette University and the University of Tennessee before beginning his NBA coaching career.

Joe Murphy/NBAE/Getty Images

Mike Fratello

Mike Fratello most recently served as head coach of the Memphis Grizzlies. Fratello's NBA coaching career started with the Atlanta Hawks, for whom he served as an assistant to Hubie Brown before handling the head coaching reins for eight seasons, one of which he was named NBA Coach of the Year (1986). His career continued with the Cleveland Cavaliers, when he guided the team for six seasons. Fratello's coaching career started at Hackensack (New Jersey) High School, and he advanced to college jobs at the University of Rhode Island, James Madison University, and Villanova University before his entry into the NBA.

Barry Gossage/NBAE/Getty Images

Alvin Gentry

Alvin Gentry has been coaching in the NBA for more than 20 years, most recently with the Phoenix Suns. Gentry began coaching in 1977 as a graduate assistant at the University of Colorado, then moved on to a full-time assistant coaching job at Baylor before returning to Colorado as an assistant coach for four more seasons. He won an NCAA Championship in 1988 as a University of Kansas assistant coach under Larry Brown, and he remained Brown's assistant when Brown took the head coaching position with the San Antonio Spurs. Gentry went on to take three NBA head coaching jobs with Miami, Detroit, and the Los Angeles Clippers before becoming an assistant with New Orleans and Phoenix.

Glenn James/NBAE/Getty Images

Del Harris

Del Harris is now an assistant coach for the Chicago Bulls after nearly 50 years in coaching. Harris landed his first NBA coaching job as assistant in 1976 with Houston, where he became head coach three years later and led the Rockets to the NBA Finals in 1981. He then moved on to Milwaukee, first as an assistant coach, and then as the Bucks' head coach for four seasons. Harris later was head coach of the Los Angeles Lakers for five years and assistant coach with the Dallas Mavericks for seven seasons. Having coached at every level of basketball competition and obtained extensive international coaching experience, Harris has shared his knowledge in instructional books, focusing mostly on defensive play.

Joe Murphy/NBAE/Getty Images

Lionel Hollins

Lionel Hollins is an assistant coach for the Milwaukee Bucks. Before joining the Bucks, Hollins was an assistant coach for the Vancouver Grizzlies, Phoenix Suns, and Memphis Grizzlies, for whom he also served as interim head coach during the 2004-5 season. He started his coaching career at his alma mater, Arizona State University, where he served as assistant coach for two seasons. As a player, Hollins was drafted by Portland and played an integral role in the Trail Blazers' winning the 1977 NBA Championship. Known for his pesky defense, he was selected for the league's All-Defensive Team three times.

Norm Hall/NBAE/Getty Images

Marc Iavaroni

Marc Iavaroni became head coach of the Memphis Grizzlies in 2007. Previously he was an assistant coach for the Phoenix Suns, Miami Heat, and Cleveland Cavaliers. With the Heat, Iavaroni was also directly responsible for player development. With the Cavaliers, he focused on developing post players and credits much of his teaching expertise in that area to his 20-year association as a student and instructor under Hall of Fame coach Pete Newell. Iavaroni began coaching as a graduate assistant at his alma mater, the University of Virginia, after a seven-year NBA playing career. Iavaroni was an assistant coach at Bowling Green State University from 1992 to 1994.

Andrew D. Bernstein/NBAE/Getty Images

Phil Jackson

Phil Jackson is the head coach of the Los Angeles Lakers. Before joining the Lakers in 1999, Jackson was head coach of the Chicago Bulls. His Lakers and Bulls have won a total of nine NBA championships, tying him with former Boston Celtics coach Red Auerbach for the most titles ever won by a coach in the league. Jackson started his coaching career with five seasons as head coach of the Albany Patroons, also leading that club to a Continental Basketball Association title. Jackson then landed a job as an assistant coach with the Chicago Bulls and became head coach in 1989. Before coaching, Jackson played in the NBA for 13 years, mainly under coach Red Holzman with the New York Knicks during their championship years of the early 1970s. As a student at the University of North Dakota, he was mentored by future NBA coach Bill Fitch.

Glenn James/NBAE/Getty Images

Avery Johnson

Avery Johnson was head coach of the Dallas Mavericks. Johnson led the club to an impressive .735 regular-season winning percentage and to the playoffs four consecutive years. He was named NBA Coach of the Year in 2005-6, and guided Dallas to a franchise-best 67 wins the following season. Johnson began his coaching career as a Mavericks assistant in 2004 after a successful 16-year NBA playing career in which he played for several clubs, including the 1999 NBA champion San Antonio Spurs. Known as a consummate court general, Johnson amassed nearly 6,000 assists during his pro career and was the nation's top assist man as a college senior, averaging more than 13 a game at Southern University.

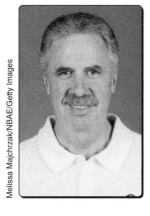

Melissa Majchrzak/NBAE/Getty Images

Phil Johnson

Phil Johnson is an assistant coach with the Utah Jazz and has been head coach Jerry Sloan's right-hand man for two decades. Johnson's expertise is widely known throughout the NBA, as reflected in the league general managers' voting him the NBA's top assistant before the 2004-5 season. Johnson started his coaching career as a graduate assistant for Dick Motta at Utah State University and became the school's head coach four years later. By the age of 27, Johnson had garnered an NBA head coaching position with the Kansas City Kings, and the following season he was named NBA Coach of the Year. In addition to the Jazz, Johnson also held assistant coaching positions with the Chicago Bulls and Sacramento Kings.

Mitchell Layton/NBAE/Getty Images

Eddie Jordan

Eddie Jordan is head coach of the Washington Wizards, a position he's held in his hometown since 2003. Jordan's previous NBA head coaching experience came in 1997 and 1998 with the Sacramento Kings, a team for which he had served as assistant coach the previous five years. Before joining the Wizards, Jordan was the lead assistant coach for the New Jersey Nets. After concluding his seven-year NBA playing career, Jordan entered coaching as a volunteer assistant at his alma mater, Rutgers University. He followed coach Tom Young to Old Dominion University, where he served as a part-time assistant, and later moved on to assistant coaching jobs at Boston College and back at Rutgers before moving on to the NBA.

Michael Martin/NBAE/Getty Images

George Karl

George Karl is head coach of the Denver Nuggets. Through 19 seasons, Karl's teams have won 834 games, and he was the sixth-fastest coach in NBA history to win 700 games. He started his career as the assistant coach of the then-ABA-affiliated San Antonio Spurs before attaining his first head coaching position with the Montana Golden Nuggets of the Continental Basketball Association in 1980. He also coached the CBA's Albany Patroons and Real Madrid in Spain. Karl then went on to become head coach of the Cleveland Cavaliers, Golden State Warriors, Seattle Supersonics, and Milwaukee Bucks before taking his present position with the Nuggets in 2005.

Courtesy of Cantelli Editore

Ruben Magnano

Ruben Magnano is presently head coach of Atenas of Cordoba, a club in Argentina's First Division professional league with whom he started his coaching career in 1992. Magnano led Atenas of Cordoba to three First Division titles, three South American Championships, and a Pan American title. Magnano became head coach of the Argentina men's national team in 2000 and made his mark in international coaching circles by leading that squad to a silver medal at the 2003 FIBA World Championships and the gold medal at the 2004 Olympic Games. He has also served as head coach of Varese, a First Division Italian League team, and Seville, a Spanish First Division professional team.

Fernando Medina/NBAE/Getty Images

Brendan Malone

Brendan Malone is an assistant coach with the Orlando Magic. Malone started his coaching career at the famous Power Memorial High School of New York City. At the collegiate level, he served as an assistant coach at Fordham University, Yale University, and Syracuse University before taking the head coaching position at the University of Rhode Island. He began his NBA career as an assistant coach for the New York Knicks. Malone then joined Chuck Daly's staff with Detroit, where his Pistons teams won two back-to-back NBA titles. After a stint as head coach of the Toronto Raptors, Malone moved on to assistant coaching jobs with the Knicks, Pacers, and Cavaliers before his current job with the Magic.

Garrett Ellwood/NBAE/Getty Images

Doug Moe

Doug Moe is an assistant coach for the Denver Nuggets and is the franchise's all-time winningest head coach. Moe began his coaching career with the Nuggets in 1974 as an assistant to Larry Brown when the club was a member of the American Basketball Association. He served as head coach of the San Antonio Spurs for four seasons, then returned to Denver in 1980 as the Nuggets' head coach. Playing his trademark up-tempo style, Moe's Nuggets teams qualified for the playoffs nine straight seasons, and he was named NBA Coach of the Year in 1988. His last head coaching position was with the Philadelphia 76ers in the 1992-93 season.

Jim O'Brien

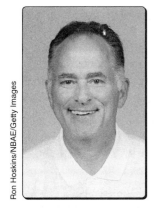

Ron Hoskins/NBAE/Getty Images

Jim O'Brien, currently head coach of the Indiana Pacers, has more than 30 years of coaching experience at the collegiate and professional levels. O'Brien entered the pro ranks as Rick Pitino's assistant with the Boston Celtics in 1997, after serving as Pitino's associate head coach at the University of Kentucky. He went on to become head coach with both the Celtics and the Philadelphia 76ers before taking the job with the Pacers. O'Brien's extensive college experience includes head coaching positions at the University of Dayton and Wheeling Jesuit College and assistant coaching posts at the University of Oregon, Saint Joseph's University, University of Maryland, and Pembroke State College.

Stan Van Gundy

Fernando Medina/NBAE/Getty Images

Stan Van Gundy is head coach of the Orlando Magic. Van Gundy's previous NBA experience had been with the Miami Heat, first as an assistant and associate head coach, then as head coach from 2003 to 2005. He also coached at the college level as a head coach at Castleton State College and the University of Massachusetts at Lowell, an assistant and head coach at the University of Wisconsin, and an assistant coach at the University of Vermont, Canisius College, and Fordham University. Basketball coaching is in the Van Gundy bloodline: His father, Bill, was a successful college coach, and Jeff Van Gundy, Stan's younger brother, was head coach of the Houston Rockets and New York Knicks.

Scott Skiles

Brian Kersey/NBAE/Getty Images

Scott Skiles was named head coach of the Milwaukee Bucks in 2008 after nine seasons of NBA head coaching experience. Skiles started his coaching career in Greece as a head coach of the PAOK Athens. He then was hired by the Phoenix Suns as an assistant coach under Danny Ainge. After two seasons, he was named the Suns' head coach and worked the sidelines in Phoenix until 2001. Skiles became the Chicago Bulls' head coach in 2003; he immediately infused the club with his trademark aggressiveness and tenacity and led the team to the second-best turnaround in the franchise's history by winning 24 more games than in the previous season.

Tex Winter

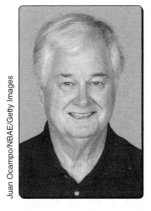

Juan Ocampo/NBAE/Getty Images

Tex Winter coached for nearly 60 years and is perhaps best known for teaching the triangle offense, a concept he learned in the 1940s from Sam Barry, his coach at the University of Southern California. From USC, he started his coaching career as an assistant at Kansas State University. After two years as head coach at Marquette University, he returned to Kansas State as head coach for the next 15 years. Subsequent college head coaching positions included the University of Washington, Northwestern University, and Long Beach State University. Winter's entry into the NBA came in 1972 as head coach of the Houston Rockets for two seasons. In 1985 he became assistant coach of the Chicago Bulls and won six NBA titles with the club. He then moved on with head coach Phil Jackson to win three more championships with the Los Angeles Lakers.

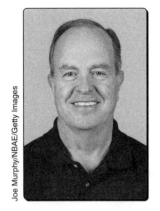

Joe Murphy/NBAE/Getty Images

Hal Wissel

Hal Wissel has coached at the college and professional level for the past five decades and remains one of the most respected shooting instructors in the sport. Wissel was an NBA assistant coach for the Atlanta Hawks, Golden State Warriors, Memphis Grizzlies, and New Jersey Nets. He also was head coach at several colleges, including the University of North Carolina at Charlotte, Springfield College, Fordham University, Lafayette College, Trenton State University (now the College of New Jersey), and University of Southern Florida, where he won the Division II National Championship. In addition to coaching, Wissel founded Basketball World Inc., an instructional venture featuring camps, clinics, videos, and books.

Brian Babineau/NBAE/Getty Images

Dave Wohl

Dave Wohl is now an assistant general manager for the Boston Celtics after serving the club as an assistant coach. Wohl started his NBA coaching career as an assistant coach under coach Pat Riley with the Los Angeles Lakers following a seven-year playing career in the league. He worked with the Lakers in two different stints, from 1982 through the NBA title-winning 1985 season, and also the second part of the 1998-99 season. In between, he was head coach of the New Jersey Nets. In addition, Wohl has been an assistant coach for the Sacramento Kings and the Los Angeles Clippers, an assistant coach and scout for the Miami Heat, and an assistant coach for the Orlando Magic.

Key to Diagrams

⟹	Player movement	○①②③④⑤	Offensive player
- - - -▶	Pass	X X₁X₂X₃X₄X₅	Defensive player
++++++▶	Shot	①	Offensive player with ball
∿∿▶	Dribble	©	Coach
————⊣	Screen	®	Rebounder
‖	Hand-off		

Note to Readers: The court diagram used throughout this book excludes many court markings so that the presentation of players' movements and passes will be as clear as possible. The NBA three-point line was included to serve as a distance reference point around the basket's perimeter. We hope this streamlined approach in no way hinders applications you wish to make to the international, college, or high school level courts.

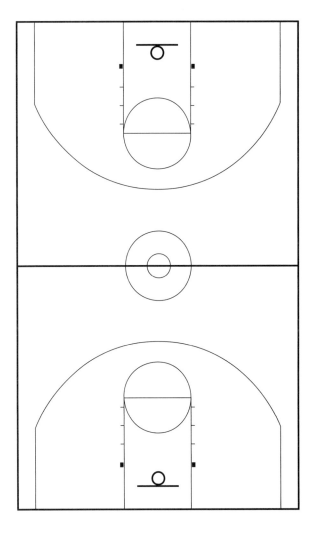

PART I

Individual Offense

chapter 1

Shooting Techniques

Hal Wissel

Shooting is the most important skill in basketball. Passing, dribbling, rebounding, and defense can provide high-percentage shot opportunities, but those shots must be converted. In rare cases, players with relatively weak shooting proficiency but exceptional athletic talent or a unique set of skills can contribute tremendously to their team in other facets of the game. All other players must develop an accurate and consistent shot. A good shooter forces the defender to cover him tightly, which opens up the floor for the offense to operate.

A key principle of team offense is spacing. Proper spacing keeps one defender from guarding one opponent and helping out on others. However, good spacing will not matter if defenders can sag off inconsistent outside shooters and into passing and driving lanes. To be successful against zones as well as man-to-man defenses, a team must have players who can consistently make the outside shot. Offensive players must maintain proper spacing so that the advantages gained by accurate shooting aren't nullified. In short, accurate shooting forces defenders to respect the offense and guard closely, which makes the defense much easier to attack.

A pure shooter has a smooth, free-flowing motion and a soft touch. Some people think pure shooters are born that way, but this is a misconception. Great shooters are made, not born. These players have shots so smooth that they might look naturally gifted, but

in fact their "gifts" are a result of practice and a proper mind-set. The thoughts of a pure shooter, such as former Boston Celtic Larry Bird, current Celtic Ray Allen, New Orleans Hornet Peja Stojakovic, or Phoenix Sun two-time MVP Steve Nash, are not on the mechanics of the shot but rather on the position and movement of teammates and defenders. A pure shooter considers faking the shot, delivering a pass, driving for the basket, or reversing direction to pull the ball out and reset the offense. For Nash and other great NBA shooters, the skill is automatic. Like other talented athletes, pure shooters perform their skills to the maximum level without conscious thought. Each was a beginner at one time, however, and each developed into a pure shooter through dedicated practice. A commitment to practice leads to improved shooting skill, which in turn leads to enhanced confidence. Shooting confidence leads to success in games and renews commitment to practicing. This is a familiar cycle of success to those who have achieved greatness.

Shooting is a skill that can be practiced alone. Once a player understands correct mechanics applied to his own shot, all he needs is a ball, a basket, and an eagerness to improve. It is helpful, however, for a player to also practice shooting under game conditions, including the pressure situations that occur late in games. A partner can help provide defensive pressure.

CONFIDENCE

Good shooting takes much more than good mechanics. Basketball is as much mental as it is physical. Developing the mental aspect is a key to shooting and performing other fundamentals. A shooter should have confidence in his ability to make the shot—every time. Confident shooters control their thoughts, feelings, and shooting skills.

To help confidence, it is important to know that the basket is big. The basket is so big that over three and a half balls can fit in the rim. This surprises most players. Realizing that the basket is so big can give a psychological boost to a player. When three balls are placed side by side over the rim, there is enough space to fit and turn your hand between each ball (figure 1.1).

It also helps confidence to keep the follow through straight up until the ball reaches the rim. Not only is this mechanically correct, but more importantly, a player will look and act like a shooter. Confidence comes from consistent success achieved through positive

feedback (results) in practice repetitions and game performance. Some players overestimate their shooting skills and range, take low-percentage shots, and eventually lose confidence in their shooting abilities. A big mistake many players make when they've missed some shots is to start thinking too much. A sure sign that a player is thinking too much is the ball being shot with a slower rhythm.

Good shooters stay confident even when they hit a cold streak and miss a few shots. After a missed shot, they don't get down; instead, they mentally correct the miss and visualize a good shot. Positive affirmation statements (such as "I'm a shooter!" "All net!" or "Count it!") can promote confident thoughts about a shot. High-percentage shooters who happen to be "off" in the first half of a contest, or even over a few games, should continually remind themselves of past success.

Players who have confidence trust their ability and don't let a shooting slump affect their confidence. The direct correlation between shooting confidence and shooting success is a consistent factor in great shooters.

RHYTHM

Basketball skills should be performed in a smooth, free-flowing, rhythmic manner, and this is especially true in shooting. Shooting involves synchronizing the extension of the legs, back, shoulders, and shooting elbow and the flexion of the wrist and fingers. Shots taken with an evenly paced lifting motion have a greater chance of going through the hoop. The initial force and rhythm for the shot comes from the down-and-up motion of the legs. We'll look at each of these movements in detail in the mechanics section, but let's summarize them here.

- Start with knees slightly flexed. Bend the knees and then fully extend them in a down-and-up motion. The legs and

Photo courtesy of Paul Wissel

Figure 1.1 Over three and one half balls fit in the rim.

shooting arm should move together—as the legs go up, the arm goes up.

- As the legs reach full extension, the back, shoulders, and shooting arm extend in a smooth and continuous upward direction. Keep the ball high with the shooting hand facing the rim. Use the down-and-up motion of the legs rather than lower the ball for rhythm. Keeping the ball high fosters a quick release and provides less chance for error. Lowering the ball tends to move the shooting hand off center, usually causing side rotation as the ball is raised for the shot. The longer the stroke, the more chance for error and the slower the release. If you like to lower the ball for rhythm, focus on keeping the shooting hand on top of the ball.

- As the arm goes up, the ball is tipped back from the balance (nonshooting) hand to the shooting hand. A good guide is to tip the ball back only until a wrinkle appears in the skin between the wrist and forearm.

- This angle provides a quick release and consistent follow-through. Direct the shooting arm, wrist, and fingers straight toward the basket at a 45- to 60-degree angle, extending the arm completely at the elbow.

- The final force and control of the shot comes from flexing the wrist and fingers forward toward the target. Release the ball off the index finger with soft fingertip touch to impart backspin on the ball and soften the shot. Keep the balance hand on the ball until the point of release.

The amount of force imparted on the ball depends on the range of the shot. For short distances, the arm, wrist, and fingers provide most of the force. Long-range outside shots require more force from the legs, back, and shoulder. A smooth rhythm and complete follow-through also improve long-range shooting.

Bill Baptist/NBAE/Getty Images Sport

Larry "The Legend" Bird shot with great confidence, based on countless hours of practice and a resulting high field-goal percentage.

An inside jump shot involves jumping and then shooting the ball at the top of the jump with the arm, wrist, and fingers applying most of the force. For an outside jump shot, lift the ball simultaneously with the upward extension of the legs, back, and shoulder.

MECHANICS

Mechanics are important, but you want to have good mechanics without being mechanical. Shots should be smooth and rhythmic. As previously mentioned, all parts of the shot should flow in a sequential rhythm (figure 1.2). To develop a consistently smooth and accurate shot, focus on only one or two mechanics at a time.

Sight

Eyes focus on the basket, aiming just over the front of the rim for all shots but bank shots. Bank shots should be taken at a 45-degree angle to the backboard. A 45-degree angle falls within the distance between the box and the middle hashmark on the lane line. The distance for the bank angle—called the 45-degree funnel—widens as the shooter moves farther from the hoop. When shooting a bank shot, aim for the top near corner of the box on the backboard.

See the target as early as possible and maintain focus on the target until the ball reaches the goal. Eyes should never follow the flight of the ball or the defender's hand. Concentrating on the target helps eliminate distractions, such as shouting, towel waving, an opponent's hand, or even a hard foul.

Figure 1.2 Shooting mechanics: *(a)* The ball is set high above the shoulder and between the ear and shoulder with the shooting hand facing the rim. Eyes are focused on the target just over the front of the rim. The knees are slightly flexed. Start the shot by bending the knees and then fully extending them in a down-and-up motion for rhythm and range. *(b)* The legs and shooting arm move together—as the legs go up, the arm goes up. As the legs reach full extension, the back, shoulders, and shooting arm fully extend in a smooth and continuous upward direction. The wrist and fingers flex forward toward the target as the ball is released off the index finger.

Balance

Good balance leads to power and rhythmic control of the shot. Your base, or foot position, is the foundation of balance, and keeping the head over the feet (base) allows you to maintain balance.

- Spread feet comfortably about shoulder width; point toes straight ahead; and align toes, knees, hips, and shoulders straight to the basket.
- Keep foot on the shooting-hand side (right foot for a right-handed shot) forward. Align the toe of the back foot with the heel of the shooting-side foot (toe-to-heel relation).
- Flex legs at the knees to provide power for the shot. Beginning and fatigued players often fail to flex their knees; then to compensate for the lack of power from their legs, they throw the ball from behind the head or shove the ball from the hip, either of which produces errors.
- Position the head over the waist and feet and slightly forward to control balance.
- Keep shoulders relaxed and inclined toward the basket.

Leg Motion

To help with rhythm and range, use a down-and-up action with the legs rather than lower the ball or step into the shot.

- Start with the knees slightly flexed.
- Bend the knees and then fully extend them in a down-and-up motion.
- Saying the key words "down and up" from the start of the shot to the release of the ball will trigger the down-and-up action of the legs that provides rhythm and force for the shot.
- The legs and shooting arm should move together. As the legs go up, the shooting arm goes up. As the legs reach

full extension, the back, shoulders, and shooting arm extend in a smooth and continuous direction forward and upward toward the target.

Use the down-and-up motion of the legs for rhythm rather than lowering the ball. Keeping the ball high fosters a quick release and offers less chance for error. Stepping into the shot might increase range, but the shot then becomes a two-count shot. Using the down-and-up method allows a shot to occur in one motion, or one count. When shooting off the catch, the "down" comes just before the catch, and the shot goes up as the legs go up, providing for a quicker release.

Hand Position

Hand position is the most misunderstood part of shooting technique. The shooting hand should be directly behind the ball; it should be kept high and facing the rim. The nonshooting hand should be under the ball for balance. Taken together, this position is called the block and tuck. The shooting hand is left free to shoot the ball rather than having to balance *and* shoot the ball.

- Place hands fairly close together with both hands relaxed and fingers spread comfortably. The thumb of the shooting hand is relaxed and not spread wide (to avoid tension in the hand and forearm). A relaxed hand position forms a natural cup; the ball contacts the pads of the fingers, not the palm.
- Place the nonshooting hand slightly under the ball. The weight of the ball balances on at least two fingers (ring finger and little finger). The arm of the balance hand is in a comfortable position with the elbow pointing slightly back and to the side.
- Place the shooting hand directly behind the ball with the index finger directly at its midpoint. The ball is released off the index finger. For a free throw, players have time to align the index

finger with the valve or other marking at the midpoint of the ball. Developing fingertip control and touch leads to a soft, accurate shot.

- Hold the ball comfortably in front of and above the shooting-side shoulder between the ear and shoulder.

Elbow-In Alignment

Keep the shooting elbow in. When the shooting elbow is in, the ball is aligned with the basket. Some players lack the flexibility to place the shooting hand behind the ball and facing front while keeping the elbow in. If this is the case, one must first position the shooting hand behind the ball and facing front, and then move the elbow in as far as flexibility allows.

Follow-Through

Consistently accurate shooters maintain good mechanics even when the ball is on its way to the hoop.

- After releasing the ball off the index finger, keep the shooting arm up and fully extended with the index finger pointing straight to the target.
- The palm of the shooting hand faces slightly down; the palm of the balance hand faces slightly up.
- Keep the eyes on the target.
- Hold the arm up in a complete follow-through position until the ball reaches the basket; then react to rebound or get into defensive position.

KEY WORDS

As important as confidence and mechanics are, the two pay off in shooting only when combined. Accurate shooting requires the meshing of positive thinking with correct technique. One way to help mesh the two is through positive self-talk. Such affirmations also speed the improvement of your shot.

Southpaw Michael Redd shows good shooting form with eyes focused on the target just over the front of the rim, balance hand slightly under the ball, and shooting hand facing the target on his jump shot against defensive pressure.

Positive self-talk uses key words (called cue or trigger words) to enhance performance. Players should select words that tie directly to correct mechanics, rhythm, and confident thinking about the shot. Key words should be concise (preferably one syllable) and personalized. Here are some common examples:

- High!—to start the shot high and to prevent lowering the ball
- Straight!—to make shooting hand go straight to the basket and to keep from turning the wrist
- Front!—to key the position of the shooting hand facing the rim
- Point!—to key the correct release of the ball off the index finger
- Up!—to key a high arc
- Through!—to key any part of the follow-through, including shoulders, arm, wrist, and finger
- Head in!—to key the follow-through of head and shoulders toward the basket and prevent leaning back or stepping back
- Legs!—to key the use of the legs
- Down and up!—to key the down-and-up action of the legs for rhythm and range

Players should identify a personal trigger they associate with correct mechanics. They will probably need to practice with various triggers until they find one that works for them.

Saying personalized key words in an even rhythm establishes the rhythm of the shot and promotes mechanics and confidence. Effective players devote time to mental practice. Relaxing and speaking the key words while visualizing the rhythm of the shot and seeing the ball go in the basket can really help execution on the court.

Some players also use "anchor" words to reinforce the visualization of a successful shot. Examples of anchor words are "Through!" "In!" "Yes!" "Net!" "Swish!" "Whoosh!" and "Face!" These words also help prevent the "paralysis by analysis" that occurs when players overthink their shots. A

sure sign of overthinking is a slow or uneven shooting rhythm.

A cue or trigger word combined with an anchor word is most effective. At first, players might try a three-word (each of them one syllable) string in rhythm, starting at the shooting motion and ending at the release of the ball off the index finger. For example, if "legs" and "through" are the trigger words and "yes" is the anchor word, the player would say in rhythm of the shot, "Legs–through–yes!" It works best to speak the words aloud.

Trigger words and anchor words are actual thoughts. Saying them reduces conscious thought and promotes automatic execution of the shot. The trigger word cues proper mechanics; the anchor word reinforces success. As shooting improves, a single trigger word might be enough. In other cases, a single anchor word is all a player needs to keep the positive thoughts—and results—coming.

REACTION OF BALL ON RIM

Learn to shoot correctly and then practice intelligently each day in order to develop an understanding of your shot. You can always benefit from having a coach watch you shoot and offer feedback, but most practice occurs when a coach is not around. Therefore, you need to get feedback in other ways. Three good sources of performance feedback are observing the reaction of the shot on the rim, internally feeling the shot, and watching shooting form on video.

Analyzing a shot's reaction on the rim can reinforce successful execution or reveal shooting errors and their possible causes. Remember that the ball goes where the shooting arm, hand, and shooting finger direct it to go. If a shot misses to the right, the shooting arm, hand, and finger were likely pointed in that direction. It's also possible that the body faced in the direction of the miss rather than being square to

Ronald Martinez/Getty Images Sport

Peja Stojakovic not only has textbook shooting form, but he also has the mentality of a great shooter, which is why he's one of the most feared perimeter marksmen in the league.

The sense of feel also yields clues. You might feel the shooting hand rotate to the right or the ball come off the ring finger (instead of the shooting finger). Either mistake gives the ball sidespin. An excellent method for developing feel is to shoot with eyes closed. A partner rebounds and tells you whether the shot was good. After a miss, the partner relays the specific direction of the miss and the reaction of the ball on the rim. By analyzing your shots, you can detect and correct errors before they become bad habits.

MENTALLY CORRECTING A MISS

Act like a shooter, feel like a shooter, be a shooter. Many players get upset over their errors, particularly a missed shot, and often dwell on the mistake to the point that subsequent play is affected. Each time you recite a negative word out loud, act with negative body language, or have negative thoughts after a missed shot, your brain is conditioned to perform the missed shot again. You must learn to "act like a shooter" rather than dwell on mistakes.

We use a computer analogy. When people type on a keyboard and make a mistake, what do they do? Do they type the same mistake again? Of course not. They erase the mistake and correct it. They backspace to delete the error, or they cut and paste in a correction. A similar process should apply to shooting errors. After a miss, you must understand why you missed by seeing the reaction of the ball on the rim or by the feel of the shot. You then immediately correct the miss using a positive trigger word that aids the correction. For example, if you feel the shot was short because you didn't use the legs, you correct the mistake while speaking the trigger word "Legs!" to key proper use of the legs.

An excellent method for conditioning successful shooting is to use a positive anchor word in association with correct mental

the basket. Or the elbow might have been out, causing the follow-through to go to the right.

If you see that the ball hits the rim and circles out, you know that you shot the ball with sidespin, which is generally caused by the shooting hand starting on the side of the ball and then rotating behind it. If you overrotate the shooting hand, the ball will hit the right rim with sidespin and roll left. If you underrotate, the ball will hit the left side of the rim and roll right. Other causes of sidespin are the ball sliding off the ring finger rather than the shooting finger, moving the hand on the ball or the ball on the palm, or thumbing the ball with the nonshooting hand.

rehearsal and visualization of a successful shot. Select an anchor word ("Through!" "In!" "Yes!" "Net!") that helps you visualize the shot going in. After missing a shot, immediately correct the miss with a positive trigger word and then visualize a good shot while saying the anchor word. This helps prevent negative thinking, which disrupts concentration and leads to more missed shots. Learning to react to a missed shot by visualizing a successful shot helps condition you to act like a shooter, feel like a shooter, and be a shooter.

JUMP SHOT

When shooting the jumper, align the ball above the shoulder between the ear and shoulder, with shooting hand facing the target and balance hand slightly under the ball. Place the forearm at a right angle to the floor. Focus eyes on the target. Jump straight up, fully extending the ankles, knees, back, and shoulders, and land in a balanced stance in the same spot as the takeoff without floating forward, backward, or to the side.

The height of the jump depends on the range of the shot. When closely guarded, generate enough force with the legs to jump higher than the defender. Also, align the ball a little higher. The top of the jump, the arm, wrist, and fingers provide most of the force. You want to feel as though you're hanging in the air as you release the ball.

Shot Fake

A good shot fake is a major plus for any shooter. The shot fake is used to make the defender believe a shot is being taken. A good shot fake creates space to shoot the jump shot over the defender. The shot fake must look like a shot. A slight upward move of the ball won't convince the defender of a shot. We like to say, "A shot fake is a shot not taken." Aggressively bring the ball up over the forehead while keeping the knees flexed.

A good shot fake gets the defender to straighten his legs, which enables the shooter to outjump the defender and get the shot off uncontested. Give the defender time to react to the fake. Reading the reaction of the defender before deciding to shoot over him, drive, or pass is basic for a successful move.

Three-Point Shot

For a three-point shot, set up far enough behind the line to avoid concern about stepping on the line. Focus on the basket. Use a balanced jump shot, shooting the ball without straining during the jump.

Successful three-point shooters excel in

- a smooth and even rhythm;
- a sequential use of the legs, back, and shoulders;
- correct mechanics, such as shooting hand facing the target;
- elbow-in alignment; and
- keeping the follow-through up until the ball reaches the rim.

On most long-range jump shots, the shooter has more time, so it's usually unnecessary to outjump the defender. You can thus use more force from the legs for shooting the ball rather than for gaining height on the jump; you can generate even more force by stepping into the shot. You want to feel that you're shooting the ball *as* you jump rather than at the top of the jump. Strive for a balanced jump that enables you to shoot without straining. Balance and control are more important than gaining maximum height on the jump. Smooth rhythm and complete follow-through are also important to long-range jump shooting. Land in balance in the same spot from which you started the shot.

Quick Release

The basic objective in basketball is to score, and the best pass is one that enables the shooter to catch the ball in shooting range and in position to shoot. Shooting range is the distance within which a player can consistently make an outside shot.

To shoot with a quick release, have hands and feet ready. Give the passer a good target with hands up above the shoulders in shooting position and knees slightly flexed. A good pass is one that hits your hands, enabling you to catch the ball in position to shoot with a quick release. Good passes make good shots. As the pass is thrown, jump behind the ball while facing the basket in position to shoot.

Good catches also make good shots. Catch the ball with the hands in a relaxed position, giving with the ball as it's caught. Let the ball come to the hands without reaching for it. Use the block-and-tuck method to catch the ball; that is, be in shooting position with the shooting hand behind the ball facing the front of the rim and the nonshooting hand under the ball. Never catch the ball with the hands on the sides and then rotate the ball into position—if rushed, you'll put sidespin on the ball. Block the ball with the shooting hand behind the ball while facing the front of the rim. Tuck the nonshooting hand under the ball.

Most shots in basketball are open shots (end of break, draw and kick out, ball passed out of double team, ball rotated versus zone or help defense, cutting off screen, pick-and-pop, long rebound, and so on). On open shots, the passer aims for the shooter's far hand, which blocks the pass. Catch the ball facing the basket and shoot in one motion. Lower knees just before the catch and extend upward on the catch in a quick, rhythmic down-and-up motion. Keep the ball high with the shooting hand facing the basket. Create rhythm by using the down-and-up motion of the legs rather than lowering the ball. Keep the ball high for a quicker release and to decrease the chance of error.

Jump behind the ball on passes that are slightly off. When you can't catch the ball with hands and feet ready to shoot in

rhythm, use a shot fake before the shot. The shot fake allows time to adjust hands and feet and establish a shooting rhythm. Use a step and turn (pivot) only when closely guarded.

Use trigger words to help learn correct mechanics, establish rhythm, and build confidence. Examples of trigger words for a quick release and rhythmic leg action are "Down and up!" to key the down-and-up action of the legs for rhythm and range, and "Up and in!" to start the shot high and prevent lowering the ball.

Shooting Off the Catch

When shooting off the catch, have hands immediately ready for shooting without needing to adjust them after the catch. An adjustment takes time and can affect the shot.

On a Pass From in Front (Inside Out). When receiving a pass from in front (inside out), block the ball with the shooting hand facing the front of the rim and tuck the nonshooting hand slightly under the ball.

On a Pass From the Strong-Hand Side. When receiving a pass from the strong-hand side, block the ball with the nonshooting hand and place the shooting hand behind the ball and facing the front of the rim. Reset the nonshooting hand under the ball (figure 1.3).

On a Pass From the Weak-Hand Side. For a pass from the weak-hand side, block the ball with the shooting hand, tuck the nonshooting hand under the ball, and reset the shooting hand behind the ball so it faces the front of the rim.

Shooting Off the Dribble

When open, dribble to the front of the shooting knee and pick the ball up facing the basket in position to shoot. Don't reach for the ball. Pick it up in front of the shooting knee with knees flexed to gain balance for the shot and prevent floating forward, backward, or to the side.

Figure 1.3 Shooting off the catch: Pass from the strong-hand side. Block the ball with the nonshooting hand and place the shooting hand behind the ball and facing the front of the rim. Reset the nonshooting hand under the ball.

Pick the ball up with the shooting hand on top of the ball and the nonshooting hand under the ball. When bringing the ball up to shoot, the shooting hand is positioned behind the ball and facing the front of the target to enable backspin. Never pick up the ball with hands on the sides and rotate it into position; when rushed, there's a tendency to overrotate or underrotate the shooting hand, resulting in sidespin on the ball upon release.

Dribbling to the Strong-Hand Side. When dribbling to the strong-hand side, dribble with the outside hand, keeping eyes on the basket. Read the defender. Create space away from the defender by taking one long dribble with the outside hand, the one far-ther away from the defender, and pushing off the pivot foot. Aim the dribble for a spot past the defender's body. Keep eyes on the basket. Protect the ball with the inside hand and the body. Jump behind the ball on the last dribble. Pick up the ball in front of the shooting knee with the shooting hand on top and the balance hand under the ball. Jump straight up and shoot a jump shot. Land in balance.

Dribbling to the Weak-Hand Side. When dribbling to the weak-hand side, dribble with the outside hand, keeping eyes on the

basket. Read the defender. Create space away from the defender by taking one long dribble with the outside hand, the one farther away from the defender, and push-ing off the pivot foot. Aim the dribble for a spot past the defender's body. Keep eyes on the basket. Protect the ball with the inside hand and the body. Make a second dribble (crossover dribble) to the front of the shooting-side knee. Jump behind the ball on the last dribble. Pick the ball up in front of the shooting knee with the shooting hand on top and the balance hand under the ball. Jump straight up and shoot a jump shot. Land in balance.

Step-Back Jump Shot

Read the defender. Fake the defender into thinking you will drive, take a quick step back from the defender, and, at the same time, dribble back with your outside hand creating space between you and the defender. Jump behind the ball and pick it up in front of the shooting knee with shooting hand on top of the ball and bal-ance hand under the ball (figure 1.4). Shoot

Figure 1.4 After an aggressive shot fake, take a quick step back from the defender with the outside foot; at the same time, dribble back with the outside hand.

a jump shot. Maintain balance by picking the ball up at the knee and exaggerating the follow-through of the shoulders, head, and shooting hand toward the basket to counter any tendency to lean the head and shoulders back on the shot.

Shot Fake Step-Through Jump Shot

You must be a threat to shoot. Make an aggressive shot fake. If the defender is aggressive, stop and read his hand position. If the defender's hand is up on the same side as the ball, step through with the inside foot past the defender's lead foot and move the head and shoulders under the defender's arm (figure 1.5).

Protect the ball with head and shoulders and move it away from the defender's reach to shoot a jump shot. Be strong. Expect to be fouled and complete the shot for a possible three-point play.

Figure 1.5 After an aggressive shot fake, read the defender. If the defender's hand is up, step through, past the defender's lead foot, moving head and shoulders under the defender's arm.

CORRECTING SHOOTING ERRORS

Error: Shooting the ball short
Correction: Establish a feel during the shot to determine whether to emphasize more force from the legs, completing the follow-through by keeping the shooting arm up until the ball reaches the basket, or by shooting with a quick and even-paced rhythm.

Error: Shooting the ball long
Correction: Raise the shooting arm higher, putting a higher arc on the shot (45 to 60 degrees); shoot with head and shoulders going forward and upward toward the rim during the follow-through.

Error: Shooting inconsistently, short and long
Correction: Extend the arm with complete elbow extension on the follow-through, rather than learning the shoulders back.

Error: Hitting the right side of the rim (right-handed shot)
Correction: The problem is either in not squaring up to face the basket or in starting the shot with the ball set in front of the head and the elbow out, which causes the arm to extend to the right on the shot. Start with the body square to the basket. Set the ball on the shooting side of the head between the ear and shoulder with the shooting hand facing the front of the rim. This allows the arm, wrist, and fingers to move straight toward the basket.

Error: Hitting the left side of the rim (right-handed shot)
Correction: The problem is either in not squaring up to face the basket or in starting the shot with the ball set on the right hip or too far to the right, which results in shoving the ball from right to left during the shot. Shoving the ball occurs when the legs are not used enough for power. Start with the body square to the basket. Set the ball on the shooting side of the head between the ear and shoulder with the shooting hand

facing front and the elbow in. Concentrate on making the shooting arm, wrist, and fingers move straight toward the basket.

Error: Lacking range, control, and consistency on the shot, missing short, long, or to either side
Correction: Set the ball on the shooting side of the head between ear and shoulder with shooting hand facing front. Emphasize the down-and-up motion of the legs and completing the follow-through by keeping the arm straight up until the ball reaches the basket.

Error: Shots hit the rim and circle out or skim from the front to the back of the rim and out, rather than hitting the rim and going through the hoop
Corrections: Avoid putting sidespin on the ball. To get backspin instead of sidespin, start the shot high with the shooting hand facing the front of the rim and the balance hand under the ball in the block-and-tuck position. Do not lower the ball for rhythm. Lowering the ball tends to move the shooting hand off center, usually causing side rotation as the ball is raised for the shot. The longer the stroke, the more chance for error and the slower the release. If you like to lower the ball for rhythm, focus on keeping the shooting hand on top of the ball. Emphasize a straight follow-through. Make sure the hand is set before shooting and focus on releasing the ball off the index finger. Practice shooting while keeping the thumb and index finger of the nonshooting hand squeezed together. Emphasize shooting the ball with one hand (the shooting hand).

Error: Shots lack control and hit hard on the rim despite what seem to be correct mechanics
Correction: The ball is likely resting on the palm. Relax the thumb of the shooting hand and set the ball on the finger pads with the palm off the ball. This enables a release off the finger pads, resulting in backspin, control, and a soft touch.

Error: Still missing, despite what appear to be correct mechanics
Correction: Ask a partner to check your eyes. If your eyes move, you're probably following the flight of the ball rather than focusing on the target, which is just over the front of the rim. Concentrate on the target until the ball reaches the basket; don't watch the ball's flight through the air.

Error: Not being in position to catch and shoot in one motion, thus reaching for the ball
Correction: Once open to shoot, give a good target with hands up in shooting position. As the pass is thrown, jump behind the ball, facing the basket in position to shoot. Let the ball come to the hands. Don't reach for the ball.

Error: A slow release after receiving a pass caused by lowering the ball before shooting it
Correction: Catch the ball in position to shoot, keeping the ball high while shooting in one motion.

Error: A slow release after receiving a pass from the side caused by facing the passer and reaching for the ball
Correction: Face the basket, turn your head to see the pass, and let the ball come to you. Jump behind the ball to catch and shoot in one motion.

Error: Catching the ball with hands on the side and rotating it into position, putting sidespin on the ball
Correction: Block the ball with the far hand and tuck the nonshooting hand under the ball. The shooting hand should always be behind the ball before the shot. When receiving a pass on the strong-hand side, the far hand is the nonshooting hand. After catching the ball, slide the nonshooting hand underneath the ball. When receiving a pass from the weak-hand side, the far hand is the shooting hand. When catching the ball, block the pass with the shooting hand. Then

reset the shooting hand by taking it off the side of the ball and setting it behind the ball so it faces the front of the rim.

Error: When shooting off the dribble, reaching to the side for the ball and starting the shot from the side of the body, resulting in a miss to the right or left of the basket
Correction: When open, dribble to the front of the shooting knee and pick the ball up facing the basket in position to shoot; don't reach for the ball.

Error: Picking the ball up off the dribble with hands on each side and rotating the ball into position, putting sidespin on the shot
Correction: Pick the ball up in front of the shooting knee with the shooting hand on top of the ball and the nonshooting hand underneath. When your hand is on top of the ball on the pickup, when you bring the ball up to shoot, your hand will face the front of the rim. This will allow you to shoot with backspin.

Error: Floating forward, backward, or sideways when shooting off the dribble
Correction: Change forward, backward, or side momentum to upward momentum. Pick the ball up in front of the shooting knee with knees flexed to gain balance for the shot and to prevent floating forward, back, or to the side.

COACHING TIPS FOR SHOOTING

• Get to know the players you're coaching. Learn to listen more than talk. A player wants to feel comfortable with you as a coach and have confidence in you before you work with him. Sometimes you'll coach a player who thinks he can't shoot. Always start with what the player is doing well.

• Coach each player individually. You don't want a player to learn everything you know about shooting. You want each player to learn what he needs to know to improve his shot.

• Encourage players to talk to you, telling you what they like and don't like. Tell a player, "I want to get you to shoot with confidence and rhythm. I want to work on the mechanic that helps the shot the most." Then he adjusts what he wants to adjust. Say, "I'm here to coach and help you, but you're going to learn to coach yourself."

• Ask questions to find out what a player is looking for. You can learn a lot about a player from his answers. When you really listen to his answers, you can gear your responses to his particular needs. Ask the player, "When you're shooting well, what are you doing?" There's no wrong answer to this question. The player's answer simply indicates his confidence level and what he knows about his own shot. If a player responds, "I just shoot!" this might indicate that he has confidence or that he's not overthinking when he shoots. If he answers, "When I'm shooting well, my shoulders go toward the basket," you know he has an understanding of what he wants to do when shooting. If he answers, "The ball is going in," this might indicate he doesn't know much about his shot.

• Keep it simple. Keep instruction brief and straightforward, yet inspiring. Players lose interest if the coaching is long, overly detailed, or boring. For the most part, players are not improving while you're talking. Get them shooting.

• Strive to keep confidence levels high. Be positive; keep encouraging players to know that they can and will achieve their goals. Motivate them to consistently do what it takes to reach their goals; never let them think they'll achieve anything less than success. Constantly tell players, "You are a shooter!"

• When a player doesn't want help, don't take it personally. In fact, only a few players might be interested in receiving much coaching. Once you have success with one or more players, others become interested in how you can help them, too.

• Never stop coaching. A player wants to see that you care about him. Be positive, enthusiastic, energized, and tenacious. This should inspire him to reach new heights.

Above all, make the game enjoyable. You become a better coach to a player when he sees that you have high spirits, a bright smile, and a sense of humor.

chapter 2

Perimeter Moves

Stan Van Gundy

Basketball is a team sport, but each player on offense must be able to execute against a defender one on one. First, players should learn how to get open to receive the ball; then they need to master basic one-on-one moves with the ball. Once proficient at performing the basics, they can add advanced moves. These moves must be so ingrained that players can select any one of them in a split-second to make the right move for beating the defender.

When I was at Miami I had the pleasure of coaching Dwyane Wade, who is adept both at freeing himself to receive the ball on the perimeter and at creating scoring opportunities once he has possession. Taller wing players, such as Rashard Lewis and Hedo Turkoglu, whom I now coach in Orlando, can also be successful with their respective assets on the perimeter, be it great driving skills, a midrange game, or a deadly outside shot.

GETTING OPEN TO RECEIVE THE BALL

Let's begin with the most basic tips to create space from a defender to receive a pass.

- Start the move to get free only when the teammate with the ball is in a position ready to pass it.
- Receive the ball in a spot on the floor from where you can effectively pass, dribble, or shoot. Know your shooting range.

- Take no longer than two or three seconds to get open. The longer it takes to get open, the longer the defense has to recover.
- Move toward the defender with normal steps without watching the passer. When you take short steps and lock in on the passer, you send a clear signal to the defender to prepare for your move to get open and receive the ball.
- Make contact with (bump) the defender with the inside shoulder and forearm without pushing. This helps freeze the defender. Then, pop out and create space from the defender. Make this separation move at a different angle, not back and forth on the same line, to require the defender even greater time to recover. Keep knees bent to stay low, and be prepared to attack upon receiving the ball.
- When popping out to receive the ball, use the hand farthest from the defender as a target for the passer. Meet the pass and catch the ball with two hands.
- While landing on the floor with the ball in your hands, immediately turn your feet toward the basket so you can start right away to play one on one and see all of the court.

Now let's look at five basic ways to get free on the perimeter, and then one special move.

V Cut

The V cut is the most common way to get open and can be executed at any spot on the floor. It's called a V cut because you follow an imaginary path in the shape of a V. To receive the ball in a high spot on the court, bring the defender low and then pop out high; to receive the ball in a low spot, bring the defender high and then pop out low.

Begin this move facing the basket. Again, it's important to get open in a spot on the court from which you can pass, drive to the basket, or make a jump shot; you also need to respect the spacing of your teammates.

Let's assume you want to get open on the right wing with the ball in the middle of the court; the defender is guarding at a three-quarter contesting position. I'll describe these moves on a one-two count sequence, but between the one and two is only a split-second, without a complete stop.

First count. To get open on the high side of the floor, take one or two steps toward the defender, shoulders squared to the basket, and then, planting the inside foot (the one nearest the baseline or the outside foot if you want to get open in a low spot on the floor) between the defender's legs, lean on the defender's chest with the right forearm and shoulder without pushing. Then pivot on the outside foot and make a crossover step with the right leg over the forward foot of the defender to freeze him.

Second count. Turning on the ball of the inside foot, push off, making a stride with the outside foot without losing balance. Make a two-count stop, landing first on the left foot (which becomes the pivot foot), followed by the right foot. At the same time, ask for the ball with the outside hand (the hand farther from the defender). On receiving the ball, make a front turn to face the basket in triple-threat position, ready to play one on one.

Triple-Threat Position

This position is called the "triple threat" because from this stance you can pass, drive, or shoot. To assume the triple-threat position, place the shooting hand behind the ball with wrist bent backward and elbow bent. Place the other hand in front and a little below the ball with arm bent about 45 degrees to protect the ball. Position the ball on the side, between chest and hip, with knees bent and trunk slightly forward (but maintaining balance). This is the proper starting position for nearly every one-on-one move.

Reverse

The reverse move is used in different phases of the game, either with or without the ball on offense (as well as on defense, for example, on the blockout). Let's now review how to make a reverse in order to get free and receive the ball.

First count. Take one or two steps toward the defender; then, planting the outside foot between the defender's legs, lean on the defender's chest with the left forearm and shoulder without pushing. Pivot on the outside foot and make a reverse, "sitting" for an instant on the forward leg of the defender to freeze him.

Second count. Take a step forward to create space between you and the defender, receive the ball, and make a front turn to face the basket in triple-threat position, ready to play one on one.

V Cut and Reverse

This move is a combination of the V cut and reverse.

First count. You start to make the V cut, as described before, but the defender is still covering you tightly.

Second count. Make a reverse, as described before.

L Cut

Here you start the move with your back to the baseline.

First count. Start near the lane about mid- to low post, facing the midcourt line; the ball is in the middle of the court, and the defender is covering face to face. Take one or two normal steps upward toward the midcourt line, then plant the inside foot (the foot nearest the lane) near or over the outside foot of the defender and lean with the inside shoulder and forearm on the chest of the defender without pushing.

Second count. Shift weight onto the ball of the inside foot, make a lateral stride and hop, land on the floor with a two-count stop, receive the ball, make a front turn to face the basket in triple-threat position, and be ready to play one on one.

L Cut and Reverse

This move is an L cut followed by a reverse.

First count. You start to make your L cut, but your defender is still covering you tightly.

Second count. Make a reverse, as described before.

Special Move: Circle Around

With a defender covering nearly face to face, bring the defender low with both hands extended overhead. When near the baseline, bring down hands (but keep them extended, as if swimming) around the inside hip of the defender to freeze him momentarily; then curl around him and pop out to the same side from which you started the move to receive the ball. Don't push the defender; go around him.

MOVES WITH THE BALL

We'll now describe the basic direct moves to master right after receiving the ball in order to play one on one with no fakes or dribbling beforehand. We describe these

One-on-One Essentials

Before looking at different moves, let's go over a few essentials for attacking a defender one on one.

- Try to read the defender's move and react accordingly. Many players decide in advance what to do with the ball, which is a big mistake. Instead, play one on one, basing your moves on the moves and reactions of your defender.
- Start the move with knees bent, keeping the ball low; then explode high for a jump shot or layup or to pass the ball to a teammate.
- Shoot after no more than three dribbles—two is better; this prevents giving the defense time to recover.
- On all drives to the basket, drive in a straight line, not in a curved line.
- When going in for a contested layup, on your last step before the shot, lean with your inside shoulder and forearm into the chest of the defender (without pushing) while also leaning against him with your inside hip and leg; this prevents the defender from recovering to block the shot.

moves as executed with the right hand, but the sequence of moves is the same when performed with the left hand.

Jump Shot

If you're in shooting range, if your defender isn't playing too tightly and his hands are down, and if there's no chance to drive past him, you can shoot a jump shot right away.

Direct Drive

If the defender allows a direct driving lane, go hard to the basket in a straight line. Let's look at all the details of the direct drive.

Terrance Vaccaro/NBAE/Getty Images Sport

Dwyane Wade can take the ball from the perimeter to the basket with the best of them.

Footwork. The first stride must be long, but not so long that you lose balance and power. The inside shoulder should be at the same level as the defender's hip. Turn the nondribbling shoulder inside to protect the ball and to get slimmer while stepping over the defender. The foot must touch the floor at the same time as the dribble to avoid walking.

The second stride after the dribble is quick and strong; stay low on the knees and don't decelerate after the dribble, but keep the change of pace alive.

Dribble. The first dribble of the direct drive is important for the success of the move. The ball is pushed hard to the ground, with the dribbling (right) hand following

the ball and ending with fingers pointed toward and as close as possible to the floor. The ball will bounce back very quickly to your hand and remain in control longer. The ball must bounce over the hip of the defender, slightly on the side of your right foot and in front of your left foot. While making the first dribble, don't watch the ground or the ball; keeping your head up, watch the basket and all of the floor to see the other defenders and your teammates. Protect the ball like a fence with the left arm bent about 45 degrees.

Crossover Step

If the defender doesn't allow a straight line to the basket, attack his forward foot using a crossover step, which I'll soon describe. But first I should mention the "sweep" of the ball, a quick movement that brings the ball from one side of the body to the other.

Sweep (or rip of the ball). Mastering the sweep is critical for playing one on one. If the ball is in your right hand and the defender has his right foot forward, sweep the ball from the right side of the body to the left side as quickly as possible. Stay low on the knees and bring the ball from chest or hip level on the right side to the left side, quickly swinging it below the knees, a move from high to low, in between. While changing the side of the ball, also rotate the right hand laterally and the left hand on the back of the ball with wrist bent backward (figure 2.1, *a* and *b*).

Footwork. As soon as you have swept the ball, put your weight on the ball of your left foot and, while maintaining balance, make a long crossover step with the right foot over the forward foot of the defender, pushing your body forward with your left foot, while at the same time making a long dribble with your left hand. The step must be long, but balance and control must be maintained (figure 2.1c). As usual, the first step must be matched to a change of pace.

Dribble. On the dribble (with the left hand), the ball must touch the floor on the side,

over the left foot and over the hip of the defender (figure 2.1d), as described for the previous move.

This is the most common sweep move, but some NBA players have their own move on the sweep. For instance, Tim Duncan makes a sweep from one shoulder to the other, whereas Allen Iverson sweeps the ball from one ankle to the other and then back to the same ankle from where he started the sweep. Kobe Bryant makes the sweep from the shoulder to the hip.

Figure 2.1 Crossover step: *(a-b)* Sweep the ball from the right side to the left side, bringing it below knee level; *(c)* make a long crossover step over the forward foot of the defender; *(d)* on the dribble, the ball must touch the floor on the side, over the forward foot.

Here are some important details on the long step and the dribble:

- After the crossover, during the long step with the right foot, you must at the same time turn the right shoulder, brushing the defender's right hip, and bring it over (or almost at the same level as) the right hip of the defender to prevent the defender from recovering. Turning the shoulder makes you thinner in order to more easily go over the defender.

- The toes of the right foot must be turned inside and toward the basket to help the body move in a straight direction rather than laterally. This is important. If the toes of the right foot are pointed laterally, the body will go in that direction rather than straight to the basket.

- The right arm is bent about 45 degrees to protect the ball.

Reverse (or Spin)

When receiving the ball on the right wing, if the defender is still leaning on the high side, immediately make a reverse (using the inside foot as the pivot foot), spin around the defender, and go to the basket with no more than one or two dribbles.

Footwork. Use the inside foot (the foot nearest the baseline) as your pivot foot, rotating on the ball of the foot, low on the knees, while making a long step toward the new direction with the nonpivot foot. For this move, turn the toes of the nonpivot foot as much as possible toward the basket to avoid moving away from the rim.

Dribble. At the same time, on the last side dribble, move the dribbling hand laterally on the ball with forearm bent about 45 degrees (with arm bent at this angle, the ball is pushed to the floor near your body rather than away from you). This brings the ball around the body and ends the move by pushing the ball hard to the floor in the new direction to get a quick bounce back.

Turn your head in the new direction before making the move; this allows you to change the move at the last second based on the defender's reaction, possibly avoiding a charging call.

BASIC COMBINED MOVES

Sometimes the relatively simple moves described so far will allow you to beat your defender. Other times, they aren't enough, and you'll need to use combined moves to create space between you and the defender and force his reaction.

Jab Step and Fake

Before a discussion of the basic combined moves, we need to cover the jab step, which is the starting point of these moves. I also want to describe the proper way to make a fake.

Jab Step

Let's say you're facing the defender with the ball on your right-hand side. The defender is in a perfect defensive stance, and you cannot shoot or drive to beat him. You must first create space between you and the defender and then force the defender to react. The jab step (so called because it's similar to a boxer's forward step) involves both the foot and the ball and is used to force a reaction from the defender and create space. This step is the base of all the basic combined moves we'll discuss.

Footwork. Start from a triple-threat position with the ball on the right side of the body. Make a forward, strong, and aggressive short step with the right foot (if right-handed) and land on the floor with the forefoot. The heel of the left foot doesn't touch the floor, which improves the pace of the next move. While making the jab step, turn the right shoulder a little inside to protect the ball and give the defender the impression you want to drive. Your right foot lands about six to seven inches ahead of the left foot. Legs are flexed; for good balance, head and trunk are straight (or slightly bent forward); and eyes are focused not below the feet but over the defender to make him think you want to go to a certain spot over him and also so that you can watch the entire court (figure 2.2).

Ball movement. Simultaneous to the quick, short step with the right foot, the ball is aggressively brought slightly to the side of the right knee (in this case) for faking a dribble with the right hand. Don't overextend the arm with the ball (to maintain balance),

and don't expose the ball too much in front of the defender.

Fake

During the fake, you'll give a true impression to the defender that you want to make a move, but instead you'll make another move based on the defender's reaction. Thus, to sell a realistic passing, driving, or shooting fake with the jab step, you must truly *start* to make a move. Many players' fakes aren't realistic enough. The fake must not be too

Figure 2.2   The jab step helps the player to create space between him and the defender.

Fernando Medina/NBAE/Getty Images Sport

Rashard Lewis uses a jab step from a triple-threat position to set up a dribble drive, pass, or shot.

defender's hip with the right hand, bringing the left shoulder to hip level of the defender. The left arm, bent 45 degrees at hip level, protects the ball.

To push the ball hard to the floor, the wrist must be bent backward and shifted behind the ball with the elbow bent to push the ball forward. Change the pace on the second step after the jab step.

The sequence is a short and quick step, followed immediately by a longer step made with the same (right) foot. Stay low and in good balance during the second step; don't decrease speed.

Jab Step and Crossover

If, after the jab step and the drive fake, the defender slides over in the direction of the jab step, take a crossover step and a dribble. The sequence might start with a hard jab step with the right foot, followed by a crossover step with the right leg.

Jab Step and Jump Shot

If the defender retreats after the jab step, shoot a jumper (if in shooting range). As usual, the jab step must be aggressive and short; knees should be flexed. Again, don't bring the ball too far from the body during the jab step; the palm of the shooting hand must be behind the ball with wrist cocked toward the chest to speed up the shot. As soon as the jab step hits the floor, and if the defender retreats, immediately bring the ball into the "shooting pocket" and go up for the jumper.

quick. You need to give the defender time to react and force him to commit a mistake, such as crossing his feet, leaning in one direction, or straightening his body. Then, based on the reaction of the defender, decide on your next move, which might be a combination of the moves we'll cover now.

Jab Step and Drive With the Same Hand

After a strong jab step with the right foot (in this example) and a drive fake with the right hand, if the defender hasn't reacted quickly enough to the jab step, take a long step with the right foot (but not so long that you lose balance) and a dribble over the

Shot Fake and Drive With the Same Hand or Crossover

This time drive to the basket after the shot fake. To sell a proper fake to the defender, bring the ball over the forehead with hands on the ball as if to shoot. While bringing the ball over the forehead, flex the legs more, and, when the defender straightens his legs as a reaction to the shot fake, explode to the basket with a drive with the same hand, or, depending on the defender's position and reaction, use a crossover.

Jab Step, Shot Fake, and Drive

This is a combination of two fakes, which must not be too frenzied. Again, take enough time on the fakes and be realistic—this is a three-count move, and every move must be made at the proper time in order to read the defender's reaction. Don't decide in advance which move to make. Always react to the defender.

Jab Step, Shot Fake, Drive Fake, and Jump Shot

This is the opposite move to the one just described. Instead of driving, fake the drive and pull up for the jumper. Stay low on the knees for the duration of the fakes, and then explode vertically for the jump shot. All the moves combined should take no longer than three seconds maximum, preferably less.

Pass Fake and Drive or Jump Shot

Fake a lateral pass with two hands, but don't extend the arms too much. At the same time, take a short step in the direction of the pass fake and shift body weight to the ball of the forward foot. Then quickly push the body in the other direction and drive to the basket or pull up for the jump shot.

DRIBBLE MOVES

To be complete on offense, you must possess an arsenal of dribbling moves. In this sec-

tion we'll describe possible moves to make once you have begun the dribble and are approaching the defender. As always, read your defender's reactions.

Change-of-Pace Moves With the Same Hand

First let's look at dribbling moves made with the same hand and in a straight direction. These moves are used to force a reaction from the defender (vertically or horizontally) and then beat him. As before, all these moves are matched by an explosive change of pace. For these moves, dribble as straight as possible, not laterally, to avoid giving the defender time to recover.

Hockey Dribble

Footwork. Freeze the defender with short, choppy steps back and forth while keeping feet nearly parallel. The steps are similar to skating slides on ice. To keep the defender clueless, combine this hockey dribble with head and shoulder fakes, shaking him from one side of the body to the other before driving hard to the basket in a straight line. Keep knees bent to drive faster to the basket. Protect the ball during the move.

Dribble. The dribbling hand is over the ball, pushing it very hard to the floor for better control, and then, on the last dribble, the hand is brought behind to push the ball hard and low over the defender during the drive to the basket. Body weight is evenly distributed on the balls of the feet during the hockey steps. Then, for the drive, body weight transfers to the foot on the same side of the dribbling hand for more power and to push the body forward past the defender.

Change-of-Pace Dribble

Approach the defender dribbling at a moderate, controlled speed, trying to get him to relax a little. When the defender's knees straighten, or when you see that he has started to relax, quickly drop your knees for a sudden sprint to the basket with a long step and a strong dribble forward.

Footwork. Avoid short and nervous steps when approaching the defender because this can signal an intended move. A head and shoulder fake in the opposite direction might help beat the defender. For the drive, body weight is brought onto the ball of the foot on the same side as the dribbling hand so you can push your body over the defender.

Dribble. The dribbling hand remains over the ball when approaching the defender. It is then brought behind to push the ball hard and low past the defender during the drive to the basket, possibly with the first bounce over the hip of the defender.

Speed Dribble: Stop and Go

Dribble quickly toward the defender. Stop suddenly for a moment, keeping the dribble alive. Raise up the head and legs a little. When the defender straightens his legs or relaxes, explode into a speed dribble using the same dribbling hand. The sequence is speed dribble, controlled dribble, wait a moment, and speed dribble. Don't ever stop the dribble— just decelerate, and then accelerate again.

Step-Back Dribble

When the defender is covering aggressively and there's no room to drive past him, make a step-back dribble to allow a chance to reassess and consider the next move.

Footwork. When near the defender and dribbling with the right hand (in this example), make a strong step with the left foot toward the defender, putting full body weight on the ball of the forward foot; at the same time, lift the right foot off the floor. Next, step back, pushing off the left foot and

then lifting it, to create space between you and the defender.

Dribble. As the left foot steps forward during the last dribble, the fingers of the right hand shift from the back to the front of the ball, pulling the ball back. Then, when the defender tries to reduce the distance, explode with a power dribble with the same hand.

Stay low throughout the move. As with all dribbling fakes, fake with the whole body, not just with the ball. If there's enough space, if you're within range, and if you can maintain balance, take a jump shot after the fake.

Brandon Roy executes the step-back dribble (left-handed) to create some room to pass, shoot, or attempt another move. Note how his head stays up and he keeps the whole court in view.

Garrett Ellwood/NBAE/Getty Images Sport

In-'n-Out

This is a crossover dribble fake. While dribbling with the right hand, take a step outside with the left foot and, at the same time, on the last dribble, shift the right hand on top and slightly laterally on the ball, bringing it momentarily into the middle of the body. The defender now likely anticipates a crossover dribble. But, at the last second, as the defender begins his lean in that direction, bring the ball back to starting position and dribble again on the right side. At the same time, take a long stride on the right side to get past the defender. Body weight must be on the ball of the left foot; the left foot then pushes the body to the right, not laterally but in a straight line. As usual, keep the dribble low for the entire movement. Add a head and shoulder fake, leaning in the opposite direction.

Change of Hand and Direction Moves

These are moves made with a change of the dribbling hand, matched always with a change of direction and pace.

Crossover Dribble

This is probably the simplest change of hand, but it's also the most dangerous because it's made in front of the defender. Nearly any player can perform a crossover dribble, but not many execute it in the fastest and safest way.

Footwork. Bring the body's weight to the inside part of the right foot, in this example, and then push the body in the new direction before taking a long but balanced step with the left foot. These are crucial details for making what some players call an "ankle-breaker crossover." On the forward step, the left foot points toward the basket, rather than laterally, to prevent going away from the rim and deviating from a straight line.

Dribble. On the last lateral dribble, when the ball bounces back to the right hand, the hand pumps the side of the ball very hard below knee level and as low to the floor as possible (to speed up the move and reduce the risk of a steal). At the same time, take a step forward with the left foot. The bounce of the ball on the crossover dribble should be on the side and over the toes of the left forward foot. The left hand is positioned laterally to stop the movement of the ball for a split second; then, right after the ball touches the fingers, the hand bends immediately backward and behind the ball for a speed dribble.

Turning the shoulders in the new direction can help this move. As usual, the move must be matched with a change of pace. Stay low for the entire movement and shortly after, then finish with a jump shot, layup, or pass to a teammate.

Behind the Back

This dribble move and the between-the-legs change of hand are safer moves than the crossover because these moves are not made with the ball in front of the defender.

One foot forward. While taking a step forward with the left foot on the last dribble with the right hand, shift the right hand in front of the ball and bring the ball behind the back; control the ball until it nearly reaches the opposite hip, and then push the ball hard to the floor. Bring the ball below the buttocks; it should bounce on the left side of the body, laterally and over the toes of the left foot. Now control the ball with the left hand while making a long speed dribble, staying low on the knees for the entire movement. As usual, change direction and add a change of pace, going to the basket in a straight line.

Two feet even. On the last dribble with the right hand, bend the knees to get into a lower position with back straight and feet parallel. With the right hand on the side of the ball, forcefully push the ball behind the back and below the buttocks from one side to the other. The ball should bounce over the left hip and on the side, even with the palm of the left hand, which stops the ball for a split second with fingers pointed toward the floor; then the palm is turned immediately backward to gain full control of the ball for a speed dribble to beat the defender.

Between the Legs

While taking a step forward with the left foot (in this example) on the last lateral, right-hand dribble, the right hand shifts laterally on the ball, pushing it between the legs to the other side of the body. The ball bounces laterally and over the toes of the left foot. The left hand (with fingers pointed to the floor) stops the movement of the ball for a split second and then shifts on the back of the ball for a speed dribble.

Reverse (or Spin)

While dribbling with the right hand (in this example), step forward with the left foot; the right hand shifts on the side of the ball, and the forearm is bent at about 45 degrees. While rotating the body in the new direction and pivoting on the ball of the left foot, bounce the ball with a hard, quick movement with the fingers of the right hand, which pushes (or, better, slaps) the ball hard to the floor. The ball should come back as quickly as possible for better control. Protect the ball, keeping it between the body and the defender.

The head should anticipate the rotation of the body in the new direction, watching the reaction of the defender in advance over the right shoulder. At the end of the reverse and the bounce back of the ball, dribble again to go to the basket.

This is a difficult move, so it's important to follow these details exactly:

- Stay low on the knees—both during the movement and on the subsequent speed dribble.
- Don't reverse with legs too close together; spread legs more than shoulder-width apart, bending the knees for a quicker and more explosive move.

- Don't overextend the arm; keep the arm near the body and slightly above waist level, bent about 45 degrees. If the angle is wider, the ball will land on the floor away from the body, reducing quickness of the move and control of the ball.
- The hand that "carries" the ball leaves the ball only after the body's reverse is nearly completed; this hand really "throws" the ball hard and low to the floor and recovers it quickly.
- Start dribbling with the left hand (in this example) only when the reverse is completed and not before—any earlier risks exposing the ball to the defender, who can slap it from behind.
- The toes of the forward foot after the reverse must be pointed straight forward, not laterally, to avoid moving away from the basket.

Half-Reverse (or Half-Spin)

The sequence of the movement is the same as for the reverse, but here, once the defender has recovered and is setting himself in your path, dribble back to where the reverse started and go in the same direction from where you began the move. Dribble with the same hand throughout the move, always protecting the ball with the body. In short, you make a half-reverse. As on the reverse, it's also important on the half-reverse to turn the head in the intended direction in advance to see how the defender reacts.

ADVANCED COMBINED DRIBBLE MOVES

After mastering the basic one-on-one live-ball and dribble moves, players can add advanced combined dribble moves to their repertoire. All these moves are a combination of two types of dribbles done in succession; they can be performed at various speeds with changes of direction.

These moves are common in the NBA. They are not circus moves to impress the crowd; rather, they are effective advanced moves for beating and countering the reactions of the defender. Players like Kobe Bryant, Allen Iverson, Mike Bibby, Steve Nash, Richard Hamilton, LeBron James, Dwyane Wade, and Tracy McGrady are among the best at executing these moves.

Dribble, Step Back, and Jump Shot

Say a defender is covering aggressively, allowing little room to maneuver. Operating within shooting range, dribble once with the right hand and take one step with the left foot. This makes the defender expect a drive to the basket, which lures him into leaning into the driving path. Now, putting full body weight on the left foot, push back and, after a small hop, land on the floor right foot first, followed by the left foot. Pull the ball back and shoot a jumper over the defender. Stay low on the knees for the entire move. You can also perform this move after the dribble with

As the opposing defense's primary concern, Tracy McGrady often must use more than one move to free himself from multiple defenders.

the right hand and the step forward with the left foot simply by stepping back with the left foot, without moving the right foot, and using it as the pivot foot, pulling back the ball at the same time, and shooting a jumper.

Dribble, Step Back, Turn, and Jump Shot

Kobe Bryant has mastered this move. The beginning of the move is the same as for the last one: Dribble toward the defender with the right hand and take a step with the left foot to make the defender expect a drive to the basket. Again, he will lean into the driving path. Now, using the left foot as the pivot foot, pull the ball back and make a rear turn to front the basket and shoot a jumper.

Dribble, Step Back, and Crossover

Simultaneous to the step back, using the right foot as the pivot foot, pull the ball back and perform a crossover dribble, followed by a drive to the basket or a jump shot. One small detail: A split second before the crossover dribble, make a head fake (but stay low on the knees) to force the defender to straighten the legs, and then make the crossover dribble.

Bill Baptist/NBAE/Getty Images Sport

Dribble, Step Back, and Reverse

Simultaneous to the step back, pull the ball back, pivot on the right foot, front the basket, and perform a reverse dribble, followed by a drive to the basket or a jump shot.

Dribble, Step Back, Crossover, and Reverse

On this move, after the step back, combine two moves—a crossover and a reverse—in the same action, always basing your decision on the reaction of the defender. Follow with a drive to the basket or a jump shot.

Dribble, Step Back, Hesitation, and Speed Dribble

After the step back, hesitate a split second, slightly raising the head and knees so that it looks to the defender like you're slowing down. When the defender stands up or relaxes, execute a hard and quick dribble to beat him. Make a direct drive or perform a crossover or a reverse dribble followed by a drive to the basket or a jump shot.

Here are other examples of combined dribbling moves, all matched with a change of speed and direction:

- In-and-out dribble followed by a cross-over dribble.
- Crossover dribble followed by a between-the-legs dribble.
- Crossover dribble followed by a reverse dribble.
- Stop-and-go dribble followed by a cross-over dribble.
- Between-the-legs dribble followed by a reverse dribble followed by a crossover dribble.
- Between-the-legs dribble followed by a behind-the-back dribble (keep feet even or one foot forward).
- Double between-the-legs dribble.

- Lateral step and dribble followed by a speed direct drive with the same hand.
- Lateral step and dribble, followed by a crossover dribble or in-and-out dribble.
- Hockey dribble followed by a crossover dribble.
- Hockey dribble followed by a lateral step and dribble followed by a speed forward dribble with the same hand or a crossover dribble.

All these moves can end with a drive to the basket or a jump shot.

SHOOTING IN TRAFFIC

For this example, let's assume a player on the right wing has received the ball and has beaten his defender, but on the way to the basket, while dribbling with the left hand toward the lane, he faces two defenders—one at the free-throw area and the other, who is coming from the weak side to help, near the basket. Here are two possible solutions.

Reverse Dribble

If the first defender at the free-throw line is positioned in the lane with his inside foot up, go toward him, perform a reverse dribble, approach the second defender near the basket, make contact by leaning on him with the inside shoulder and hip to freeze him, and shoot a layup.

Hesitation and Change of Pace

If the first defender is at the free-throw line with his feet parallel, use a hesitation dribble, faking with the head and shoulder, and then explode to the basket on the other side, dribbling straight to the basket with the left hand. Again, make contact by leaning on the second defender with the inside shoulder and hip to freeze him, and then shoot a layup.

TEACHING POINTS

• To master their one-on-one moves, players must work a lot on ball handling: stationary ball handling and on the move, dribbling with one and two balls, practicing the basic dribbles, and then progressing to the more advanced dribbles.

• They must learn not just to push the ball on the dribble but also to "pump" it very hard and low to the floor. A speed dribble must be kept lower than a stationary dribble.

• Coaches should teach these moves gradually. Focus first on the most basic and simplest moves. Then work on the combined and more difficult moves, first at moderate speed and without a defender. Finally, add a defender who initially guards at 50 percent effort before progressing to defend at game pace. Don't hurry; teach the moves step by step.

• Teach your players to be prepared to use a variety of moves based on the reaction of their defender. They must learn to read and react rather than deciding in advance which move to execute.

chapter 3

Post Moves

Kareem Abdul-Jabbar

When archived footage of my playing career is shown, it almost always features me shooting the "sky hook" shot, even though I had a wide array of offensive moves. Fans forget that I was a pretty good passer, and that 11 times during my pro career I was named to the first or second NBA All-Defensive Team.

Still, having a signature, or money, move certainly contributed to my success, and has helped many post players excel during the course of their careers.

But such moves aren't easily acquired. It took me countless hours of practice to master the sky hook. Along the way toward mastery, a player will encounter many disappointments and doubts about whether the move is worth all the time and effort. In my case, I'm glad I stuck with it.

But I was fortunate to realize (and to be often reminded by my coaches) that no player, regardless of stature, can excel with only one move. Since my days on the court, this has become all the more true—today's post game requires an even greater repertoire of skills.

Yes, the bigs, as centers and forwards are often called, are still expected to do the blue-collar work of setting screens, rebounding, blocking shots, and throwing outlet passes, but more and more post players are required to be scoring threats from 15 to 20 feet, to fill the lane on the primary break, and to apply defensive pressure farther from the opponent's basket.

In fact, considering the way the game is played today, I recommend that every player—even small forwards and guards—learn how to play in the post and to master a couple of moves with their back to the basket. This will not only make them more versatile and valuable offensively but also give them insight into aspects of playing the position, which can be useful on defense (for example, when the player they're guarding enters the lane, or when they're asked to help defensively in the lane area when a teammate overplays or gets beat by an opponent). I am particularly proud of the improvements of Lakers' center Andrew Bynum. We worked for hours in practice on all the aspects of the post game, and his hard work has paid off.

Developing a post game typically takes longer than it takes to grasp the basics of perimeter play. The most important thing for the post player is to approach the task with the right mind-set. Post play is a physically demanding job that involves aggressiveness, toughness, and persistence. Size is not as critical as attitude. A player in the post must be mentally ready to fight for position, collide inside the lane and on screens, and jump maybe two or three times to grab a rebound, all the while getting banged around by defenders. It's not a role for the faint of heart.

It also helps to be basketball smart. By that I mean developing a keen sense as to where missed shots will bound to off the

Even 7-foot-4 Ralph Sampson found the sky hook very difficult to defend.

rim, anticipating how an opposing player will attack or defend, and maneuvering to the most advantageous location on the court for your team as a receiver, screener, passer, or defender.

A post player must also commit to improve each year, to add more moves, and to refine his skills. Tim Duncan provides a great example of this. Although he has already won four NBA titles and is a two-time NBA MVP, every summer he masters a new move, either facing the basket or with his back to it.

The essential physical tools of post play (quickness, agility, stamina, strong hands, jumping, coordination, and a sturdy upper and lower body) must also be developed. An out-of-shape post player is a lame duck on the basketball court, bound to be exposed, if not embarrassed, very early in the game. Check out the Orlando Magic's Dwight Howard for a clear idea of what proper conditioning for post play looks like.

These assets, in addition to the aforementioned array of skills—from basic footwork to refined techniques—are desirable for any players seeking to be successful in the post. The rest of the chapter should be helpful in developing and improving players in this key facet of the game.

PRINCIPLES OF OFFENSIVE POST PLAY

Before we go deep into post moves and countermoves, let's first review some basic principles of playing in the post.

Use Both Feet

Post players need to maintain strong position, always keeping their balance. Balance in the post is particularly important because of the more physical game that occurs there. Balance is best maintained by staying low, with legs bent and feet wider than shoulder-width apart. The post player should receive the ball with both feet on the floor so he can use his left or right foot as his pivot foot. He must have both feet on the floor as much as possible to take a position, to slide in a certain direction, and to shoot. For example, if he wants to make a power shot and doesn't jump from both feet, the defender has an easy job knocking him off balance.

Make Contact With the Defender

An imperative in establishing low-post position is effective physical contact with the defender. When the low-post player reaches his spot near the basket, he must immediately recognize where the defender is and how he is moving. Thus, the post must use all his moves to make physical contact with his defender so he can gain the best position and know where the defender is (i.e., if he is completely behind him or if he's overplaying on the high or low side).

The post must "see" his defender through touch. He knows where the defender is by feeling his presence through contact. His offensive moves will be determined by his feel for where the defender is located. All physical contact must be made within the rules with the buttocks, legs, and arms. The post player must also react to the defender and maintain proper positioning for those two or three seconds it takes to provide a proper target for teammates to get him the ball. A post must have the aggressive desire to make contact with the defender. Remember that it's not stature or bulk that's most important but rather the size of the post player's will and heart.

Receive the Ball

When he thinks it's the right time to receive the ball, the post player calls for it by yelling "Ball!" or signaling with a move of the hand or head. The post then gives a definite target to the passer—usually the open hand that's away from the defender, with the arm extended outside or bent at a 45-degree angle. I suggest that the low post not try to receive the ball with both arms and hands straight unless the defender is far away. It's much easier for the defender to reach for the ball and steal or deflect it from behind when the low post keeps both arms extended. Then the post, continually adjusting his position to the moves of the defender, must stay open for those two or three seconds to receive the ball. He forces the defender to maintain position in the lane by using his body to constantly attempt to back into the three-second area. This constant movement should distract the defender, momentarily

freeing the post to receive the ball under minimum pressure.

As soon as the ball is in the hands of the post, the other hand immediately slaps it tightly, gripping the ball with the fingers, with one hand beneath and the other hand over the ball (to avoid the ball being slapped from below), forearms bent at chest level, and elbows pointed outside and forming a T with the body. As soon as he touches the ball, the post looks inside the lane over his top shoulder to be aware of exactly where his defender is and to see if a teammate is cutting into the lane.

Attack in the Direction of the Pass

All coaches advise passers to "pass the ball away from the defender," and this axiom holds true when getting the ball to the post. As soon as the post receives the ball, he must go to the rim on the side from where he received the pass because normally the defender can't cover the post in that direction. Only if the post sees that that direction is blocked by the defender should he then use a countermove. Before making any offensive moves, the post should usually check for a double team. If he senses a double team is arriving, he can wait a count for the double team to develop and then pass to the open teammate created by the double team.

Read the Defense

"Read the defense" is a principle valid for all players on the court, both on the perimeter and in the lane. The post player reads what his defender is doing and then reacts to his moves, attempting to force a defensive mistake, such as jumping to a fake or leaning or sliding in one direction or another. It's sometimes fine to use strength and power for scoring a basket, but the most outstanding players on the post capitalize on the mistakes of their defender rather than relying on their own strength and size.

Barry Gossage/NBAE/Getty Images Sport

Effective post players like Tim Duncan keep a sure grip on the ball while reading the defense prior to making their move.

post is double teamed, or inside on a cut.

Sell a Good Fake

To fake means to show one move while intending to make another. To really sell a fake, the post must actually start the movement. To make an effective shot fake, a player must bring the ball slightly over the forehead, holding the ball firmly with two hands while giving the impression that he wants to shoot; he should be looking toward the rim or in the direction he's pretending to go. At the same time, his legs are bent, ready to explode up for a shot or forward for a drive.

Some players tend to overfake or underfake. A post is overfaking when he extends his arms too much with the ball over his head; in this case, he'll also extend his legs, thus losing the necessary power and strength to go straight up for a shot or forward for a drive. By underfaking, I mean not moving the ball enough to fool the defender, thus not drawing a reaction.

Make a Move at the Count of Three

Basketball is a game of quickness and reaction. The most dangerous situation for the defense is when the ball is in the hands of a post near the basket. However, keeping the ball too much in the post's hands in this position gives the defense the opportunity to rotate and trap the post. So, when a player receives the ball in the post position, he must decide within no more than three counts to play one on one or to pass the ball—either outside to a teammate, who is spotted up when the

Shoot With Defender's Contact

If under the basket the defender is on the side of an offensive player who's going up for a shot, the offensive player puts his inside leg between the defender's legs and leans to make contact with his shoulder against the chest of the defender, who's either jumping up or coming down after jumping on a fake. The post should then shoot with the opposite hand. This contact freezes the defender and gives him less chance to block the shot. He must be mindful not to push the defender away with the shoulder or the nonshooting arm.

Be a Good Free-Throw Shooter

A post asset often underconsidered is the ability to make a free throw. With all the banging that occurs near the basket and all the fouls being whistled in the lane, the post player must work on becoming a good free-throw shooter. The "Hack-a-Shaq" strategy, referring to Shaquille O'Neal and a defense's tendency to foul a post player who hits a low percentage of free throws, is applied often, and not only in the NBA. Thus, coaches must spend time teaching the proper technique for shooting free throws. Posts with above-average free-throw percentages, such as Yao Ming and Mehmet Okur, are money in the bank for their teams.

The principles just discussed should be reflected in the way a post player performs the post moves and shots described in the upcoming sections.

GETTING OPEN

Let's look at ways to get open when a post is guarded individually, analyzing various situations depending on ball position and how the defender is guarding the post.

Low Post on the Ball Side

Defender in a three-quarter overplaying stance. Before asking for the ball, the post must gain a strong position. He works with his feet and buttocks first and with his arms and hands second. Assume a position facing the passer with the inside forearm bent 45 degrees and parallel to the floor and leaning on the chest of the defender. The simplest way to get the ball is to freeze the defender momentarily without pushing with the inside forearm, and then, with a small hop, to extend the outside foot and outside arm to give the passer a target. But this simple move cannot be done every time, so here are the moves of the post when the defender is overplaying him in a three-quarter stance.

- Reverse (facing the defender)

  Feet: Face the defender with the head up (or with the head leaning on the defender's chest to create space). Put the foot nearest the midcourt line between the defender's feet, make a reverse, stepping over the front foot of the defender with a big and strong step, and then open up to the ball. At the same time, "sit" on the front leg of the defender and ask for the ball.

  Arms: While making a reverse, use the arms to freeze the defender and prevent him from jumping the pass. Raise both arms, bent 45 degrees, with palms open and up. If the defender tries to come over the shoulder, put a forearm under his elbow and lift it high (without fouling) and ask for the ball with the opposite hand. If the defender tries to anticipate by putting his arm below the post's bent arm and under the armpit, the post pushes down the defender's arm and asks for the ball with the opposite hand.

- Step-over (facing the passer)

  Feet: This move consists of a short but strong fake step toward midcourt with the forward foot, followed by a long step over the forward foot of the defender (figure 3.1a), sitting on his leg and getting open for the ball.

  Arms: While making the fake step, put your inside arm over the forearm of the defender's inside arm for a second, then "swim" (i.e., bring the inside arm high and then down, as if swimming) over the defender with some contact (figure 3.1b) but not enough to draw a foul. Then ask for the ball (figure 3.1c).

Figure 3.1   Step-over: *(a)* the first and second steps; *(b)* bring down the forward arm of the defender; and *(c)* ask for the ball.

Defender in front. Many times the defender will guard the post by being completely in front of him. In this case, there's more than one way to get open to receive the ball.

• *Keep the position.* If the ball is on the right wing of the half-court, the first and easiest way for the post player to get open for a pass under the basket is to keep his body parallel to the baseline, putting his forward leg (the one nearest the sideline) between the defender's legs, with his hip against his buttocks, his corresponding arm bent 45 degrees and over the defender's shoulder, and his other arm extended high with the palm of the hand up, asking for the ball. Using the outside arm this way, the post generally avoids fouling, whereas if he puts his forearm against the defender's back, he might tend to push to get open.

• *Ball reversal.* If the defender gets a good position and the ball handler can't pass directly to the post, the post player signals with his hand to reverse the ball to the wing on the weak side of the court. Meanwhile, he pins down the defender and then receives the ball from the wing (or from the teammate at the top of the lane).

In the previous moves, to receive the ball safely and prevent the defender from recovering, it's important to release the position only when the ball is in the air and over the head of the defender, not before.

• *Step back and turn around.* The post can also take a short step back before turning around the defender and going in front of him. In turning around, he makes a big step over the front foot of the defender, and then "sits" on his front leg.

• *Release contact and come back.* The post can release his contact with the defender, step to the middle of the lane, come back, and then, once the defender regains his normal defensive position, choose from two options. If the defender body checks him or guards him face to face, he can spin around the defender, or, if the defender is in a helping defensive stance with the inside foot forward, he can make a V cut—that is, a step in one direction, followed by a step in the opposite direction.

Low Post, Ball at the Top of the Key (Duck In)

The pass to the post from the top of the key or from the high to the low post is one of the most effective for a high-percentage shot near the basket. However, the post must get open when the ball is on this spot of the court, and he must seal the defender behind him. The move to get open under the basket is usually called "duck in." There are two ways to get open to receive the pass from the top of the key; which you choose depends on how the defense is guarding the post.

Defender body check or face to face. If the defender is in this position, the post puts his forward foot between the feet of the defender and makes a turnaround move; this is followed by a long, quick, and aggressive step over the front foot of the defender and, simultaneously, a swim move over the defender's front arm. If the defender tries to anticipate the pass with his front arm high, the post pushes the defender's arm up for a moment, with his forearm bent and at the middle of the defender's forearm. If the defender tries to anticipate the pass by extending his arm below the armpit of the post, the post pushes the defender's forearm down.

Defender in a three-quarter overplaying stance. With the defender in this position, the post makes a short fake step with the forward foot to close the distance from the defender. He then momentarily grabs the wrist of the defender's forward arm, pushing it down and "swimming" over; he makes a long and aggressive step over the front foot of the defender, sits on the defender's front leg, and asks for the ball.

High Post, Ball on the Top of the Lane

If set on the high post, at one of the corners of the free-throw area, or at the free-throw line, the post can get open using the same moves described for getting open on the low post. He can make a reverse move when facing the defender or use a step-over move when he has his back to the basket.

Low Post on the Weak Side: Baseline Cut

The low post is set on the weak side of the court, away from the ball, and wants to cut to the ball, positioned at the opposite wing. Again, he must read what the defender is doing and react. A key point on all the post cuts from the weak to strong side is that he must force a defender's reaction when he starts to step into the lane. If he starts to move when he's under the rim or near the ball, he won't have enough space to react and will be forced to receive the ball away from the basket.

Defender body check or face to face. The post puts his foot nearest the midcourt line between the defender's legs, makes a reverse to seal the defender, and asks for the ball.

Defender in a three-quarter overplaying stance. The post makes a V cut, stepping in one direction, and then goes in the opposite direction; at the same time, he pushes down the defender's extended arm and then makes a big step over the defender's front leg.

Defender double reaction. After reacting to the post's V cut, the defender might change his three-quarter contesting stance to a face-to-face defense. In this case, the post uses a combination of the two described moves: After the V cut, he brings the defender high, and then makes a reverse with his forward foot nearest the midcourt line, facing the baseline and sealing the defender, and prepares to receive the ball.

Ball reversal. If the post tries to cut to the ball but is overplayed by the defender, the ball handler can't directly pass him the ball, in which case the ball is reversed to the other side of the court on the wing or the corner. While the ball is in the air, the post goes deep into the lane, seals the defender under the basket with a step-over or a reverse, and asks for the ball.

Using a Screen

A screen is an offensive way to free a teammate. Most screens are made by a post player for a perimeter player. However, on these offensive plays, the inside player can also get open himself.

- *Horizontal screen.* On a screen along the baseline, right after the screened teammate has cut, the post opens himself to the ball by stepping over the defender's feet or using a reverse to seal the defender and asks for the ball.

- *Vertical screen.* When the post is screening down a teammate with his back to the ball handler, right after the cut of the screened teammate, the post reverses to open himself up to the ball and seal the defender and then asks for the ball.

- *Fake a screen.* Instead of making a vertical or horizontal screen, the post can fake the screen; once near his teammate, instead of setting the screen, he immediately opens himself up and asks for the ball.

POST MOVES AND SHOTS

The moves presented in this section are not necessarily part of a center's tools. Some will work for some players, and others will not. Within team play, the coach should discover which of these moves are most effective for his post players. Having a number of moves to use is a definite advantage. The post player must leave no move to chance; he must know what he can and can't execute.

We'll now look at post moves with the back to the basket and when facing the basket.

Low Post Back to the Basket

The post must master the drop step. The drop step is a lost art, but it's a move that's at the base of every move with the back to the basket, particularly at the low- and midpost position, but also at the high-post position.

Based on the position of the defender, the post can make a long drop step toward the baseline or to the middle of the lane. A key point: If he's at the low-post position, he must set himself above the block to make enough space to go to the baseline or to the middle of the lane. On all drop-step moves, the player starts the drop step while the ball is in the air, but he does not release contact with the defender (because doing so allows the defender to steal the ball). Being parallel to the board after the drop step gives an advantage to the post because he can then shoot (a power shot or a dunk) with the protection of the rim, which avoids the weak-side defender's help.

The greatest master of the drop step was Kevin McHale, the Boston Celtics' center in the 1980s. What made McHale even more effective is that in addition to the best drop step, he had a whole repertoire of moves to counter the reaction of a defender. While a pass was still in the air on the way to him, he would make the drop step to "hook" the back foot of the defender. Current players could learn a lot about setting up an opponent for a post move by watching old footage of McHale.

Drop Step to the Baseline

After the drop step, the post's moves and shots are based on the reaction of the defense.

Defender on the high side—shoot with one or no dribble. Imagine that the ball is on the wing. The post gets position at the mid- or low post on the ball side, and he has sealed the defender on the high side (nearest to the midcourt line) with an arm bent at 45 degrees by leaning on the chest or on the crook of the defender's overplaying elbow.

Walter Iooss Jr./NBAE/Getty Images Sport

Kevin McHale wasn't the biggest post player, but his long arms and crafty maneuvers made him very tough to guard, as defender Mychal Thompson demonstrates by having to hook his opponent here.

While the ball is in the air, the post makes a long drop step with the baseline foot, with toes pointed as much as possible toward the baseline and touching the floor with the heel and then with the toes. With this step, the post "hooks" his back foot around the back foot of the defender, turns the front foot to the baseline, and rotates his body to be parallel to the board. The move is finished with a dunk or power shot near the basket. While making the drop step, the buttocks must block out the body of the defender, putting the post's body between the basket and the defender, who can't recover.

Depending on the distance from the basket, this move can also be done with one dribble. In this case, the post makes the dribble between the legs to protect the ball with his body and avoid the recovery of the defender. He bounces the ball very hard on the floor and bends his legs at the same time to jump with all his strength to the basket. One thing to note here: If, after the drop step, the post shoots a power shot with a defender behind him, he must not shoot with his arms straight over his head and his body completely vertical but rather with his torso and arms leaning forward; this prevents the defender from blocking the shot from behind.

Defender behind, fake to the middle, power dribble, and shoot. In this situation, the defender is set behind the post player, between him and the basket, and the ball is already in the hands of the post. Right after he has received the ball, the post holds it tightly with both hands, elbows outside; his head is turned inside the lane to see where the defender is and if there's a chance to pass to a teammate who's cutting. He then brings the ball toward the outside shoulder (the one nearest the midcourt line), turning his head toward the lane to give the defender the impression he wants to go to the middle. As soon as the defender reacts and slides in the direction of the fake, the post makes a drop step toward the baseline, hooks the rear foot of the defender to seal him, points the

toe of the drop-step foot toward the basket, and, at the same time, makes a strong power dribble with both hands and shoots a power shot or a dunk.

Defender recovers on the baseline. If, after the post's drop step to the baseline the defender recovers to the baseline and blocks the path to the basket, the post front pivots, goes to the middle of the lane, and, after a dribble, finishes with a jump hook, hook, jump shot, or an up-and-under shot. Let's look at each of these.

• *Jump hook.* After the baseline drop step, the post takes one step into the lane with the same foot, dribbles once (always inside the body to protect the ball), and keeps his toes pointed toward the sideline. Then, jumping on two feet, he executes a jump hook, bringing the ball laterally away from the defender and over his head, protecting it with his other forearm and shoulder. Once the ball is overhead, he releases the ball with a flip of the wrist. As he makes the step and the dribble in the lane, he must stay low on the legs. If his legs are straight or not bent enough, he loses power and strength, and it's easier for the defender to bump or push him away. A split second after landing on the floor, he prepares to catch the rebound in case the shot is missed.

• *Hook.* If there's enough space, the hook shot is an option. Though used less frequently by today's players, the move is nearly impossible to stop, even by bigger and stronger defenders. This shot can be taken with or without a dribble. The toes of the forward foot should point as much as possible toward the basket. While jumping off the front foot, bring the ball outside with the arm nearest to the midcourt line, starting the shot a little above the shooting shoulder and bringing up the corresponding leg bent at the knee. The nonshooting arm, bent about 45 degrees and pointing toward the basket, lifts the ball up and releases it at about shoulder level. With the shooting arm extended overhead, the ball is released with a flip of the wrist and fingers; the fingers end up pointed toward the center of the basket.

One important detail to remember is to turn the head and watch the basket in advance while turning the body to prepare the shot. Doing so helps locate the defender and focus the eyes on the rim. Also, if the foot of the high leg is pointed toward the basket, the body will automatically move in that direction. If the foot is pointing in another direction, the body will move away from the basket, which results in two negatives—the ball will be farther from the basket, making the shot more difficult, and the player will have a greater distance to cover to rebound a missed attempt.

• *Jump shot.* If the player is squared to the basket in a proper balanced position and with enough space, he can take a jump

shot—if the defender is far enough away to let him shoot.

• *Up-and-under shot.* If the defender completely recovers the position under the basket and tries to block the shot, the post fakes a shot and brings the ball up with both hands a little above the forehead, while bending the legs and watching the basket as if he would like to shoot (figure 3.2a). As soon as the defender is in the air, the post makes a long but balanced stride through and over the body of the defender with the outside foot (the foot nearest the midcourt line), while at the same time bringing the ball from one ear to the other (figure 3.2b). In this case, he must not bring the ball to chest level because there's no space for this move, and he would lose time. He then goes under the body of the defender and shoots (figure 3.2c). When making the step through,

Figure 3.2 The up and under consists of *(a)* a shot fake, followed by *(b)* a strong step under the arms of the defender, and ending with *(c)* a layup.

With his size, agility, and power, Andrew Bynum will be a special NBA post player if he continues to expand and improve his positioning, footwork, and repertoire of moves.

Stephen Dunn/Getty Images Sport

Defender recovers—drop step baseline, dribble, and shot. If the defender slides up and recovers on the drop step to the middle, the post takes a drop step to the middle, using the foot nearest the baseline as his pivot foot, reverses, takes one dribble (bouncing the ball in front of the body to protect it), and goes up for a dunk or a shot off the glass.

Spin

If the defender stays behind the post and pushes him with the forearm, a great move is the quick spin around the defender to take a shot right away, if possible, without a dribble. The spin is most common to the baseline but can also be to the middle. The keys to this move are staying low, using the foot nearest the baseline or midcourt line as the pivot foot, rotating on the heel, pointing the toe of the pivot foot toward the basket, and taking a long step with the other leg. To avoid the defender touching or slapping the ball from behind, keep it at chest level and in the middle of the body during the entire spin. The best ever at the spin-and-go move was Hakeem Olajuwon of the Houston Rockets, who had great footwork, agility, and quickness.

the post turns his body and becomes as slim as possible to more easily and quickly get under the body of the defender and to the rim.

Drop Step to the Middle

Defender on the low side—shot with no dribble or one dribble. Once the post has sealed the defender on the low side, he makes a drop step on the baseline to the middle (using the same technique described for the baseline drop step) and has these options: finishing with a dunk, shooting a power shot off the glass, shooting a jump hook or a hook, taking a jump shot, or shooting an up-and-under shot.

High Post Back to the Basket

A high-post position gives the center the opportunity to shoot jump shots and pass to cutters who have beat their defenders.

The high-post player can also set picks for guards above the circle. Pick-and-roll skills should be part of this game (i.e., attacking the hoop or taking the jump shot from 12 to 16 feet).

When receiving the ball with his back to the hoop, because of the distance from the basket, the post has basically two immediate options from the high-post position: the drop step and drive and the spin and drive.

Drop step and drive. The execution is the same as described before. Go to the rim with a long, quick step, dribble once, shoot off the glass, jump on one or two feet to take the shot, or dunk.

Spin and drive. Fake on one side and then spin, or spin immediately upon receiving the ball and shoot after no dribble or one hard dribble.

Make sure during these moves that the lane is free. Because the move is so quick, there's little chance (or no chance) to make a countermove if another defender is in the lane.

Face-Up Moves and Shots

The post must be able to face the basket and master some basic face-to-the-basket moves and shots. Decent ball-handling skills are essential to use these moves effectively. At either the low or high post, the post player must make a front or reverse pivot to face the basket. These moves initiate facing the basket and allow the post to read the defender's position and decide which move to make to get to the basket.

Low-Post Front Pivot

The front pivot to face the basket can be done to the middle of the lane or to the baseline. Once he has received the ball with his back to the basket with the defender completely behind him, and when there's no chance to make a drop step or a spin, the post first creates space from the defender.

To do this, he makes a good fake with the ball, bringing it a little over the shoulder nearest the midcourt line if he wants to go to the baseline or the opposite if he wants to go to the middle of the lane. At the same time, he turns his head to watch the feet of the defender to try to sell him a move in that direction. Then he uses the foot nearest the baseline as his pivot foot, touching the floor with the heel first and rolling on it to quickly turn and face the basket. During the entire front pivot, the post stays low on his knees. The ball is brought to the side at chest level with the wrist bent behind. The head is near perpendicular to the floor for good balance, and eyes are on the rim. If he has his head forward, his body will come forward too and thus be out of balance. For a quicker move, he should start to front pivot while making the fake with the ball. Using the front pivot, he'll stay closer to the basket.

• *Jump shot.* If the defender goes for the fake and gives the post the space he needs, the easiest shot is the jump shot. While turning, keeping legs bent, bring the ball at forehead level to a shooting position with the shooting hand behind the ball and bent. Keep both feet pointed toward the basket to maintain balance. Release the jump shot right away, shooting with the help of the backboard if front-pivoting to the baseline.

• *Up and under.* If the defender recovers and is still between the post and the basket and tries to block the shot, the post makes an up-and-under move, taking a step into the lane long enough to beat the defender, and finishes with a layup with the left hand if he's on the right side of the court and the right hand if he's on the left side of the court.

• *Reverse and shoot.* Start with the usual ball-and-head fake and the front pivot; when the defender recovers and closes the path in that direction, reverse pivot to go the opposite direction and then shoot a hook.

Low-Post Reverse Pivot

In the NBA, the defender usually stays between the basket and the post and tries to push the post away from the lane, using his forearm against the post's back and hip. In such a case, set with back parallel to the baseline and inside forearm (the arm nearest the lane) bent at 45 degrees against the defender's chest; now ask for the ball with the other hand. After receiving the ball, face the basket and pivot away from it on the foot furthest from the defender to create space. The heel should touch the floor first, preparing for the roll and push on the forefoot for a drive or jump shot. Stay low on the knees during the entire reverse pivot. Bring the ball to the side at chest level with wrist bent behind. The head is near perpendicular to the floor for good balance, and eyes are focused on the rim. If the head is forward, the body will come forward too, causing imbalance.

As I said at the beginning of the chapter, especially when facing the basket, the post must be able to put the ball on the floor and master three types of dribble: the crossover, the spin, and the step-back. He must also be mindful not to dribble too much (no more than twice) before shooting to prevent the defense from collapsing on him. The post has a great selection of shots when facing the basket.

• *Jump shot.* If after the reverse pivot the defender backs off to prevent the post from driving, and if there's enough space, take a jumper. Keep the ball high. A shot fake is often to the shooter's advantage in this situation.

• *Up and under.* If after the reverse pivot the defender remains between the post and the basket and tries to block the jump shot, make a shot fake followed by an up-and-under move (using the mechanics described earlier).

• *Rip the ball and drive.* If the defender leaves space to get to the rim on the baseline or in the middle of the lane, rip the ball from one side of the body to the other, bringing it below knee level; then make a long step with the leg opposite to the ball to go over the defender's hip. Dribble to avoid walking and protect the ball with the nondribbling forearm bent at hip level. Finish with a dunk or a power shot.

• *Crossover step.* If the defender doesn't allow space for a straight drive to the basket and has a leg forward, make a crossover step simultaneously with a dribble. Then quickly rip the ball from one side of the body to the other, bringing it below knee level. Take a step and a dribble over the forward leg of the defender and go to the rim. The toes of the nonpivot foot point toward the basket; if pointed in a different direction, the body will go in that direction instead of toward the rim. Bounce the ball over the hip of the defender so he can't recover. Protect the ball with the nondribbling hand bent and at the defender's hip level.

• *Drive and spin dribble.* If after the first drive the defender recovers and cuts off a straight path to the basket from the baseline or the middle of the lane, spin dribble (also called a reverse dribble) and drive to the opposite direction. The velocity of the ball on the spin dribble should be very fast so the ball comes up rapidly from the floor for a quick catch-and-shoot.

• *Drive, step-back dribble, and shot or crossover dribble.* Work on this combination move only after mastering the step-back. If the defender recovers after the straight drive to the basket, make a step-back dribble to create space, and then shoot or make a crossover dribble and drive to the basket. To step back, make a hop backward, pushing on the nonpivot foot; at the same time, bring the ball back with the same hand.

• *Sikma move.* This maneuver is named after Jack Sikma, a seven-time all-star center for the Sonics and Bucks in the late 1970s and '80s. After receiving a pass with back to the basket, keep the ball at forehead level. Then, using either foot as the pivot foot, take a step forward, turn to face the basket, and, at the same time, bring the ball overhead to shoot a jump shot. This shot is virtually impossible to block because the ball is so high and seems to go behind the head before it's released. Teams that grew frustrated with Sikma's success would sometimes have their guards sag off the perimeter and try to swat the ball from behind, but this rarely worked.

High-Post Front and Reverse Pivot

From the high-post position, the post can use many of the shots described for the low post facing the basket, either with a reverse or front pivot.

- *Front pivot, jump shot.* Once the ball is received, and if the defender allows space right away to face the basket with a front pivot, or after a fake on one side and the front pivot on the other side, the post makes a jump shot.
- *Front pivot, up-and-under.* This is the same move described for the low post, but here a dribble might be necessary to go to the rim.
- *Sweep the ball and drive.* The technique is the same as for the low post, but here the dribble and step must be longer because the post is further from the basket.
- *Crossover dribble.* When the post rips the ball during the crossover, if the defender closes the path to the rim, the post makes a crossover step and a dribble to go over the defender. Because of the distance from the basket, the high post must dribble only once to get to the basket to avoid the other defenders.

Additional Moves

I call these additional moves because players must develop complete body control, foot-work, and ball handling before practicing and using these moves in games.

Jump stop. The jump stop is usually used at the high-post position (either when facing the basket or with the back to it) after a drop-step move, an up-and-under, or a spin. The post must be in the air when he picks up the dribble. When he starts one of the

described moves and sees the defender is in his path to the basket, he can pick up the dribble with both hands and, pushing himself laterally with the foot opposite to the new direction, hop and land with the other foot on the opposite spot in the lane. He moves a couple of feet away from the defender and in the opposite direction. Depending on the defender's position, the post takes a jump shot, power shot, or jump hook; fakes a shot and then shoots; makes an up-and-under move; or tries any other move he has confidence in.

Power slide. This move requires teammates to clear out the low-post position, freeing the post to play one on one toward the baseline or the middle of the lane without risk of the double team. As soon as the post receives the ball, he leans his inside shoulder on the chest of the defender; at the same time, he makes a power slide and dribbles to the lane, dribbling hard with the hand away from the defender and forcing him to move back inside the lane. After one dribble (two at the most), the post makes contact with the defender (without pushing or charging) for an open shot under the rim. If the defender tries to overplay the power slide, the post uses any of the moves and shots already described, such as the drop step and power shot, the jump hook, or the hook. The post's back is usually parallel to the baseline at the start of the move. It helps a great deal if the post is taller or stronger than the defender. If he's not, the move can be rendered ineffective by a bigger and stronger opponent who's allowed to push and shove.

TEACHING AND LEARNING POST PLAY

When I played, the coach's job was easier because players stayed attentive during practice, like learning-motivated students listening to a professor. Now, with athletes who come to the game with less discipline and many more distractions, a coach needs to command players' attention by convincing them that the knowledge and instruction he's imparting is useful and will improve their skills and performance. A coach wins the confidence and respect of his athletes because they see the benefits of what they're learning.

To reinforce these points, it helps if the coach can provide proof of the payoff through the use of video. Show players what they looked like on the court prior to their teaching and development, and then contrast that with recent footage highlighting specific techniques and tactics in which they've demonstrated significant improvement. The coach must praise and reinforce the things players do well.

Young post players are often taller (sometimes much taller) than their peers, and are often less confident about and less secure in relationships with the people around them. This can create negative self-esteem issues that they carry onto the basketball court. So, especially with a big player, the coach must have an open and positive relationship, correcting mistakes, but above all emphasizing the progress being made and what the player is doing well. This can provide a real confidence boost and spur the player on to work hard to reach his potential.

I started this chapter by saying that the growth of the post requires more time and attention. Indeed, there simply isn't enough space allotted here to cover everything a player needs to be effective on the post. For example, I didn't get into the skills and determination needed to be a successful rebounder. This is not to suggest that rebounding is not an important part of effectiveness at the post. Please seek other sources for information on that aspect of post play.

Before closing this chapter, I want to make one more essential point for both the coach and the player: Be patient. Most post players develop a bit later than their counterparts, and their coordination might not catch up to their size for several years. Don't try to rush the development process. Teach proper footwork first because that's the foundation on which all progress is made. Then, because the post usually moves in a limited and congested space, it's important to master how to get open. I call this initial stage of learning the post the crawling phase.

When getting open is no longer a problem, work on the primary post moves, such as the drop step and the front and reverse pivot. Practice the basic shots diligently, both facing the basket and with the back to it. Practice the power move, the jump shot, the hook, and the up-and-under. This stage is what I call the walking phase.

Finally, when a player has good command of footwork, moves to get open, primary moves with the ball, and shots needed to be successful in the post, it's time to add difficulty and seek refinement. Countermoves and advanced moves, passing, and mastering a go-to move comprise the running phase of post-player development.

When coaches and players approach the challenges of post-play instruction and learning in this manner, everyone benefits. Though other positions are certainly important, championship teams almost always have very capable, if not superb, post play. Keep that in mind the next time you dream of cutting down the nets.

chapter 4

Screens and Screen Plays

Phil Johnson

Screens, also called picks or drags, are vital to any type of offense because it's practically impossible to defend all the options available to the offensive players when they execute their screen plays properly. Every coach should teach and drill all players on how to set screens and how to use them based on reactions of the defenders.

Over the course of my career I've been fortunate to work with some of the best screen combinations in basketball history, including the famous John Stockton and Karl Malone duo. Currently, I have the pleasure of working with one of the best screening combos in today's game: Deron Williams and Carlos Boozer. Watching these players develop such superb technique, gain such a keen sense for each other's moves, and adjust in a blink of an eye to defenders' efforts to stop them is one of the things I appreciate most about coaching.

The principle of screening—shielding an opponent from covering the player to which he is assigned—is easy to understand. However, learning to execute the play effectively in various ways in different locations on the court and against good, smart defenders is more difficult.

GEORGE FREY/AFP/Getty Images Sport

Karl Malone sets an effective screen for teammate John Stockton to initiate a textbook pick-and-roll play, which the duo executed together many times in their careers.

SCREENING BASICS

Let's start with some simple guidelines that even young and inexperienced players can grasp with proper teaching. An on-ball screen, in which one player screens for a teammate with the ball, is a good place to start. For this situation, we'll look at rules for both the screener and the player receiving the screen.

Screener Rules

- See the teammate with the ball to best time the screen.

- Establish a solid stance (wide and low) at the proper angle for the ball handler to use an advantage against the defender.

- After setting a screen, pivot to face the ball and present a target for the ball handler.

The screen's angle is of foremost importance because the angle influences whether the defender has an easy or difficult time fighting the screen. As a rule, try to present the screen to the defender at a 90-degree angle, which gives him the widest space to cover when chasing the screened player.

Screen Receiver Rules

- See the screener, and either stay stationary or move in a way that helps the screener set a good screen.

- Use the angle and placement of the screen to your best advantage—get an open shot or drive toward the basket.

- Read the defense. Is the defender covering the ball stopped or slowed by the screen? Has the player guarding the screener switched to help out his screened teammate to defend you? Whatever the case, sense the defense's reaction and move accordingly.

When receiving the screen, don't move too quickly before the screen is set, and don't cut the screen off at full speed. Sometimes the screened player can beat the defender getting off the screen at full speed, but many other times, reading the defense, using a change of pace, and going the opposite way of the defender is the best way to exploit the screen.

Sam Forencich/NBAE/Getty Images Sport

Deron Williams gets picked up by teammate Carlos Boozer's defender and dishes the ball to him for a basket.

Often the ball hander who has used the screen is picked up by the help defender or the original defender, who recovers quickly after being screened. In such a case, an open shot or drive to the hoop is probably not possible, so at this point the ball handler becomes a passer.

Passer Rules

- See the full court and all teammates, but be especially aware of the screener.
- Read the reaction of defenders involved in the screen.
- Make a good, crisp pass away from the defender.
- Use the lob pass if necessary.

READING THE DEFENSE

Now we need to get deeper into the tactical decisions and actions necessary to make screens effective. The game of basketball is extremely fluid, with the pace of the action, player matchups, types of defenses employed, and a host of other variables changing all the time. Thus, offensive players must constantly examine the current situation and choose their tactics accordingly.

Such is the case when determining how best to set and use a screen, based on the defensive personnel, their positions on the court, and their actions. A keen awareness of the present defense and proper execution of the following countermoves will increase chances for success.

Screened Player's Reads

Setting up a defender to be screened and then capitalizing on the defense's response to the screen are underappreciated offensive maneuvers. Let's look at several options for using a screen.

Curl. If his defender trails, the screened player circles, or curls, around the screener and cuts to the basket to receive the ball (figure 4.1). He cuts as close as possible to the screener (brushing his shoulder) to avoid giving the defender a chance to get through the screen.

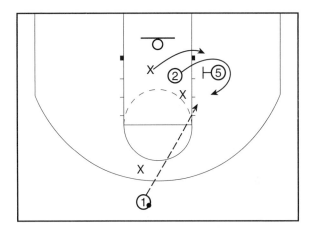

Figure 4.1   If his defender trails, the screened player curls around the screener.

Curl and slip. If the screened player curls around the screen and his defender trails, and the screener sees that his defender leaves him to help out (figure 4.2), the screener cuts (slips) to the basket to receive the ball.

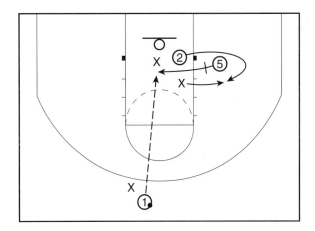

Figure 4.2   If the screener's defender helps out on the curl, the screener (5) slips to the basket.

Bump and pop. If, during the curl around the screener, the screened player sees his defender going over the screen to beat him on the spot (figure 4.3) while the screener adapts his screen by making a drop step, the screened player executes a "bump"—that is, he pushes himself off the screener and pops away. By popping out, the screened player can elude the defender, pushing with his hand against the back or the hip of the screener and taking a step or a hop away.

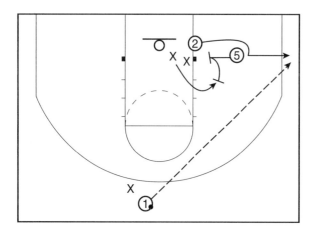

Figure 4.3 If his defender goes over the screen, the screened player bumps the screener and pops away.

Bump and slip. If the screener's defender jumps out (also called showing or hedging) to cover the screened player who has bumped and popped away from the screen and then received the ball (figure 4.4), the screener (5) quickly slips to the basket to receive a pass from the screened player.

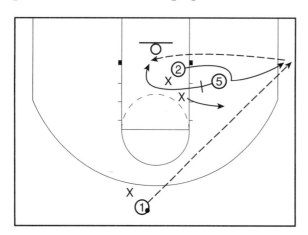

Figure 4.4 If the screener's defender jumps out to slow down the screened player, the screener slips to the basket for a pass from the screened player.

Screener's Reads

On all screens, the screener must offer a passing option to the ball handler, either rolling to the basket, popping out, or going in the opposite direction of the screened player. Thus, the screener must watch the reactions of the screened player, as well as watching his defender and the screened player's defender, and move accordingly. In general, the screener should go the opposite direction of the screened player. For example, if the screened player goes to the baseline, the screener goes high in the opposite direction. We'll review the screener's reads while describing the different types of away and on-ball screens.

SCREEN PLAYS

The proper choice of screen to use depends on the player's location on the court and the number of offensive players involved. The four categories to select from include off-the-ball screens, on-the-ball screens, high-post rub cuts, and special screens.

Off-the-Ball Screens

These screens involve three players: the passer, the screener, and the player for whom the screen is set.

Back Screen

This screen is also called a blind screen because the screener comes from behind the defender so that he can't see the arrival of the screen. Here are the options for the screened player based on the reaction of the defender:

- If his defender runs into the screen (figure 4.5), the ball handler (1) makes a lob pass to the screened player (2) while the screener (5) rolls to the ball.
- If his defender slides high on the screen (figure 4.6), the screened player cuts low while the screener pops out.
- If his defender slides low on the screen (figure 4.7), the screened player cuts over the top of the screen while the screener pops out.

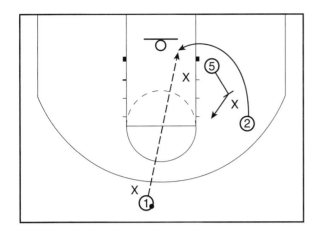

Figure 4.5 If his defender runs into the screen, the screened player receives a lob pass.

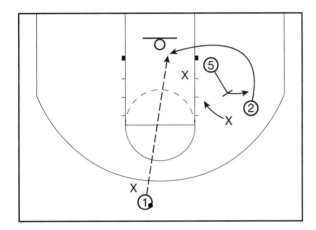

Figure 4.6 If his defender slides high, the screened player cuts low.

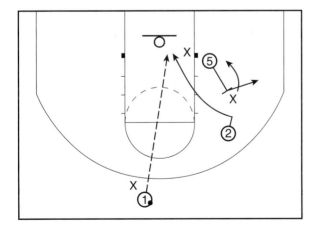

Figure 4.7 If his defender slides low, the screened player cuts over the top.

- If his defender anticipates the cut (figure 4.8), the screened player bumps and pops out away from the screen while the screener rolls to the basket.

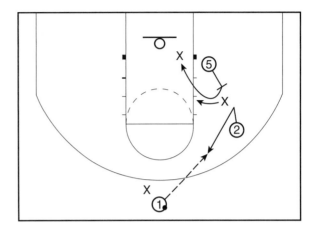

Figure 4.8 If his defender anticipates the cut, the screened player bumps and pops out.

- If the ball handler can't pass directly to the screened player (figure 4.9), the screener pops out, receives the ball, and passes to the screened player, who has posted up.

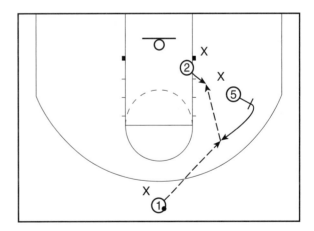

Figure 4.9 If the screened player can't receive the ball, the screener pops out, receives the ball, and passes to the screened player on the post.

Down Screen

The screen is set near the baseline. The player who receives the screen waits and then sets up his defender when he's near to receive the screen; then he runs into the screen. Here are the options for the down screen, again depending on the defender's reactions:

- If the defender trails the screened player (figure 4.10), the screened player curls around the screen, and the screener pops out to the corner.

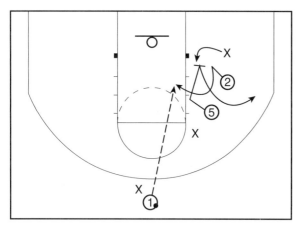

Figure 4.10   If his defender trails, the screened player curls around and the screener pops out to the corner.

- If the defender anticipates the cut of the screened player (figure 4.11), the screened player cuts behind the screen, and the screener comes high.

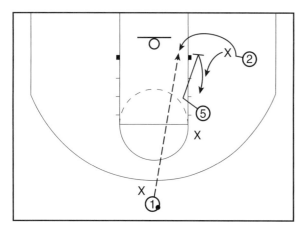

Figure 4.11   If his defender anticipates the cut, the screened player cuts back, and the screener comes high.

- If his defender slides under the screen (figure 4.12), the screened player bumps and pops out to the corner, and the screener cuts into the lane.

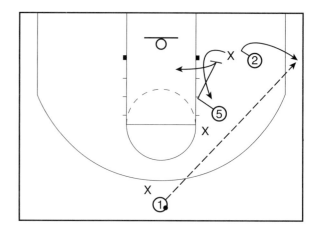

Figure 4.12   If his defender slides under the screen, the screened player bumps and pops out, and the screener cuts into the lane.

Flare Screen

With the ball in the hands of a player positioned past the free-throw line extended, the high post, with his back to the sideline, sets a side screen for a teammate. Here are the options for the flare screen based on the defender's reactions:

- If his defender slides behind the screen (figure 4.13), the screened player flares away from the screen, and the screener cuts to the basket.

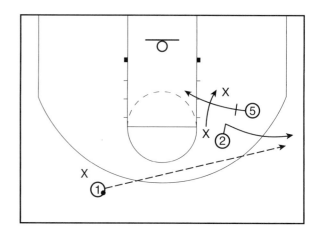

Figure 4.13   If his defender slides behind the screen, the screened player flares from the screen, and the screener cuts to the basket.

• If his defender anticipates the cut (figure 4.14), the screened player cuts directly to the basket, and the screener pops out.

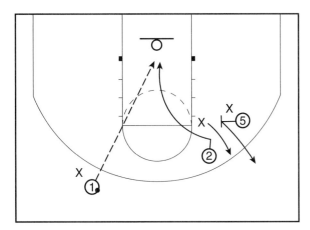

Figure 4.14 If his defender anticipates the cut, the screened player cuts to the basket, and the screener pops out.

• If his defender slides over the top of the screen (figure 4.15), the screened player goes away from the screen and then cuts into the lane, and the screener pops out.

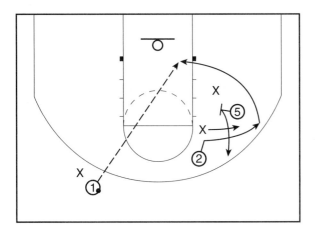

Figure 4.15 If his defender slides over the top, the screened player goes away and then cuts into the lane, while the screener pops out.

Cross Screen

A cross screen is run by two players, both set at the blocks on the two sides of the lane. Here are the options for the cross screen based on the defender's reactions:

• If his defender slides under the screen (figure 4.16), the screened player cuts high over the screen while the screener opens up to the ball in the opposite direction of the screened player.

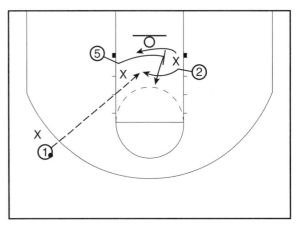

Figure 4.16 If his defender slides under the screen, the screened player cuts high over the screen while the screener goes high in the opposite direction.

• If his defender slides over the screen (figure 4.17), the screened player comes out low along the baseline while the screener opens up and goes high in the opposite direction of the screened player.

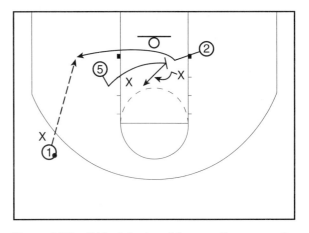

Figure 4.17 If his defender slides over the screen, the screened player comes out low, and the screener goes high in the opposite direction.

- If his defender anticipates the cut (figure 4.18), the screened player stops near the basket to receive a lob pass while the screener opens up to the ball and goes in the opposite direction of the screened player.

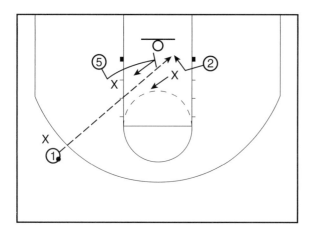

Figure 4.18 If his defender anticipates the cut, the screened player stops near the basket and receives a lob pass while the screener goes in the opposite direction.

Flex Screen

This screen is so called because it is the beginning of the flex offense. Basically, the flex is a back screen set along the baseline (figure 4.19). The reads and options for the screened player and the screener, always based on the reactions of the defense, are the same as described previously for the back screen but in this case are run along the baseline.

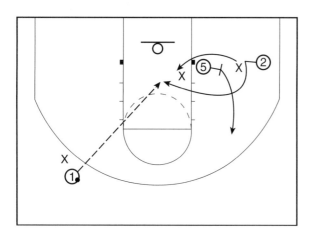

Figure 4.19 The flex screen is a back screen run on the baseline.

Corner Pin Down Screen

This screen is run by a player at the midpost position for a teammate in the deep corner (figure 4.20). The reads and options for the screened player and the screener, always based on the reactions of the defense, are the same as described previously but are run on this spot of the half-court.

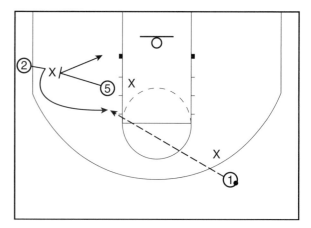

Figure 4.20 The corner pin down screen is a screen at the midpost position, set in the deep corner.

On-the-Ball Screens

These screens directly involve two players: the ball handler and the screener.

Side Screen

The side screen is brought by the screener fronting or with his back to the sideline. Here are the options for the side screen:

- If the ball handler's defender trails the ball handler (figure 4.21), the ball handler drives over the top of the screen while the screener rolls to the basket in the opposite direction of the ball handler's drive.
- If the ball handler's defender slides under the screen (figure 4.22), the ball handler pulls up for a jump shot while the screener rolls to the basket in the opposite direction of the ball handler.

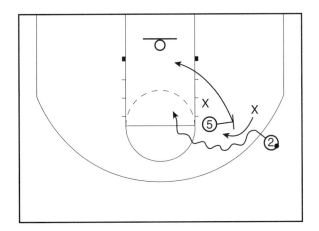

Figure 4.21 If his defender trails, the ball handler drives over the top of the screen while the screener rolls to the basket in the opposite direction.

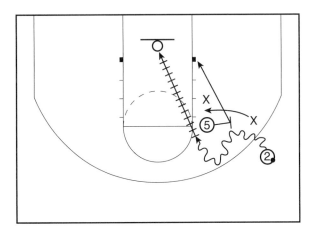

Figure 4.22 If his defender slides under the screen, the ball handler pulls up for a jump shot while the screener rolls to the basket in the opposite direction.

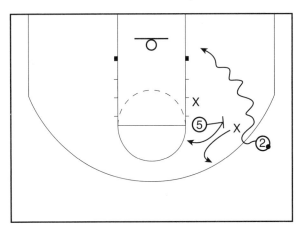

Figure 4.23 If the defender anticipates the ball handler's drive, the ball handler drives to the baseline while the screener rolls to the basket in the opposite direction.

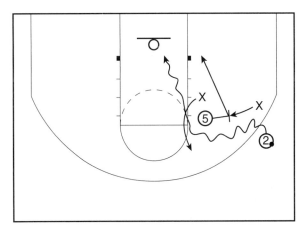

Figure 4.24 If the screener's defender shows up too late, the ball handler splits between the two defenders and drives to the basket while the screener rolls to the basket in the opposite direction.

- If the ball handler's defender anticipates the drive around the screen (figure 4.23), the ball handler drives to the baseline while the screener rolls to the basket in the opposite direction of the ball handler's drive.

- If the screener's defender shows up too late (figure 4.24), the ball handler splits between the two defenders and drives to the basket while the screener rolls to the basket opposite the ball handler's drive.

- If two defenders double team the ball handler (figure 4.25), he takes two dribbles away from the screen and

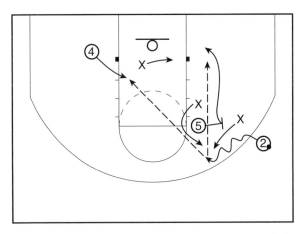

Figure 4.25 If the ball handler is double teamed, he takes two dribbles away and can pass to the screener or to the teammate whose defender helped.

passes to an open teammate—either to the screener, who has rolled to the basket in the opposite direction of the ball handler's drive, or to the teammate whose defender helped out on the roll of the screener.

- If the ball handler's defender forces him to the baseline, the ball handler has three options (figure 4.26):

  Drive to the middle and pull up for a jump shot.

  Pass to the screener (5), who has rolled to the basket.

  Pass to the teammate, who has made a flash cut from a low-post position on the help side to the corner of the free-throw area on the ball side.

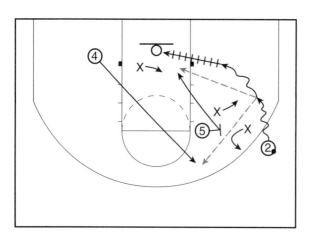

Figure 4.26 If his defender forces him to the baseline, the ball handler can drive to the middle; pass to the screener, who has rolled to the basket; or pass to the teammate, who has flashed to the elbow.

High Screen

The high screen (also called a midscreen) is set in the middle of the court outside the three-second lane. Here are the options for the high screen:

- If his defender trails him (figure 4.27), the ball handler drives around the screen while the screener rolls to the basket in the opposite direction of the ball handler.

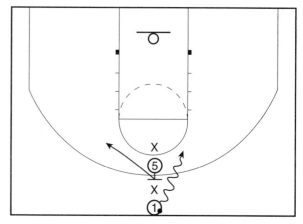

Figure 4.27 If his defender trails him, the ball handler drives around the screen while the screener rolls to the basket in the opposite direction.

- If his defender slides under the screen (figure 4.28), the ball handler pulls up for a jump shot, and the screener rolls to the basket.

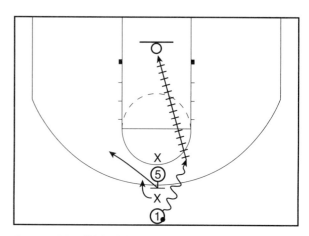

Figure 4.28 If his defender slides under the screen, the ball handler pulls up for a jump shot while the screener rolls to the basket.

• If his defender pushes him outside (figure 4.29), the ball handler passes to the screener, who has rolled to the basket.

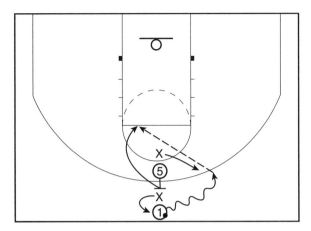

Figure 4.29 If his defender pushes him outside, the ball handler passes to the screener, who has rolled to the basket.

Horns Screen

This screen is part of an offense called horns (also called V), which uses a midscreen and roll. This on-ball screen employs a second high screener, which gives the ball handler options of driving off a screen to either side of the free-throw lane (figure 4.30).

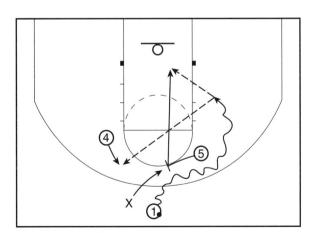

Figure 4.30 The ball handler's reads and options for the horns screen are the same as for the high screen; the nonscreener goes in the opposite direction of the screener.

The reads and options are the same as for the high screen except that the other player (nonscreener) reacts to the screen's action. If the screener rolls to basket, the nonscreener pops out. If the screener pops out, the nonscreener rolls to the basket.

High-Post Rub Cuts

These screens involve three players: the screened player, the screener, and the passer.

UCLA Screen

This vertical back screen set at the corner of the free-throw area is from the famous UCLA offense created by John Wooden, winner of 10 NCAA titles. The ball handler passes the ball to a wing and then "rubs" off the screen (figure 4.31). After the screen, the screener rolls to the basket or pops out. The reads and options for the screened player and the screener, always based on the reactions of the defense, are the same as described earlier but are run at this spot of the court.

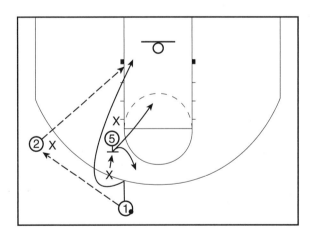

Figure 4.31 The UCLA screen is a vertical back screen set at the corner of the free-throw area.

Hawk Screen

This diagonal screen was used in one of the most common NBA offenses at one time, created and popularized by coach Hubie Brown while he was on the bench for the Atlanta Hawks. The screen is set at the free-throw line area when the ball is at the wing (figure 4.32). The ball handler (1) drives to the wing while the high post (5) back screens for 2; 5 then rolls to the basket in the opposite direction of the ball handler's drive. The reads and options for the screened player and the screener, always based on the reactions of the defense, are the same as described before but are run at this spot of the court.

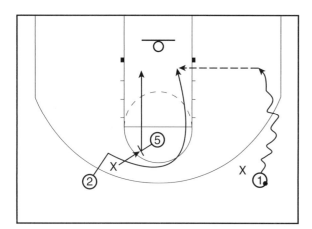

Figure 4.32 The hawk is a diagonal screen at the free-throw circle used when the ball is at the wing; the screener rolls to the basket in the opposite direction of the screened player.

Special Screens

Now let's look at four special screens that involve more than three players.

Screen the Screener

This special screen combines a baseline screen and a down screen. The continuous screen-the-screener action puts pressure on the defense, which must defend two types of screens at once. Screen-the-screener action is initiated by the ball handler (1) making a crosscourt pass to the other guard (2) and then setting a down screen. 3 comes off 4's baseline screen, and 4 pops out high off 1's down screen (figure 4.33).

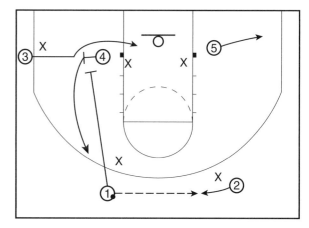

Figure 4.33 The screen-the-screener action is a screen run for a player who has just set a screen.

2 first looks to pass to 3, who is coming off the baseline screen or posting up. 2 can also pass to 5 for a post feed (figure 4.34). If 3 is not open, 2 passes to 4, who is popping out off 1's down screen, or to 1, who's rolling to the basket off the down screen.

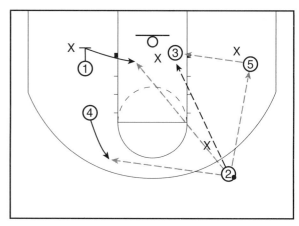

Figure 4.34 The ball handler (2) can pass to 3, 5, 4, or 1.

Continuity: 2 passes to 4 and sets a down screen for 3 (figure 4.35). 5 comes off 3's baseline screen, and 3 pops out off 2's down screen as 1 clears to the corner.

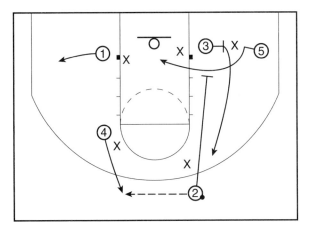

Figure 4.35 The same action can be run on the other side of the floor.

Double Screens

The double screen, in which two players typically screen shoulder to shoulder, can be set up either parallel at the free-throw line or perpendicular to the baseline.

Parallel Double Screen. 4 and 5 set a double screen parallel to the free-throw line. The ball handler (1) dribbles to the wing spot. 2 breaks up off the double screen set by 4 and 5. If his defender trails, 2 can curl and cut to the basket to receive from 1 and shoot (figure 4.36). When the defender cheats and

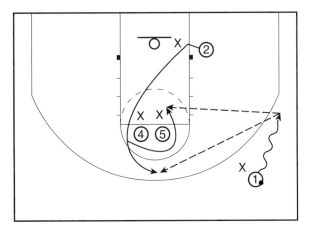

Figure 4.36 The ball handler (1) can pass to 2 at the top of the circle or on the curl around the double screen set by 4 and 5.

goes over the screen, 2 flares and receives the ball for a jump shot.

If 5's defender steps out and hedges or switches on the screen, 5 slips to the basket to receive the ball (figure 4.37). If 4's defender helps out on 5's slip, 4 rolls to the basket, and 1 lobs a pass to 4. 5 also has the option of screening for 4, who cuts to the basket and receives the ball from 1 (figure 4.38).

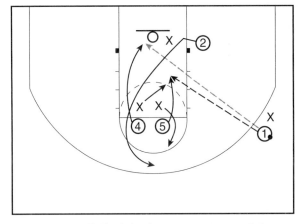

Figure 4.37 If 5's defender steps out or switches on the screen, 5 slips to the basket and receives from 1. If 4's defender helps, 4 rolls to the basket and receives from 1.

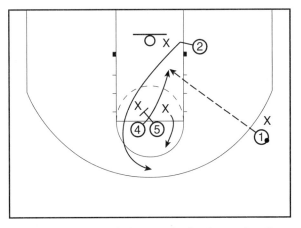

Figure 4.38 5 can also screen for 4, who receives from 1.

Perpendicular Double Screen. 4 and 5 set a double screen for 2 perpendicular to the baseline. The ball handler (1) sets up at the top of the lane. 2 cuts along the baseline off the double screen set by 4 and 5 (figure 4.39). If 2's defender trails, 2 curls around the screen and cuts to the basket to receive a pass. If the defense cheats and goes over the screen, 2 fades to receive and shoot.

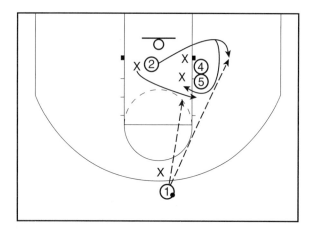

Figure 4.39 If 2's defender trails, 2 curls and cuts to the basket; if 2's defender goes over the screen, 2 fades for a shot.

If 5's defender steps out and hedges or switches on the screen, 5 slips to the basket for a shot (figure 4.40). If 4's defender helps out on 5's slip, 1 can lob a pass to 4. 5 also has the option of setting a screen for 4, who cuts to the basket (figure 4.41).

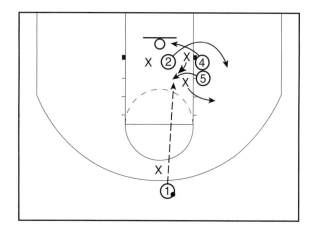

Figure 4.40 If 5's defender shows or switches, 5 slips to the basket; if 4's defender helps on the 5 slip, 4 cuts into the lane to receive a pass from 1.

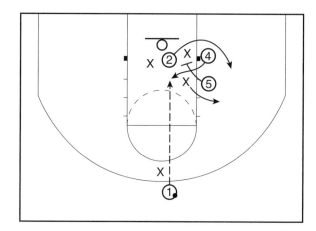

Figure 4.41 5 can also set a screen for 4, who cuts to the basket.

Stagger Double Screen. This special screen uses a series of down screens to get good shooters open. Usually it starts with the big men out and the shooters inside. The stagger double screen is started with 3 setting a cross baseline screen for 2, the shooter. 2 then continues out off 5's down screen (figure 4.42). The ball handler (1) looks to pass to 2, coming off the down screen, or, if the defenders switch, tries to pass to 5, who is rolling to the basket.

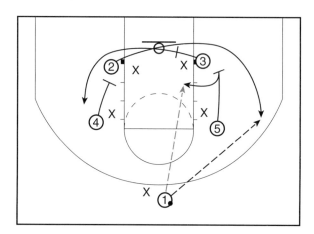

Figure 4.42 1 looks to pass to 2 or passes to 5, who rolls to the basket if the defenders switch.

If 2 and 5 aren't open, 1 looks to pass to 3, popping out on the opposite wing off 4's down screen (figure 4.43). If the defenders switch, 1 looks to pass inside to 4.

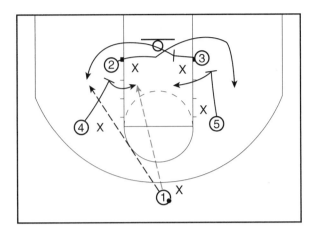

Figure 4.43   If 2 and 5 aren't open, 1 passes to 3, who pops out off 4's screen, or to 4, who rolls to the basket.

Single/Double Screen. The single/double screen is similar to the stagger double screen, but here the shooter starts out under the basket, with 3 and 5 setting a perpendicular screen to the baseline double screen on one side of the lane and 4 setting a single down screen on the opposite side (figure 4.44). 2 then has the option of going either way.

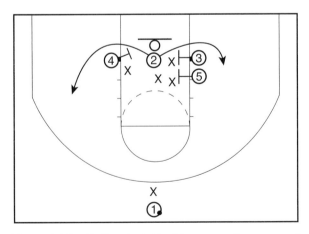

Figure 4.44   On the single/double screen, 2 can pop out on the left or right side of the court.

If 2 goes off the double screen set by 3 and 5, 3 then goes opposite off 4's single down screen (figure 4.45). 1 can pass to 2, coming off the double screen; to 5, who rolls to the basket; to 3, coming off 4's down screen; or to 4, who rolls to the basket after setting the screen for 3.

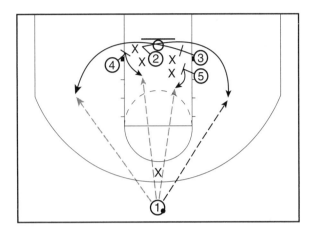

Figure 4.45   1 has several options—he can pass to 2, coming off the double screen; to 5, who rolls to the basket; to 3, who comes off 4's screen; or to 4, who rolls to the basket after setting the screen for 3.

If 2 decides to go off 4's single down screen, 3 pops out off 5's down screen (figure 4.46). 1 can pass to 2, to 3, inside to 4, or inside to 5 if defenders switch.

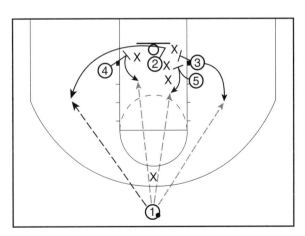

Figure 4.46   If 2 pops out from 4's screen, 3 pops out off 5's screen; 1 can then pass to 2, to 3, to 4, or to 5 if defenders switch.

REACTIONS TO THE DEFENSE

Offensive players not directly involved in the screens being set during a given possession must nevertheless remain alert. Here are some guidelines for these players to make the most effective response to the defense's reaction to the screen(s).

Hedge and Over. If 4's defender (X4) hedges and 1's defender (X1) goes over the screen, 1 has two options:

- Dribble out of the screen and away from X4, who hedged, and then pass to the screener (4), who cuts low (figure 4.47).
- Dribble between the two defenders (X4 and X1) if X4 has delayed the hedge and leaves enough space for the drive (figure 4.48). 1 can pass to 4, to 5 (if X5 helps), to 3, or to 2, who has spotted up.

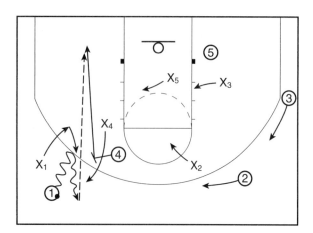

Figure 4.47 On X4's hedge, 1 can dribble out and away from the screen and pass to 4 as he rolls to the basket.

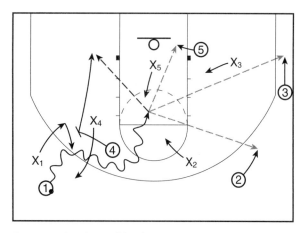

Figure 4.48 1 can drive between the two defenders and pass to 4, to 5 (if X5 helps), to 3, or to 2, who spots up.

In both situations, the key is to keep the dribble alive while going away from the screen; meanwhile, the other three teammates spot up for a possible kickoff pass. If the offensive players keep good spacing, the defenders are forced to rotate, increasing the possibility of getting an open shot.

Hedge and Under. If X4 hedges and X1 (the screened defender) goes under the screen (usually when the screened player is not a great shooter), 1 can try driving inside the lane to create shooting possibilities for himself or his teammates (figure 4.49).

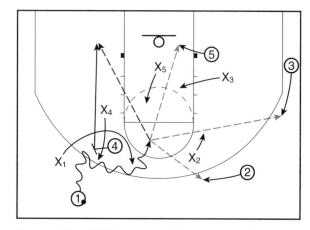

Figure 4.49 If X4 hedges and X1 goes under the screen, 1 can try to drive inside to create shooting possibilities.

Trap and Rotate. If X1 and X4 trap 1, the other offensive players spread out on the half-court. 1 dribbles out of the trap, while the screener (4) slips the screen early. This should allow an outlet pass to 4, cause the defense to reposition, and create an opening for a teammate inside or on the perimeter (figure 4.50). If 4 receives and X5 helps on him, 4 can pass to 5 under the basket (figure 4.51).

Push to the Baseline. When defenders force the ball handler (1) to drive to the baseline, 4 rolls to the basket after the screen while the nearest teammate (2 in this example) flash cuts to the free-throw area (figure 4.52). 1 can pass to 4 or 2.

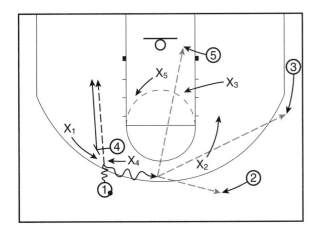

Figure 4.50   1 dribbles out of the trap, 4 slips the screen early and receives from 1, while teammates spread out to create passing options for 1.

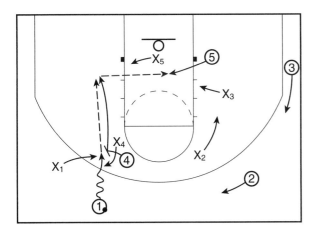

Figure 4.51   If 4 receives and X5 helps, 4 passes to 5.

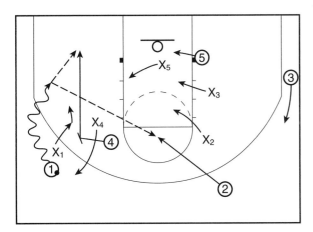

Figure 4.52   If 1 is forced to drive to the baseline after the screen, the screener (4) rolls to the basket while 2 flash cuts to the free-throw area.

FAVORITE JAZZ PLAYS

The shot clock in the NCAA and NBA or a high school team's up-tempo style can force a coach to design quick plays for the offense. The Utah Jazz have relied on a half-court offense for many years. Lacking a superior one-on-one player, we needed to set screens, move without the ball, and execute plays with as much precision as possible. We spent a lot of practice time working on execution on our different offensive sets and taking care of every detail—the real difference between success and failure of a play. A proper angle or cut, the timing of setting a screen, and when and where to pass the ball are some of the key elements that can lead to a score.

We tried to push the ball upcourt and fast break on every possession to buy ourselves more time to execute our offense if we didn't get a good shot quickly. We had the reputation for involving all five players in executing whatever offensive set we called. We worked to achieve good shot selection and put ourselves in advantageous offensive rebounding positions.

Setting screens for good post-up position can be achieved by using smaller players to screen for bigger teammates. We also used big players to down screen for smaller players in many of our offensive sets.

The importance of moving without the ball, setting screens, and reacting to what the defense gives you is paramount. To accomplish these goals, teams must do the following:

• Read and react to the defense (play against your man). Players often decide in advance what they're going to do instead of reacting to the defender who's facing them.

• Stay in good physical condition. Basketball is hard work. At every level of competition, the player who's in great shape will usually prevail, especially when fatigue sets in at the end of a game.

- Play as a team. Making the extra pass, being willing to get the ball to a teammate who's in better position, setting a pick to take pressure off a teammate—these are the kinds of things that make a team gel.

- Have good passing abilities, including these skills and tendencies:

  Post entry passing—knowing how, when, and where to pass the ball to the center is key for the success of a play.

  Perimeter passing—moving the ball quickly and sure-handedly around the arc makes the defense work and can create shot, drive, and entry pass opportunities.

  Post passing—finding cutters and other open teammates is a great skill for a center, because from his position, he can normally see the entire court and thus create many options for teammates who cut around him or spot up for a shot after they pass to him.

- Maintain court balance and spacing, two concepts emphasized by coaches at every competitive level. Poor court balance means offensive players are too clustered, too spread out, or otherwise easy to guard and not positioned to threaten the defense. Proper distribution and placement of personnel allows an offense to dictate the action and exploit weaknesses in the defense.

Now I want to share four basic plays we've found to be very effective for the Jazz.

Cross-Screen Play

On this play we use a cross screen and a double parallel screen at the free-throw line. We form a box set, with 2 on the low post and 5 on the high post or the corner of the free-throw area on the left side of the court. 4 is on the low post, and 3 is on the corner of the free-throw area on the right side of the court.

1 dribbles to the left-wing position, which

signals 2 to make a cross screen for 4, who cuts into the lane and then posts up (figure 4.53). After setting the screen, 2 reads 4's move and then cuts high off the double screen set by 5 and 3 at the free-throw line (figure 4.54). 1 passes to 2.

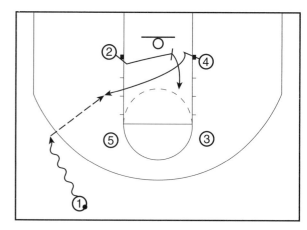

Figure 4.53 1 dribbles to the wing, and 2 makes a cross screen for 4, who posts up.

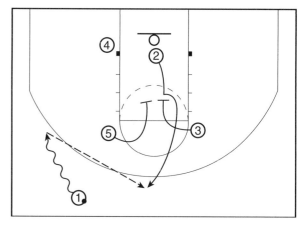

Figure 4.54 2 reads 4's move and then cuts high off the double screen set by 5 and 3 to receive the pass from 1.

Up Screen Play

This play involves a back screen and down screen. We start from the same set, but this time, while 1 is dribbling on the left side, 2 back screens for 4, who cuts down and posts up in the low-post position (figure 4.55). 1 can pass to 4 in the low post, or to 2, who opens up after the screen, facing the basket.

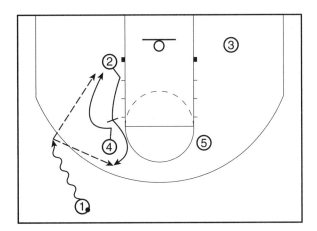

Figure 4.55 1 drives on the wing, while 2 back screens for 4, who posts up and receives from 1. 1 can also pass to 2 after the screen.

If 1 passes to 2 at the corner of the free-throw area and 2 can't shoot, 5 screens down for 3 and then rolls to the basket (figure 4.56). 2 can pass to 3, to 5, or to 4, who ducks in. If 2 passes the ball to 3 and 3 can't shoot, 3 passes to 5, who posts up after rolling to the basket.

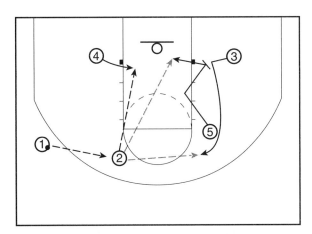

Figure 4.56 If 2 can't shoot after the pass from 1, 5 screens for 3 and then rolls to the basket; 2 can pass to 3, to 5, or to 4.

Diagonal Screen Play

For this play we initially use a diagonal screen, and then a diagonal back screen followed by screen-the-screener action. 1 dribbles to the wing on the left side of the court; 2 receives a diagonal screen from 5 and then posts up on the low post (figure 4.57). 1 passes to 2; after the screen, 5 rolls out of the lane.

If 2 doesn't receive the ball, he sets a diagonal back screen for 4, who moves to the low post on the ball side (figure 4.58). After the screen, 2 receives a down screen from 5 via screen-the-screener action. 1 can pass to 4 in the low post, to 2, who comes off the screen of 5, or to 5, who rolls to the basket after the screen.

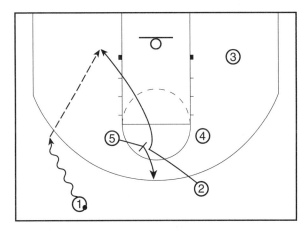

Figure 4.57 1 dribbles on the wing, 2 receives a diagonal screen from 5, and 1 posts down; 1 passes to 2 as 5 rolls out of the lane.

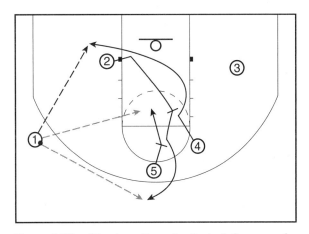

Figure 4.58 If he doesn't receive the ball, 2 screens for 4, and then 5 screens for 2. 1 can pass to 4, 2, or 5.

Another solution is a baseline cut by 3, who, taking away the weak-side help, rubs around 4, comes off to the corner, and receives a pass from 1 (figure 4.59).

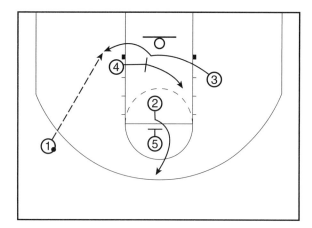

Figure 4.59   The baseline cut by 3, who rubs around 4 and receives the pass from 1.

Pick-and-Roll Play

For this play we use a high-post rub cut and a side screen, followed by a perpendicular double screen on the baseline. The set is two guards (1 and 2) and two posts (4 and 5) at the corners of the free-throw area; one forward (3) is below the free-throw line extended. 1 dribbles on the left, and 2 uses the high-post rub screen of 4; 2 then posts up in the low-post area (figure 4.60).

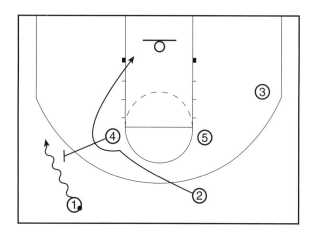

Figure 4.60   1 dribbles on the left; 2 receives a screen from 4 and then posts up.

4 leaves the lane to set a side screen for 1 (figure 4.61). 4 can then roll to the basket or flare, depending on his shooting ability and the reaction of the defense. If 2 doesn't receive the ball in the lane, he cuts off the double screen set by 5 and 3 (figure 4.62). 1 can pass to 4, 2, 5, or 3.

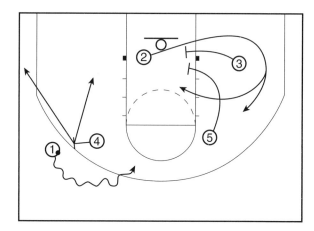

Figure 4.61   4 screens for 1 and then rolls or flares.

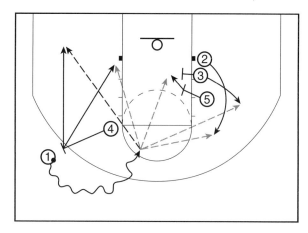

Figure 4.62   If 2 can't receive the ball, he cuts off the double screen set by 5 and 3; 1 can pass to 4, 2, 5, or 3.

FINAL POINTS

Screens can be a double-edged sword because if players are unable to read and execute the proper moves and options based on the reaction of the defenders, screens can lead to turnovers and disrupt the flow of the offense. Much practice focused on repeated perfect execution is required for all the moves and options related to screens before a team can fully incorporate them into its offense. My suggestion is to initially run screens in practice with all the options but without defenders. Then add defenders, who first defend at 50 percent. Finally, once your players have mastered all the moves, have defenders play with game aggressiveness.

PART II

Team Offense

chapter 5

Attacking Offense

Avery Johnson

Playing 16 years in the NBA with different teams, different styles of play, and different coaches, I have learned what I like and don't like on offense. The system I wanted to implement sprang from my overall philosophy of being the aggressor, not a reactor, on the basketball court. Once that system was determined, the next step was to identify and come up with a plan for developing each of the basic elements of the system to ensure it had a strong foundation in our basketball organization and team. From there, we could work on the details and fine-tuning, such as situation-specific attacks and individual plays, to be successful against a variety of defenses in all types of circumstances.

Key to the success of any system is that all players and coaching staff buy in fully, accepting individual responsibility to contribute in their respective roles and committing to doing their best for the success of the team. Those two elements—a clearly defined system and 100 percent commitment of the entire roster and staff to making it work—are critical to the success of any basketball team.

ATTACKING THE DEFENSE IN TRANSITION

Our offensive style is apparent immediately after we get the rebound on our defensive end. After a missed shot by the opponents, with the ball in our possession, we want to *go*. Of course, the first and most important part of starting an offense is not to let the opponents grab the offensive rebound. This means every player must do whatever needs to be done to keep his man off the defensive board. The blocking-out technique can vary from coach to coach, but the *must* for each defender is to prevent his man from grabbing the offensive rebound.

Missed Shot

Immediately after we get the rebound, the rebounder makes the outlet pass as we convert to our offense. We don't always want our point guard to come back to receive the outlet pass from the rebounder. We also want our shooting guard and small forward to be ready to receive the outlet pass in case the point guard is not in position.

So our first key concept for running in transition is to have multiple players ready to receive the ball and attack the basket. I always use the word "attack" on offense because this communicates to my players the aggressive style we're seeking on the court. Once the ball is to the outlet, our other big man (the one who didn't get the rebound) sprints to a position under the offensive rim. Two wings run the sidelines. The point guard pushes the ball hard down the floor.

Let's now go over what I call the three areas we have when we attack the man-to-man defense: the passing ahead area, the decision area, and the breaking area.

• *Passing ahead area.* If the player receiving the outlet pass sees an open teammate

Glenn James/NBAE/Getty Images Sport

Guard Jason Terry initiates the offense at the opponent's end, looking upcourt to see if any wing men are in an advantageous position to receive the ball for a quick score.

ahead of him, he immediately passes the ball to him. If he can't pass ahead, the ball handler quickly brings the ball downcourt, not too close to the sideline to avoid a trap. We want the ball to spend very little time in the passing ahead area, so we push it forward quickly but with control (figure 5.1).

• *Decision area.* Once the ball crosses the midcourt line, whatever player has the ball must quickly decide what he's going to do with it.

Say the ball is still in the ball handler's possession at the spot shown in figure 5.1. At this point, the ball handler must determine instantly if it's best to pass to the big man near the hoop, get the ball to the wing popping open, or hit a cutter breaking free toward the basket. Another possibility is to

use a high screen for a pick-and-roll play (figure 5.2). In any case, the ball handler must keep his dribble until he decides what to do with the ball. Whatever the choice, he must commit to it and force movement from the defense.

• *Breaking area.* As the ball advances forward, near the key (figure 5.3), it's now in the area of the court where we break off to form our triangle.

5 runs a low pick-and-roll. Remember that picks are always based on angles, so 5, the screener, makes a jump stop, picking 1's defender at a proper angle, while 1 cuts at a proper angle. This keeps 1's defender from easily getting under the pick. Terminology might vary from coach to coach (some coaches call this action drag or side screen), but the concept is the same.

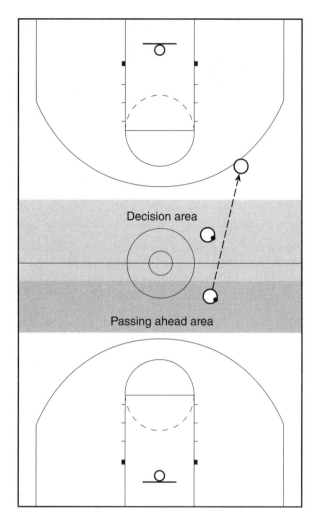

Figure 5.1   Passing ahead area and decision area.

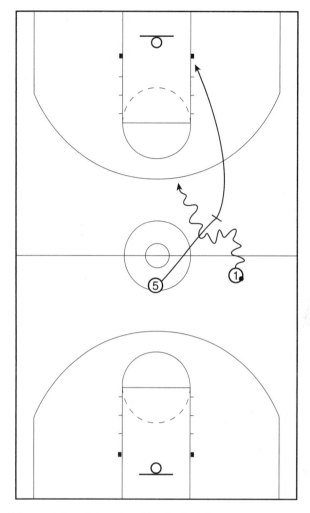

Figure 5.2   Pick-and-roll in the decision area.

In this situation, 4 goes to the right side of the key and then ducks in or goes to the low post on the left side, or he replaces 5, who then moves to the low post (figure 5.4).

For my teams, it's crucial we don't keep the ball on the same side of the floor. If nothing positive develops, we reverse the ball to the other side of the half-court. We swing the ball to the other side in any possible way, swinging it through the post or via a pick-and-roll, but we *must* swing the ball.

If we don't find a shot that I call an "80 percent efficiency shot," which means a direct drive to the basket and a layup (very rare against good defenses), we must swing the ball to the other side of the court.

Let's review the complete action. 5 screens for 1, who goes around the screen and passes to 3. After the screen, 5 exchanges positions with 4. After the pass, 1 can go to the strong or weak side of the court (figure 5.5).

Let's assume 1 goes to the strong side. Depending on his skills, 5, now on the low post, might have these options:

- Flash cut toward the ball while 4 screens for 3 (figure 5.6).
- Screen on the ball and roll to the basket or step back (figure 5.7).
- Flash cut to the high post (figure 5.8).

Another way to swing the ball to the other side of the court is via zipper action (figure

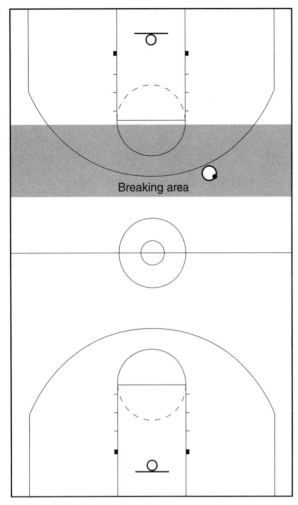

Figure 5.3 Breaking area: As the ball handler drives forward, we break off to form our triangle.

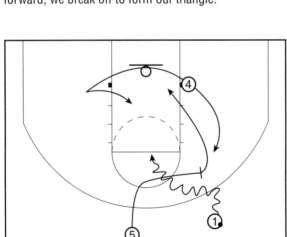

Figure 5.4 On a low pick-and-roll of 5, 4 goes to the right side of the key and then ducks in or goes to the low post on the left side, or he replaces 5.

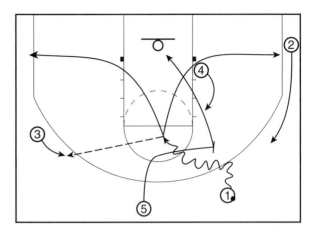

Figure 5.5 Review of the complete action: 5 screens for 1, who passes to 3; 5 changes places with 4.

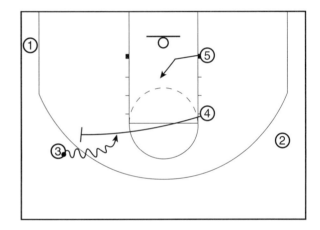

Figure 5.6 5 flash cuts to the ball while 4 screens 3.

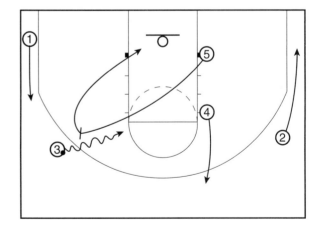

Figure 5.7 5 can pick-and-roll, or pick and step back.

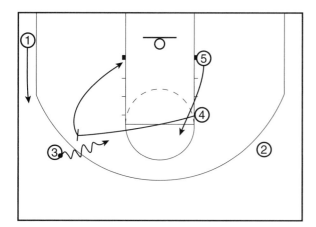

Figure 5.8   5 flash cuts to the high post.

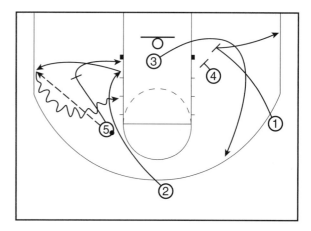

Figure 5.10   5 passes to 2 and screens for him; 3 goes around the double pick set by 1 and 4.

5.9). 2 cuts around 4, comes up, stops for a second to freeze his defender and avoid getting denied, pops out, receives the ball from 1, and passes to 5, who has screened for 3 and popped back to receive the ball.

After he comes off the screen from 5, 3 continues his cut and curls around the double pick set by 1 and 4, while 5 passes to 2 (figure 5.10). We get to the point we wanted to reach by passing the ball to the other side of the floor, where the shooting percentage usually goes up. In fact, when you swing the ball you have more chances for an open shot or a drive to the basket because the defense must rotate and adjust to a new and quickly developing situation, which of course is more difficult to defend.

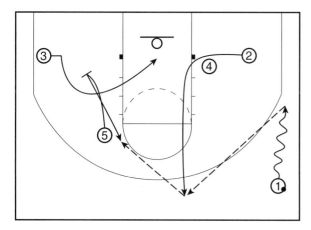

Figure 5.9   Zipper action for swinging the ball: 2 cuts around 4, receives from 1, and passes to 5, who pops back after setting the pick for 3.

In short, if we can't get at least one of our 80 percent efficiency shots, which means a straight layup, and if the defense catches up, we want to do whatever we can to get the ball to the other side of the floor. This keeps the defense moving, thereby improving our percentage for getting a good shot. We can swing the ball to the other side by posting up or via a pick-and-roll or an isolation play. Whatever your system, apply the rules of our offensive philosophy to play your offense and do what you're comfortable with.

Made Basket

Let's move to another offensive situation. The opponents have scored a basket, so we now have the problem of getting the ball inbounds. Usually the defender of 5 (X5) will go down to cover the defensive basket as a safety, so we'll try to get 5 into position to set a pick for 1, the receiver, who then makes a banana cut to receive the ball (figure 5.11). So we're trying to use something similar to a brush pick to free the receiver of the out-of-bounds pass.

If, while driving the ball down the floor to the basket, 1, the receiver of the inbounds pass, is trapped, we teach our players to then square the floor. We try to form a square with three other teammates (4, 3, and 2 in this case), thereby offering the ball handler

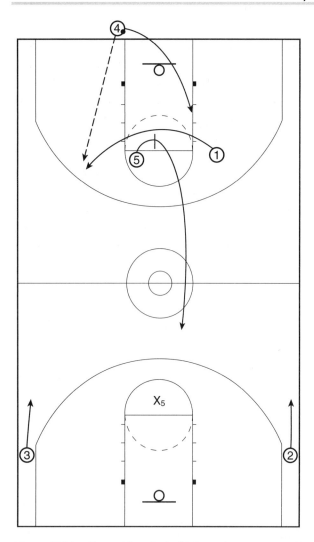

Figure 5.11 For getting the ball inbounds on a press, 5 screens for 1 and then heads downcourt.

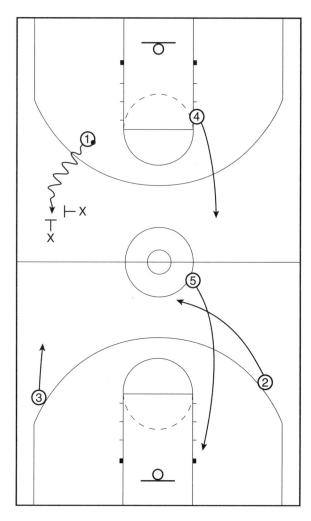

Figure 5.12 If the ball handler is trapped, we square the floor with three other teammates: 4, 3, and 2.

different choices (figure 5.12). Good passing and squaring the floor are key against trapping. If it's impossible to pass the ball out of the trap, one corner of the square goes to the middle of the square to help the ball handler get rid of the ball.

If we get the ball into the half-court but there's a trap on a sideline, we again form our square to release the pressure. Players square the floor in position to receive the pass.

As you can see in figure 5.13, 2 won't set himself at the same level as 1, but higher than 1, thereby becoming a pressure-release

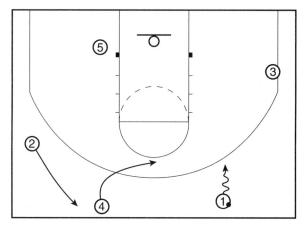

Figure 5.13 2 sets up higher than 1 to release pressure.

player and offering 1 a better angle to pass, while also stretching the floor as much as possible.

I now want to discuss the situation in which the ball handler, who is trapped, picks up his dribble. We teach players in this situation that the ball handler must be in a strong position and look to break through the trap to pass the ball out, either stepping strongly between the two defenders or else pivoting away from the trap and passing the ball. The trapped player must never be in a surrender position, with ball high overhead, or afraid of losing the ball.

ATTACKING THE DEFENSE ON THE HALF-COURT

We can now review our options once the ball is brought to the area of the half-court that we call the breaking area, where we attack the basket aggressively.

Drive Inside

After he reaches the offensive half-court, let's imagine that our ball handler (1) has beaten his defender and is driving to the baseline. Depending on the opposing coach's defensive philosophy, a team might collapse on the driver with three defenders and, in this case, open a passing lane to the corner to 4 (figure 5.14).

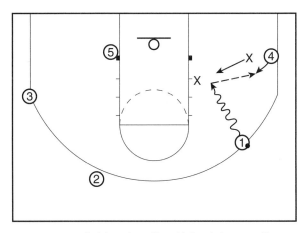

Figure 5.14 1 drives baseline. If the defense collapses on him, 1 passes to 4 in the corner.

But many teams create a defensive wall with two defenders (X5 and X1), who deny the pass to the corner. In this case, it's important for 1, the ball handler making the baseline drive, to make the right decision; it's also critical to have good spacing among teammates. For this reason we need to set a player at what I call a dunking position, which means under the rim. In this case, 5 slides into the middle of the key, and 3 drifts to the baseline to spot up in front of the ball handler and give him another good passing lane (figure 5.15).

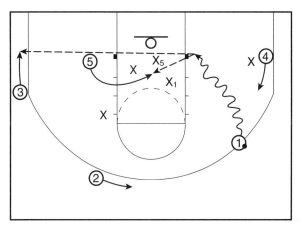

Figure 5.15 1 drives baseline. If the defense denies him the pass to the corner, we create two passing lanes for him.

An important detail: 5 will stay in front of the basket with his hands up to try to get the ball into the middle of the key; in doing so, he'll also keep the baseline passing lane free.

When the ball handler starts a baseline drive, he must not "jump on the trampoline." That is, he shouldn't jump into his shot, especially against teams that like to take the charge. During the drive, the ball handler must avoid committing a charging foul or losing control of the ball.

When 1, the ball handler, is trapped, and if defenders have their hands up, he can pass the ball out of the trap to 3 in the opposing corner with a step-through pass. If defenders have their hands down, he can make what I call an ear pass—that is, a pass near the ear of a defender.

If it's not possible for the trapped ball handler to pass to the teammate on the other corner of the court, he can pivot away from the trap and pass to 2 (figure 5.16), our pressure-release player outside.

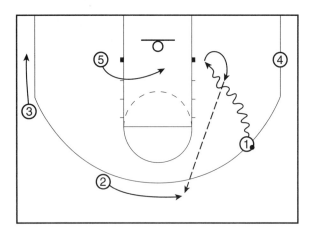

Figure 5.16 If on the baseline drive 1 is trapped and can't pass to the other side of the court, he passes outside to 2.

Again, I put a lot of emphasis on fundamentals and particulars. One of these particulars is that my players must always play to minimize turnovers and lost possessions. I emphasize teaching them how to avoid losing the ball and different ways to pass the ball out of a trap on the baseline To summarize, the ball handler has these options:

- Make a step-through pass.
- Make an ear pass.
- Make a pivot pass.
- Keep the dribble alive and pop away from the trap. In this last case, it's better to overdribble than lose the ball on a turnover.

Top-Side Closeout

Now we've swung the ball successfully, and the defender of the offensive player receiving the ball closes out on the top side of the ball handler. In this case (figure 5.17), 5 flashes out of the key for a pick-and-roll, but the defense forces the ball handler to the sideline, and then X5 traps 3 with X3.

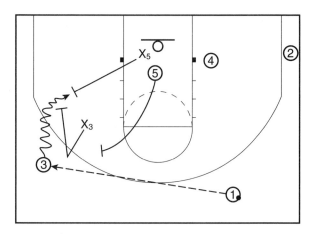

Figure 5.17 When 3 receives the ball from 1, X3 closes in on the top side; 5 picks and rolls, and then X5 traps on 3.

What should happen next depends on the shooting skills of 5. Let's say he's not a good shooter. In this case, after the screen he rolls to the basket and gets to the dunker spot in the key, under the basket, asking for the ball; meanwhile, the other big man (4) sprints outside because we always want our big men (4 and 5) to be on a "string" (figure 5.18). 4 must get himself outside of the three-point arc, squared to the basket. 1 must also give himself up, becoming the pressure-release player to receive the ball from 4 and swing it to the other side of the floor. But to get to this scenario, players must stretch the defensive rotation, quickly getting the ball to the other side.

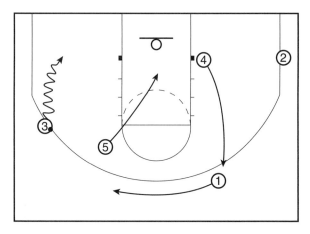

Figure 5.18 In this defensive situation, if 5 is not a good shooter, he rolls to the basket; 4 then gets out to the three-point line.

Maybe your 5 man is not good at the dunker spot. Always suit your philosophy to your personnel, exploiting your players' strengths and limiting their weaknesses. In this case, you might send 4 to the corner, establish your point guard (1) as the pressure-release player, and get 2 involved (figure 5.19).

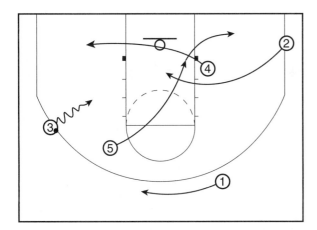

Figure 5.19 On the same defensive situation, if 5 is not good inside, he goes to the low post, 4 flashes to the corner, and 2 cuts into the lane.

This is how we square the floor. Yes, we like to have 4 and 5 on a string, but we can also make an adjustment, as just described, to suit the game or personnel situation.

I now want to take a step back and examine the pick-and-roll of 5 for 1, who's trapped by the two defenders, X5 and X1. One of the keys in this situation is the separation of the offensive big man. If he stays near the trap, and this happens often, he gives another advantage to the two defenders who have trapped him. When your big man separates from the pick, he must go low and away from the trap to put pressure on the defender, who then rotates. 2 then becomes the pressure-release player, 4 the player at the dunker spot, and 3 the player who spots up to stretch the defense (figure 5.20). Again, the ball handler must always take care not to lose the ball. When the ball is swung, you as the coach must tell the player who

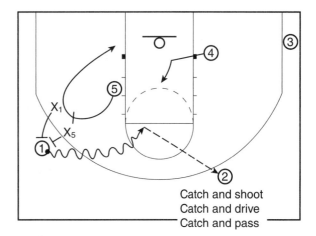

Figure 5.20 On a trap on 1, 5 separates from the trap and goes low and away from the trap.

received the ball not to hold it. He must catch and shoot, catch and drive, catch and pass—anything but hold it. He can't allow his defender to catch up to him.

Attacking the Post-Ups

When the ball is passed to the low post, some teams double team on the first or the second dribble; others double team when the ball is in the lane or when the ball is in the air and reaches the low post's hands. In this situation we again need to square the floor (figure 5.21) with the other four offensive players.

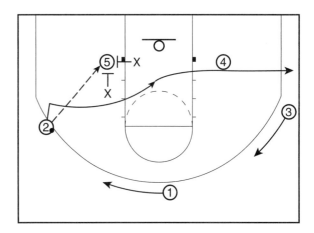

Figure 5.21 On a pass to the low post, we square the floor with the four other players, ready to beat the trap on the low post.

Glenn James/NBAE/Getty Images Sport

Dirk Nowitzki spins and drives from the low post to beat the Celtics attempted trap and take the ball to the hoop.

When possessing the ball, the low post's first job is to be strong and avoid making turnovers. He must get the ball out of the trap in whatever way necessary—either dribbling out or passing to the other side of the floor. If the low post receives the ball from the top of the key and the trap is set by X1 (the passer's defender) and X5, I use the key word "Angles!" This indicates the trap is coming from the strong side of the court, which means there might be a chance to split the trap and score right away. The low post reads the angle at which the trap is coming, watching for the opportunity to split the trap and score inside the key (figure 5.22). As an alternative, he can pass the ball out of the trap.

It's more difficult to split the trap if the trap comes from the weak side of the floor (because of the angle), and there's also the risk of committing a charge while splitting the trap. It's easier to split the two defenders if the trap is run from the strong side of the court. It's all based on the angles, and

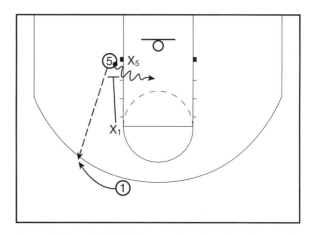

Figure 5.22 With the trap coming from the strong side of the court, 5 tries to split the trap or else passes the ball outside.

players must be able to read the angles. Your star player must not give in to weak double-teams because this gives your opponent an opportunity to steal the pass; he must try to split the double team and go for a score.

Let's review the moves offensive players must execute on the trap on the low post when the trap comes at the top of the key (figure 5.23). 2 passes to 4, who is trapped by X4 and X2. 4 passes the ball to 2, and 2 swings the ball to 1. 5 picks and rolls on 1, and then separates (figure 5.24). 1 swings the ball to 2, 2 swings it to 3 on the weak side, and 3 attacks the basket or passes to 4 (figure 5.25).

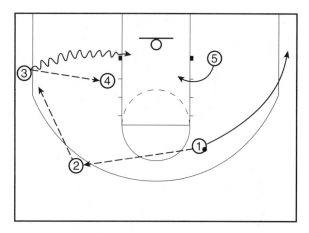

Figure 5.25 We reverse the ball from 1 to 2 and from 2 to 3 for a drive or a pass to 4.

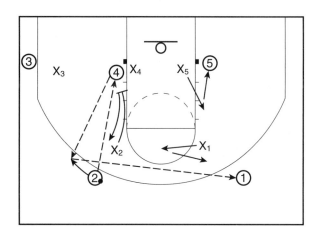

Figure 5.23 Review of the moves on the strong-side trap: 4 passes the ball back to 2, who swings the ball to 1 on the weak side.

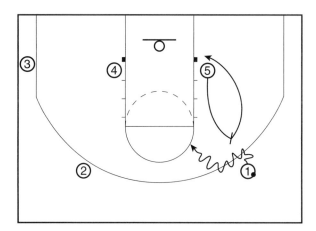

Figure 5.24 After the pick-and-roll, 5 separates.

I again want to emphasize that when we reverse the ball on the weak side, we don't want to be passive on offense. We want to do something with the ball. The receiver on the weak side must "show and go," or he can execute a quick drive to the basket—but he can't be passive!

Middle Pick-and-Roll

Another defensive situation to face and beat is the reaction of the defense to the middle pick-and-roll. Say the screener's defender jumps out in advance and traps, or maybe he waits until the screen is set and then jumps out to help or traps. Again, the response to this situation is fundamental: the separation of the screener after the screen and squaring the floor.

After the separation, 5 can receive the ball from 1, and now there are two things that the low-post player must avoid: dribbling toward the sideline and picking up the ball, and holding the ball.

As I've mentioned, we want to attack the defense when we swing the ball to the weak side, so 5 must make an aggressive drive to the basket to pressure the defense (figure 5.26). 5 will either be free to shoot, or he can drive and kick the ball to an open teammate.

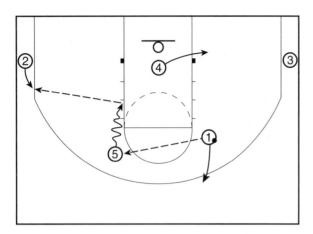

Figure 5.26 When 5 receives the ball from 1, he can drive to the basket or pass the ball to 2 in the corner.

If your center doesn't like to put the ball on the floor and roll, instead of separating and driving, we attack this way: 5 rolls under the basket, and 4 becomes the pressure-release player (he's also on the string as quickly as possible because we need to use a better ball handler, someone faster than 5). 4 then quickly receives the ball from 1 and attacks as described before (figure 5.27). Again, we need to know the skill level of our players so we can switch positions based on their strengths and weaknesses.

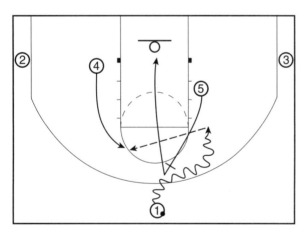

Figure 5.27 If 5 doesn't handle the ball well, he rolls under the basket and 4 becomes the pressure-release player.

If your team has a hot player who's unstoppable in a particular game, we want to set up 4 and 5 on the low posts and 2 and 3 on the wings. The defense wants the ball out of the hands of 1, your hot player, so they'll try to trap him. The answer here, again, is to square the floor. 2 comes up to become the pressure-release player, 5 flashes to the high-post area at the free-throw circle, and 4 runs to the corner. 1 dribbles back to stretch the trap and then passes to 2. But 2 might be covered, so 1 must be able to quickly read the situation and pass to 5 to make this work (figure 5.28). 1 can't turn the ball over or fall into a surrender position.

When 2 receives the ball from 1, he attacks the defense immediately and drives to the basket to force the defenders to rotate (figure 5.29). He can then shoot or pass to 5 or to another open teammate.

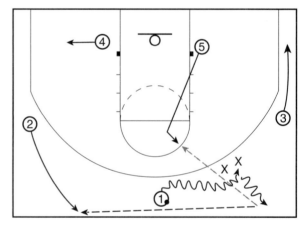

Figure 5.28 If the defense traps a hot player, 2 becomes the pressure releaser, while 5 flashes to the high post on the strong side.

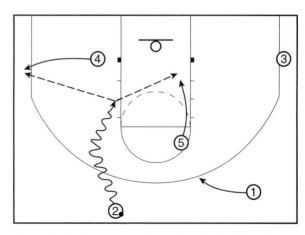

Figure 5.29 As soon as 2 receives the ball, he attacks the basket and either shoots or passes to another teammate.

FINAL POINTS

When you're experiencing tough stretches and accompanying fatigue, it can be easy to slack off during practice. Guard against that. The lack of aggressiveness might carry over to games. I've been known to turn a light shoot-around on game day into a highly intense competitive practice. Only players with an attacking attitude can be effective in my system, and if they're going to be attacking in games, I want them attacking in practice, too.

An attacking offense takes time and commitment to run, but if you stick with it, the rewards are well worth the effort. Before we conclude, let's review the concepts we've discussed in this chapter:

- From a broad philosophy of play, isolate a system and its individual components. Master those essential components and then work on each detail, such as specific plays and situation-specific tactics.

- The key offensive principle is to attack. Players can't be passive or hold the ball. The more pressure applied against a defense, the more likely it will crack.

- A fast pass beats the fastest dribbler every time, so find ways to move the ball as quickly as possible via the pass, especially to the weak side, where the shooting percentage should be higher.

- Stretch the defense by squaring the floor.

- On the pick-and-roll, the screener must separate from the pick.

- The other four players on the floor must always be ready to help the ball handler.

Every player and coach is accountable to the offensive system—no exceptions. Good and bad days come and go during the course of a season, but a system and the commitment to its success should never waiver. Trust in your system and make it work.

chapter 6

Triangle Offense

Phil Jackson and Tex Winter

Tex and I have been coaching together since 1989, when I became head coach of the Chicago Bulls and he remained with the organization as an assistant. Tex is an original thinker about basketball and has played an invaluable role in establishing a system of play and coordinating our efforts on the offensive end of the court.

This system is much more than a series of plays—it's a philosophy, a consistent way of thinking and executing that kicks in each time we gain possession of the ball. In the transition from defense to offense, players move in a natural, purposeful flow so that we're in position and rhythm when we bring the ball into the half-court.

Over the years, this style of play has been called the triangle offense, the triple-post offense, and the sideline triangle offense. Tex doesn't claim to have invented it, but he has mastered teaching it and instituting it, not simply as a sequence of movements but rather a set of concepts and rules that guides an offensive attack.

To describe it, we would say this offense is a sideline triangle on one side of the court and a two-man game on the other side, in which the offensive options are dictated by the positioning and reactions of the defenders. But it really isn't all that complex. In fact, the triangle—the label we'll use for brevity's sake—is an offensive system that can be applied to all levels of competition.

It is old-school basketball in that it's founded on the basics: exact court spacing, execution of fundamentals, and constant movement of ball and players based on certain rules. Winning requires a five-man coordinated effort, and we get that when we get our teams to run it properly.

The primary misconception about the offense is that it is designed around a gifted player. Yes, Michael Jordan, Scottie Pippen, Shaquille O'Neal, and Kobe Bryant have thrived in the system, but those four all-time greats would excel and score in any system. What the triangle really does is help players who aren't so gifted contribute to a team's success at the offensive end. The system, or method of play, as Coach Winter likes to call it, uniquely offers an offense the option to play unselfishly as a unit while still allowing players creative individuality in their offensive decisions.

The triangle offense requires players to be self-reliant and in control of their game. The system provides a framework that frees both the athletes on the court and the coach on the sideline from having to call a particular play or isolation on numerous occasions during a game. I do not want to, nor is it best to, dictate how a Michael Jordan or a Kobe Bryant applies his amazing scoring ability one possession after another.

I'm convinced that highly structured, non-spontaneous basketball does not win championships. My belief was, and is, that a team on the floor knows best what is going on and the players must be confident that they can read the defense and react accordingly. This style of play does, however, require players to be disciplined and willing to submit their personal ambitions to the best interests of the group. This is essential for the system to achieve optimal results.

The system also runs better when players' games are well-rounded, not one- or two-dimensional. Complete players well-versed in fundamental movement, ball handling, screening, and shooting skills will perform the tasks demanded of them within the offense more effectively and consistently. Basketball played at its best is a reflexive sport, and I want my team to play a fluid, instinctive, complete game.

I rejected the idea of relying solely on a point guard to bring the ball up the court and make all the ball-handling decisions. Ultimately, a good defensive opponent will pressure and destroy a team with a single point-guard orientation. A two-guard offense allows players to share the ball handling and passing duties and prevents a defense from ganging up against one player out front.

SEVEN PRINCIPLES OF THE SOUND OFFENSE

An effective offense, to my way of thinking, features the following dimensions.

1. *Penetration.* Players must penetrate the defense, and the best way to do this is the fast break, because basketball is a full-court game, from baseline to baseline.

2. *Spacing.* I am a fanatic about how players distribute themselves on the offensive end of the court. They must space themselves in a way that makes it most difficult to defend, trap, and help. Players must align a certain number of feet apart. In high school, I'd recommend 12 to 15 feet spacing, in college, 15 to 18 feet, and in the NBA, 15 to 20 feet. Proper spacing not only exposes individual defensive players'

Multidimensional players like Michael Jordan, Ron Harper, and Scottie Pippen, shown here back in the 1996 Finals, are perfectly suited to run the triangle offense.

vulnerabilities, but also ensures that every time the defense tries to trap, an offensive player will be open.

3. *Ball and player movements.* Players must move, and must move the ball, with a purpose. Effective off-the-ball activity is much more important than most fans and players think because they're so used to watching only the movement of the ball and the player in possession of it. But there is only one ball and there are five players, meaning most players will have the ball in their hands 20 percent or less of the time the team is in possession of the ball.

4. *Options for the ball handler.* The more options a smart player has to attack a defender, the more successful that offensive player will be. When teammates are all moving to positions to free themselves (or another teammate with a pick), the ball handler's choices are vastly increased.

5. *Offensive rebounding and defensive balance.* On all shots we take, players must go strong for the rebound while retaining court balance and awareness to prevent the opponent's fast break.

6. *Versatile positioning.* The offense must offer to any player the chance to fill any spot on the court, independent of the player's role. All positions should be interchangeable.

7. *Use individual talents.* It only makes sense for an offense to allow a team to take advantage of the skill sets of its best players. This doesn't preclude the focus on team play that is emphasized in the six other principles, but it does acknowledge that some individuals have certain types and degrees of talent, and an offense should accentuate those assets. Michael Jordan taught me this.

Finally, I want the offense to flow from rebound to fast break, to quick offense, to a system of offense. The defenses in the NBA are so good because the players are so big, quick, and well coached. Add the pressure that the 24-second clock rule applies to the offense to find a good shot, and the defense gets even better.

The triangle offense has proven most effective, even against such obstacles, when players commit to and execute the system. The offense hinges on players attending to minute details in executing not just plays but also the fundamentals underlying the plays. Once players have mastered the individual techniques required of their roles, we then integrate those individuals into a team. Once this is done, the foundation for a good offense is solidly in place. The team can then go on the court with the confidence and poise so essential to success.

This method of play is as old as basketball. The triangle set is adjustable to the personnel, but such adaptations can be made without altering the essence of the offense. The only necessary adjustment from one season to the next involves tailoring the series of options based on each individual's talents. Now Tex and I will present the triangle offense in detail, including some of those variations and options to optimize its use for specific teams.

COURT SYMMETRY

Proper spacing gives the ball handler ample room to respond to help and traps and also puts the onus on the defense to cover a larger area in which it can be attacked at more angles. So the offense starts in a symmetrical alignment of players, forming a triangle on both sides of the half-court (figure 6.1).

In the triangle offense, the role of the players is totally interchangeable. There's no need for the guards, forwards, and centers to play only in their typical spots on the floor—the spots can be filled by any player. Once the spots are filled, the offense is run by where the ball is positioned on the court and by how the defense is moving.

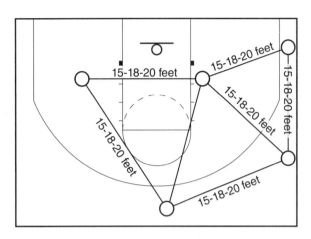

Figure 6.1 Proper spacing of the triangle on the half-court.

LINE OF DEPLOYMENT

One of the assets of the triangle offense is the chance to isolate the post and attack his defender. We want to talk now of the "line of deployment," a basic concept. With this term we mean an imaginary line traced from the forward with the ball to the center in the low post, his defender, and the basket.

To play a standard defensive position between the center and the basket, the defender of the center must play behind him, as long as the center remains on the line of deployment (figure 6.2). But when being defended in this way, it's easy for the forward to pass the ball to the center.

If the center's defender wants to prevent an easy pass, he must overplay him, either on the baseline side or the high side, losing in this way his alignment with the center and the basket, so the forward can make a quick pass to the open side of the center. The center must master the technique of shaping up on the post, playing the line of deployment. After receiving the pass, the center can either shoot or pass out to a teammate in position to do something constructive with the ball (figure 6.3).

Noah Graham/NBAE/Getty Images Sport

Spacing and ball movement are key elements of the offense's effectiveness. With the ball in the low post here, if Shaq can't make a scoring move, he can kick the ball out to Kobe at the top of the key or to the wing, or perhaps spot an open player on the weak side.

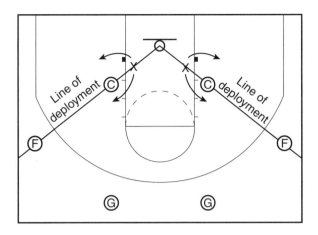

Figure 6.2 The line of deployment.

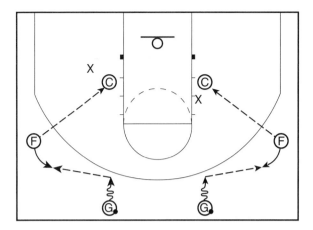

Figure 6.3 Stressing the line of deployment, we are successful in passing the ball to the post.

Passing Principles

Before getting further into the offense, we want to emphasize one essential skill to make it work. Passing is underrated these days, but it's the key to executing the triangle offense. Players must understand and adhere to the following principles when passing the ball.

- *Pass when the defender is three feet from the ball or closer.* The closer the defender covers the offensive player with the ball, the less time the defender has to react to the passer's movement. This principle of good passing is violated more than any other.

- *See the passing lanes and the receiver, but don't stare at the target receiver.* Use peripheral vision without making a blind pass.

- *Use fakes with a purpose without overfaking.* Purposeful fakes allow a passer to get the ball past an opponent based on how the defender reacts. The passer should keep poised and attuned to all passing lanes while executing fakes.

- *Eliminate all unnecessary movements.* Use quick wrist and finger action, shortening as much as possible the action of the pass.

- *Pass quickly to an open teammate,* who will typically have no more than three seconds after he receives the ball to make a play. For every second under the three seconds it takes for the receiver of the pass to execute the play, the better basketball player he becomes. For every second over three seconds, the poorer he becomes. Moving the ball so quickly makes the defense adjust and might force them out of position, increasing the chances of passing lanes and scoring opportunities.

- *Pass the ball to a teammate's open side* is another rule often violated by the best players. The passer must have a view not only of his defender but also of the passing lane and the receiver's defender. The receiver should help the passer by becoming a good target and keeping the defender from the passing lane with an effective seal-off.

- *Anticipate receiving the ball and be thinking ahead where (to what teammate and location) to throw the ball next.* This is a skill the best players share. If players don't have this ability, you need to build an offensive pattern that ensures the quick movement of the ball to keep the defense busy.

By thoroughly indoctrinating the players on the line of deployment theory, we feel we have been successful in getting the ball to our center, and this has been true despite a concentrated effort by opponents to prevent the pass to the post.

FORMING THE SIDELINE TRIANGLE

Most offenses require an entry pass to start a play, but this is not the case with the triangle offense. The triangle offense can be initiated with any of several pass options, depending on defensive adjustments and offensive strategies.

Andrew D. Bernstein/NBAE/Getty Images Sport

Talented wing players like Kobe Bryant can use the triangle's spacing to their advantage to drive past their man, draw defensive help, and then pass to an open teammate for a basket.

First Pass (Strong-Side Fill)

Following are the options for the first pass, strong-side fill.

Guard to Wing

- *Outside cut.* The ball handler (1) dribbles in the pro lane, passes to the wing (3), cuts outside him, and goes to the corner, forming a triangle with 5 and 3. Here we must again talk about spacing—3 must set himself at a proper distance away from the sideline to let 1 cut behind him (as well as to allow the other types of cuts, which we'll explain soon).
- *Slice cut.* 1 passes the ball to 3, moves toward him, and then cuts away and goes to the corner (figure 6.4).

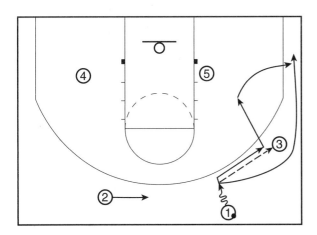

Figure 6.4 The strong-side fill: guard outside and slice cut.

- *Blur screen cut.* 1 passes the ball to 3, cuts inside, brushes off the center (5), and moves to the corner.
- *Basket cut.* 1 passes the ball to 3 and then cuts to the basket, coming off 5 and moving to the corner (figure 6.5).

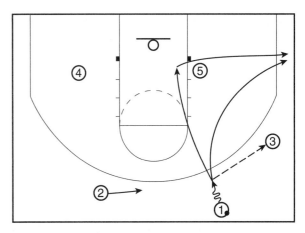

Figure 6.5 The strong-side fill: guard blur screen and basket cut.

On all the cuts of the strong-side guard (1), the other guard (2) moves to the middle of the floor for defensive balance and then plays two on two on the weak side.

Wing Dribble Entry

1 dribbles toward 3, which signals 3 to go to the basket and then to the corner; meanwhile, 5 moves to the high post, and 2 goes to the middle of the court. Then 4 cuts into the lane and takes the center position, while 5 replaces 4 in the wing spot with a weak-side cut (figure 6.6).

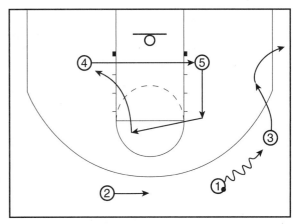

Figure 6.6 The strong-side fill: 5 takes the weak-side wing and 4 takes the post.

Center Corner Fill

- 1 passes to 3; 5 goes to the corner; 4 cuts, high or low, into the lane and replaces the center; and 2 cuts to the weak-side wing spot, replacing 4 (figure 6.7). 1 moves to the top of the circle, and proper spacing is maintained.

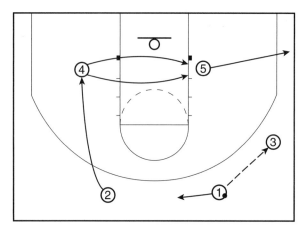

Figure 6.7 The strong-side fill: 5 goes to the corner; 4 replaces 5.

- Another option: 1 passes to 3, 5 goes to the corner, and 1 (or 2, whichever is the better post player) replaces 5 in the post (figure 6.8).

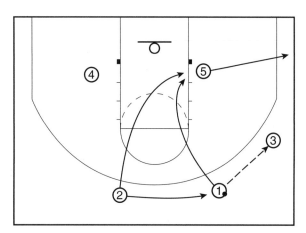

Figure 6.8 The strong-side fill: 5 goes to the corner; 1 (or 2) replaces 5.

First Pass (Weak-Side Fill)

Following are the options for the first pass, weak-side fill.

Weak-Side Guard Fill

1 passes to 3; the weak-side guard (2) can then fill the corner in two ways (figure 6.9):

- with a basket speed cut, or
- after a back-pick off the wing (4).

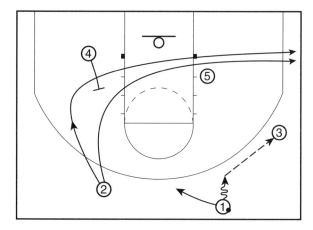

Figure 6.9 The weak-side fill: guard basket cut or through a screen by the weak-side wing.

Weak-Side Forward Fill

1 passes to 3; 4 makes a baseline or over-the-top cut and fills the corner; 2 replaces 4 in the wing position (figure 6.10). Note that the court is once again balanced.

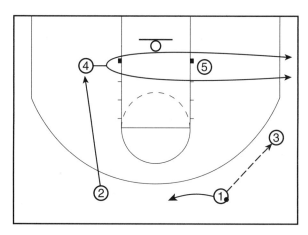

Figure 6.10 The weak-side fill: forward baseline or over-the-top cut.

Second Pass

After we form the triangle on the strong side of the court, four passes could become available for the strong-side wing. We call these four passing options "second pass" because they're made after the first pass to the wing position, which initiates the offense. There are four spots on the court where these passes could be directed, and each of these spots offers a multitude of offensive options.

Assuming that 1 passes to 3 and then fills the corner, 3 reads the defense and takes the following looks to pass (figure 6.11):

First look: to the center (5).

Second look: to the weak-side guard (2) at the middle of the half-court at the top of the circle.

Third look: to the weak-side wing (4) on the backdoor step.

Fourth look: to the strong-side guard (1) in the corner.

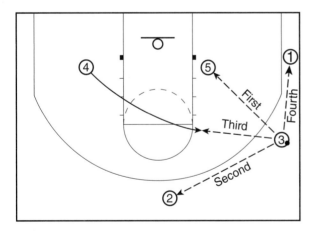

Figure 6.11 The first look: pass to the center; the second look: pass to the weak-side guard; the third look: pass to the weak-side wing stepping on the backdoor; and the fourth look: pass to the strong-side guard in the corner.

First Look: Pass to the Center

We'll now show one of the simplest options of this offense; it's as old as basketball, but still quite effective. It's called split cuts or split the post or sometimes post cuts. The play starts with the entry pass from 1 to 3 and 1's outside cut to the corner to form the sideline triangle, while 2 goes to the middle of the court (figure 6.12).

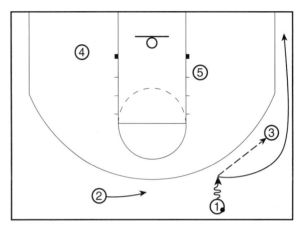

Figure 6.12 Setting the sideline triangle: pass to the center. 1 passes to 3 and goes to the corner.

Option 1. 3 passes to 5, makes a fake to cut inside the lane, and then cuts on the baseline side of 5 while 1 cuts as close as possible behind 3. The passer is the first cutter and cuts to the side of the teammate he is trying to free (5) (figure 6.13).

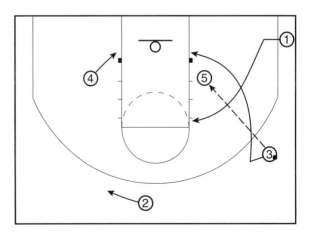

Figure 6.13 The split speed cuts of 3 and 1.

3 can also make a change-of-pace cut and attempt a screen for 1 (figure 6.14). 2 spots up opposite to the ball at the fan spot, and 4 gets near the lane for the rebound. After the pass to the post (5), 3 can also start a speed cut and then screen for 2 (figure 6.15). 3 might also make a speed cut and then screen for 4, while 1 speed cuts on the baseline (figure 6.16).

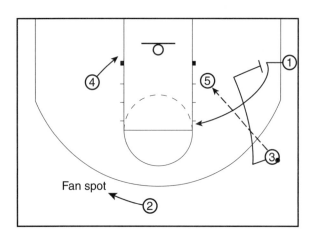

Figure 6.14   3 can also screen for 1.

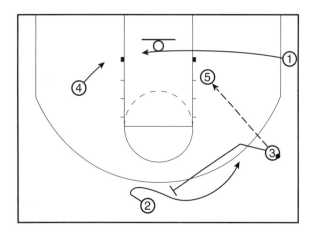

Figure 6.15   A speed cut and then a screen of 3 for 2.

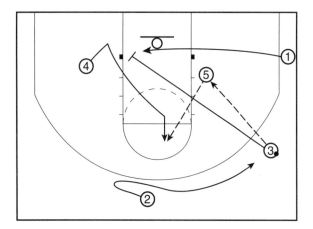

Figure 6.16   A speed cut by 3 and a screen for 4.

The post (5) can also kick the ball off to 2, who has spotted up on the weak side at the fan spot, also called the garden spot because it's a nice and open spot on a court for shooting if the defensive man attempts to double team the center (figure 6.17).

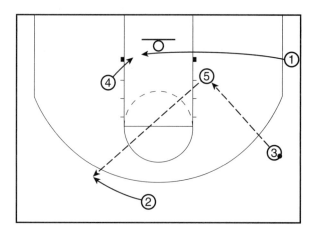

Figure 6.17   5 can make a fan pass to 2 at the garden spot.

Option 2. 3 passes the ball to 5; 1 speed cuts to the baseline and, if open, receives a drop pass from 5; 3 makes an over-the-top speed cut (we call this an action zone speed cut). Meanwhile, on the pass from 3 to 5, 2 spots up at the garden spot to receive the ball from 5, and 4 cuts behind the defense to the freeze spot (figure 6.18). The freeze spot is a point on the court where he keeps his defender busy while waiting for a possible screen.

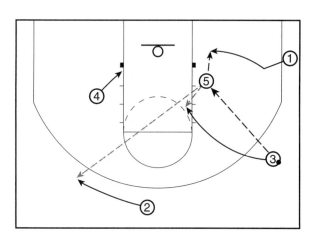

Figure 6.18   1 speed cuts, and 3 over-the-top speed cuts. 4 works behind his defensive man, moves out of his vision, and freezes in the deep basket area for a pass or rebound.

If 1, 2, or 3 aren't open, 1 continues his cut, rubs off 4's screen, and moves out for defensive balance, while 3 cuts into the lane and screens for 4 (screen-the-screener action) and 2 replaces 3 (figure 6.19). 4 pops out to the free-throw area and receives the ball from 5, or, if 4 is not free, 5 can also pass to 3, who has rolled to the basket after the screen. If he has no other choice, 5 can pass to 2. If 3 doesn't receive from 5, he fills the corner on the weak side (figure 6.20).

2 passes to 4 (or can pass back to 5) and then moves to the top of the circle. If 4 is not free for a shot, he passes to 1 and then cuts

to the low-post position, while 5 takes the weak-side wing spot (figure 6.21). Now we have formed the triangle on the other side of the floor, and we can restart our offense. As we like to say, "We are always in our offense and ready to operate!"

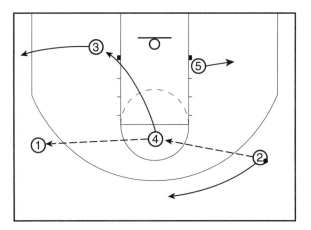

Figure 6.21 With no solution, we create a new triangle on the other side of the floor and are ready to continue with continuity.

Option 3. After the pass to 5, 3 makes a rebound screen cut (starting to cut as if going to the rebound in the lane, but instead going to screen), while 1 step fakes on the baseline to set the defender up and cuts off 3's screen to a position in front of 5; 2 and 4 spot up opposite to the ball (figure 6.22). 5 passes the ball to 2 or 4, whichever one is open.

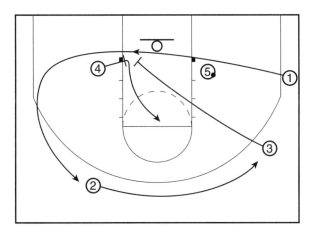

Figure 6.19 3 screens for 4 with screen-the-screener action.

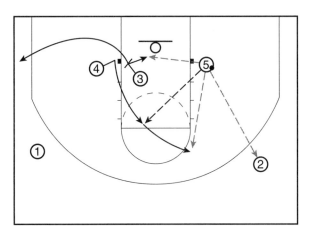

Figure 6.20 All the passing options of 5.

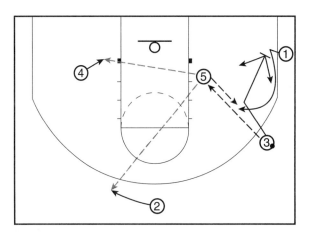

Figure 6.22 3 passes to 5 and then rebound screen cuts. 3 will make a basket cut if he has a direct line to the basket or will step back or out if the defense gets caught behind the center.

If neither 2 nor 4 is open, 1 continues to the free-throw line area, where he can cut into the lane, screen for 2, who has come back to the ball, and then roll to the basket or pop out after the screen (figure 6.23). 5 can pass to 1, 2, or 3, who, after setting the screen, pops out in the corner.

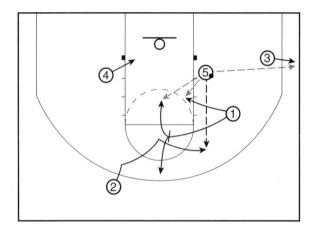

Figure 6.23 The options of 1 and the passing choices of 5.

Second Look: Pass to the Weak-Side Guard on Top of the Circle

Option 1. If 5 is not open, 3 can pass to 2 at the top of the circle; if 2 is open, 2 can shoot as the first option, or pass to 5, who ducks into the lane (figure 6.24).

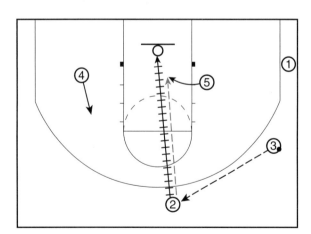

Figure 6.24 3 can pass to the weak-side guard at the top of the circle if open as the result of a sagging or doubling defense.

If 5 is not open on his duck into the lane, 3, after the pass to 2, runs a rebound screen cut, while 1 step fakes on the baseline to set the defender up and cuts off 3's screen on the way back to defensive balance. 2 can pass to 1 if he's open (figure 6.25). 4 fakes a cut and comes back, as does 5. This action keeps the defense occupied off the ball.

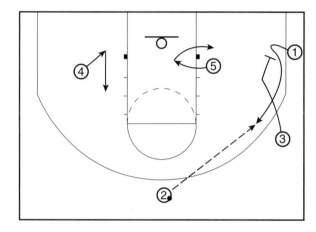

Figure 6.25 3 makes a rebound screen cut.

2 can pass to 1 if he's open, or, if the defense is sagging, can dribble weave the ball to 1. 2 passes to 1 on the dribble interchange, at about the midpoint, or 2 passes up to 1 and 1 passes to 3, who has stepped back into the corner after the screen (figure 6.26). 4 reverses back to the basket area as the dribble-weave action takes place to get into rebounding position, and 5 posts deep or rebounds if a shot goes up.

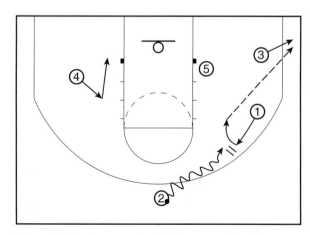

Figure 6.26 2 passes (or dribble weaves) to 1.

Option 2. We call this play pinch post action. 4 starts to pop out to the ball when 2 receives the ball from 3, but 4 is overplayed, so he reverses to the basket (in a backdoor cut) to receive an over-the-top pass from 2; meanwhile, 1 gets back for defensive balance, and 5 keeps his defender busy, moving in and out of the lane ready to rebound or freeze at the basket for a pass (figure 6.27). 2 passes to 4.

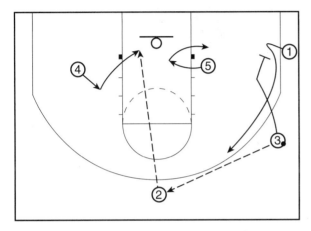

Figure 6.27   Pinch post action: a backdoor cut by 4.

If 4 can't receive on the back door, he pops out to the high-side post area at the elbow and receives the ball from 2, who speed cuts off 4 and receives the ball back via a short flip pass off 4's front hip (figure 6.28). 2 must have his hands in a ready position to catch the ball on the two-man play, while 3 screens for 1. After the screen, 3

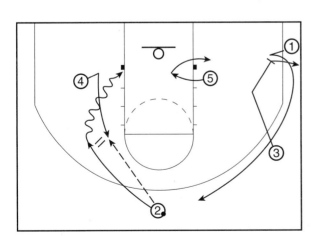

Figure 6.28   The two-man play between 2 and 4.

steps back to the corner, 1 moves back for defensive balance, and 5 keeps his defender busy and then freezes for a second at the block.

2 drives to the basket, and 4 reverse pivots with the pass—he opens up to the ball, reads the defense, and reacts accordingly. If there's a direct line to the basket, he dive cuts to the basket and receives a return pass from 2. If 2 is double teamed, 4 opens up to the ball with a reverse pivot and holds for a return pass from 2 (figure 6.29). 5 freezes at the block, ready to receive a possible pass from 2, and 3 spots up for a possible kickoff pass or cuts to the front of the rim for a pass or to go after a rebound.

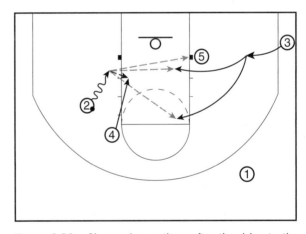

Figure 6.29   2's passing options after the drive to the basket.

Third Look: Pass to the Weak-Side Wing on the Backdoor Step

Option 1. 3 passes to 4, who has flashed to the elbow on the ball-side high post, and 2 makes a backdoor speed cut to the basket. If 2's head and shoulders are by his defender, 4 makes a quick drop pass to 2 (figure 6.30). 2 should reach ahead for the ball, catching it knee-high.

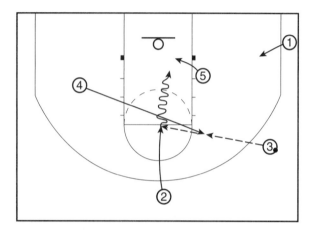

Figure 6.30 3 passes to 4; 2 makes a backdoor speed cut, receives, and drives to the basket.

3, after making the pass to 4, runs a rebound screen cut, while 1 step fakes to the baseline and comes off the screen of 3. 1 gets back for defensive balance, and 3 reads the play and prepares for the rebound off the front of the rim. 5 freezes at the block and anticipates a possible pass from 2, in case his defender switches to help 2's defender on the drive (figure 6.31). 4 then

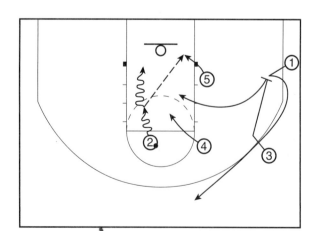

Figure 6.31 2's options on the drive to the basket.

reverse pivots and reads the defense, staying behind the ball or diving to the basket, ready to receive a pass from 2 if 4's defender drops to cover 2.

Option 2. 3 passes to 4, who has flashed to the elbow on the ball-side high post, and 2 makes a backdoor speed cut to the basket. If 2 is not open, he cuts into the corner, and 3 cuts right after him to receive a pass from 4 (figure 6.32). 3 can drive to the basket for a layup, or he can drive and kick off to 5 on the block, or to 2, who spots up in the corner.

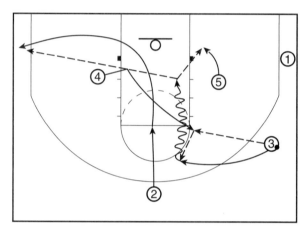

Figure 6.32 3 receives the ball and drives to the basket, or he kicks off to 5 or 2.

If 2 is not open and 3 can't receive the ball, 4 dribble weaves to 1 coming out of the corner, or passes to him on the step back to the corner (figure 6.33). If 1 receives the ball on the dribble weave, he drives straight to the basket, or he can take a jump shot or

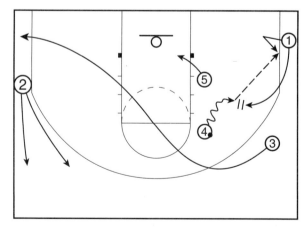

Figure 6.33 The dribble weave or pass from 4 to 1.

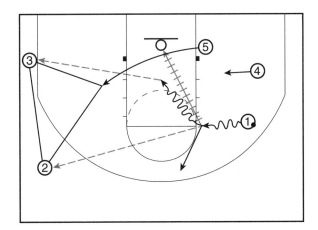

Figure 6.34   1's options for driving to the basket.

make a fan pass to 2 or 3, spotted up at the wing and in the corner, while 5 flashes to the low post from the other side of the floor (figure 6.34).

If nothing happens with the pass to 2, we have formed a triangle on the other side of the court with 2, 5, and 3, with 1 at the top of the lane and 4 on the weak-side wing spot, and we create continuity in our offense.

Fourth Look: Pass to the Strong-Side Guard in the Corner

3 passes to 1 in the corner, and 1 looks at the basket with a threat to shoot. After the pass, 3 makes a banana cut to the basket and can try to receive the ball, while 5 gets to the high post at the ball-side elbow (figure 6.35).

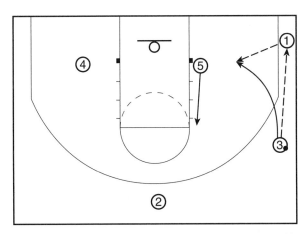

Figure 6.35   The fourth look: pass to the strong-side guard.

Right after 3's cut, 5 screens and rolls on 1, who drives to the top of the key, where he can pass to 5 on the roll; 3 continues his cut and is screened by 4 on the weak side (figure 6.36); 2 fans away as 1 dribbles out of the corner, spotting up opposite to the ball.

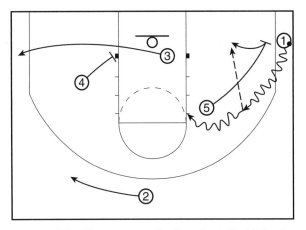

Figure 6.36   The screen and roll on the ball of 5 for 1.

1 can shoot or drive to the basket or pass to 2, who has spotted up (figure 6.37). 1 can also pass to 4 or 5 if there's help on the basket penetration. If nothing happens, we have formed the triangle on the other side with 3, 4, and 2, while 5 becomes the weak-side wing and 1 sets up at the top of the lane.

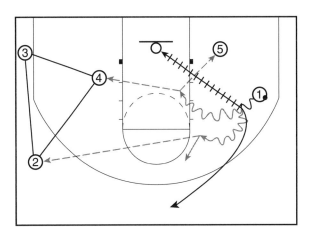

Figure 6.37   1's options, and the triangle on the other side of the court.

SOLO CUT SERIES OF OPTIONS

After 1's pass to 3, instead of cutting to the corner to create the triangle, 1 makes a speed cut to receive the ball at the free-throw line area or under the basket, if he's free (figure 6.38). 4 moves to 15 to 18 feet from the basket and holds; 2 gets to the top of the circle and holds.

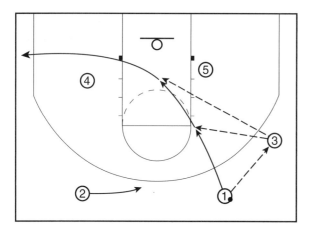

Figure 6.38   The solo cut series of options: 1 passes to 3 and speed cuts.

3 gets into triple-threat position and looks to the post (5) for a pass. 1 holds position in the corner opposite the ball. 3 passes to 5 and makes what we call a solo cut to either side of 5 (figure 6.39). 2 spots up on the garden spot, away from the ball, while 4 screens down for 1, and 1 pops out in the corner.

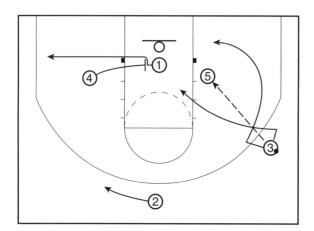

Figure 6.39   3 passes to 5 and makes a solo cut behind or over the top of 5.

As 3 cuts by 5, 5 has a cleared area for a shot, and 2 works behind the sweet spot. 3, if he doesn't receive the ball on the cut, screens for 4, who can come high to the free-throw line area or cut to the basket to receive the ball from 5 (figure 6.40). 5 can instead pass to 2.

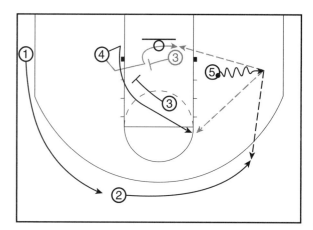

Figure 6.40   3 screens high or low for 4, and 5 has passing options.

Let's now assume that 3 can't pass to 5. 3 then passes to 2 at the top of the circle and then makes a rub cut off 5, while 5 steps up to pinch post off 3's cut. On the weak side, 4 screens for 1, who can pop out flat to the corner, or out and up. 2 has several options for passing (figure 6.41): He can pass to 3, 1, or 4, who has rolled to the basket after the screen for 1, or to 5 on the pinch post.

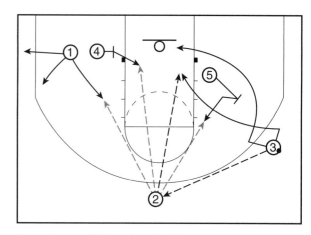

Figure 6.41   If 2 receives the ball, he has several passing options.

PRESSURE RELEASES

We must be able to overcome the problem of the defense, which puts a lot of pressure on our offensive players. Here we'll show methods of pressure releases and penetrating the front-line defense.

Moment of Truth

Following are some terms we use: We define "moment of truth" as the position of 3, the wing in front of the defensive player defending the ball. 1 is ready to pass the ball to the wing (3) as he reaches the moment of truth, and 3 must coordinate his pop-out so he can receive the ball at the wing position as 1 reaches the moment of truth (figure 6.42).

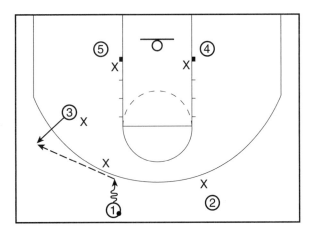

Figure 6.42 The moment of truth is when the wing on the ball side pops out to receive the ball when 1, the guard, picks up his dribble three feet in front of his defensive man.

Therefore, we call the line of truth the imaginary line across the floor three feet in front of the defensive player guarding the ball handler (figure 6.43).

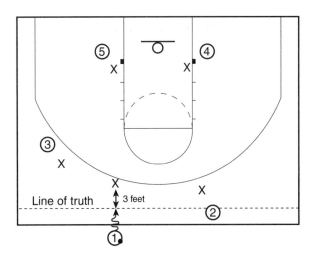

Figure 6.43 The line of truth is the imaginary line three feet in front of the ball handler's defender.

Lag Principle

If 1 reaches the moment of truth and 3 is not open on the pop out, we apply the "lag principle," a guard-to-guard pass. 1 passes to 2 as 2 lags behind the line of truth, by three feet or more, as a safety valve. Then 2 passes to 4 as he pops out to receive the ball (figure 6.44). All three players involved in these two quick passes must coordinate their moves and timing for a successful wing entry—much dribbling is required to execute these actions properly.

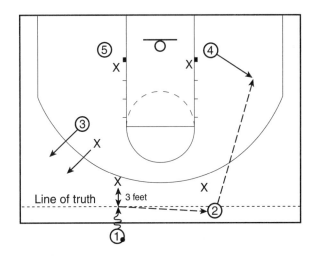

Figure 6.44 The lag principle: if 3 is not open, the other guard (2) steps behind the line of truth as a pressure-release player. 1 executes a lag pass. Since the ball has not penetrated the front line of defense, we do not number this pass.

Blind Pig Action

If 2, the player who should receive the lag pass, is overplayed, 4 flashes to the top of the lane, 1 passes quickly to 4, 2 speed cuts down the back side for a backdoor cut, and if he's open receives a drop pass on the cut to the basket (figure 6.45).

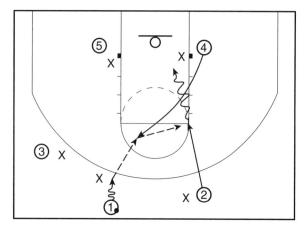

Figure 6.45 Blind pig action—if 2 is overplayed, 4 flashes to the high post, receives from 1, and passes to 2.

If 2 is not open, he continues the cut to the weak side freeze spot, and 1 cuts over the top of 4 and receives the ball from him (figure 6.46). 1 drives to the basket or dribbles onto the operating spot, on the wing or in the corner.

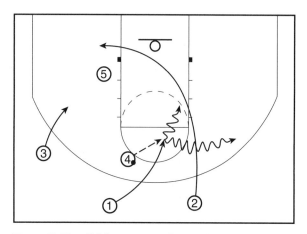

Figure 6.46 If 2 is not open, he continues the cut, and 1 cuts over the top.

If 1 is not open on the cut, he continues to the basket area and then steps out, looks for a late pass from 4, and holds position. 4 then drives to the other side of the court for a dribble weave and meets 2 coming off the down screen set by 3 (figure 6.47). After the pass, 4 has centered the court and can operate on either side. 4 can also pass directly to 2, who has popped out to the corner after 3's screen and fills the wing spot to form the triangle.

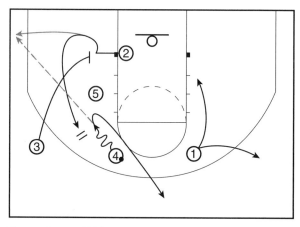

Figure 6.47 With no possible pass to the cutters, 4 drives on the other side of the court and makes a handoff pass to 2.

Options for 4: 4 can pass to 3 and, instead of screening for him, screen down for 1, who moves to the top of the floor (figure 6.48). 2 holds the freeze position and reads

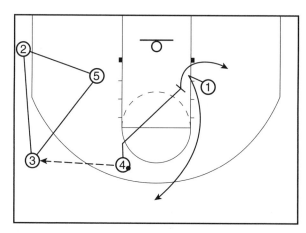

Figure 6.48 4 passes to 3 and then screens for 1; in this case, 2 pops out and we form the triangle.

the action, while 3 holds the wing position, instead screening down for 2. If 4 goes away to screen for 1, 2 pops out to the corner area and a sideline triangle is formed by 3, 5, and 2. 4 can also pass to 1 and set a screen for him (figure 6.49).

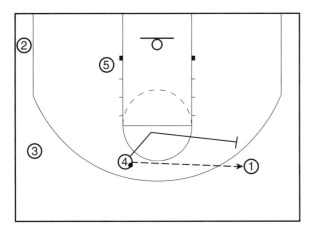

Figure 6.49   4 passes to 1 and sets a screen for him.

1 has the following options (figure 6.50):

- Make a drop pass to 4 on 4's roll to the basket (screen-and-roll two-man play).
- Drive right to the basket.
- Penetrate to clear for a jump shot.
- Penetrate and pass the ball to 5 on the block; to 3, who's holding on the weak side; or to 2 in the corner spot.

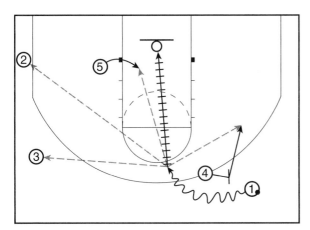

Figure 6.50   1 has different passing and shooting options.

If no teammate is open, we can form the sideline triangle with 3, 5, and 2. 1 can pass to 3 and then get to the top of the circle; 4 can go to the wing spot.

After the blind pig (see figure 6.45) and 2's cut, 4, with the ball at the top of the circle, passes it back to 1 and then goes away (figure 6.51).

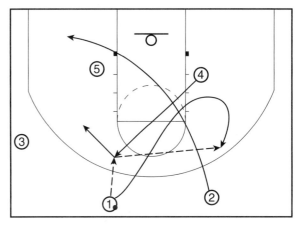

Figure 6.51   4 passes the ball back to 1 and goes away.

4 sets a second screen (a staggered screen) for 2, who has come out of the lane and has received a first screen from 3. 1 is isolated on one side of the court and can play one on one, while 2, if not open for a shot, has come off the screens set by 3 and 4 and is back in the center of the court for defensive balance (figure 6.52).

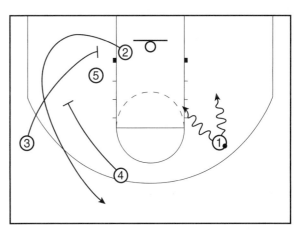

Figure 6.52   2 receives a staggered screen set by 3 and 4; 1 plays one on one on one side of the court.

If 1 can't beat his defender to the basket, he can pass the ball off to one of his four teammates, who have spaced out on the weak side (figure 6.53). Again, we form the sideline triangle with 4, 5, and 3, while 2 sets himself up at the top of the circle and 1 at the weak-side wing.

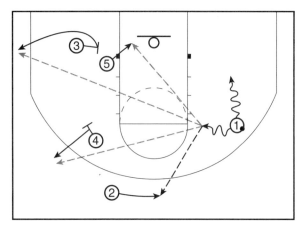

Figure 6.53   1 has several passing options.

Wing Entry on the Blind Pig

4 has flashed to the top of the circle, and 2 speed cuts into the lane and continues to the corner. But this time 1 can't pass to 4, so he passes to 3, and then 1 receives a back screen from 4. 1 speed cuts, and 3 looks for a high over-the-top pass to 1 (figure 6.54). Note that the right side of the court is clear.

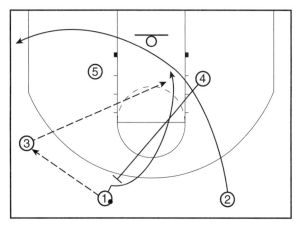

Figure 6.54   The wing entry on the blind pig: 1 passes to 3, and 4 back screens for 1 into the cleared area.

After setting the screen for 1, 4 sets a side screen for 3, who drives around 4 to the lane (we call this action wing screen and roll). 1 spots up in the corner or at the wing spot, or comes back for a dribble weave interchange with 3. After the screen for 3, 4 screens for a third time, now in the corner for 2, who comes up for defensive balance (figure 6.55). 5 freezes in the weak-side post area.

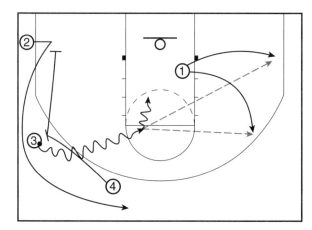

Figure 6.55   The two consecutive screens of 4 for 3 and then for 2.

After the screen, 4 continues to the weak-side rebound position, and 3 posts down after the kickoff pass to 1 (figure 6.56). 5 sets himself in the lane to possibly rebound a shot by 1.

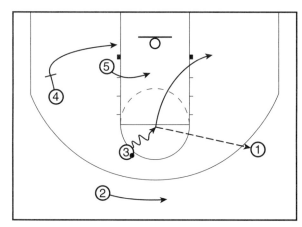

Figure 6.56   4 and 5 set themselves for a possible rebound.

If 2 is overplayed or has violated the lag principle, 2 cuts first and 4 cuts second, right off 2's tail (we call this a blur screen). 4 receives the ball from 1, 1 speed cuts off the back side of 4. 3 screens for 2, who comes up for defensive balance. 1 can also make a high pass to 2 if open (figure 6.57).

If 3 can't receive the ball on the cut, 1 screens on 2 (we call this action "guard squeeze action"). 2 cuts off 1's screen to a position three feet in front of 5, and 5 passes the ball to 2, if open. After the screen, 1 rolls to the free-throw area and can receive the ball from 5 (figure 6.59).

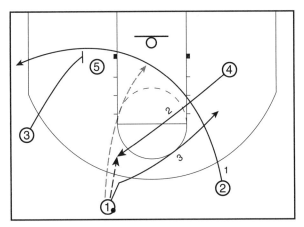

Figure 6.57 If there is no pass for 2, 2 cuts first, 4 cuts second, and 1 cuts third after the pass to 4.

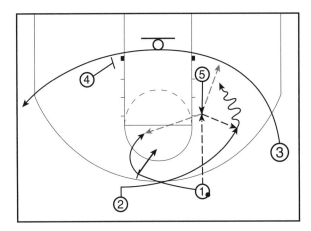

Figure 6.59 5 can pass to 2, 3, or 1, who steps back after setting the screen.

WING REVERSE

If 1 can't pass to 2 or 3, he can pass to 5, who has flashed to the high-post position at the elbow on the ball side, as usual, respecting the spacing of his teammates. 3, on the pass to the high post (5), cuts backdoor (we call this action wing reverse). 5 drop passes the ball to 3, if 3 is head and shoulders past his defender (figure 6.58).

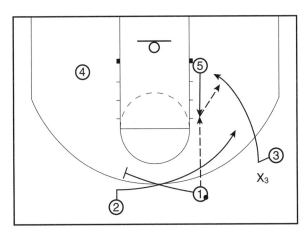

Figure 6.58 The wing reverse: 1 can also pass to 5 and screen for 2, while 5 can pass to 3 on the backdoor.

FINAL POINTS

Winning basketball is a matter of fundamentals and details, but you also need a tough attitude to reach the top. Players are now quicker and bigger than in the past, but this system of play, based on fundamentals, has proven effective for nearly 60 years. The system helped win college games in the 1960s and 1970s, and helped win games in the NBA during two different periods—first with the Bulls of Jordan and Pippen's time, and second with the Lakers of Bryant and O'Neal's time. In short, the triangle offense has proven to be ageless and tremendously effective. We hope this chapter gives you insight into basketball at a deeper level. This style of play takes basketball back to a teaching level and, at the same time, liberates players to elevate their skills at both an individual and team level. We solicit your attention to the details of the fundamental skills as the necessary tools to carry out the triangle offense. Always remember, "It's the execution that counts."

chapter 7

Princeton Offense

Eddie Jordan and Pete Carril

Offensive basketball is comprised of five elements: cutting, passing, dribbling, screening, and shooting. The aim of our offensive attack is to have five players working together using each of those elements at the proper time, in the most effective manner, as the game situation dictates. These are the premises on which the Princeton offense, or high-post offense, was founded.

At Princeton University in 1967, we adopted an offensive system based on backdoor cuts, screens, and a great deal of movement without the ball. What appealed to us about this style of play was that it involved, indeed relied on, the efforts of five players, not just one or two. The offense also was very flexible and unpredictable and could be started in many ways.

The basic idea is to spread out the court with a high formation, keeping players above the free-throw area extended except when they cut to the basket. All five players are in constant motion, reading reactions of the defenders and determining the best manner of attack. This prevents the defense from providing weak-side help and leaves it vulnerable in many ways. A common result is that the defense tires over the course of a game, and we try to take great advantage of that extra step gained by the offense.

And we don't look for just any shot. We want shots to come within the flow of players' movements, with little or no defensive pressure, and well within the shooter's high-percentage range.

OFFENSIVE FUNDAMENTALS

The offense is successful only when players execute with patience, poise, and unselfishness. Each offensive player must blend with his four teammates and share a mind-set and complementary skills to form a cohesive attack with multiple options. For this to happen, every player must be sound in all offensive fundamentals.

Cutting

Most of the time, the defender dictates to the offensive player which direction to cut. Is the defender denying the ball from being passed to a player? If so, the offensive player makes a backdoor cut, faking a move toward the ball or away from the basket and then quickly cutting behind the defender to create an opening through which the ball handler can pass. If the defender is playing below or slightly off the player he's guarding, the offensive player makes a high cut to receive the pass.

When cutting in any offense, players must be aware of what their teammates are doing and try to anticipate the cuts and moves they'll be making. If all four teammates without the ball make a basket cut or backdoor cut at the same time, a traffic jam is produced in the lane area, with no player open to receive a pass. For cuts to be effective, they must be executed with good court awareness and familiarity with teammates' tendencies on the offensive end.

Finally, when an offensive player starts any type of cut, that cut should be completed so that the passer can anticipate where the player will be and deliver the ball with accuracy. So, even if a defender recovers to prevent a back cut from being successful, the offensive player should maintain the continuity of movement he initiated in case the ball handler has committed to the pass. If he stops in midcut to the basket and his teammate passes the ball to where it appeared he was moving, a sure turnover results.

Passing

No other facet of the game fosters offensive teamwork like quick, accurate, and unselfish passing. Conversely, a team riddled with players who dribble with no purpose and shoot low-percentage shots when they have the ball is sure to be dysfunctional.

Great passers have tremendous basketball instincts. They can see the play unfolding even at its initial stages and deliver the ball to the right spot at the right time with the right touch. The best pass isn't made when it's one of the few options left for the ball handler. Rather, productive passes are those that achieve a specific aim on the offense.

Not every great pass is an assist. Often it's the pass that leads to the assist that's more important to the score. Hockey rewards assists on such passes, and most basketball coaches value them similarly.

Passing becomes contagious when all players on a team accept the notion that the objective of an offense is to get the best possible shot on each possession. Even the best scorers on the team must subscribe to this approach. Remember that the quality of passing determines an offense's quality of shots.

Dribbling

We want all five players on offense to be able to dribble, but we also want each one of them to use the dribble in a selective and savvy manner. Too much dribbling is non-

Caron Butler rises for a jumper but sees an open teammate with an even better shot and passes the ball for an assist.

productive and actually stalls an offense. We ask our players to have a purpose in mind before putting the ball on the floor.

The dribble can be an effective way to create or maintain proper offensive spacing. A short dribble can create a better passing angle to a teammate. Dribbling is also one (but not the best) way to reverse the ball to the other side of the court. And just the threat of the dribble to the basket should prevent the ball handler's defender from guarding too close for fear of getting beat for an open shot or layup.

Gregory Shamus/Getty Images Sport

Screening

Screens are essential for the long-term effectiveness of an offense. The best basketball programs have always used screens as a crucial part of their offensive attacks, even when isolations, one-on-one moves, and quick-shooting fast breaks became popular for a while.

Screening encourages teamwork and flow and serves to gain a specific advantage over the defense. For example, a screen on the defender of a particularly good shooter can provide that shooter the space he needs to drill a three-pointer. A screen across the lane on a post defender can open up a big man to receive a pass near the hoop for an easy basket.

Screening technique is important because ineffective screens contribute nothing to an offense and can actually diminish offensive flow through wasted time and movement and unnecessary fouls. A screen is not simply a matter of bumping and pushing a defender to help a teammate get open. In fact, good screening is an art.

Basketball is a precise sport, and screens must be executed with the same precision as a pass or a shot. Timing between the screener and the screened player is key. The screener must also determine the best angle at which to approach the defender, both to prevent the defender from fighting over the screen and to give his teammate an opportunity to get open to receive, pass, drive, or shoot the ball.

Shooting

As in passing and cutting, when a player decides to shoot he must do so, because the worst thing in shooting is indecisiveness. We want our players to shoot without unnecessary dribbling. Too much dribbling tends to make teammates stand around and watch the ball handler rather than continuing to move to get free for an open shot.

Rules

To the untrained eye, the Princeton offense may seem a bit helter-skelter, with players moving all about the court in no apparent pattern. And though part of the offense's success stems from its lack of structure and its unpredictability, players certainly have a number of rules to follow in executing it.

- If an offensive player without the ball is loosely guarded, the player can come toward the ball to receive a pass or direct handoff. This can be a good start to an offensive possession and is an effective way to make the defense move in order to see what openings might develop.

- Proper spacing is a must for every offense, but particularly for the Princeton offense. Because all five players are involved, they must keep proper spacing with teammates. Maintaining proper spacing creates opportunities for one-on-one situations as well as driving and drifting actions.

- When a player is guarded too closely, overplayed, or guarded by a defender who's watching the ball, the offensive player makes a backdoor cut. After one or two successful backdoor cuts, the defender will guard the offensive player less aggressively. The concept here is for offensive players without the ball to move away from defensive pressure; they don't stand stationary or try to fight the pressure.

- The ball handler should use a one-hand pass, usually a bounce pass, off the dribble when passing to a teammate cutting backdoor. The one-hand pass is quicker, and defenders are less likely to see it coming.

- Players must not decide in advance what to do but instead react to the movements of the defense. They must continually read the situation on the court.

When run effectively, the offense will yield open backdoor scoring opportunities, such as the one Antawn Jamison has here.

Taking and making good shots from the perimeter forces defenders to come out, and a defense that is spread across the court is much more vulnerable; it even makes smaller and slower offensive players seem taller and faster.

Players should only take shots they know they can make. Every player in the offense must have a keen sense of his individual aptitude in this regard. Indeed, knowing when not to shoot is just as important as knowing when to do so.

INITIAL SET

The initial set is a 2-3 alignment with two guards, two wings, and one high post (figure 7.1). When playing with a high post, you need a player in this position who's able to

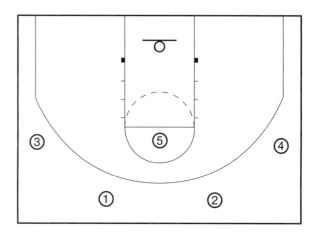

Figure 7.1 A possible initial set: a 2-3 alignment.

pass, dribble, and shoot, because he's like a big point guard. The offense is designed in such a way that it's possible to start the play on either side of the floor using different entries, either with a pass or dribble.

From this set the offense can evolve to three players out and two inside at the low-post (figure 7.2) or to four players on the perimeter and one at the low post (figure 7.3). None of these sets is permanent but is constantly changing.

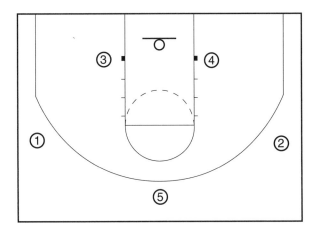

Figure 7.2   Another possible set: a 3-2.

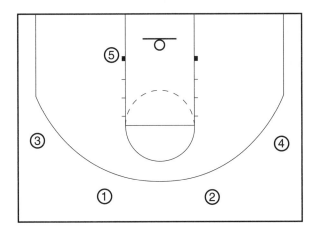

Figure 7.3   A third possible set: four outside and one inside.

Pass

Pass to the Wing. This is the easiest way to start the offense, but not the most common because many times the wings are overplayed. 1 is the ball handler in this example, but it could also be the off guard, 2. 1 passes to 3, the wing on his side. 1 can then cut to the same side as the ball or to the other side of the court.

Pass to High Post and Guards Cut or Exchange. If 1 can't pass to 3, the wing, or reverse the ball to 2 because both are overplayed, he passes to 5, the high post, who has flashed to the free-throw area. 1 and 2 cut and go to the low-post positions on the same side as the cuts, while the two wings (3 and 4) replace the guards (figure 7.4). After the entry pass to the high post (5), 1 and 2 can exchange positions with the wings (3 and 4).

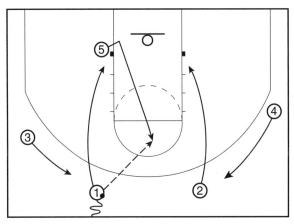

Figure 7.4   The entry pass to the post; guards cut to the low post.

Dribble

Dribble Clear. If none of the other four teammates is free, 1 begins the play by dribbling toward one of the wings, a signal for the wing to clear out and cut backdoor to the basket, or else post down low (figure 7.5). 1 dribbles toward 3, who clears out and cuts to the basket.

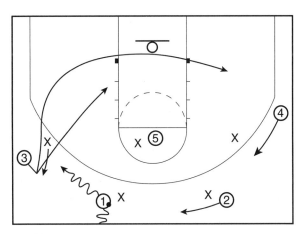

Figure 7.5   The entry: dribble clear.

Dribble Weave. Another way to beat an aggressive defense that prevents the direct pass is to make a dribble weave. 1 dribbles toward 3 and then makes a short kickoff pass (or, if possible, a hand-off pass) to 3 if the defense plays loose; 2 and 4 can exchange positions (figure 7.6).

Screen

Midscreen on the Ball. 1 can also use a midscreen set by 5 as an entry on the offense (figure 7.8). 2, who is overplayed by his defender, cuts into the lane as soon as he sees 5's screen on 1 and goes to the opposite corner; 4 and 3 come high, and 1 passes to 3.

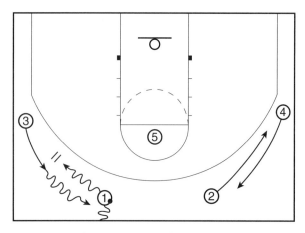

Figure 7.6　The entry: dribble weave.

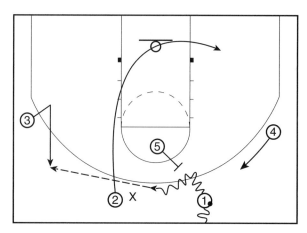

Figure 7.8　The entry: midscreen on the ball.

Reverse Dribble. The ball handler (1) can also dribble in one direction, make a reverse dribble, and then pass the ball to the wing (4), who has exchanged positions with 2 (figure 7.7). 1 can also pass to the post (5), who has popped out to the free-throw lane to get free.

Midscreen on the Ball and Reverse Dribble. 1 receives a midscreen from 5 but can't pass to 3 because he's overplayed, so he makes a reverse dribble and passes to 2, who has come off the down screen of 4 (figure 7.9).

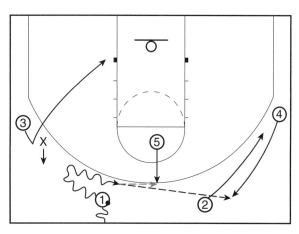

Figure 7.7　The entry: reverse dribble.

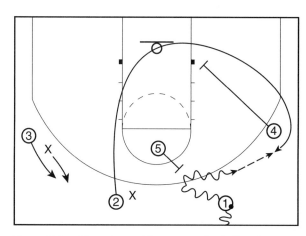

Figure 7.9　The entry: midscreen on the ball and reverse dribble.

Midscreen on the Ball and Dribble Weave.
1 receives a midscreen from 5 and dribbles toward the wing (3), but 3 is overplayed, so 1 makes a dribble weave with him for a short kickoff pass or a hand-off pass, while 2 and 4 come up (figure 7.10).

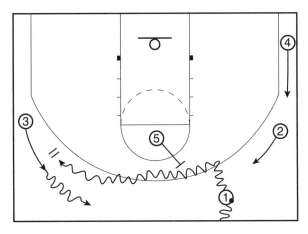

Figure 7.10 The entry: midscreen on the ball and dribble weave.

BACKDOOR CUT

A trademark of the Princeton offense is the backdoor cut, one of the most basic and best ways of playing without the ball to beat an overaggressive defender. Players don't need to fight the defender; rather, they run away from the pressure. The word "backdoor" describes exactly how this cut is done, but to use the move most effectively you need players who can make the pass to the cutter with proper timing and technique, usually via a one-hand bounce pass. All players on the offense must master the backdoor cut, whether they're post or perimeter players.

We'll now describe some situations for using the backdoor cut. The backdoor cut can be a pressure releaser, and it's also used to get a player the ball on his way to the basket when his defender has lost sight of him or of the ball.

A key point to the backdoor cut is good timing between the cutter and the passer. The cutter must not make a banana cut; rather, he cuts at an angle and calls for the ball only when he's sure to be open, giving the passer a target with his hand to indicate where he wants to get the ball. The passer must pass quickly, preferably with a one-hand bounce pass.

Wing

Direct Backdoor Cut. If the defender of the wing (3) tries to deny his receiving the ball, 3 makes a strong step toward the ball to create an overreaction from his defender, cuts hard behind him, and, if possible, receives the ball from 1 for a layup (figure 7.11).

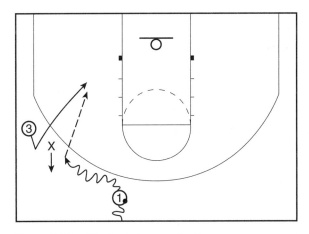

Figure 7.11 The backdoor cut by the wing.

Both Wings Backdoor Cut. With the ball in the hands of the post (5), both wings can fake going up and then make backdoor cuts if they are aggressively overplayed.

Backdoor Cut With the Help of the Center.

This is another classic backdoor situation that requires perfect spacing and timing. The post (5) flashes to the high-post area and receives the ball from 2; 4 fakes going up and then cuts backdoor to receive the ball from 5 for a layup (figure 7.12).

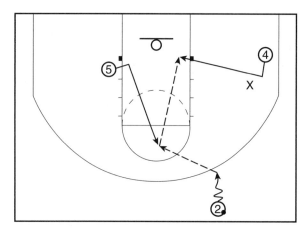

Figure 7.12   The backdoor cut with the help of the center.

Guard

Backdoor Cut With the Pass From the Other Guard.

If the guard (2) is overplayed and 1 can't pass him the ball, 2 makes a direct backdoor cut (figure 7.13).

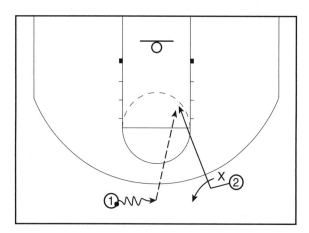

Figure 7.13   The guard's backdoor cut: The guard passes to the guard.

Backdoor Cut With the Pass From the Wing.

If the wing (4) wants to pass to 1, but 1 is overplayed, 1 fakes going toward him and then cuts backdoor (figure 7.14).

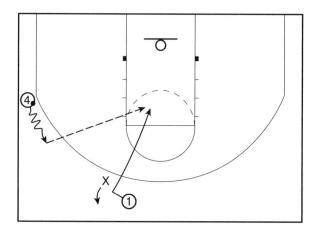

Figure 7.14   The guard's backdoor cut: The wing passes to the guard.

Backdoor Cut With the Pass From the Center.

The guard (1) can also make a backdoor cut, playing with the post, 5, who flashes to the high-post area, receives from 2, and passes to 1 on the backdoor (figure 7.15).

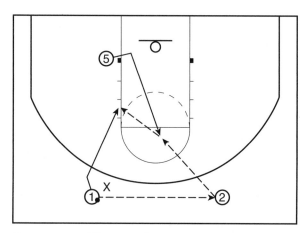

Figure 7.15   The guard's backdoor cut: The guard passes to the post; the post passes to the guard.

Post

High-Post Backdoor Cut. If the defender of the high post (5) denies the pass reversal when the ball is in the hands of the wing (1), 5 fakes to go toward the ball and then cuts behind the defender to receive the ball from 1 for a layup (figure 7.16).

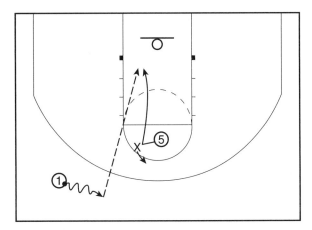

Figure 7.16   The high-post backdoor cut.

Low-Post Backdoor Cut. The backdoor cut can also be made from the low post. If 5's defender denies his receiving the ball while he's flashing to the high-post area, 5 makes a strong backdoor cut to receive the ball and shoot under the basket (figure 7.17).

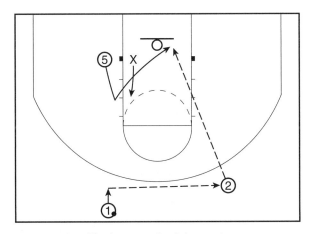

Figure 7.17   The low-post backdoor cut.

BASIC ACTION

As we've said, the initial set is a 2-3 formation, with two guards (1 and 2), two forwards (3 and 4) near the free-throw line extended, and one post (5), who can start from the low-post position and then flash to the high-post area at the elbows or at the free-throw area.

This is the initial formation, but remember that all the players are interchangeable on the court and also that we can start the action on both sides of the court or by passing to the high post. As we mentioned, the four perimeter players must be able to play both the guard and wing position because they'll often exchange their positions on the court. The "basic" has three set options:

- Pass and screen away from the ball.
- Pass and cut away.
- Pass and follow the ball (high split).

Pass and Screen Away From the Ball Set

We'll now show different options for the screen away from the ball based on defenders' reactions.

Option 1. 5 flashes to the high-post position and receives the ball from 1; 1 then screens away from the ball for 2, who cuts backdoor and moves to the other side of the court, where he receives a down screen from 3.

As you can see just from these two simple moves—one side screen and one down screen—we keep all the defenders busy and create several options for shooting. 5 can pass to 2 on the backdoor when he comes off the screen set by 3, or, if 2's defender cheats on 3's screen, when he runs back under the basket. 5 can also pass to 3, who rolls to the basket after the screen; or 3 can post down low and receive the ball from 1 (figure 7.18). Finally, 5 can also pass to 1, who pops out after setting the screen.

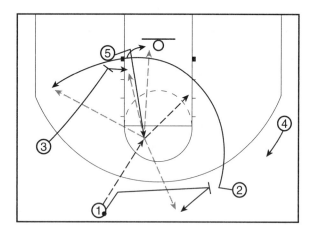

Figure 7.18 Pass and screen away set, option 1: 1 passes to the high post and screens for 2, and then 3 screens for 2.

Option 2. 2 passes the ball to 5 and then screens for 4, who goes backdoor, while 2 pops out. 5 can pass to 4 for a layup when 4 comes out of 3's screen, or, if 4's defender cheats on 3's screen, when he runs back (figure 7.19). 5 can also pass to 2, who pops out after the screen, or to 3, who rolls to the basket after setting the screen, or 3 can post down low and receive the ball from 4.

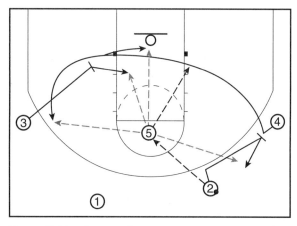

Figure 7.19 Pass and screen away set, option 2: 2 passes to the high post and then screens for 4; then 3 screens 4 again.

Option 3. Let's now assume that 1 can't make the entry pass to 3 or to 5, and he can't reverse the ball to 2 to start the offense on the other side of the court. 1 then drives toward 3 for a hand-off pass, while 2 and 4 exchange their spots (figure 7.20). 3 passes to 4 and 4 passes to 5, who has flashed to the elbow, while 3 cuts to the other side of the court. 5 can pass to 3 (figure 7.21).

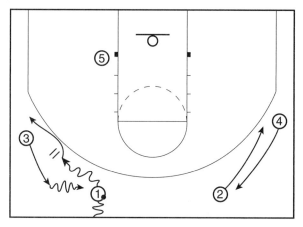

Figure 7.20 Pass and screen away set, option 3: a hand-off pass from 1 to 3 and an exchange between the other two perimeter players.

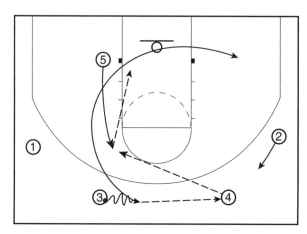

Figure 7.21 Pass and screen away set, option 3: 3 passes to 4, 4 passes to 5, and 3 cuts off 5.

4, after passing to 5, screens for 2, who goes backdoor, cuts to the other side of the floor, and is screened for by 1, who then goes to the corner. 5 can pass to 2 on the backdoor, or to 4, who, after setting the screen for 2, rolls to the low-post position or pops out. 2, if he doesn't receive the ball from 5, continues his cut and rubs off the screen set by 1. If 2's defender cheats on 1's screen, 2 runs back and receives the ball from 5 under the basket (figure 7.22).

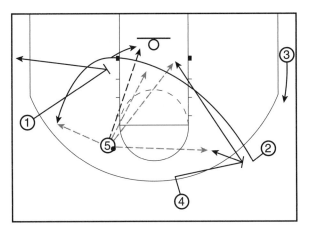

Figure 7.22 Pass and screen away set, option 3: 4 screens for 2 and then 1 screens for 2; 5 has several passing options.

If there's no solution, 5 makes one or two dribbles to the other side of the court and passes to 3. 4 then back-screens for 5, who receives the ball from 3. 3 can also pass to 4, who has popped out after the screen (figure 7.23).

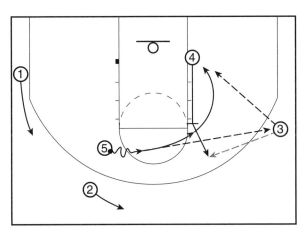

Figure 7.23 Pass and screen away set, option 3: 5 passes to 3 and 4 screens for 5.

Option 4. 2 reverses the ball to 1, and 1 passes to 3, while 2 cuts to the other side of the court. 1 screens down for 2, while 5 pops out of the lane (figure 7.24).

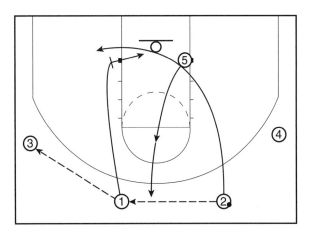

Figure 7.24 Pass and screen away set, option 4: 2 passes to 1, 1 passes to 3, and then 1 screens for 2.

3 passes to 5 and screens down for 2, while 4 screens down for 1. 5 can pass to 2 or 1, who come out of the down screens of 3 and 4, respectively, or to 3 or 4, who have rolled to the basket after the screens. If nothing happens, 5 passes to one of the two guards—to 1, in this example (figure 7.25).

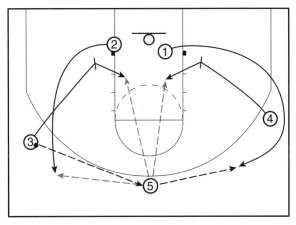

Figure 7.25 Pass and screen away set, option 4: 3 passes to 5, and then 3 and 4 screen for 2 and 1.

After the pass to 2, 5 then screens away for 1, who goes backdoor, while 2 dribbles to the other side of the court. 2 can pass to 1 on the backdoor, or to 5, who rolls to the basket after the screen (figure 7.26). After the pass to one of the guards, who came up after the screen, 5 can also post down low.

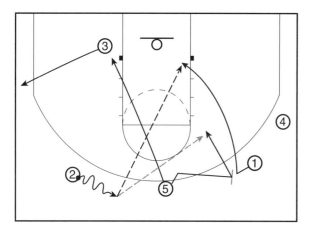

Figure 7.26 Pass and screen away set, option 4: 5 picks and rolls for 1 or cuts to the low post.

If, after the pass to 2, 5 posts down low, he can then flash to the high-post area at the elbow, while 2 passes to 1 and cuts to the other side of the court. 5 receives the ball from 1, then 1 screens away from the ball for 4, who goes backdoor, while 1 pops out. 5 can pass to 2 on the cut or when 2 comes out on the other side of the floor, or 5 can pass to 4 on the backdoor or to 1, who has popped out after the screen (figure 7.27).

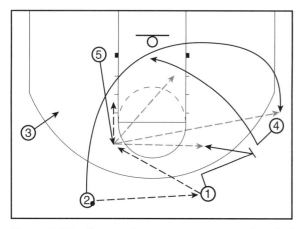

Figure 7.27 Pass and screen away set, option 4: 2 passes to 1 and cuts; 1 passes to 5 and then screens for 4.

Option 5. 1 passes to 2, cuts and screens for 5, and then goes out on the wing on the other side of the court. 5 goes to the high-post position and receives from 2, who then screens for 4, who goes backdoor. 5 can pass to 4 on the backdoor, to 1, who pops out after the screen, or to 2, who rolls to the ball after screening for 4 (figure 7.28).

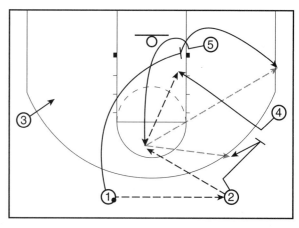

Figure 7.28 Pass and screen away set, option 5: 1 passes to 2 and screens for 5; 2 passes to 5 and screens for 4.

Pass and Cut Away Set

We always want to have the four perimeter spots occupied, and we also want to constantly move the defense so we don't have a weak and strong side of the court. For this reason, we tell our players that they can also pass the ball and cut away from the ball. Here is an example; from the previous plays, you can see that the pass and cut away is an important move of this offense.

2 passes to 1; 5 flashes to the high-post position at the elbow opposite the ball; 1 passes to 5; 2 cuts to the other side of the floor; 1 cuts and goes to the opposite side of the court, timing his cut after the cut of 2 (figure 7.29). 5 can pass to 2 or to 1 on the cut.

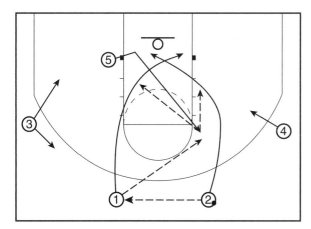

Figure 7.29 Pass and cut away set: 2 passes to 1, 1 passes to 5, and 2 cuts away.

While he's coming out of the lane, 1 receives a down screen from 4 (or he can replace 2). 5 can pass to 1 off the down screen of 4, or to 4, who rolls to the basket after the screen for 1. If 5 can't pass to 1 or 4, he dribbles toward 3, who, if he's over-played, goes backdoor and can receive a pass from 5 (figure 7.30). 3 can also screen down for 2, and 5 can pass to 2. In this case, if 2 can't shoot, he can pass to 3, who has posted down low.

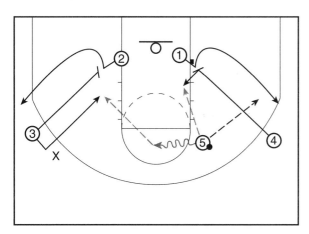

Figure 7.30 Pass and cut away set: 4 screens for 1, and 5 has several passing options.

Pass and Follow the Ball (High Split)

As we've said, in this offense the post must be a good passer and able to read different defensive situations. 2 passes to 1 and cuts to the opposite side of the court, while 5 flashes to the high-post position at the elbow opposite the ball to receive the ball from 1. 5 can pass the ball to 2 on the cut or after 2 comes off 3's screen (figure 7.31).

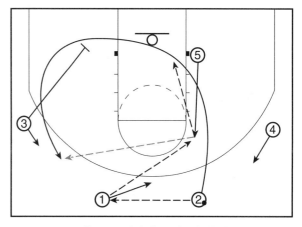

Figure 7.31 Pass and follow the ball (high split): 2 passes to 1; 1 passes to 5; 2 cuts off 5 and receives a screen from 3.

If this solution is not possible, these are the alternatives:

- After the pass to 5, 1 follows the pass, while 4 fakes a split and goes backdoor to receive from 5 (figure 7.32). 5 can also pass to 1, who pops out.

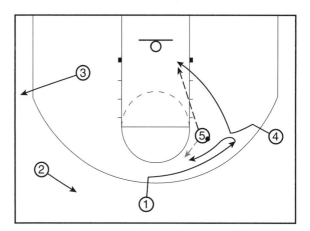

Figure 7.32 Pass and follow the ball (high split): 1 follows the pass to 5, while 4 goes backdoor.

- 1 screens for 4, and 4 receives the ball for a jump shot or a drive to the basket (figure 7.33). 5 can also pass to 1, who rolls to the basket.

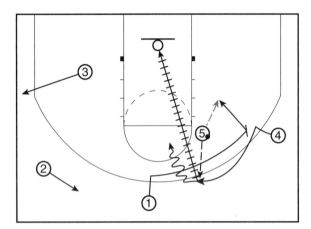

Figure 7.33 Pass and follow the ball (high split): 1 picks and rolls with 4.

- 1 screens for 4, 4 goes backdoor, and 1 pops out for a jump shot (figure 7.34).

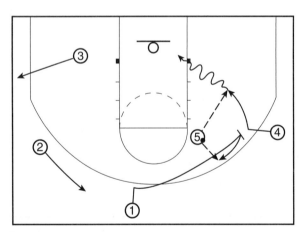

Figure 7.34 Pass and follow the ball (high split): 1 picks for 4 and pops out.

- 1 splits with 4, who goes backdoor and then to the low post; 1 then pops out to the wing area (figure 7.35).

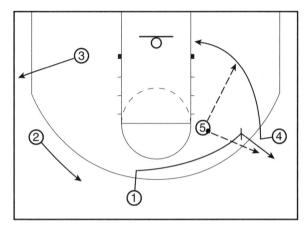

Figure 7.35 Pass and follow the ball (high split): 1 splits with 4, who goes backdoor.

- After the pass to 1, 5 is back-screened by 4 and receives the ball from 1 (figure 7.36). 1 can also pass to 4, who pops out after the back screen.

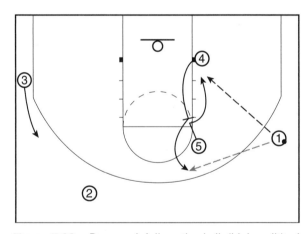

Figure 7.36 Pass and follow the ball (high split): 4 back-screens for 5 and then pops out.

OPTIONS TO "BASIC"

No matter what type of offense you run, you must have different options to start your play in case the defense stops your primary entry option. As we've said, there are two basic options for starting a play: either with a pass, as we described previously, or with a dribble. In this section we'll review options for starting the offense with a reverse dribble.

Reverse Dribble

Option 1. 1 can't pass to one of his teammates, so he starts to dribble toward 2, who cuts away from the ball to the opposite side of the court; 1 then reverse dribbles toward 4, who goes backdoor (or screens for 2) and then to the low-post position; 5 flashes to the elbow on the weak side (figure 7.37).

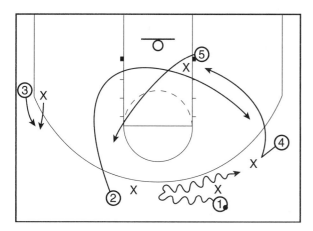

Figure 7.37 Reverse dribble, option 1: 1 reverses the dribble, 2 cuts away, 4 cuts backdoor, and 5 flashes to the high post.

After the reverse dribble, 1 passes to 2, receives a side screen from 5, and gets the ball from 2 for a jump shot or a drive to the basket. 2 can also pass to 5, who has rolled to the basket after the screen. 2, after the pass to 1, can also screen down for 4, and 4 can receive the ball from 1 (figure 7.38).

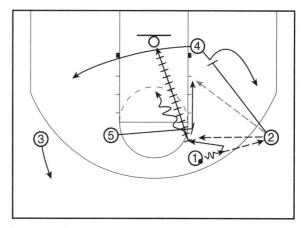

Figure 7.38 Reverse dribble, option 1: 1 passes to 2 and is screened for by 5. 2 can then pass back to 1 and screen for 4.

Option 2. 2 dribbles toward 1, then reverse dribbles and passes to 3; 5 has flashed outside the lane to receive the ball from 3. 2 and 1 cut to the same side of the court from which they started and are screened respectively by 3 and 4 (figure 7.39). 5 can pass

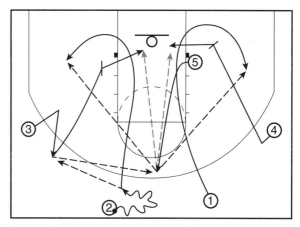

Figure 7.39 Reverse dribble, option 2: 2 reverses the dribble and passes to 3, 3 passes to 5, and then 4 and 3 down-screen for 1 and 2.

to 2 or 3 off the screens or to 4 or 5, who
have rolled to the basket after the screens.
5 passes to 1 and goes to the low-post area,
while 4 goes outside the three-point arc. 1
passes to 2 (figure 7.40).

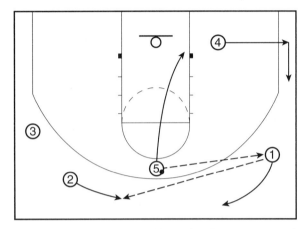

Figure 7.40 Reverse dribble option 2: 5 passes to 1
and goes on the low post, while 1 passes to 2.

2 then starts to dribble toward 1, who cuts
in the lane and comes out on the other side of
the court, brushing off the screen of 3. 2 makes
a reverse dribble and passes to 1 or to 3, who
rolled to the basket after the screen (figure 7.41).
1 passes to 3, while 5 side-screens for 2 and then
pops out (figure 7.42). 3 can pass to 1, who spots
up, to 2, to 5, or to 4, who spots up.

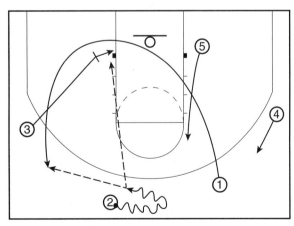

Figure 7.41 Reverse dribble option 2: 2 reverses the
dribble and passes to 1, coming off the screen of 3, or to
3 as he's rolling to the basket.

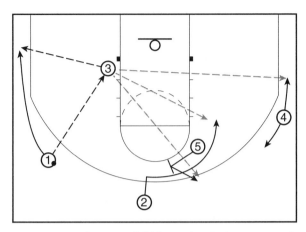

Figure 7.42 Reverse dribble, option 2: 1 passes to 3,
and 3 has several passing options.

Option 3. 2 is overplayed, so 1 dribbles
toward him; 2 makes a backdoor cut and
gets out on the opposite side of the court.
1 reverse dribbles and has these options on
the strong side:

- 4 screens for 2 and then rolls to the
  basket (figure 7.43).
- 4 fakes the screen and cuts to the
  basket.
- 4 posts up down low (figure 7.44).

1 can also pass to 2, receive a screen from
5, and get the ball back from 2; 1 then plays
pick-and-roll with 5 (figure 7.45).

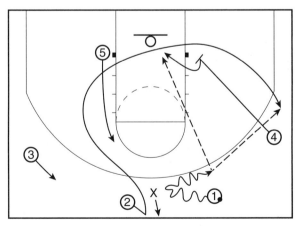

Figure 7.43 Reverse dribble, option 3: 1 reverses the
dribble and passes to 2, coming off the screen of 4, or to
4 as he's rolling to the basket.

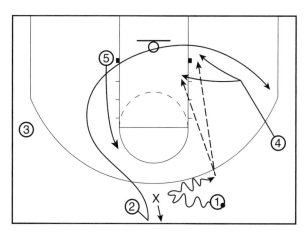

Figure 7.44 Reverse dribble, option 3: 1 reverses the dribble and passes to 4, who has faked a screen or posted down low.

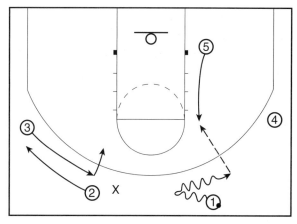

Figure 7.46 Reverse dribble double screen high option: 1 reverses the dribble and passes to 5, while 2 and 3 exchange.

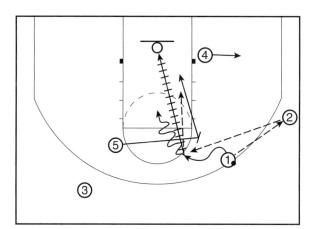

Figure 7.45 Reverse dribble, option 3: 1 passes to 2, receives the ball back from 2, and plays pick-and-roll with 5.

Reverse Dribble with Double Screen High

1 dribbles toward 2, who is overplayed and can't receive the ball, so 2 and 3 exchange spots as 1 reverses the dribble and passes to 5, who has flashed to the elbow (figure 7.46). 3 and 1 double-screen on the other side of the court. 5 has these options:

- Pass to 2, who rubs off the double screen high or low.
- After a couple of dribbles, pass to 4, who cuts backdoor if he's overplayed (figure 7.47).

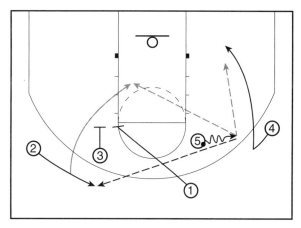

Figure 7.47 Reverse dribble double screen high option: 5 can pass to 2 or to 4 on the backdoor.

- Pass to 2, who fakes to rub off the double screen and then cuts backdoor.
- Pass to 1, who pops out of the screen (figure 7.48).

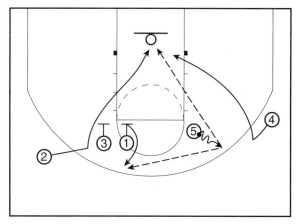

Figure 7.48 Reverse dribble double screen high option: 5 can pass to 2 on a backdoor cut or to 1.

Chin

This action, called chin, starts with a back pick by the high post on the weak side of the half-court.

Option 1. 2 passes to 1, then rubs off the back screen set by 5 and gets to the other side of the court, while 1 passes to 3 (figure 7.49). 3 can pass to 2. If 2 can't receive the ball, 5 screens on the other elbow for 1, who receives the ball from 3 for a shot or a drive to the basket (figure 7.50). 5 can roll to the basket in the opposite direction of 1 and receive from 3.

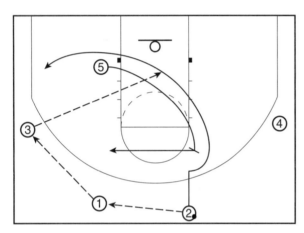

Figure 7.49   Chin, option 1: 2 passes to 1, and 1 passes to 3; 2 rubs off the back screen set by 5.

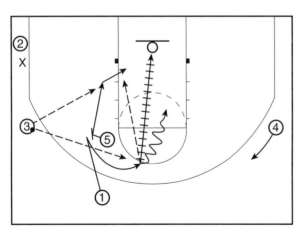

Figure 7.50   Chin, option 1: 3 can't pass to 2, so 5 screens and rolls on 1.

Option 2. 2 passes to 1, rubs off the back screen of the high post (5), and cuts to the other side of the court. 1 passes to 3 and 3 dribbles to the right, while 5 screens for 1, who cuts to the opposite side of the court and replaces 4, who gets to the guard position (figure 7.51). 3 passes to 4 and 4 passes to 1, while 3 rubs off the back screen set by 5 and goes to the ball-side corner. 1 can pass to 3 (figure 7.52).

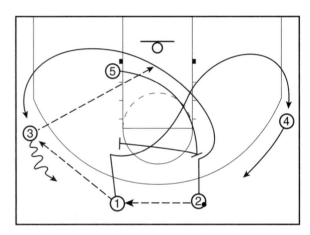

Figure 7.51   Chin, option 2: 2 passes to 1 and is screened by 5; 1 passes to 3 and is screened by 5 on the other side.

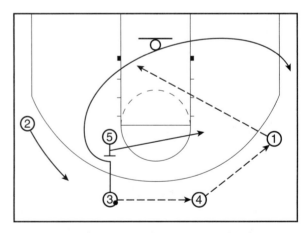

Figure 7.52   Chin, option 2: 3 passes to 4 and 4 passes to 1, while 3 is screened by 5.

If nothing happens, 5 flashes to the other elbow and back-screens for 4 (figure 7.53). 1 can pass to 4. If 4 can't receive the ball, he comes back and back-screens for 5. 1 can pass to 5 or to 4, who pops out from the screen (figure 7.54).

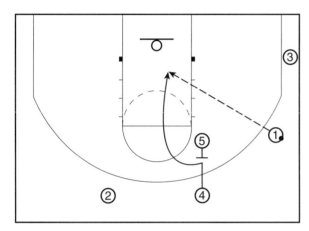

Figure 7.53 Chin, option 2: 5 back-screens for 4.

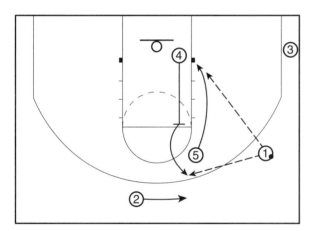

Figure 7.54 Chin, option 2: If there's no solution, 4 back-screens for 5 and pops out.

Chin Pass to Strong Side (Flare Action)

Option 1. 2 passes to 3 and receives a back screen from 5, who has flashed to the strong-side elbow. 2 posts down low on the ball side, while 5 pops out after the screen (figure 7.55).

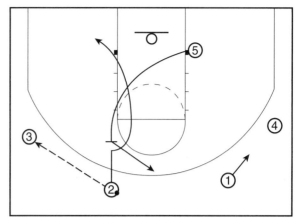

Figure 7.55 Chin pass to strong side, option 1: 2 passes to 3, is back-screened by 5, and posts down low.

3 passes to 5 and then screens down for 2, while 1 makes a flare screen for 4. 5 has several options (figure 7.56):

- Pass to 2, who comes off 3's screen.
- Pass to 4, who comes off 1's screen.
- Pass to 3, who rolls to the basket after setting the screen for 2.
- Pass to 1, who rolls to the basket after setting the screen for 4.

4 can also make a backdoor cut if his defender slides over the screen.

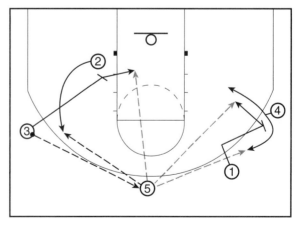

Figure 7.56 Chin pass to strong side, option 1: 3 passes to 5 and screens down for 2, while 1 makes a flare screen for 4; 5 has several passing options.

Option 2. 1 passes to 2, screens on the ball, and pops out to replace 2. 2 dribbles on the other side of the court, while 1 posts down low on the weak side and 5 gets to the other elbow (figure 7.57). 2 passes to 4, rubs off the back screen of 5, and goes out on the ball side, while 5 pops out after the screen (figure 7.58). 5 receives the ball from 4, and 1 screens for 3, who pops out and receives from 5 (figure 7.59).

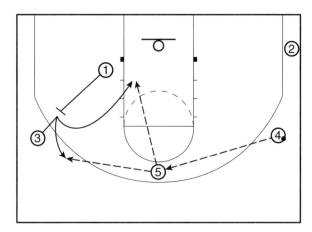

Figure 7.59 Chin pass to strong side, option 2: 5, who popped out, receives from 4, while 1 back-screens for 3.

Sets Out of the High Pick

One of the possible entries on this offense is the high pick. From this entry we can start different sets.

Option 1. 5 flashes to the elbow, then pops out and sets a high screen for 1. 2 cuts into the lane, is screened for by 3, and gets out to the other side of the court, replacing 1 (figure 7.60). After the screen, 5 rolls outside.

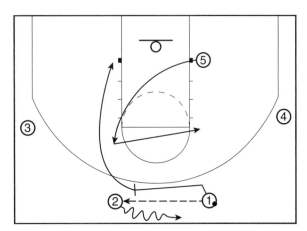

Figure 7.57 Chin pass to strong side, option 2: 1 passes to 2, screens 2, and then pops out and posts down low on the weak side.

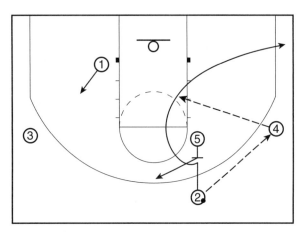

Figure 7.58 Chin pass to strong side, option 2: 2 passes to 4 and is back-screened by 5.

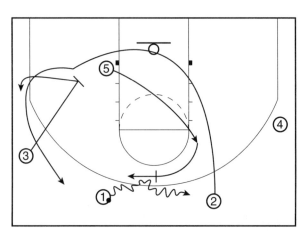

Figure 7.60 Sets out of the high pick, option 1: 5 pops out to screen for 1, while 2 cuts into the lane and is screened by 3.

1 reverses the dribble and passes to 5; 5 passes to 2 and then posts down low; 3 gets outside the three-point arc. 2 passes to 3 and screens on the ball. 3 drives to the basket or passes to 2, who has rolled to the basket (figure 7.61).

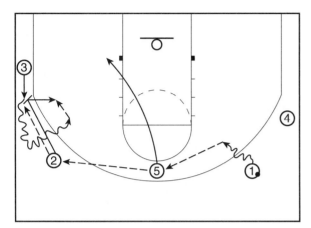

Figure 7.61 Sets out of the high pick, option 1: 1 passes to 5; 5 passes to 2; 2 passes to 3 and then screens for him and rolls.

Option 2. 5 flashes to the elbow, pops out, and sets a high screen for 1, while 2 cuts down low (figure 7.62).

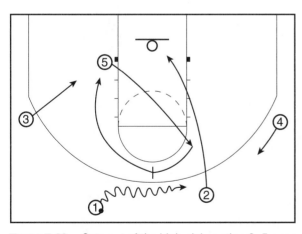

Figure 7.62 Sets out of the high pick, option 2: 5 pops out to screen for 1, while 2 cuts into the lane.

After the screen, 5 runs down and forms a double screen with 3 for 2, who rubs off and gets out to the three-point arc. 1 dribbles toward 4 for a hand-off pass to him. 4 dribbles to the other side of the court and passes to 2. If 4 is overplayed, he can go backdoor while 1 is dribbling toward him. 2 can also pass to 5, who rolls to the basket, or to 3, who can pop out or curl around 5 (figure 7.63).

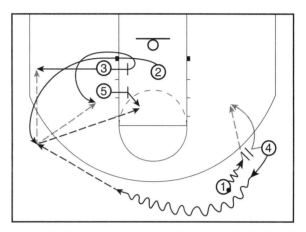

Figure 7.63 Sets out of the high pick, option 2: 5 and 3 form a double screen for 2; 4 receives a hand-off pass from 1, drives, and passes to 2, who has several passing solutions.

IMPLEMENTING THE OFFENSE

Some coaches are reluctant to adopt this offense. It's wise to be cautious before accepting and implementing any particular manner of attack. However, any drawbacks to this offense are more imagined than real. We're convinced this style of offensive play has far fewer shortcomings and many more appealing features than the popular alternatives, so let's address what we've heard coaches cite as their major concerns.

• The offense is too slow to develop. True, this offense requires a bit of patience. It might very well take a while before the offense gets an open, high-percentage shot during a possession. And that's the point: It forces the defense to work over longer stretches, reacting to the players' and the ball's movement. But just because the offense might require more passes and more seconds might tick off the shot clock before a field-goal attempt is made doesn't mean the offense is slow. Indeed, it's far faster than an offense in which players dribble too much, cuts are made too slowly or not at all, and passes are deliberate and telegraphed. In our offense, the ball never remains in one player's hands for more than a couple of seconds, and the players without the ball are constantly moving (cutting or screening). Plus, we don't have to waste time calling out plays or resetting the offense; players can flow immediately to new solutions

without losing time. And, typically, there's more than one good opportunity to score per possession—but if the first backdoor cut is open for a layup, hey, we'll take it.

• The offense is difficult to teach. Because execution is the key to any set, as with any offense, you need to take care and practice details when learning it and all its options. Think of it this way: You're not teaching an offense but are teaching the game of basketball, including all the basics a player must master to play the game well. If a player can master the fundamentals involved in this offense, he can play in any other type of offense. By adopting and working on this offense, a coach improves not only his players' offensive skills but also their defensive skills, because they must work on any type of defensive situation that occurs on the court, including screens on and off the ball, every type of cut, blocking out in difficult situations, and so on.

Ned Dishman/NBAE/Getty Images Sport

Sound fundamentals must be taught and executed in any successful offense, including the Princeton or high-post offense.

under basket

Under basket

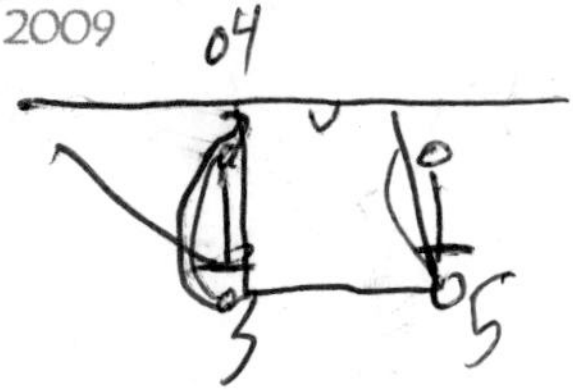

thanks for coming to John's 50th!
April 11, 2009

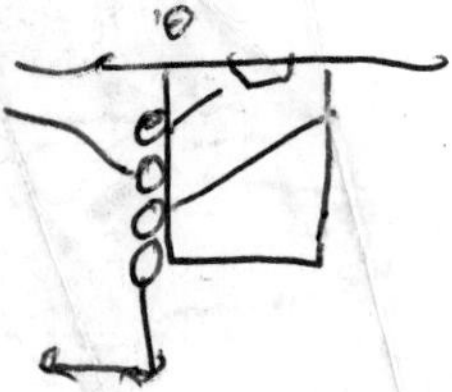

o4

1 or 2

Sideline

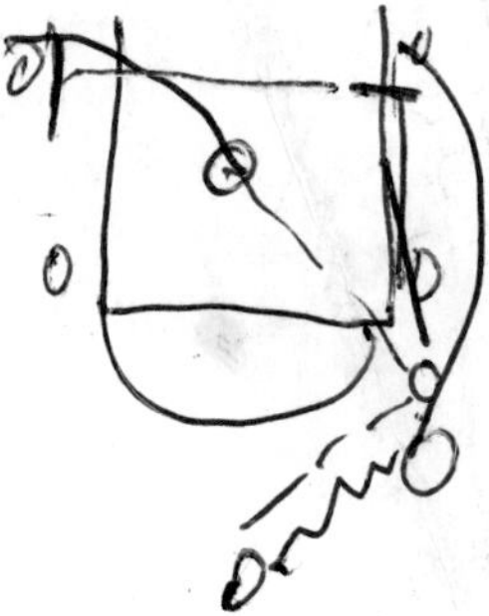

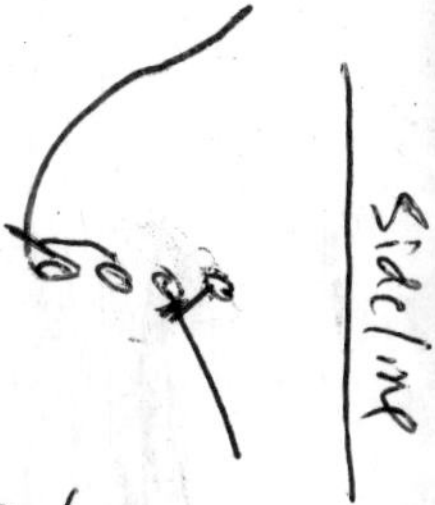

Color

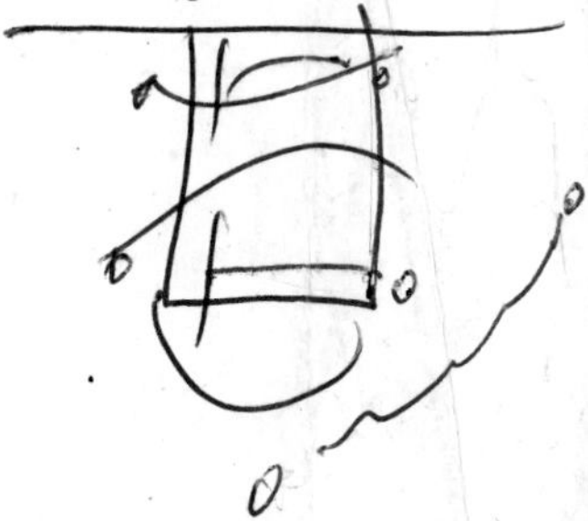

over the hill

• **This offense hampers players' scoring averages, and the best scorer on the team gets fewer touches.** Would you prefer to have a happy scoring leader who's averaging 30 points a game on a losing team riddled with dissension caused by selfishness and a one-pony style of attack, or would you prefer having every player participate in and contribute to the offense of a successful and cohesive team, though no individual averages more than 18 points? And, considered from a different angle, which team would you rather defend—the team with only one threat or the team with five threats? Basketball is a team sport, and the team wins, not a single player. Besides, gifted offensive players can and do shine in the Princeton offense, though their scoring stats might not be as gaudy as another team's gunners.

• **This offense gives more freedom to the players, so the coach has less control.** This is true. But, then again, a coach's sense of control in other offenses is no more than an illusion. Ultimately, the fundamentals and execution of players determine the success of any team. We as coaches can't shoot, pass, dribble, or make the hundreds of on-court decisions for players during the course of a game. The last thing any coach should want are robots on the court. Instead, we find great satisfaction in seeing our players take the principles they've been taught and practiced and apply them most effectively during competition. And we know our players appreciate the respect we show for their unselfishness and decision-making skills by allowing them such freedom.

FINAL POINTS

A few final points on teaching and practicing this offense: Emphasize working on those things that matter—the skills needed and situations most likely to be encountered in a game. Don't waste hours of practice time on drills that don't mean much when it comes to how your players and team perform in competition. If you watch what your players are doing when they play, they will show you what to teach them.

When you do work on a drill that's directly related to game performance, put maximum effort and concentration into it. The quality of work is more important than quantity, though the best drills should be repeated often and done right. With this offense, as with others, taking shortcuts only adds to shortcomings. Winning is in the details, and we hope you have learned enough about the Princeton offense to at least seriously consider it as an option for your team.

chapter 8

Flex Offense

Ruben Magnano

Basketball in Argentina is more similar to the European style of play than to the brand of ball most common in the NBA, where one-on-one and pick-and-roll are more popular. But, as the NBA has become more international, with nearly 20 percent of its players coming from outside the United States, those distinctions are blurring. More and more aspects of the European or Argentinean style of play are finding their way into not only the professional ranks but other levels of play in the States as well.

One of the first points I emphasize to my players is that offense starts with defense. And since we want fast action in our offense, we want to pair it with very aggressive defense. This gives our players a chance to make quick transitions from one end of the court to the other. In doing so, we can create high-percentage, quick scoring chances off the primary or secondary break. Those of you who have watched one of our fine players, Manu Ginobili,

through the years have seen how he pushes the ball up the court and so often converts transition opportunities into scoring plays.

Pushing the pace upcourt and creating scoring opportunities before the defense can get into position is one of Manu Ginobili's fortes.

Andrew D. Bernstein/NBAE/Getty Images Sport

135

We want to attack the opposing defense as soon as we gain possession of the ball. But please don't confuse this emphasis on a running game with playing in a rush. Among the great John Wooden's many words of wisdom is the reminder to "Be quick, but don't hurry." And that certainly applies here. With proper teaching and correction through repeated practice, players will recognize the difference between effective speed of movement on offense and hasty, counterproductive activity.

TRANSITION GAME

On the primary break, players should fill the proper lanes and seek to create overload situations for high-percentage shots. We have different ways to fill the lanes on the court on a primary and secondary break.

Two Players on the Wing on Same Lane, Ball Side. For example, if 2 and 3 run on the same lateral lane and the ball is driven on offense on the same lane behind them, the player who is forward (2 in this case) continues his run and cuts under the basket until he reaches the other corner. 3, who is behind 2, stays in the same lane and goes in the corner on the same side. At the same time, 4, the other wing on the lane opposite 2, cuts into the three-second area to receive the ball; if he does not receive it, he posts up in the low-post position (this is the rule for the first trailer), while 5 runs as a second trailer and stops himself outside of the three-point line (figure 8.1).

One Player on the Wing, Ball Side. Another transition situation occurs when 3 (guard or small forward) is behind the ball. 3 runs to occupy the other open lateral lane, independently from what the first trailer, 4, is doing (figure 8.2).

Trailer, High Over the Ball on Lateral Lane. 4, one of the trailers, is high over the ball and on a lateral lane; he runs to receive the ball and shoot a layup. If he can't receive and shoot inside the lane, he posts up on the

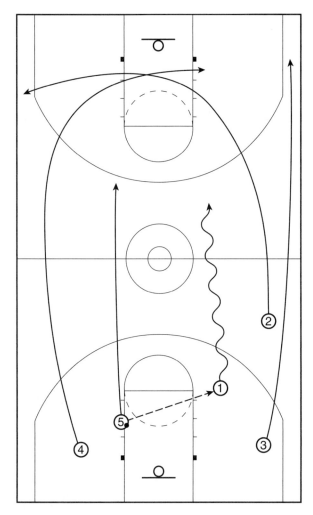

Figure 8.1 The fast break: two players on the wing on the same lane, ball side.

same side of the ball, while 2 and 3 run on the lateral lanes, and 5 is the second trailer (figure 8.3).

These transition options should never preclude players from improvising when an easy basket is possible. You don't want to hamper players' creativity, but you do want to provide some basic principles and structure.

Our transition ends with players set on the court this way: two guards, 2 and 3, on the corners outside the three-point line, our power forward, 4, in the low-post position, and 5, our center, the second trailer, outside the three-second lane; the ball is in the hands of 1 (figure 8.4). From this setup we start our flex offense.

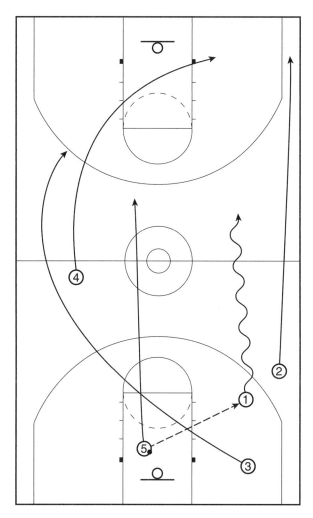

Figure 8.2 The fast break: one player on the wing, ball side.

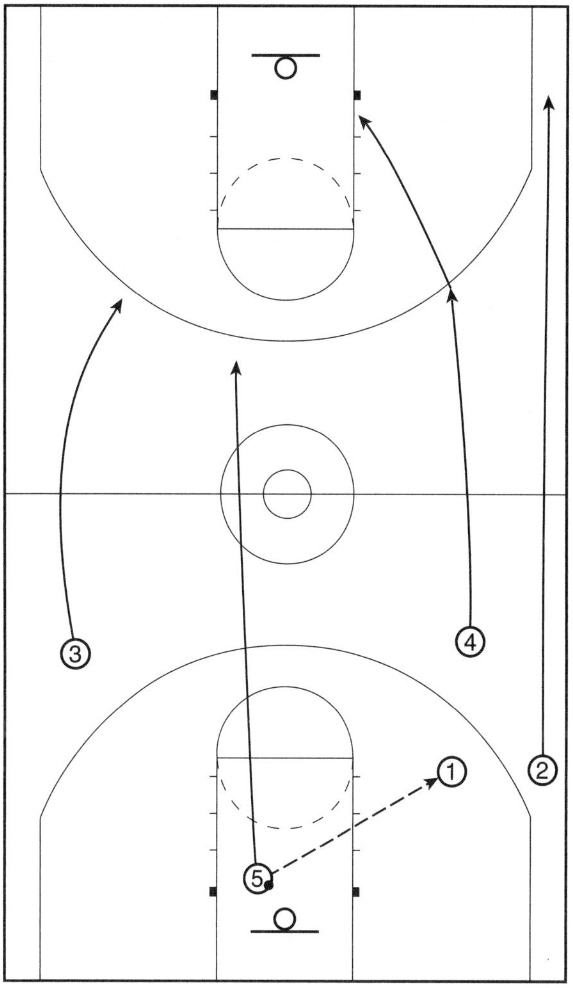

Figure 8.3 The fast break: trailer high over the ball on the lateral side.

FLEX OFFENSE CHARACTERISTICS

Though we want to use the transition game whenever we gain an advantage on the break, we prefer a more tactical, controlled half-court attack that involves all players. We encourage a flowing attack with quick and continuous passing and cutting, without as much physical contact as many European and NBA teams seem to favor.

That doesn't mean our style of attack is soft. The success of not only Manu Ginobili but also Andres Nocioni, Carlos Delfino, Fabricio Oberto, Walter Herrmann, Luis

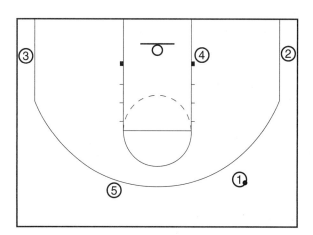

Figure 8.4 The end of transition and setting the flex offense.

Scola, and other Argentinean players should dispel any such notion. All of these players benefited from a strong grounding in the fundamentals of the game and playing in a system that emphasized a team concept.

My preference for the flex offense was born many years ago, when I started coaching at the youth level in Argentina. The appeal then, as now, was that the offense incorporated a lot of movement, with several offensive options for all of the players in different positions on the court, either facing the basket or with their backs to it. This seemed the best way to keep all players involved and a good way to introduce them to the essential skills of passing, shooting, and driving with the ball, as well as playing without the ball.

Over time, my teaching of the offense and modifications to it allowed for even quicker learning and better execution. And, as Argentina's National Team coach, I continued to employ the flex offense for additional reasons:

- We lacked a dominant center, as none of our players had great size or great back-to-the-basket inside moves. So it served no advantage to station a player on the low post.

- Our players' off-the-ball skills were usually stronger than their individual moves with the ball. The offense's emphasis on movement played more to our strength.

- We sought to take advantage of our players' versatility. They were accustomed to and very capable of facing the basket, shooting from outside when open, and cutting and driving to the basket as opportunities arose. This served to open up the lane and to expose larger and slower defenders' weaknesses, which we could exploit.

- Every player in the offense could become a scoring threat, making it more difficult for opponents to focus defensively on just one or two positions.

Flex Offense Essentials

- Correct use of fundamentals, including playing one on one, passing, shooting, and playing facing the basket as well as with the back to it
- Moving without the ball—a must for every player in every position on the court
- Proper spacing and timing in the execution of fundamentals
- Being able to perform at various positions on the court
- Reacting to the reaction of the defense: reading the defense and making countermoves
- Screening the screener—because the player setting a pick for a teammate who has just screened for another teammate is often left wide open
- Emphasis on two types of screens for perimeter players: vertical and back screens
- Overloading one side of the court

- The offense entailed a lot of movement, with continuous cuts and screens; we found this wore opponents down as the game progressed.

In the course of running the offense, we also found our players liked the freedom to locate favorite positions on the court in which to receive a pass for a shot. Their confidence and comfort level in shooting from those spots led to a higher shooting percentage.

In teaching the flex, we believe players learn best if they first see a demonstration of the complete play. We walk them through the offense and all its options at a slow enough pace for them to grasp the spacing and actions we're seeking. Only after that do we examine the different phases. Once it appears players have a basic understanding, we put all the pieces together again in a real game situation.

We found that breaking the flex down into separate parts first and then trying to assemble it was not effective, because players need to establish a global picture and sense of flow of the attack to really grasp the elements and nuances later on. In addition to aiding their learning, showing players the flex in its entirety serves to motivate them as students because they see the many opportunities for themselves and potential for success as a team.

HALF-COURT ATTACK

The flex is our primary offense in the half-court and what we instinctively run when nothing happens in transition during a possession. The offense starts with 1 passing the ball to 5. Simultaneous to that pass, 2 brings his defender on the back screen of 4 and looks for a pass from 5 inside the three-second area. 2 reads the reaction of his defender and, based on his position, either cuts over or cuts behind 4's screen; if he doesn't receive the ball, he posts up. 4, right after the screen for 2, receives a screen from 1 in a screen-the-screener play (figure 8.5). After setting the screen, 1 pops out.

The same movement is made on the other side of the court with 5, who passes the ball to 4. 2 makes a back screen for 3 and receives a screen from 5 (screen-the-screener play) right after he screens for 3; then 5 pops out (figure 8.6). 4 now has two options: to pass to 3 inside the three-second area or to pass to 2, who comes up after 5's screen.

Melissa Majchrzak/NBAE/Getty Images Sport

A power forward like Luis Scola, who is adept at setting screens, moving without the ball, and sharing the ball with teammates, makes the flex offense even more effective.

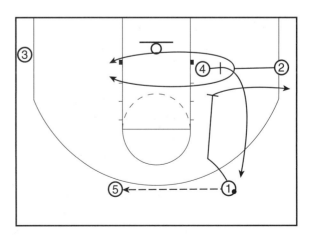

Figure 8.5 The back screen and screen-the-screener action.

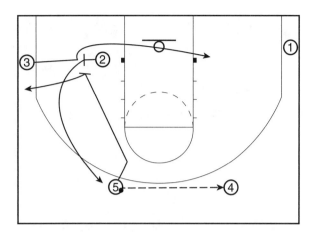

Figure 8.6 The same action on the other side, and the possible solutions.

In this last option, we repeat the initial movement, with 1 receiving a back screen from 3 and then cutting into the lane, and 4, who—after passing to 2 and after receiving the back screen from 3—screens for 3 (figure 8.7). For this screen-the-screener play to work, all players on the court must read the situation (both the teammate with the ball and the teammates off the ball, who are setting and using the screens) and then react to the reaction of the defenders.

As you can see, none of the five offensive players stay at a certain position while running the offense; they move in all positions on the court, with the center, power forward, and perimeter players playing both inside and outside.

If the ball is passed in the corner to 2, in this example, the player at the low-post

position on the ball side, 1, makes a vertical back screen for 5, who goes to the low-post position. 2 can pass the ball to 5 in the low post or to 1, who pops out after the back screen (figure 8.8).

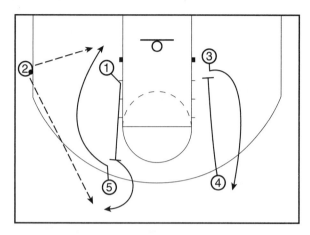

Figure 8.8 All players play in all positions on the half-court.

Option 1. Every play is as effective as the different options and countermoves. Basketball is a game of chess—you need to study and react to the moves of your opponent. Here we show the first option. 1 passes the ball to 5 and makes a vertical screen for 4, who comes up and receives the ball from 5. After the screen, 1 rolls to the low-post position on the other side of the court (figure 8.9). When 4 receives the ball, 1 makes a back screen for 3 and then receives a vertical screen from 5 (screen-the-screener play). 4 passes the ball to 1 (figure 8.10).

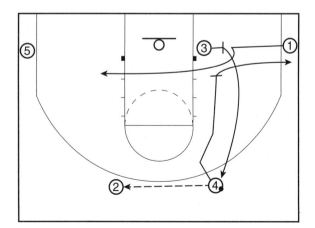

Figure 8.7 The repetition of the initial movement.

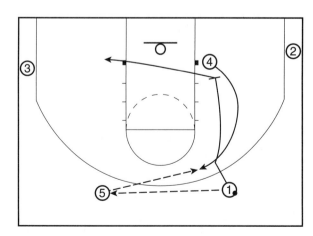

Figure 8.9 Option 1: 1 passes to 5 and screens for 4.

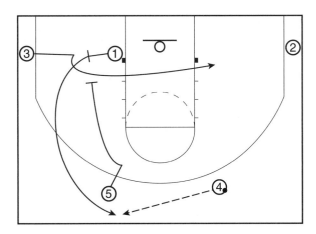

Figure 8.10 Option 1: The play is run with the same two moves, using the back screen and screen-the-screener action.

The ball is in the hands of 1; 2 and 3 are on the weak side. 2 can now choose which screen to use:

- the screen of 3, for cutting and receiving in the lane, or
- the screen of 4, for coming up high.

Based on which screen 2 exploits, 3 chooses from two options (figure 8.11):

- to stay and receive a screen from 4 (screen-the-screener play) if 2 cuts into the lane, or
- to cut into the lane and go out to the other corner, using the screen of 5.

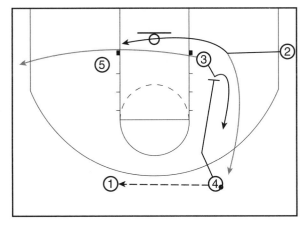

Figure 8.11 Option 1: The move of 3 is based on the move of 2.

1 has four choices for the pass. He can pass

- to 2, who comes off from a screen of 3 or 4;
- to 3, who comes off 5's screen;
- to 5 in the low post on the ball side; or
- to 4 in the low post on the opposite side of the court.

Let's come back to the situation when the ball is in the hands of 4. 3 can decide to go to the low-post position or, as we show here, to exploit the vertical screen of 5 and come up to receive the ball from 4 (figure 8.12). In this case, it will be 1 who moves to the low post opposite to the ball.

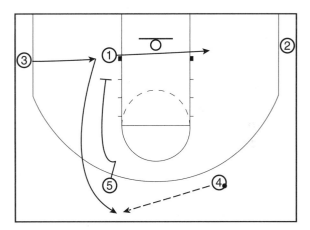

Figure 8.12 Option 1: 3 can go to the low post or use the vertical screen of 5.

With the ball in 3's hands, 2 can choose which screen to exploit (figure 8.13). In any case, we always follow our basic rule, which is to give the man with the ball (in this case, 3) four passing options.

Option 2. The play starts and is run as basic flex (figure 8.14). Then 3 uses 1's screen, and 5 screens 1 in a screen-the-screener play (figure 8.15).

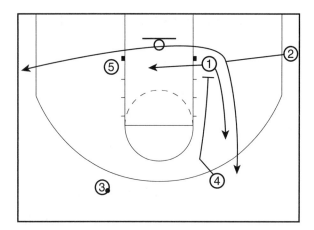

Figure 8.13 Option 1: With 3 with the ball, 2 can choose which screen to use.

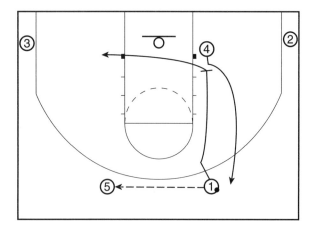

Figure 8.14 Option 2: The play starts as basic flex, with 1 down-screening 4.

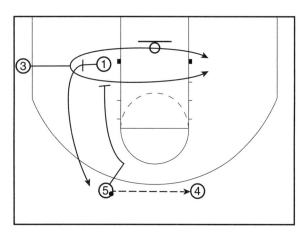

Figure 8.15 Option 2: 5 screens the screener.

But when we reach the point of the play in which 3 screens for 2 and the defenders start to change between 2 and 3, we want 2 to curl around 3 and come high to make a back screen for 4, while 3 exploits the screen of 5 on the other side of the lane and then goes to the other corner of the court (figure 8.16).

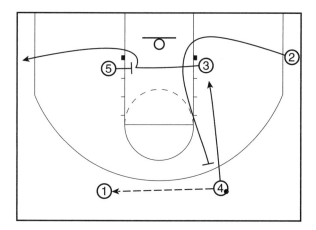

Figure 8.16 Option 2: When defenders change, 2 curls around 3 and screens for 4.

1 now has several options. He can

- pass to 4 after the back screen of 2;
- pass to 2, who pops out after the screen;
- pass to 3, who comes out of the screen of 5; or
- pass to 5, who, after the screen for 3, rolls to the basket.

The idea behind this last movement is to take advantage of the space given to the offensive players, above all to 3, after the defensive change.

Option 3. When we need to give the ball to the low post, we run this move, starting immediately at the end of the transition. 1 passes the ball to 5; at the same time, 2 exploits the back screen of 4 and goes to the low post on the other side of the court (figure 8.17).

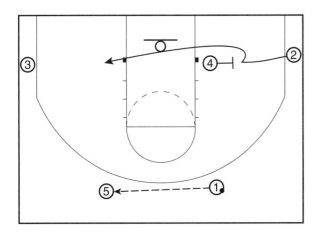

Figure 8.17 Option 3: the beginning of the play for passing to the post.

5, instead of skipping the ball to the other side of the court, makes a return pass to 1, who has gotten open, while 4 ducks into the lane to receive the ball from 1 and play his defender one on one (figure 8.18).

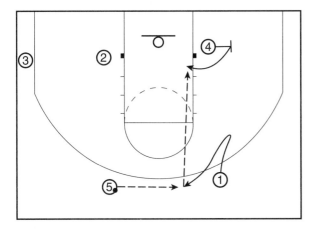

Figure 8.18 Option 3: 4 screens and rolls in the lane and receives from 1.

DRILLS FOR THE FLEX OFFENSE

The players must know all the options of an offensive set perfectly, but they must also practice the different shooting solutions generated by all the moves of the offense. For this reason we run the following shooting drills to practice shooting in the flex offense.

Shooting With Two Players

This is a shooting drill we use to practice getting off the vertical screen and on an overload in the corner. We run this drill with two coaches, who are the passers.

We start with two lines of players, each with a ball, outside the baseline (figure 8.19). The first two players come on the court at the low-post positions, pass the balls to the coaches, and then make these moves: 2 cuts on the baseline and comes off the screen of 3, and then 3 comes high: they receive the balls, shoot, grab their own rebound, and go to the opposite line from which they started the drill. The next two players will invert the exit: 3 comes off the screen of 2, and 2 comes high.

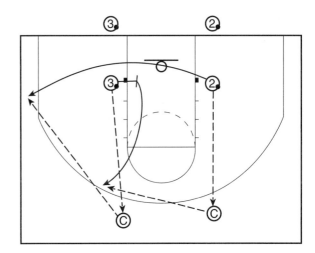

Figure 8.19 Shooting drill with two players.

Shooting With Three Players

This drill is done with three players, with two balls and two coaches as passers. 5 and 2, with the balls, pass to the coaches, and 2 moves with 3 for a specific move. In this case, if 3 chooses to exploit the screen of 5, 2 then cuts to the baseline to the opposite corner of the half-court (figure 8.20). The coaches can then pass to the shooters or else pass to 5, who rolls to the basket after the screen for 3.

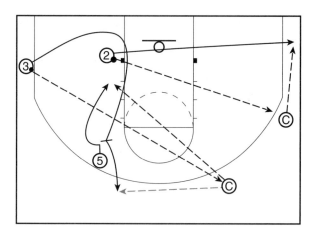

Figure 8.21   Shooting drill after a back screen.

Shooting With Two Screens

In this drill, 2 can choose which screen to exploit: the one set by 4 or the one set by 5. Here we play four offensive players against four defenders (figure 8.22). 1, with the ball, can pass to 2, who's coming off one of the two screens, or pass to 4 or 5, who are rolling to the basket after setting the screens.

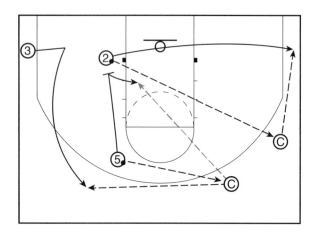

Figure 8.20   Shooting drill with three players.

Shooting After a Back Screen

This drill is the same as the previous one, but here 3, instead of using 5's screen, goes around 2 and back-screens for 5, while 2 cuts across the baseline to the opposite corner (figure 8.21). The two coaches can now

- pass to 5, who uses the back screen of 3;
- pass to 2 in the corner, who has an advantage over his defender; or
- pass to 3, who pops out after the screen.

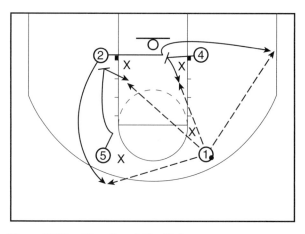

Figure 8.22   Shooting drill with two screens.

2 decides which screen to use based on the move of his defender. If 2's defender chooses to slide through the screen, screener 5 then changes the angle of the screen, and 2 fades from the screen to get enough space and time to receive and shoot (figure 8.23).

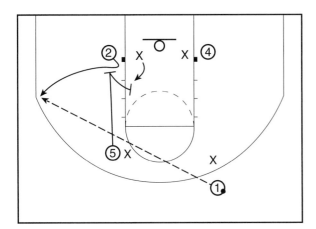

Figure 8.23 Rescreen of 5 for 2 if the defender slides through.

In another case, 2's defender follows behind him. 2 then curls around, receives the ball, and shoots or passes to 5, who has rolled to the basket after setting the screen. 1 can also pass directly to 5 on the roll (figure 8.24).

Note that if 2 decides to use 4's screen (instead of 5's) he'll move in the same way, as shown in figure 8.24.

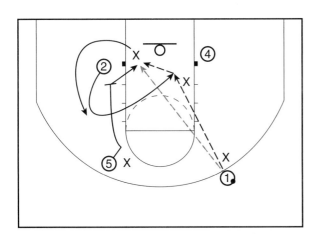

Figure 8.24 Curl of 2 if the defender follows behind.

Shooting on Screen-the-Screener Action

Another four-on-four drill. We run this drill to practice the screen-the-screener play. 1 passes to 3; when the ball reaches 3's hands, 4 makes a back screen for 2 and then immediately receives a high screen from 1 (figure 8.25). 4 goes high and receives the ball from 3.

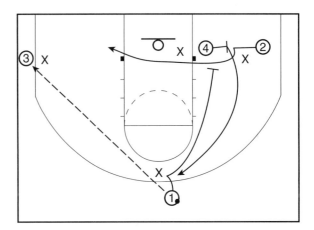

Figure 8.25 Shooting drill on screen-the-screener action.

4 makes a skip pass to 1; when the ball is in the hands of 1, 2 screens for 3 and receives a screen from 4 (figure 8.26). We then play until we can't find an effective shooting situation.

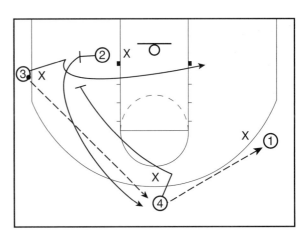

Figure 8.26 Continuity of the drill on both sides of the floor.

FINAL POINTS

Many coaches, especially early in their careers, are searching for a "miracle offense." They mistakenly believe that one special offensive attack is used by winning coaches around the world. The point they miss is that every team is different, and what works well for one team very likely won't work for another. That's why coaches—at any level of the game—must tailor their offense to their personnel.

I have found the flex offense to be the best offensive attack for "my" players. In short, it gives our team the best chance to be successful and achieve our goals. Our particular version of the flex came from no one specific coach or program but from many different coaches and experiences I've learned from over the years. And of course I am still learning—all the time.

Embrace the opportunities available to learn to be a better coach, whether they come in the form of a clinic, a conversation, a book, or a DVD. Perhaps after reading this chapter and the others in this section, you have not found the exact attack that fits your philosophy or the strengths of your team, but I hope you have found at least a few valuable insights or drills to increase your knowledge and effectiveness as a coach.

I encourage you to be receptive to new ideas from other coaches—young or old, having high or low winning percentages, famous or lesser known; you might be amazed at what you can learn. The basketball universe is home to few real geniuses, so remain curious, open-minded, and willing to adapt to a variety of approaches.

Here's a closing point I hope you'll take to heart. Even after you have devised the best offensive strategy and tactics possible for an opponent, in the end it's your players who must execute the plan. While you should take individual talents and matchups into account in developing a game plan, success still hinges on how well that plan translates to action on the court. With this in mind, teach and prepare your athletes as well as you can, and remember they are humans, not robots. If you've been coaching long at all, you might agree that seeing five teammates space themselves properly to move about the court in a fluid, purposeful, and ultimately successful manner is as beautiful a sight as any in the game.

PART III

Fast Break

chapter 9

Fast-Break Principles

George Karl and Doug Moe

All coaches have their own personalities that are reflected in the style of play of their teams. In our case, we're pretty assertive guys and not very patient. So we prefer to play up-tempo and create offense through defensive pressure. And, when we get the ball, we want to force the action.

Nothing against coaches who choose to have their teams walk the ball up the court, run set plays, and execute a more methodical offensive attack. That's just not us. We favor the fast-break offense for several reasons:

- It's harder to prepare for and defend because it has no strictly defined positions or set plays.

- It hurries many opponents, setting a tempo faster than they prefer to play.

- It wears down the opposition, who will typically like to run less than your players and won't be as well conditioned to run more.

- Run properly, it produces more easy and open shots than an attack that allows the defense to get in place.

- It's generally more fun for players because they get more shot attempts, use a greater variety of skills, and get to be involved more, both through more passing and more frequent substitutions.

History shows that every championship team has good chemistry, good spirit, tough defense, a positive, unselfish offensive energy, and a play-hard intensity that doesn't waver. So, in addition to our personal prefer-

ence, we have a solid rationale for employing a high-speed attack. Let's look at each of those five reasons in greater detail.

Be hard to guard. Because only the point guard in our system has what could be called a defined role, the opponent is challenged to match up with us every time we break down the court. And because the whole offense is based on players responding to each situation, the defense has no real notion of how the attack will materialize on any given possession. This lack of predictability is very unnerving to opposing coaches and players, and a big plus for the fast-breaking team.

Rush the opposition. The very pace of a high-speed, fast-break offense often unsettles opponents. Their comfort zone is disrupted because they have to think and move faster than they do against other teams. Rather than dictating a more leisurely tempo, they are now reacting to—and trying to keep up with—what seems to them a helter-skelter style of play. When this happens to the opposition, you've got them where you want them. Not only will their defense suffer many breakdowns, but their transition game and offense will move into a quicker mode than normal as well, which leads to turnovers and poor shot selection on their end of the court.

Fatigue the opponent. You can't count on the opposition being out of shape; any coach worth his salt will have his players fit enough to compete and win. But being in condition to run a standard, set offense and being physically prepared to play a high-speed, fast-break attack for a full game are two different levels of conditioning. And a winded or tired player is a very vulnerable player. So what you'll see during long stretches of continuous play and in the second half of games is the opposing team suffering defensive breakdowns, coming up short on its shots, and having to go deeper than it would prefer on its bench. Just watch how opponents of the better fast-breaking teams start tugging on their shorts during every dead ball. The pace takes its toll on athletes who aren't trained to handle it.

Produce more and easier looks. At its most fundamental level, winning comes down to scoring more points than the opponent. We believe the best way to do that is to create more possessions and scoring chances than the opposition. A successful fast-break attack generates more shots. In addition, because the defense won't have time to get in position every time down the court, it is more likely that one offensive player will get free for a jumper or a layup, which should increase your shooting percentage.

Use players' preferred style. Although not a determining factor in our deciding to commit to the break, another plus is that players are enthusiastic about playing a fast-paced style. Whether a freshman in high school or a second-year pro, most athletes are going to want to display their talents in an open-court situation rather than be confined in a more restrictive half-court attack. But taking part in a fast-break offense isn't easy. Those who contribute to a fast-break system must sacrifice as well, as we'll see when it comes to putting such an attack in place.

IMPLEMENTING THE FAST BREAK

Becoming a running team doesn't happen with a snap of the fingers. It's a process that involves firm and clear instruction and correction by the coach, and gradual acceptance by players until the system becomes second nature to them.

What's essential is that everyone involved in the program understands that the team and coaching staff are committed to playing that style all the time. The fast break starts with establishing an unquestioning mind-set that eliminates hesitation and doubts, and instead thrives on a full-speed-ahead attitude and instincts developed through countless repetitions.

Apply Defensive Pressure

Every championship team has high energy on defense. That go-hard intensity you're looking for from players on the offensive attack must also be evident when the opponent has possession.

Good fast-breaking clubs bring their defense to the offense; they don't wait and react to what the offense does. This makes sense when you consider the unfamiliar, up-tempo pace at which you want the opposing team to play.

Perimeter pressure is especially important to prevent, or at least discourage, their guards from playing catch outside, running the clock, and slowing the game down until they decide to shoot or dump it inside to the post. We've benefited from coaching some outstanding defenders over the years. T.R. Dunn was a tremendous perimeter defender with the Nuggets' teams of the 1980s. Of course, Gary Payton earned his reputation as one of the NBA's all-time best defensive guards (hence his nickname, "The Glove") playing in Seattle on some of the Sonics' fine teams.

Yes, we want defenders to go for steals when the percentages are with them. Such takeaways should lead to easy buckets on the other end. But we don't want our players taking chances, foolishly reaching, fouling, or getting out of position to allow an easy score. The key is for defenders to play hard and smart, and to assess the risk–reward of each possible steal attempt. Good, sound defensive pressure should disrupt an offense enough to generate a high number of turnovers without taking too many chances.

Rebound the Ball

Obviously, besides turnovers and steals, the only other way to gain possession (other than after an opponent has scored) to start the break is to rebound missed shots by the opposition. So there's no way to overemphasize the importance of rebounding in a running system.

Where so many teams that want to run fail is in too few of their players attacking the defensive boards. Instead, they have three or four guys cherry-picking, out at half-court looking for an outlet pass from the only guy on the squad who's going after the ball. To prevent that from happening, we demand that four players (all except the point guard) attack the glass every time the opponent shoots. They are not allowed to start toward the offensive end until they or a teammate claim the rebound.

Sprint the Court

Once possession is gained, the scene on the court should look like runners exploding out of their starting blocks to run a race. Our guys must think full-speed ahead and take off without hesitation.

A great rebounder and shot blocker like Marcus Camby on the defensive end is a great asset to a fast-breaking team.

Only with this mental approach can players fully accept the physical challenge of playing our energy-sapping style. The best up-tempo teams don't just run, they sprint—the whole game. Breaking through that mental barrier of the natural inclination to rest or run less than full speed is perhaps the biggest hurdle to becoming a full-court fast-break club. This approach is something a coach must insist on every day in practice and in games, and correct immediately if the pace of the team up and down the court starts to slow.

Move the Ball

The effort required to sprint the court is worthwhile only when combined with equally fast movement of the basketball. Nothing puts the brakes on the break quicker than a player holding the ball in a stationary position. Quick passes, on

Terrance Vaccaro/NBAE/Getty Images Sport

Carmelo Anthony has an array of skills to finish on a break, be it from the perimeter, midrange, or at the basket, as shown here.

perhaps create a turnover or deny what would have been a good shot attempt that trip down the court.

Moving the ball also has the beneficial effect of wearing down an opponent. Making the defense work continuously through each possession just to keep up with the ball and to try to deny passing lanes will take its toll over the course of a game.

Take Quick, Good Shots

The final piece of the puzzle is to insist that players shoot the ball quickly. If players pass the ball around the perimeter and run the clock down while looking for a perfect, wide-open shot each time down the court, you're in trouble. They need to have the green light and take immediate advantage of shot opportunities on the primary and secondary breaks. If the shot clock comes into play when you have the ball (and you aren't simply expending time at the end of the first half of the game), this should send a warning signal. We don't recommend anything like a "chuck and duck" shooting mentality, but the whole basis for this system is a relentlessly fast attack.

To do this, players must develop a good sense of what is and isn't a "good" shot for them, and be very confident in what they define as good. Their sense of good versus bad shots comes largely from the coaches' feedback during practices. Once their good shots have been defined, players must be prepared—even eager—to take those shots during games.

We do not set strict rules, but our players must understand their roles and be conscious of their offensive ability and the range of their shot. For example, Carmelo Anthony has great offensive skills and is free

the other hand, are impossible for even the quickest defenses to stop. It's quite simple—if you move the ball faster than the defense can react, someone will have an open shot.

Of course, it helps if those quick passes are accurate. Hitting a teammate in stride where the ball can be caught easily and converted quickly into a shot attempt is the goal. Sloppy passes that require a receiver to make an adjustment just to gain possession allow the defense to catch up to the ball and to shoot on a fast break whenever he wants. Other players, such as Marcus Camby and Kenyon Martin, are not our best options for the first shot on the fast break or when they're open on the perimeter, because they possess different offensive skills.

EXECUTING THE FAST BREAK

When it comes to running our break, the rules are few. The freedom we allow execution-wise has a purpose—we want players to learn to think for themselves and react instinctively in the most effective manner in each situation. That's because each situation on any given break presents unique challenges and opportunities. If we were to preprogram players to always move to a certain spot on the court or always run the same pattern, we'd make life much easier for our opponent and miss a lot of scoring chances along the way.

This less-structured approach is a good basis for player development. Through being forced to make many fast decisions on the fly repeatedly every practice, they gain a good sense of what the game is about and how to play it. Mind you, it won't always be pretty, but it's essential that you stand firm behind what you're teaching and stay positive with the players.

When we were implementing the offense in Denver, we had an exhibition game in Wyoming versus Golden State. The Warriors just killed us, and we committed 30 or more turnovers. After the game, everyone was commenting on how poorly we were executing the break and even suggesting that we might want to slow down our offensive attack. So they were surprised when we sounded so optimistic after the blowout. From our perspective, our pressure defense was great, our rebounding was great, and our running was great. What we hadn't quite developed yet was a feel for the passing game.

Starting Point

As we mentioned before, only one position on our team has a defined role in our break. The point guard is responsible for receiving the ball from the rebounder (assuming the point guard hasn't rebounded the ball). We'll emphasize once again just how important defensive rebounds are to making a fast break successful. When the opposition shoots, your players must crash the boards with all their might and make sure they get the ball quickly to the point guard, who should either come to the ball or create a clear passing lane between himself and the rebounder. We want our point guard to receive the outlet pass as far away as possible from the defensive basket (figure 9.1). He's our main target when we start the fast break. However, if there is good defensive pressure on him, making this first pass extremely difficult, we want the guard to quickly come in closer and get the ball (figure 9.2).

Once the ball is in hand, the point guard quickly brings the ball up the middle of the court, where defenders can't use the sideline to trap him. We believe having the ball in our point guard's hands places pressure on the defense. The point guard can penetrate to the basket, pass the ball to an open teammate, shoot a pull-up jumper, or

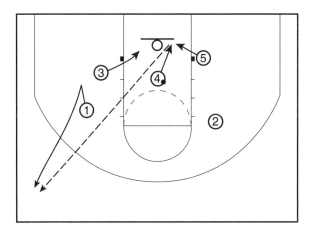

Figure 9.1 We want to make the outlet pass to the point guard as far as possible from the basket.

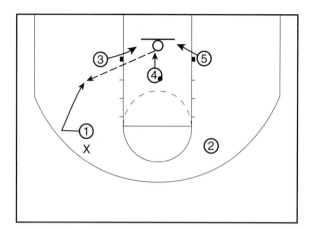

Figure 9.2 When pressured by the defense, the point guard might receive the first pass closer to the rebounder.

even launch a three-pointer on occasion. In our system, as in many fast-break attacks, the point guard is the key cog in initiating the offense and making the first key decision in the frontcourt.

Winging It

Once possession is gained, the two players closest to the wings (roughly the free-throw line extended on each side of the court) should sprint to those spots. We want them as wide as possible to create space to allow more room for the point guard to receive the ball from the rebounder. Then, as the point guard takes off with the ball, the wings dash down opposite sides of the court, staying wide until they reach the free-throw line extended on the offensive end (figure 9.3). The most difficult thing to teach the players who run on the wings is to stay wide. The wider they are, the better the passing lanes, thereby increasing our chances to score.

Again, we don't force any rules on the wings. Depending on the defensive situation, they must read and react. In short, the two wings can cross in the lane (figure 9.4), they can stop at the free-throw line extended (figure 9.5), they can play give-and-go with the point guard (figure 9.6), or they can try any other option the defense allows.

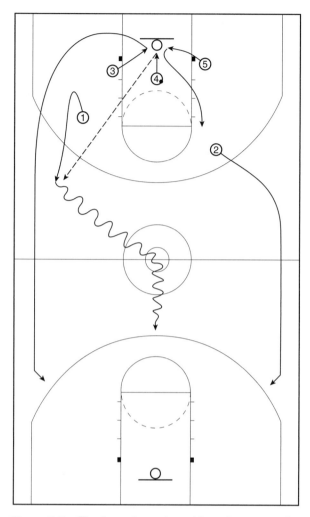

Figure 9.3 The two wings stay wide and run near the sideline.

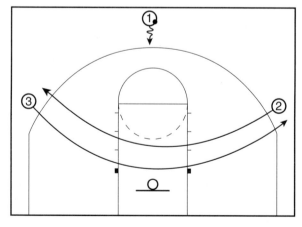

Figure 9.4 Depending on the defense, the wings can cross in the lane.

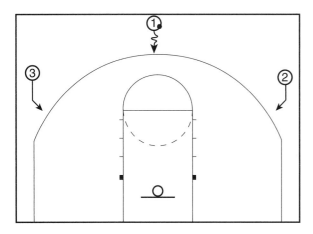

Figure 9.5 The wings can also stop at the free-throw line extended.

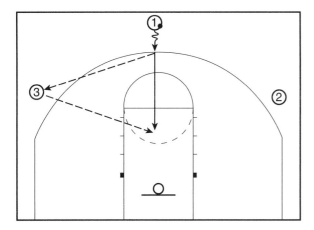

Figure 9.6 The wings can also play give-and-go or try any other option the defense allows.

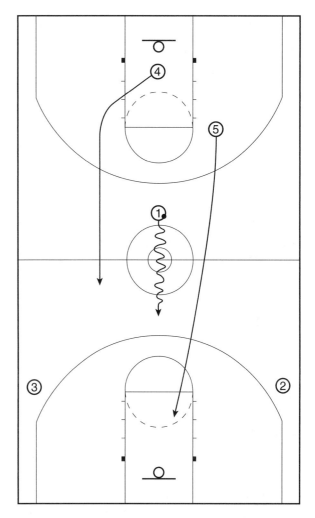

Figure 9.7 The big men (4 and 5) are usually the trailers—but not always.

Ideally, your 2 and 3 players will fill the role of the wings most of the time. They'll usually be faster than your big men and better able to convert a scoring opportunity during the initial onslaught. But we don't have any strict rules on this because in some cases the 4 or 5 could fill the wing lane.

Support Troops

Assuming your 4 and 5 players gain the majority of your defensive rebounds, they'll most often be the last two team members up the court. If 4 grabs the rebound, he'll fill the lane between the point guard and a wing on one side of the court. 5 will trail the point, moving to a position near the top of the key (figure 9.7).

As with the wings, the spacing of the two trailers is important. They should be far enough apart that they both can't be covered by one defender, and they must stay aware of what's happening as they run upcourt, ready to alter their paths as necessary.

PRIMARY BREAK

As you'd expect, quickness and speed are vital to the primary break. By "primary break" we mean a fast break run when there's a real advantage over the defenders.

In all situations in which there's an offensive advantage, defenders are outmanned and kept off balance, creating a variety of possible mismatches. The defense simply can't cover all spots on the court. Instilling this notion in our players is not as simple as it seems, and coaches must teach and practice these situations regularly, using a few basic and practical rules to increase the odds that the advantage will go to the offense.

However, before discussing the fast-break rules and how to teach them, we want to say something about the mental game. We're convinced the first ingredient of an effective fast break is the mental switch, the "offensive transition"—that is, rapidly changing the mind-set from defense to offense within a split second. This quick switch must occur after a basket, a defensive rebound, a steal, a turnover, a sideline or baseline inbounds play, or a made shot or free throw.

Following a score by the opponent, if the inbounder is slow to inbound the ball, or, following a defensive rebound, if the rebounder doesn't make a quick outlet pass, the fast break will almost certainly be affected. We think an extremely quick "mind switch" is the basis of an effective fast break.

The second fundamental aspect of the fast break is running. The main rule here is that players must always maintain proper spacing on the court. If the offense runs a two-on-one fast break and the two offensive players are too close to each other, one defensive player might effectively guard the two players and prevent what should have been an easy basket (figure 9.8).

These are the premises from which a coach can build the primary break, and without these two vital aspects, we don't think a primary break can be successful. Basketball is a game of habits, and these two habits must be taught and practiced to be reinforced. It's a big mistake to skip the teaching and learning of these basics. Failing to do so is like driving a Ferrari equipped with motorbike tires: You won't get anywhere!

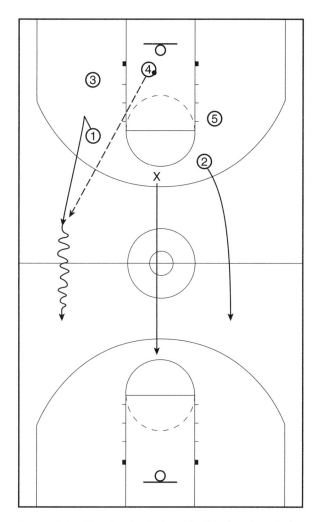

Figure 9.8 Spacing is vital on the fast break and also on the two on one.

Coaches personalize their fast-break approaches, as can be seen from coach to coach. Some coaches run their primary break on the sideline or in the middle of the court (figure 9.9); others want the two wings to cut at the free-throw line extension or else work off a give-and-go move.

We're different from the majority of coaches because we don't give our players specific rules. We tell them to react to what the defense gives them. This doesn't mean our philosophy is necessarily better than that of others—just that it works best for us. As always, you'll want to gear your approach around your players.

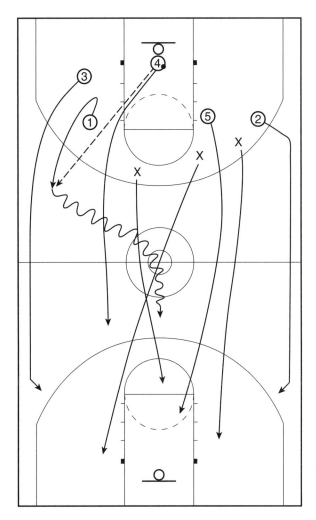

Figure 9.9   A primary break run in the middle of the court.

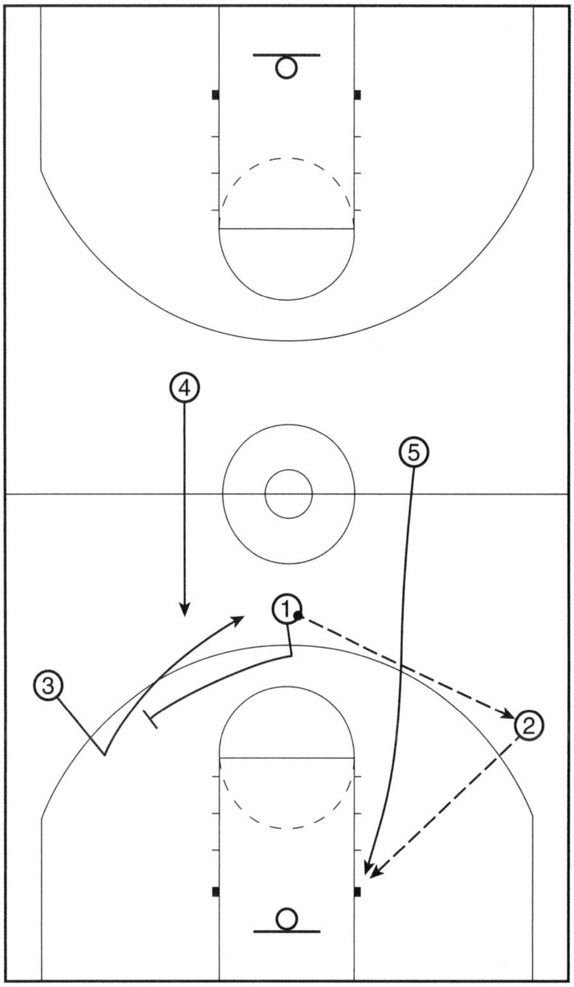

Figure 9.10   Two trailers post down and reverse the ball.

SECONDARY BREAK

The secondary break occurs after the primary break has failed to produce a basket. In this case, the team quickly tries to take advantage of the defense—which is still not yet set—and find a quick-scoring play. On the secondary break, all five offensive players are involved. Normally, the secondary break lasts just a few seconds and tries to punish the ill-formed defense (characterized by poor matchups and bad rotation).

There are many ways to run the secondary break, but the break typically involves one or two trailers, generally the big men, who are used for reversing the ball and posting down on the low-post position (figure 9.10) or for a stagger screen for an outside shot (figure 9.11).

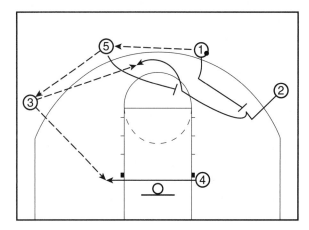

Figure 9.11   A staggered screen formed by the two trailers.

We don't have an established secondary break. If we don't score right away, we immediately run our passing game, which in effect *is* our secondary break, including cuts, backdoor plays, the give-and-go, and screens on and off the ball.

Again, we want to underline that the game and the decisions belong to the players, who react to the defense, and that they don't depend too much on the input of the coaching staff. The players must be responsible for their moves and decisions: We don't want to call every play like a teacher in a classroom directing her students.

One of our favorite and most respected coaches, Dean Smith, was convinced that to have a good passing game without rules you needed five very smart players on the court—which is not always possible. He believed that if you lacked savvy players, you needed to set rules, lest your passing game be ineffective. With all due respect to Coach Smith (and there is much that is due), we happen to think differently. We believe players must have the freedom to make the proper decisions on the court based on the reaction of the defense. However, based on the number of ACC and national championships Coach Smith won and the dozens of All-American players he coached, maybe, just maybe, Coach Smith was on to something.

DRILLS FOR THE FAST BREAK

Our practices typically last no longer than 75 to 90 minutes. We believe you get more out of high-speed, high-concentration practices than you do long sessions, when physical and mental fatigue set in.

Our typical practice focuses on the fast break and teamwork. More isolated drills have their place with developing players, especially in the off-season and preseason, but once the competitive season gets under way, our emphasis shifts to helping our squad execute as a unit.

Standard Practice Session

Three-line full-court fast break
10 to 15 minutes

Five-player passing game fast break
15 minutes

Half-court defense with a fast break
30 to 40 minutes

Scrimmage
20 minutes

The three group drills we run to develop and sharpen our execution on the break are the three-line and five-player breaks and what we call a "beep-beep" drill. Here's how they work.

Three-Line Drill

We run this drill as a way to teach our wings to stay as close as possible to the sidelines. They must start to run only when the point guard receives the ball and starts the dribble. We form three lines, toss the ball off the backboard, and start the fast break without the defense (figure 9.12). Players are free to cut at the free-throw line extension, make a give-and-go, or try any other variation as long as they maintain proper spacing.

Five-Player Passing Game

The second drill is a five-player passing game drill without the defense (figure 9.13). We run this drill until one player asks for a time-out because he's out of gas. Players can run any options they want on the passing game, but everything must go at full speed.

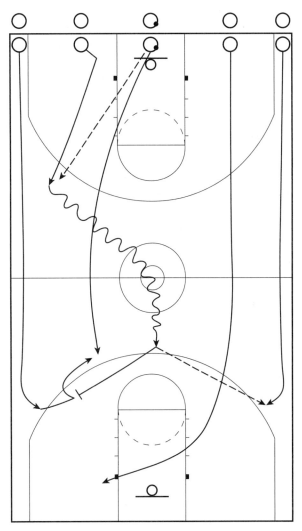

Figure 9.13   Five-player passing game drill without the defense.

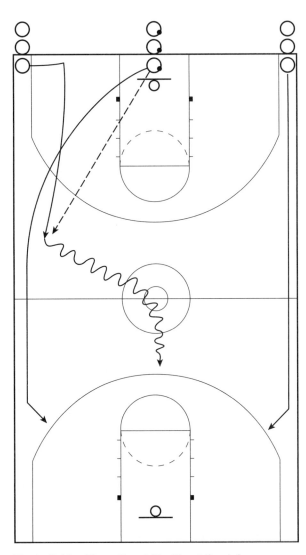

Figure 9.12   Three-line drill without the defense.

Beep-Beep

We call this five-on-five drill "beep-beep" after the cartoon character the Roadrunner. We tell our players the rule is that the point guard must bring the ball down as quickly as possible on offense and either shoot as quickly as he can or make only one pass, and that whoever receives the pass must shoot immediately (figure 9.14). The defense then switches to offense and runs the play down the other end of the court. This drill works the fast break and conditioning at the same time.

We run all our drills at top speed to help our players maintain the essential habit of sprinting the court. The pace also raises the level of competition during practice, which

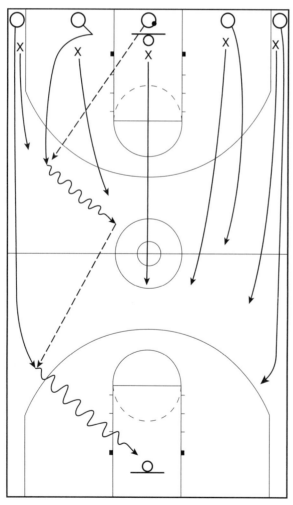

Figure 9.14 The beep-beep drill.

in turn challenges players to step up their performance each time on the court, not just in games.

FINISHING UP THE FAST BREAK

Many coaches are reluctant to adopt the fast break as a primary offensive attack, citing the various challenges to playing an up-tempo style. To close the chapter, we'll address the common concerns coaches have about committing to a running system. Just remember that no system is flawless, and whatever means of attack you choose will require fine-tuning to your situation and personnel.

• **What happens when the team lacks a capable point guard?** Admittedly, this is probably the Achilles' heel of the fast-break system. It's very difficult to have much success without a playmaker who can put pressure on the defense each time down the floor. At the high school level, what you must do is ensure your feeder schools are developing players who can step into this role when they come of age. At the college level, you must make your point guard position a priority for at least every other recruiting class. And at the pro level, you need to draft or trade for at least a starter and capable backup point guard if you hope to have success running the fast break.

• **Can the break be effective without an especially fast team?** That's like asking if you can rebound without a tall team. The answer to both is yes, but it sure helps when players have the physical tools so they don't always need to work that much harder than the opposition just to keep on a level playing field. If your team is overmatched from a speed standpoint, you can still run the break effectively with superior conditioning, hustle, smarts, techniques, and tactics. The important thing is that the players don't consider their lack of speed a handicap or use it as an excuse when they come up short.

Sharp cuts, quick passes, and fast thinking can offset faster feet.

• Don't fast-breaking teams commit too many turnovers to win consistently? If you adopt a fast-break system, you must accept that you'll incur more turnovers. That's not because your team is being loose with the ball or playing too risky—it's just that there are so many more possessions, trips down the court at a high speed, and passes to be thrown and received. That all adds up to a higher turnover total for a fast-break team than for a half-court club. We don't like a high number of turnovers, but we believe a more important statistic is turnover ratio. As long as we consistently have fewer turnovers than our opponents, our per-game turnover average isn't that much of a concern.

• Won't the team wear down over the course of a season? Yes, the cumulative effect of a running game can take its toll in a season as long as the NBA's. That's why we keep our practices short and more intense. It also helps to have a decent bench, so you can call on your 8, 9, and 10 players to give your starters occasional rests. At the college and high school levels, you can maintain a higher pace over the season because the season and length of games are shorter. Plus, players are younger and less susceptible to the kind of fatigue that athletes encounter in their pro careers. We always felt that the conditioning factor—both in a particular game and over the course of a season—was in our favor because we were well trained to maintain the fast break better than our opponents were.

chapter 10

Primary and Secondary Breaks

Mike D'Antoni, Alvin Gentry, and Marc Iavaroni

More than half our points are scored off our fast break. That includes both the baskets we make quickly off the initial offensive surge at our end of the court (primary breaks) and the baskets we score quickly afterward once all our players make it into the frontcourt, before the defense is able to fully recover (secondary breaks).

A successful running game starts not with Xs and Os but with a proper state of mind. Basketball is a game of reaction; players must react immediately to new situations and change instantly from defense to offense. Players don't have time to think about where they should go or what they should do; they must simply respond in a flash. The rebounder who hesitates in throwing the outlet pass, or the guard who fails to anticipate and break to the pass to push the ball up the floor, will render what appears to be a perfect fast break on paper ineffective on the court. A "move it, *now*" mind-set is essential to the success of a breaking team.

The second prerequisite for the fast break is understanding *how* to run. That means as soon as we gain possession—or as soon as it appears we'll gain possession—of the ball, we're off to the sprints. The rebounder, or more likely the recipient of the outlet pass, should high-tail it up the court with the ball, looking for a free teammate further down the floor. Everyone else is sprinting to the offensive end. There should be no wasted motion. That's easier to say than do because proper running and sprinting technique take a willingness to work and a high level of conditioning. Watching videos showing correct running mechanics and then practicing these techniques will help establish the basics; then it comes down to applying those same movements at full speed in game situations.

The simple part of instituting a running system is selling the players on it. Few athletes in today's game want to walk the ball up the court and hold it for the full 24 seconds each possession. They want to play up-tempo—just as they play in full-court pick-up games when given the chance. The fast-break style appeals to players' natural preference to make something happen, and quickly. The style is a lot of fun when it works. But what most players fail to appreciate, at least at first, is what it takes to execute a consistently effective, fast-paced, full-court offense.

Coaches are often reluctant to commit to a running-style game for fear of too many turnovers. That's understandable; a helter-skelter-type break almost invariably leads to a high percentage of lost possessions, even before the team can attempt to score. In our system, however, we remain in control. In fact, our turnover total is among the lowest in the NBA, and is extremely low given the number of additional opportunities we create with the break.

In this chapter we'll explain how we do it. You might be limited by the personnel of your team, or your league might have rules that limit your commitment to such a system, but even so, you're sure to find many elements here to benefit your offensive attack.

ELEMENTS OF THE BREAK

Before getting into the specifics of how we run our primary and secondary breaks, let's first look at the core components that make our style of play possible.

Personnel

Every team must have a good point guard who can see the whole picture on the court. Naturally, it helps if that point guard is Steve Nash, the two-time NBA MVP, who is like a second coach on the court. But not every point is going to have Steve's tremendous court vision, superb passing skills, and fantastic ability to anticipate on the court. What's essential, though, is that the point guard can read situations and pass the ball quickly with no wasted dribbling.

Nothing undermines a fast-break offense quicker than a point guard who fails to advance the ball upcourt or who misses an open teammate in position to score. Every player without the ball must be in motion, sprinting the court, cutting, and using screens—doing whatever it takes to get open. If a point guard fails to deliver the ball to teammates who are making such an effort, before long they'll stop moving as quickly and persistently on the floor. When that happens, your fast break is effectively shut down.

To complement a capable point guard, successful running teams also have quick athletes who are totally committed to this style of play. Amare Stoudemire is one of the quickest power forwards in the NBA, and Leandro Barbosa is also very fast. Players with such quickness love the opportunity to use that asset, and the fast-break game creates those situations.

Conditioning

A high level of physical conditioning is mandatory for any team committed to running the fast break. All players, including reserves, must be in top shape and have the stamina to sprint the court from the opening tip to the final buzzer. For reaching the best possible shape, we run a lot in practice, and we do all our drills, on full- or half-court, at maximum

Barry Gossage/NBAE/Getty Images Sport

Steve Nash is a transition team's coaching staff's dream due to his amazing court vision, decision-making ability, ingenuity, and passing skills.

speed, from the usual full-court break drills to shooting drills.

Defense

Fast-breaking teams are sometimes accused of playing poor defense. Critics point out that we allow opponents more points than other teams do and that our opponents' field-goal percentages aren't the best. What they neglect to mention is that we typically outscore our opponents by more points than almost anyone.

Our defense has to fit our running offense, so we're not going to play a sit-and-wait, slug-it-out style favored by more physical, deliberate teams. When we play well defensively, we disrupt the opponent's flow and create loose balls and turnovers that we can convert quickly into baskets. Our fast break is most productive when we're aggressive on the defensive end, stealing the ball, stepping into the passing lane, contesting shots, and blocking out.

We harass the opposing offense, keeping them unsettled by the pace of our game and forcing them into taking bad shots. When that happens, they often miss, and then we're off to the races. We're dictating the action and making our opponent exert a great deal of energy in the transition game. The result is that we create more and better scoring opportunities for ourselves, taking our opponent out of its comfort zone and wearing it down over the course of the game.

Rebounding

Obviously, the more possessions you have, the more chances you have to run the fast break. The most common way to get the ball is to take the defensive rebound, which is easier said than done. All five players must be alert on every opponent's shot and block out the offensive players; they need the strength of will to prevent opponents from getting into the paint and grabbing rebounds. This task is demanded not only

of the big men but also of the guards and small forward—an example is small forward Shawn Marion, a great rebounder and among the best in the league.

Ball Handling

We strongly believe that every player, from the starting five to the last of our reserves, must have good ball-handling skills if we're going to run a sound fast break. If the ball is in the hands of Nash the majority of the time on the primary or secondary break, there will be more than one occasion when the play requires our forwards and centers to drive when running the fast break. When we talk of ball handling, we include the skills of dribbling the ball at full speed as well as executing proper passes at proper times.

Shooting

When a player is free on a primary fast break, he has the green light to shoot. Yes, players must exercise good shot selection— taking shots within their range that they can shoot with confidence—but they must not hesitate to put the ball up when scoring opportunities present themselves. I get much more upset when players fail to shoot open shots than I do when they miss the shots (unless, of course, an open shooter passes to a teammate who has an even better shot).

A signature of our break involves players spotting up on the three-point arc, ready to launch a shot. This feature really spreads the defense because the players who have hustled back to defend must decide whether to extend out to the perimeter or stay back in the lane to deny easy layups. Often we'll catch defenders in no-man's land, unsure of what to do, in which case our man on the arc can shoot, fake, and drive, or fake a shot and pass to a teammate in better position to score.

Ideally, every player on the team will have excellent shooting mechanics, but that's rarely the case. Regardless of how much instruction they receive and practice they put in, some players are going to have idiosyncratic technical flaws in their shooting motion. That doesn't always mean they're incapable of shooting at a high percentage, especially if they're consistent in their technique, release the ball quickly, and get decent elevation at release. Again, shot selection comes down to each player understanding what a good shot is for him.

Barry Gossage/NBAE/Getty Images Sport

Fast, agile, and versatile, Amare Stoudemire can get out front for a slam on a primary break or fill the lane with the best of them on a secondary break.

PRIMARY BREAK

A standard way of defining the primary break is the first two or three seconds a team has the ball after transitioning from defense to offense. This is when the opposing defense is most vulnerable. Once we gain possession, there's no hesitation—we're sprinting toward our end of the court.

We fast break on every possession in the following situations:

- A defensive rebound following a missed field goal or free throw.
- An out-of-bounds play, whether after a score or a violation. (Normally, the power forward is supposed to make the inbounds pass, but we don't strictly follow this rule. Any player nearest the ball after an opponent's score can make the inbounds pass if doing so gains us precious seconds in getting the ball upcourt.)
- A steal by the defense or a turnover by the offense.

Although a very fast player with good ball-handling and shooting skills might be called a "one-man fast break," rarely is a team successful if it relies on a single player to convert in its transition game. Rather, the two most common primary break scenarios involve two offensive players and three or more offensive players on the attack.

Two-on-One Break

When two players fast break against one defender, the offensive players must keep good spacing between them, which is the secret of any fast break. This prevents the single player back on defense from covering both offensive players.

As the two offensive players move toward their basket, the ball handler should stop (but continue to dribble) near the corner of the free-throw lane, while the other offensive player, keeping proper spacing, cuts at a 45-degree angle to the basket (figure 10.1). At this point, it is up to the ball handler to read the situation and react based on what the defender does. If the defender moves out to cover him, the ball handler passes the ball to an open teammate. If the defender sags back or hedges toward the offensive player without the ball, the ball handler takes the open shot or drives to a point where an unimpeded shot can be taken.

We don't have definite rules for players in our fast break except that they maintain proper spacing and an eagerness to run. Of course we try to correct them when they

make the wrong decision on a two-on-one fast break, but we generally allow their court sense to determine the best option.

Break With More Than Two Players

After a basket by the opponents, let's assume that 4, the power forward, makes the inbounds pass to 1, the point guard, and the two other perimeter players—2, the shooting guard, and 3, the small forward—run as wide as possible (exaggerating, we tell them to "touch" the sideline to give them precise lanes to occupy) and go deep into the two corners of the offensive half-court (figure 10.2).

These three players must recognize that with the fast break they can go straight

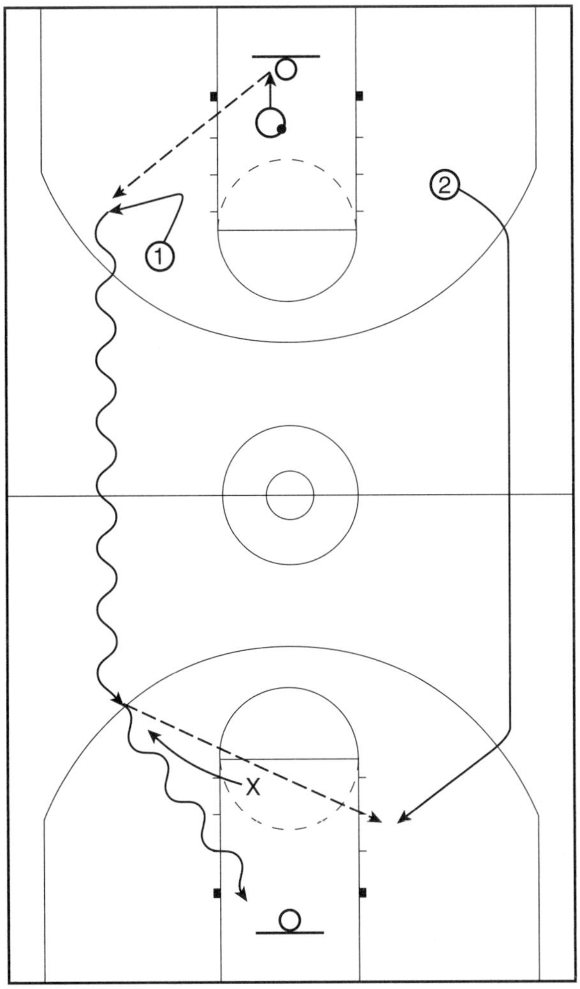

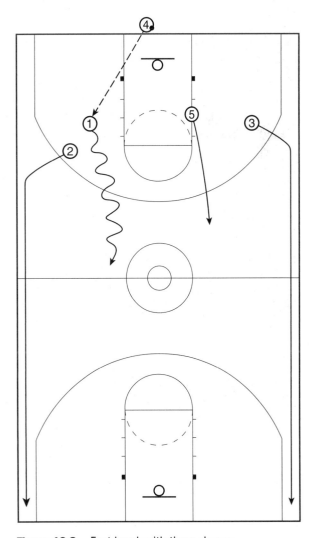

Figure 10.1 Two-on-one fast break.

Figure 10.2 Fast break with three players.

to the basket and score with a layup, but without the fast break there's no advantaged situation in which the offense outnumbers the defense. In this case, the two wings run until they reach the baseline and then stay deep in the corners; in this set, the spacing is very important—you want to force the defenders to cover a wider area. 5, who is the first trailer (4 has made the inbounds pass and is the second trailer), sprints the floor, following the first three players on the fast break. 5 has two options:

- He can, once he reaches the free-throw line extended, receive the ball and shoot, or cut into the lane at a 45-degree angle and receive the ball for a shot under the basket (figure 10.3).

- He can stay in the middle of the floor to reverse the ball to the other side of the court.

In this second case, 1 moves the ball to an area in which he can take advantage of spacing and possibly pass the ball to 5 to try to score with a layup.

Alternatively, 4, a shooter who made the inbounds pass, sprints on offense and spots up for a three-point shot (figure 10.4). The players' movements can also create the chance for a three-point shot by 2 or 3, who are spotted deep in the corner, or a shot by 5, who, in this case, is the first trailer (figure 10.5).

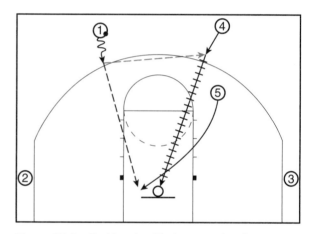

Figure 10.4   Fast break with the second trailer.

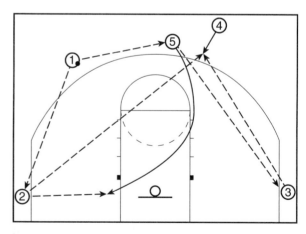

Figure 10.5   Three-point chances on the fast break.

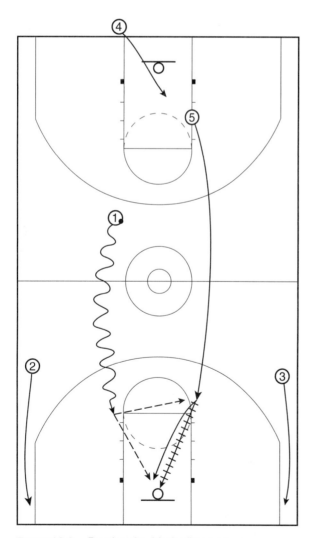

Figure 10.3   Fast break with the first trailer.

If there are no quick solutions on our primary fast break, we immediately run a pick-and-roll play. 4 sets a screen on 1, and they play a quick pick-and-roll. This action can create a situation in which 1 can pass to perimeter players 2 or 3, who are in the deep corners, for a three-point shot; 1 can pass to 5, who has cut into the three-second lane; 1 can make a layup; or 4 can shoot from the lane, rolling to the basket after setting the screen for 1 (figure 10.6).

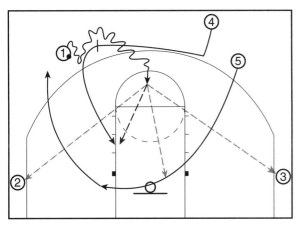

Figure 10.6   With no solution on the primary break, we run a pick-and-roll.

SECONDARY BREAK

Our secondary break is in the hands of Steve Nash, who is an unbelievable passer and creator of scoring options for himself and his teammates. Again, such a player is the base of the success of our fast break.

We play our secondary break in a different way from other teams. We post up our centers and power forwards for no more than a few seconds because we want to take advantage of the quickness of our big men and their shooting skills from the outside. As you'll notice, we always want to have at least three, if not four, players on the perimeter, and we give them the green light to shoot if they're free. We also want to reverse the ball as quickly as possible to create open shots on the perimeter. Let's now look at some of our plays generated from the offensive transition.

Roll 4 Pop

If in this case 4 is the first trailer and 5 is the second trailer, 4 cuts into the lane and posts up, while 5 stops outside the three-point line.

1 passes the ball to 5 and goes in the opposite direction; 5 reverses the ball, passing it to 3, who comes high. At the same time as the pass from 5 to 3, 2 cuts along the baseline, using the screen of 4, and then moves into the opposite corner, replacing 3 (figure 10.7).

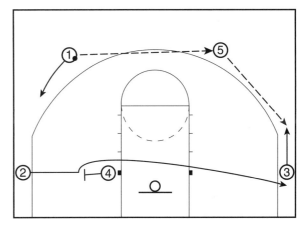

Figure 10.7   Roll 4 pop.

If 3 can't pass to 2, 1 screens down for 4, who comes high and receives a stagger screen from 5, who, after the screen, sets up in the short corner. 4 goes to the middle of the court and receives the ball from 3. 1, after setting the screen, returns to his original position (figure 10.8).

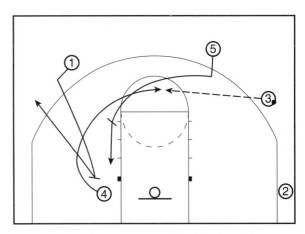

Figure 10.8   A stagger screen for 4 by 1 and 5.

4 drives to the basket, where, if he can't shoot, he kicks the ball to a teammate on the perimeter: either to 5, who pops out to the corner, or to 1, 3, or 2 (figure 10.9). At least one of these four players on the perimeter will be free for a shot.

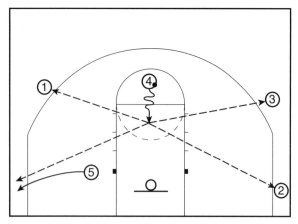

Figure 10.9   Passing options for 4.

Roll 1 Pop

The play starts like the previous one but this time is run for 1. 1 passes to 5; 5 passes to 3, who comes high. At the same time as the pass from 5 to 3, 2 cuts on the baseline, using the screen of 4, and then moves to the opposite corner, replacing 3 (figure 10.10).

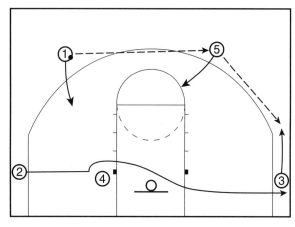

Figure 10.10   Roll 1 pop.

1, after the pass to 5, starts to cut down; this time he doesn't screen for 4, but receives a screen from 5, goes high in the middle of the half-court, and receives the ball from 3. Right after the screen, 5 rolls to the basket and moves to the short corner on the other side of the court, while 4 goes to the angle of the free-throw area (figure 10.11).

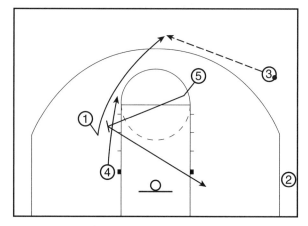

Figure 10.11   After receiving a screen from 5, 1 receives the ball from 3.

1 passes the ball to 4, cuts around him for a possible hand-off pass, and then goes out to the corner. Meanwhile, 3 cuts into the lane and moves to the short corner on the other side of the court. 4, if he can't shoot or drive to the basket from this position, drives toward 2 for a hand-off pass. 2 can penetrate or pass to 4, 5, 3, or 1 (figure 10.12).

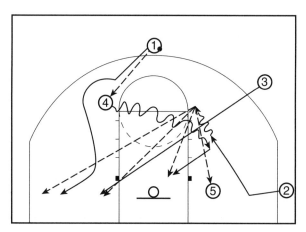

Figure 10.12   4 can shoot, drive, or make a hand-off pass to 2, who has several options.

Through Flare 1 Man

Starting from our set after the offensive transition with 5 as the second trailer, 4 as the first trailer on the low post, and 2 and 3 in the deep corners, 1 passes the ball to 2, who comes high, or to 5, in this case, and then cuts to the opposite side of the court in the low-post area (figure 10.13). 3 screens for 1, who comes off the screen and receives the ball from 5. After the screen, 3 moves to the low-post area (figure 10.14).

If 1 isn't free to shoot, he passes the ball to 3, receives a screen from 5, goes to the middle of the court, and receives the ball back from 3. He can now drive to the basket or drive and kick off the ball to 2, 4, 3, or 5, who rolls after the screen (figure 10.15).

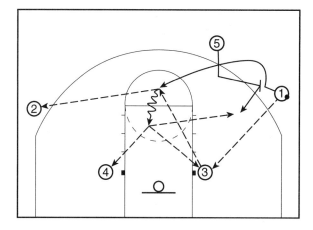

Figure 10.15   Option for the drive of 1 or a penetration and kickoff pass.

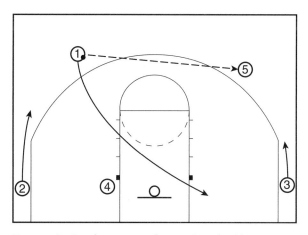

Figure 10.13   1 passes to 2 or to 5, as in this case.

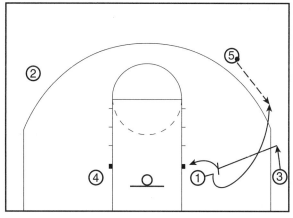

Figure 10.14   3 screens for 1 and moves to the low post.

PRACTICE

Running teams must run a lot during practice. This goes back to one of the basic aspects of the fast break, maintaining a running attitude, a state of mind that's developed in practice.

We do some work on half-court in practice, but once the season starts we devote most of the 90 minutes to full-court running. Sometimes execution is sloppy, but we don't want to compromise our running. Our style of basketball is based on quickness and speed, not on power and set plays, so our players must be able to react immediately to any defensive situation. This is why we practice all the possible plays of the secondary break at full speed.

We divide the team into perimeter players (point guards, guards, and small forwards) and big men (power forwards and centers). Our big men have different skills from most big men on other teams; they don't post up much, but they can face the basket and also drive and shoot from the outside. One of our main offensive rules is that we want the middle of the court open.

In the following drills we'll show how we work with our big men, while on the other side of the court, our perimeter players practice shooting off the different options of our secondary break.

DRILLS FOR PRIMARY AND SECONDARY BREAKS

You cannot simply ask the team to run on offense if you do not run in practice and you do not practice the different solutions that will be applied on the court. Here are some simple drills we run to cover the different options on the break.

Double Drag

We set up one coach on one side of the half-court and another coach at the free-throw line, while a line of big men, each with a ball, are in the middle of the half-court.

The first player passes the ball to the coach on the perimeter; the second player passes the ball to the coach at the free-throw line. These two players then set a stagger screen (we call this a "double drag") for the coach on the perimeter. The first player picks and rolls to the basket, receives a pass from the coach at the free-throw line, and shoots a layup or a dunk; the other player, after the second pick for the coach outside the three-second lane, pops out, receives the ball from the coach on the perimeter, and shoots from outside (figure 10.16).

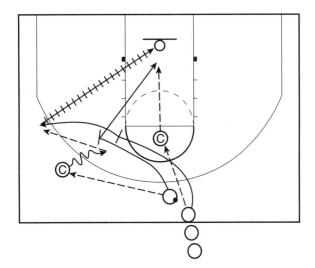

Figure 10.16 Double drag drill.

Dribble Drags

We set up one coach in the corner without the ball, one coach with the ball on the same side outside the three-point line, and one line of players. The coach with the ball starts to dribble toward the other coach, who comes high and receives a hand-off pass. The first player in line makes a screen for the second coach, then rolls to the basket to receive the ball from the second coach, who has dribbled around the screen (figure 10.17).

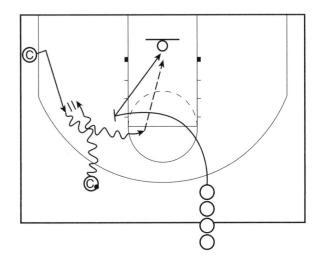

Figure 10.17 Dribble drags drill.

Rim Runs

We set up one coach with a ball on a wing and another coach on the opposite wing, without a ball; players form a line in the middle of the half-court.

The drill starts with the coach with the ball dribbling toward the baseline and then receiving a side screen from the player at the front of the line. The coach goes around the screen and reverses the ball, passing it to the coach on the other side. After setting the screen, the player rolls to the basket on the side opposite the ball and receives a lob pass for a layup or a dunk (figure 10.18).

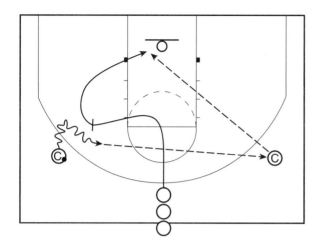

Figure 10.18   Rim runs drill.

The same drill can be run with a different finish. The coach dribbles toward the baseline and receives a screen from the player, but this time, after the coach goes around the screen and reverses the ball to the coach on the other side of the court, the player cuts straight to the opposite short corner, receives the ball, and takes a jump shot (figure 10.19).

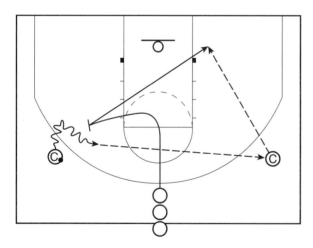

Figure 10.19   Rim runs drill with a different solution.

Read the Defense: Step Up

If the defense wants to force the ball handler to the sideline, we counter this defensive move with a step-up move. Following is the drill for practicing this move.

We run this drill on both halves of the half-court, with a coach with the ball on the wing and a line of players behind him. The coach starts to dribble to the baseline, and the first player follows him; then the player comes back and screens. After the screen, he rolls to the basket, going inside the lane, and receives the ball from the coach for a layup or a dunk (figure 10.20).

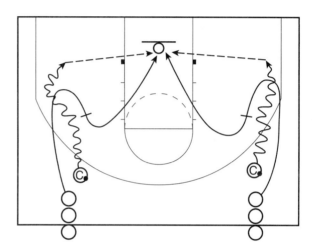

Figure 10.20   Read the defense: step-up drill.

Pinch Post Series

We set up two lines of players at the baseline, facing the midcourt line. Each player has a ball. Two coaches are in front of the two lines.

The first player of each line passes the ball to the coach at the head of the line, then posts up at the corners of the free-throw area and receives the ball back; after the pass, the coach cuts around the player. While cutting around, the coach, acting as a defender, tries to hit the ball so that the offensive players must face a game situation. We run this drill with two finishes:

- The player drives right away to the basket for a layup or a dunk after faking a hand-off pass. As soon as the player receives the ball, he protects it, watching over his shoulder to get used to locating the defender, and then drives to the basket. Because two players are involved simultaneously, they must coordinate their drives to the basket.

- The player can also turn, face the basket, and make a jump shot (figure 10.21).

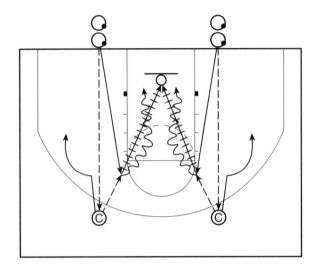

Figure 10.21 Pinch post series: driving and shooting.

- The initial routine is as described before, but now the player receives the ball and dribbles outside the lane toward the coach, who after the pass has cut toward the corner. The player then makes a hand-off pass to the coach, who dribbles toward midcourt and passes the ball back to the player, who has rolled to the basket for a layup or a dunk (figure 10.22).

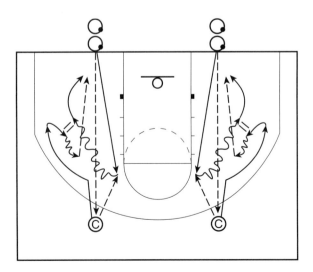

Figure 10.22 Pinch post series: hand-off pass and layup.

- The initial routine is as described before, but now the player makes a hand-off pass to the coach, who dribbles toward the baseline. The player then screens for the coach, who dribbles toward midcourt and passes the ball to the player, who, after the screen, can roll to the basket for a layup (or dunk) or to the short corner for a jump shot (figure 10.23).

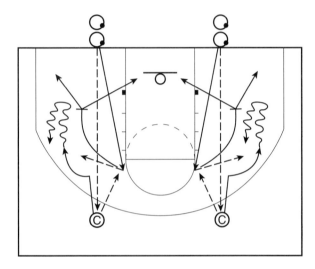

Figure 10.23 Pinch post series: hand-off pass, screen, and layup or jump shot.

FINAL POINTS

We've discussed the primary and secondary breaks, the practices, and the drills, but we would now like to say a few words about the foundation on which to build your running game—that is, all players must be in superb physical condition *and* have the proper mental approach.

We have spoken of endurance, stamina, and strength—all physical skills that a player builds through hours of conditioning on the court and in the weightlifting room. As we mentioned, we run all-out in practice; we do everything at full speed to build up the conditioning necessary to run for an entire 48-minute NBA game.

Yet you create this style of play not only through conditioning and drills but by talking to your players, giving them examples to follow, designating leaders who are totally committed to the running game, and instilling the idea that every player on the court will have a chance to score as long as he trusts this style of play. In short, you need to work on the physical and technical aspects of the fast-break game, yes—but you must also tend to the mental side. You must motivate your players to buy into this system. Once they do, they'll find it's an effective and exciting way to play basketball.

PART IV

Special Plays

chapter 11

High-Percentage Plays

Lionel Hollins

Coaches must adapt their offense to the rules of their team's level of play—particularly to the rules of the clock because there's a big difference between playing with the 24-second clock of the NBA and the WNBA, the 35-second clock of NCAA men's basketball (30-second clock of women's), and no shot clock in high school.

In the NBA the time factor is crucial; the 24-second clock forces every team to create offensive options as quickly as possible. We don't have the chances to create a continuity of offense as high school and college teams do; we must create plays that offer two or more options within a few seconds.

In professional basketball we base play more on individual matchups and one on one. We use plays to isolate our best offensive players, with fewer passes and players' movements compared to high school and college basketball.

No matter what level of play you're coaching, you're always looking to create the most and best opportunities to score. In this chapter we'll look at high-percentage scoring plays that have worked with teams I've been associated with. You can adapt these plays as necessary for the rules of your team's level of play and to best use the skills of your players.

OFFENSIVE PRINCIPLES

I would like to describe some high-percentage offensive plays that our team has used effectively in the NBA—our offensive philos-

ophy centers around a few simple principles. Conscious of the 24-second clock, we get the ball as quickly as possible to the man we want to run the play; this allows him time to survey the situation and make a play for himself or a teammate. In keeping with our quick-striking emphasis, we strive to get to the shot with one or two passes to reduce the chance of a steal by our opponents.

We frequently use screen-the-screener plays, where the player who makes the screen then receives a screen himself right away (which forces defenders into difficult recoveries). We also use the staggered screen—a series of two or three screens in a row, which are very difficult for a defender to get through. With these screens, the defender must go through a maze of screens to cover his man. If he's a poor defender or doesn't like physical contact, he'll never get through all the screens, and the shooter will get an open shot. Or, in some cases, another defender must help, which leaves another offensive player open.

Like all NBA teams, we use pick-and-roll in many situations. We set high and middle screens, side screens, "elbow" screens (at the corners of the free-throw lane), and step-up screens. When you have a big defender who doesn't like to leave the basket area or who isn't mobile, the pick-and-roll is very effective. If you have a point guard who is a three-point shooter and a penetrator, it's tough for the defense to decide how to play the screens. We also use any of our big men in the screens and different ball handlers

Cameron Browne/NBAE/Getty Images Sport

The priorities of the point guard in this offense, in this case Mike Conley, are to drive and distribute the ball to teammates where and when they are most likely to score.

to take best advantage of whomever we want to exploit, such as a weak or slow defender.

Personnel can dictate just how much you rely on the pick-and-roll. One season we had forwards and centers who could shoot from outside. We could force other teams to rotate to cover our big men on the perimeter, which allowed us pick-and-pops for jump shots and fake-and-drive situations. Our opponents were often forced to double team our post, which afforded us open jump shots and drive-and-kick situations on the perimeter.

We call most of our plays from the bench, but our point guard also has opportunities to call plays. We want to have control of the game on offense, but we give our point freedom to alter the play when the defensive situation changes.

We want to attack matchup advantages involving our two or three best offensive players. We also want to fast break after an opponent's missed shot when we have the numeric advantage. If we lack that advantage, we flow into our early offensive set, a transitional set with different options read by our point guard.

As common sense dictates, if we have a player with a hot hand we want to milk or a matchup we want to exploit, we set up those plays after our opponent's made field goals or free throws.

PERSONNEL SKILLS

These are the skills we look for from our starting five:

- 1 is the point guard, with good court vision and passing and dribbling skills. He also needs to be a good penetrator.

- 2 is a big guard, a good outside shooter, a good passer, and able to put the ball on the floor and post up smaller players.

- 3 is the small forward, our best shooter from the three-point range and a capable post player.

- 4 is the power forward, who can score inside and is quick and agile enough to move outside for the shot or drive to the basket.

- 5 is the center—tall but agile, aggressive on the boards, and able to run the floor.

SCORING PLAYS

We start the game with our "special 1" play for our top scorer. We want him to score the first basket of the game to build his confidence. We then run plays for our other scorers, mainly our 2 (off guard) and 3 (small forward), while trying to include solutions for every player on the court. We want to get everyone involved offensively as early as we can. We use a lot of isolation plays for our top scorer, as well as for the other four players on the court.

Special 1

This is an excellent play to use at the start of a game, usually for your top scorer. Put 5 and 4 outside the three-second lane, 2 at

Joe Murphy/NBAE/Getty Images Sport

Rudy Gay, who can play the 2 or 3 position, is a threat to score from a variety of areas on the court.

the low post, and 3 at the wing below the free-throw line extended.

1 drives the ball on offense, dribbling to the left side of the court, where the top scorer is set. When 1 reaches the free-throw line extended, 2 makes a diagonal screen for 4, who cuts to the basket to receive the

ball from 1. Usually once or twice a game 1 can make a lob pass to 4 when 4's defender (X4) moves to the top of the screen and no defender can help. If 4 can't receive the ball off the screen, he sets up at the low post, where 1 hits him with a pass (figure 11.1). If there's no pass open to 4, 5 screens for 2 (screen-the-screener action), who comes off the screen to receive from 1, or 5 can roll and receive from 1.

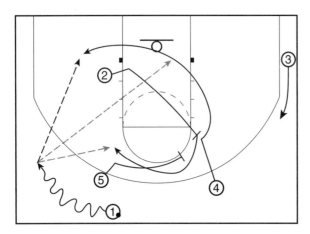

Figure 11.1   The special 1.

Utah

We took this play from the Utah Jazz, who ran it for Karl Malone. Here 2 and 3 form a stack on the left side of the court, 5 is out at the top of the three-second lane extended opposite the stack, and 4 is just outside the three-second lane on the right side of the court. 1 drives the ball on the left side of the court, staying high; 2 curls around 3; and, as soon as 2 rubs around the shoulder of 3, 3 pops out of the lane to receive the ball from 1. 1 can also pass to 2 on the curl. If 2 doesn't receive the ball on the curl, he continues the cut and screens for 4, who crosses near the baseline and receives the ball from 3.

After screening for 4, if the defenders are cheating too much, 2 is vertically screened by 5 (screen the screener), and 1 holds the ball for a moment before passing to 2 (figure 11.2). Another solution for 3 is the pass to 5, who has rolled to the basket after setting the screen for 2.

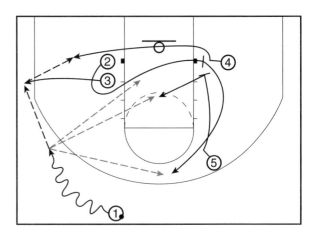

Figure 11.2   Utah.

You can run this play as described if your point guard draws a lot of defensive pressure and has a difficult time passing the ball to the low post. If you can get your 3 man free, you relieve the pressure on the point guard and get a bigger passer to the post.

Utah Special

We also run a variation of the Utah in which we try to get the ball to 4. Here 4 sets up on the right corner of the free-throw area, 5 is at the top of the key, 2 and 3 form a stack on the left side of the court, and 1 dribbles on the left side. 2 rubs off the shoulder of 3, and 3 moves into the deep corner. 2 continues his cut and screens for 4, who receives a lob pass from 1.

After setting the screen for 4, 2 is screened for by 5 (screen the screener; figure 11.3). 1 also has the option to pass to 2 or to 3 in the corner.

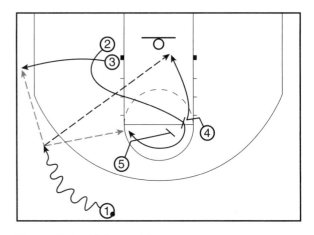

Figure 11.3   Utah special.

55

This is an excellent play. 2 sets up on the low post on the left side of the court, with 4 on the opposite side outside the three-second lane; 5 is at the corner of the free-throw area on the same side as 4; 3 is outside the top of the key.

1 dribbles to the left side of the free-throw line extended, which signals 2 to make a baseline screen for 4. 1 feeds 4 in the low post, and then 1 and 3 make a fake split—1 screens at the free-throw area for 3, who first fakes to cut to the screen before cutting backdoor to the basket. 1 pops back outside of the lane as a spot-up player in case the defense double teams 4 (figure 11.4).

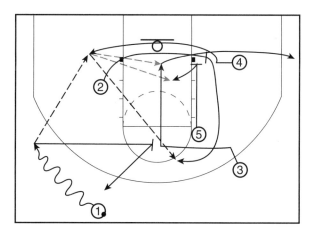

Figure 11.4   The 55.

If 3 doesn't receive the ball, he comes out of the lane and moves to the corner. After setting the screen for 4, 2 receives a vertical screen from 5 (screen the screener) and pops out. 4 plays one on one or passes to 3, 2, or 5, who has rolled to the basket after setting the screen.

You form a triangle on the weak side of the court, with 1 as the spot player on the strong side of the court. If 4 is double teamed, he passes out of the double team to his teammates around the perimeter (1, 3, or 2) or to 5 near the basket. Note the good rebounding positions maintained by the offense.

43 Post

Our defenders tend to bump and switch a lot on our best scorer to keep him away from the post, so we want to get him the ball while he is moving. We run this play out of our flex set.

4 is at the low post, 2 is in the corner, 5 is at the top of the key, and 3 is at the free-throw line extended. 1 dribbles on the right side and passes to 5, while 2 make a flex cut past 4 (figure 11.5).

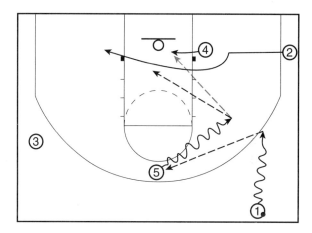

Figure 11.5   The 43 post.

If 2 is open out of the flex cut, 5 gives him the ball; 5 can also hit 4, who has ducked into the three-second lane.

If there's no option, 5 dribbles back toward 1. 1 receives a hand-off pass from 5 and dribbles to the center of the floor. In the meantime, 4 screens for 2, and, after the screen, opens up to the ball and receives from 1. Meanwhile, 2 continues his cut and receives a screen from 5. 1 can also hit 2 off the screen of 5, or 5, who has rolled to the ball (figure 11.6).

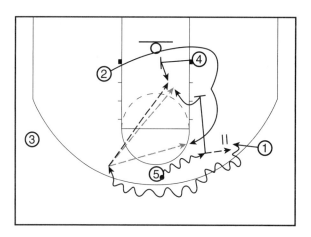

Figure 11.6   The 43 post: other solutions.

We like to use this play for two purposes: to get our shooting guard's jump shot or to get the ball to our power forward inside the lane while he is on the move.

3 Quick

This play is run for the 3 player in the post. He posts up in the low-post position on the right of the court. 4 is on the left corner of the free-throw lane; 5 is on the opposite side, outside the three-second lane; 2 is on the right side of the free-throw line extended; and 1, with the ball, is in the middle of the court.

1 passes to 4 and then goes in the opposite direction, spotting up outside the three-point line; 2 runs to the corner.

As soon as 4 receives the ball from 1, 3 makes a flash cut to the lane. If he doesn't receive the ball right away, he moves to the opposite low-post position, and 4 tries to get him the ball.

After the pass, 4 dives opposite diagonally and replaces 3 at the right low post. 5 holds his position for a moment and then flashes to the left corner of the free-throw lane and, if his defender goes to double team 3, receives the ball to take a jump shot (figure 11.7).

3 has three options for where to start the play: on the right low post, on the left box, or on the left wing.

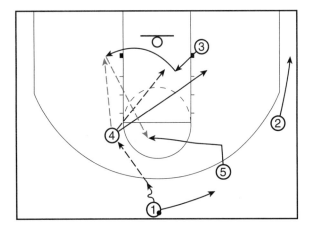

Figure 11.7 The 3 quick.

50

The following play is one of the best for getting the power forward to the front of the basket. Start this play on the right side of the basket with 1 dribbling to the free-throw line extended, 5 at the free-throw line, 3 and 4 forming a stack on the left side of the court, and 2 outside the lane on the left side.

2 fakes a cut into the lane and then cuts off 5 and moves into the right corner. 3 pops out of the stack and moves to the corner. As soon as 2 rubs off his shoulder, 5 steps out. 1 hits 5, who then hits 4, who has flashed into the lane (figure 11.8).

5's defender can't help inside on 4 because that leaves 5 open for the outside jumper. We spent a lot of time in practice working on this high–low post play.

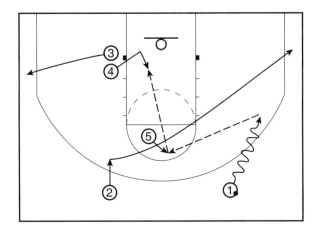

Figure 11.8 The 50.

52–53

We run this play for our 2 or 3. The set is the same as the previous one, but this time 2 (or 3), after making the cut on 5, posts up on the low post and receives the ball from 1.

After 2's cut, 5 opens to the ball and can receive from 1 or 2 (if 2 is double teamed). Meanwhile, 3 pops out of the stack and replaces 2 (figure 11.9).

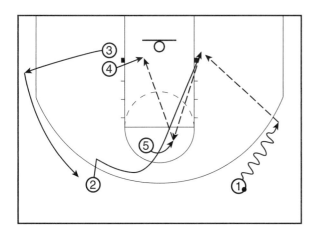

Figure 11.9 The 52–53.

Fist Out–Isolation 4

This play, usually called "single–double" because it forms a single screen on one side of the lane and a double screen on the other side, is a standard play in the NBA to run along the baseline.

4 is on the left low post, 5 is on the right low post, and 2 and 3 are under the basket. 3 screens for 2, and then 2 runs off, curls around 4, and moves to the opposite corner. 3 cuts off 5 and moves up to the three-point spot.

1 passes the ball to 4, who has popped out to the short corner or to midpoint (halfway between the lane and the sideline). 4 faces the basket. This play works excellently when 4's defender is a slow post player. If 4 is quick, he can beat his defender and get to the basket with one dribble (figure 11.10). Obviously, if your 4 player is not quick, this play won't work as well for you.

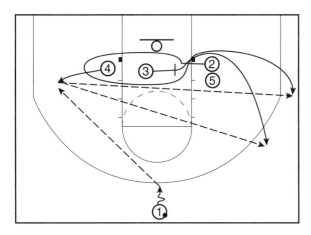

Figure 11.10 The fist out—isolation 4.

If 4 can't get a shot off, he can skip the ball to 2 or 3, who have spotted up for the shot. 5 is in good rebounding position, or he can receive the pass.

Fist Counterplay

We run this play for our 5, and it is effective if the defenders switch. 5 and 4 are on the opposite low-post positions, 3 screens across for 2, and 2 goes outside the three-second lane.

If there's a switch of defenders, 3 curls around 4 and goes either over the top or back off and then under 5, making a figure-eight cut. 1 has the ball at the top of the key. After the switch, X2 is guarding 3 on his back side, waiting for 2 to come off 5 (figure 11.11). 3 now turns and comes out on the other side, rubbing off the shoulder of 5. 1 passes to 3, and 3 passes to 5. 1 can also pass to 2, and 2 to 4.

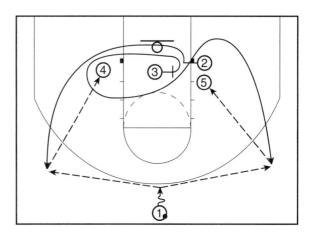

Figure 11.11 The fist counterplay.

Fist 1

When your point guard is covered by a weaker defender, this play is a good choice. The set is a box formation, with the two big men, 5 and 4, on opposite corners of the free-throw area, and 2 and 3 on the low post at opposite positions.

1 starts to drive to the right side of the court, which signals to 4 to make a vertical screen for 2, who comes high to the middle of the floor to receive the ball from 1.

After setting the screen for 2, 4 steps out and screens for 1, who then also receives a staggered screen from 3 in the middle of the lane, and from 5, also in the lane. 3 then comes out of the lane on the other side of the court. 2 passes to 1 (figure 11.12). If 1 can't shoot, 5 screens for 1, and the two players play pick-and-roll. 2 can instead pass to 3—or to 4, who has opened up after setting the screen.

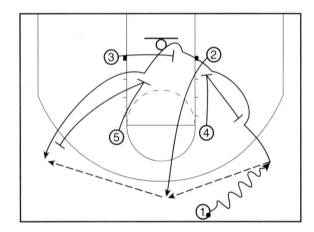

Figure 11.12   The fist 1.

Turn 42

This is another play designed for our 4 player that we run after a time-out. 4 and 2 form a stack on the left side of the court, with 2 near the baseline. 5 sets up high in the middle of the court. 3 is on the wing on the free-throw line extended. 1, outside the three-point line, is on the side of the court where the stack is positioned.

2 curls off 4, rubbing against his shoulder, and moves to the wing at the free-throw line extended, receives the ball from 1, and passes it to 4 in the low post. 1 then cuts into the lane and moves to the opposite corner. Normally, when 4 receives the ball in the low post, X2 will sag back and try to help on 4. In this case, 5 will come over and screen for 2, and then roll to the basket or pop out for a jumper (figure 11.13).

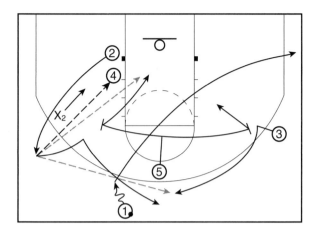

Figure 11.13   The turn 42.

We also have another option: 5 makes a screen away from the ball for 3, and then rolls to the ball. 2 can pass to 4, 3, or 5.

Zipper

4 and 5 are on the corners of the free-throw lane, and 2 and 3 are at the low-post positions. 1 dribbles to the left side of the court, while 4 screens down for 2, who comes up to receive the ball from 1. 3 can either cut near the baseline and go to the opposite corner or clear out to the corner on the same side. 5 brings a high pick for 2, then rolls to the basket to receive from 2 (figure 11.14). If X4 helps on 5, 4 replaces 5, who can receive and shoot.

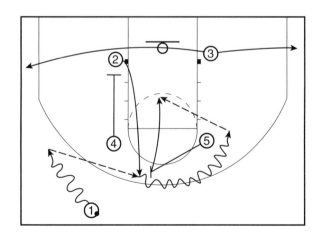

Figure 11.14   The zipper.

Zipper Special

If 2's defender overplays him and he can't receive the pass from 1, we run the same play, but now as soon as 2 comes high, he receives a screen from 5.

1 passes to 2, who can shoot or pass the ball to 5, who rolls to the ball after the pick; or 5 and 2 can play pick-and-roll (figure 11.15).

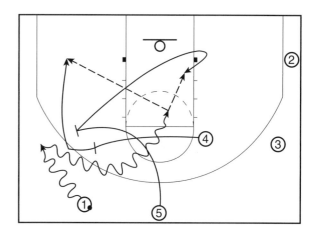

Figure 11.16   The open–close.

this play to isolate our 4 man or our other big man (5).

Position four players near the baseline: 2 and 3 in the opposite corners, and 4 and 5 in the opposite low-post positions, while the point guard (1) dribbles in the middle of the court. The two post players flash to the corners of the free-throw area. 1 passes to one of the high posts (4 in this case) and then moves to the wing position on the same side as the pass.

As soon as 4 receives the pass, 5 makes a diagonal cut into the lane and goes to the low-post position on the same side of the ball. 4 has the chance to play one on one and drive to the basket. If 3's defender (X3) helps, 4 dishes the ball off to 3 in the corner for a three-point shot, or he passes to 5, if 5's defender (X5) tries to help (figure 11.17).

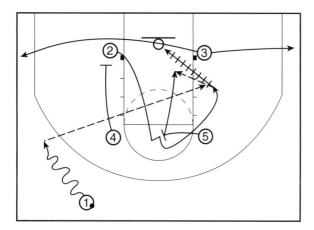

Figure 11.15   The zipper special.

Open–Close

We run this offensive option versus a blitz defense—when the defense double teams the ball handler coming off the screen.

1 dribbles on the left side of the court. 2 is in the deep corner on the opposite side, 3 is outside the three-point line, 4 is outside the free-throw lane, and 5 is in the middle of the court. 5 runs to set a screen, then slip cuts to the basket and goes to the low post on the opposite side. 4 follows and sets a pick for 1; 4 then rolls to midpoint. 1 can pass to 4 or to 5, who has ducked in (figure 11.16).

2X Isolation 4

We use the following plays at the end of the quarter but also during the normal course of the game if there are seven to eight seconds left on the clock. The aim of these plays is to create space and isolate one player to give him a chance to play one on one. We call

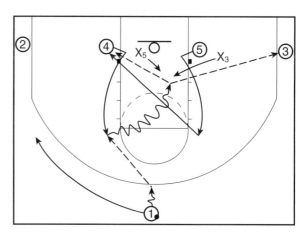

Figure 11.17   The 2X isolation 4.

2

This play can be called to isolate the point guard, especially if he has an excellent drive to the basket. Start from the same set as described before, with four players at the baseline.

1 has the ball in the middle of the court and drives right to the basket. If he penetrates on the right side of the lane, 5 clears this side, moving to the other low-post position. Meanwhile, 4 ducks into the lane behind 1 (figure 11.18).

If 1 can't score, based on the help and reactions of the defenders, he can pass to 4 or 5, or he can dish off to 2 or 3 in the corner for a three-point shot.

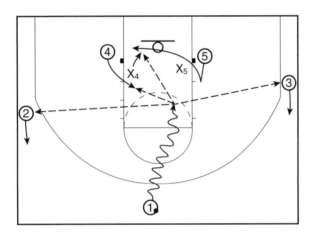

Figure 11.18 The 2.

2 Clear

This play starts similarly to the 2X isolation 4 play but is run when 4 and 5, who flash cut to the corners of the free-throw area, are overplayed and can't receive the ball. 1 dribbles toward the free-throw line extended, while 5 makes a diagonal cut into the lane and posts up on the low-post position on the same side as the ball. 3 clears out to the opposite corner, and 2 comes high. 1 passes to 4, who flashes high after the cut of 5, and 4 drives to the basket (figure 11.19).

You can also leave 3 in the corner to receive the ball if his defender helps on 4.

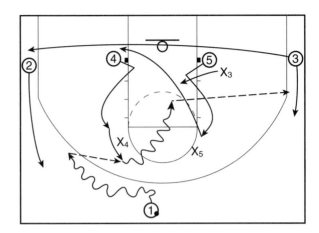

Figure 11.19 The 2 clear.

TEACHING POINTS

In practice, we teach the whole play and then break each play down to its parts, and players work on these situations, such as the pick-and-roll, the staggered screen, the duck into the lane, and screen-the-screener plays.

We break down sessions at both ends of the court for the big players and the small players. For instance, while the big men work on picking and rolling to the basket and to the midpoint for a jump shot, on the other half-court, the guards work on feeding the screener and the duck-in man. They also work on coming off screens for jump shots.

If we want to practice on a post play, we have our big men work on post position and the guards on feeding the post and cutting. Then we bring them together and put the whole play into action. Doing it this way, we are able to teach the play better, show the different positions their responsibilities, and get players a lot of repetitions.

FINAL POINTS

When planning your offensive strategy, strive to create an offense that uses the strengths of your players and also hides their weaknesses. Don't, for example, use a staggered screen for a player who's not a good shooter. Don't base a play on a drive to the basket and a kickout for a player with relatively weak ball-handling and dribbling skills.

Another mistake some coaches make is to adopt a play because it has been used by a famous or winning coach, failing to consider that every team has different players with different skills and that one winning offense doesn't guarantee success for another team at another level of competition.

Finally, coaches must always remember that the success of a play depends mainly on the sound fundamentals—passing, shooting, dribbling, playing without the ball, the ability to read defensive situations—of the players involved, not on the play itself. The details are important, and the details of any play are the sound fundamentals. Without sound individual and collective fundamentals, such as how to set and use screens, there can be no winning offense.

chapter 12

Out-of-Bounds Plays

Brendan Malone

Well-executed out-of-bounds plays, as well as other special-situation plays, can be critical because late in a game they often make the difference between a win and a loss. All NBA teams run several of these plays, practicing them until they are automatic. Another name for the out-of-bounds play is the inbounds play.

There are keys to success at every level of basketball, but two stand out in our league. One such key is *detail,* which applies to individual fundamentals as well as to team offense and defense. Maybe more than any other team sport, basketball is a game of details, as well as of finesse and strength. A player might miss a shot by a fraction of an inch, costing his team the game. A screen set at a slightly improper angle won't be effective in freeing up your shooter for his shot. A pass that is a trace too slow or barely off target will likely result in a steal. When it comes to running out-of-bounds plays, detail is as important as ever. When a team is working on the fundamentals necessary to run a baseline or sideline out-of-bounds play, the coach must attend to every detail.

Another key is *execution.* To perfectly execute a play, and to *know* that the play will be executed perfectly every time, teams must practice the play over and over until it becomes automatic. Never assume that players will run a play in a game properly after they've practiced it only a few times. Execution doesn't come naturally to all

players. You must run the play initially at moderate speed without the defense, then with the defense playing at 50 percent, and finally with the defense playing as they would in a game.

Run each out-of-bounds play many times during each practice. Players must have complete knowledge of the entire play. They must master the play's first option as well as all the other options. They also must master the timing of the different actions of each option.

As coach, you need to make sure every player understands not only *how* to run the out-of-bounds play but *why* to run it; you want the skills of the play to be automatic, but you don't want your players to play like robots. You want smart players who are conscious of the reasons behind each play. But before inserting and teaching specific plays, it's useful to specify to players what you consider the keys to making your team optimally successful in such situations.

BASIC CONCEPTS

Before we get into each play, I want to emphasize some concepts I feel are important in the effective and successful execution of the out-of-bounds play.

• *Get the ball inbounds.* This is top priority. The inbounder can't waste time or commit a turnover because he has locked into a single idea for the inbounds play. He needs to get the ball into the court, be it underneath or outside of the lane—this is the first aim of the play!

• *Make your best passer your inbounder.* The inbounder must pass the ball into the court with speed and accuracy, preferably to particular teammates, so use your most reliable passer for the best execution of the inbounds play. If your best passer is out of the game, designate a player who handles the ball a lot, usually a 2 man or a 3 man.

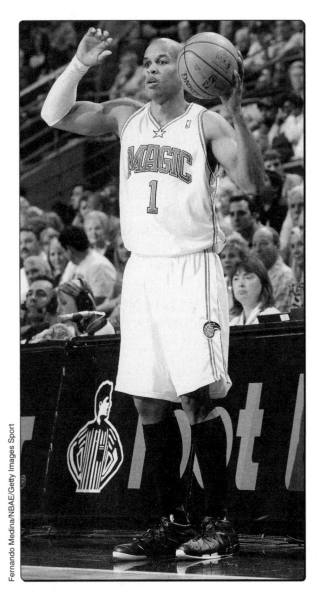

The inbounder should be the best passer on the court at the time.

Your inbounder should always be the best passer you have on the court at the time.

• *Your best scorer should be the first option to receive the pass.* Don't use your best scorer as the inbounder. This player should be the first option to receive the inbounds pass. Your team's best shooters must get into position to receive the inbounds pass in the right spot when the passer is ready to inbound the ball.

• *Use fakes.* The inbounder will be aggressively pressured and in many cases should use pass fakes and other deception to get the ball inbounds. The inbounder might fake a pass up and then throw a bounce pass; he might fake a bounce pass and then make a pass over the top. He should also use eye and head fakes to throw the defender off, looking in one direction and passing in the other.

• *Make good screens.* You'll usually use your big men to set screens and get their teammates open. But you can also use your 2 or 3 man to screen your big man or to force a defensive switch, or in screen-the-screener action to get the ball to the 2 or 3 man for shooting. The player who receives the screen must set up his defender. Meanwhile, the screener should screen a body, not the air, and, after the screen, he must step to the ball. Two other important points: Remind your players that the screener will always be freer than the teammate who is screened for, and make sure the screened player waits for the screen and doesn't rush his shot.

• *Screen the screener.* This action is common in the NBA but is especially effective in inbounds situations. "Screening the screener" simply means that the player who first makes the screen then receives a screen himself. In most cases, the screener's defender won't have time to react to the second screen.

• *Back screener will always be open.* In certain situations, such as at the end of a game when opponents put a lot of pressure on your best shooter, the player who sets the back screen is always open. This player might become your first option—the player who gets the shot—or, if he can't shoot, have him play pick-and-roll.

• *Don't panic.* The inbounder must keep his poise. He should be counting, and if he can't make the inbounds pass by the count of three, he should call a time-out. If no time-outs are left, he should throw the ball off a defender's leg.

CALLING THE PLAYS

Different teams have different names for their inbounds plays. Some teams use the name of another team (New York, Indiana, and so on); other inbounds plays might be called a "quick," "special," or "home-run." Sometimes numbers are used to indicate the player or players involved. For instance, if we call "53," it means the play is run for our big man, 5, and our small forward, 3; if we call "42," the play is run for our power forward, 4, and our 2 guard.

An out-of-bounds play can occur during a game or after a time-out. In either case, the coach calls a particular play, and the inbounder communicates the call to his teammates.

Remember that repetition and close attention to details will ensure the flawless execution of your out-of-bounds plays.

BASELINE OUT-OF-BOUNDS PLAYS

In the NBA, most out-of-bounds plays are against a man-to-man defense, so most of the plays described here reflect that. On page 202, we show one play versus a zone defense.

"Series" Plays

The first play I want to introduce is one we call "series," which includes sequences

Jonathan Daniel/Getty Images Sport

With .7 seconds remaining in overtime, Hedo Turkoglu hits a game-winning shot off an inbounds play in which the opponent's defenders switched on a screen-and-roll.

designated by an action and a number. The first number designates the receiver of the inbounds pass, and the second number designates the receiver of the guard-to-guard pass. The action is designated by the second part of the call and will be explained soon. It's not imperative that we line up in the same spots each possession, but we must get to the proper spots to receive the inbounds pass and execute the action.

The first number (the receiver of the inbounds pass) catches the ball in the "catch area," which is an area around the elbow extended on the side of the inbounder. The second number (the receiver of the guard-to-guard pass) catches the swing pass even with the catch area on the opposite side of the free-throw lane.

The proper receiver must make himself available to receive the ball in the proper area at the time the passer is ready to make the pass. Also understand that the pass doesn't have to go directly to the catch area from the out-of-bounds pass. If the defense prevents this pass, the ball can go through the corner to the catch area and you'll still have the same option.

Here are the different action sequences for "series."

42 Strong

1 is the inbounder; the other four players are set on a flat formation on the baseline: 5 and 3 are near the sidelines on the corners; 4 and 2 are on the low-post areas above the blocks.

4 (the receiver in the "catch" area) fakes to go to receive the ball from 1 and then pops up toward the midcourt line and outside of the three-point line. 2 (the receiver of the guard-to-guard pass) makes the same movement. 1 passes the ball to 4 and then enters the court and replaces 4 (figure 12.1).

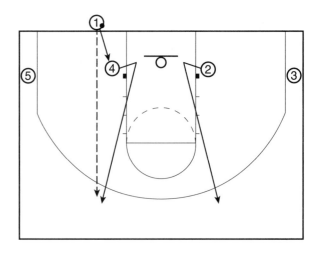

Figure 12.1 42 strong: the set and the start of the play with 1, who passes to 4.

4 swings the ball to 2; 5 comes off the shuffle screen of 1; 4 screens the screener, 1; and 2 has the following choices:

- pass to 5,
- pass to 1, or
- pass to 4, who rolls to the basket after setting the screen for 1 (figure 12.2).

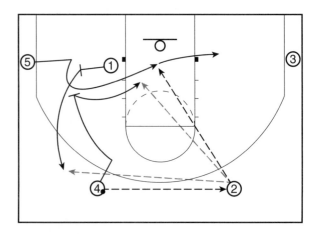

Figure 12.2 42 strong: the passing choices of 2.

24 Weak

The set is similar to the previous one, but now 4 and 2 invert sides and roles: 2 receives the pass in the catch area, and 4 receives the guard-to-guard pass; 1, after the pass to 2, enters the court and replaces 4 (figure 12.3).

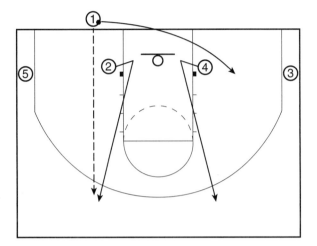

Figure 12.3   24 weak: the set and the start of the play with 1, who passes to 2.

Now 2 swings the ball to 4, and 5 sets a flare screen for 2. 5 reads the defense—if his defender jumps out, he slips the screen and cuts to the basket (figure 12.4). 4 has the following choices:

- pass to 2, or
- pass to 5, who slips the screen or rolls to the basket after setting the screen for 2.

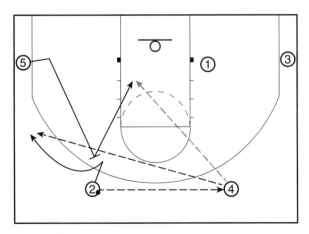

Figure 12.4   24 weak: the passing choices of 4.

43 Counteraction

The set is similar to the previous one, but now 2 and 5 are in the corners near the sidelines and 3 and 4 are on the low-post areas above the blocks. 4 pops up and receives the inbounds pass in the catch area. 3 also pops out to take his defender high, while 1 enters the court and goes out to the three-point line. 3 then makes a backdoor cut to receive a lob pass from 4 (figure 12.5).

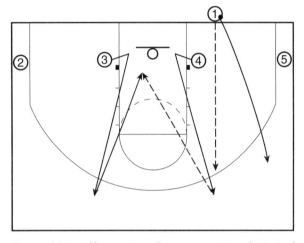

Figure 12.5   43 counteraction: same set and start of the play, but now 1 passes to 4 and 3 makes a backdoor cut.

43 Triple Action

The set is similar to the previous ones, but now 5 and 2 are near the sidelines above the blocks, and 4 and 3 are on the low-post areas, with 4 the receiver in the "catch" area, and 3 the receiver of the guard-to-guard pass.

4 pops out over the three-point line and receives the inbounds pass from 1, while 3 also pops out over the three-point line. After the pass to 4, 1 enters the court and cuts opposite to the ball (figure 12.6).

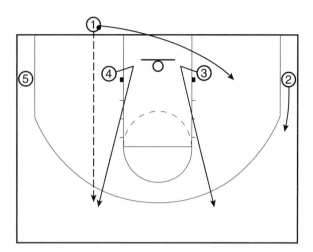

Figure 12.6   43 triple action: same set and start of the play with 1, who passes to 4.

1 screens for 2, who cuts into the lane and receives another screen from 5. 4 swings the ball to 3 and cuts down to the lane to make a third screen for 2, who pops out over the three-point line. 3 dribbles toward 2 and either passes 2 the ball or chooses one of these options (figure 12.7):

- pass to 4, who goes to the ball after the screen,
- pass to 5, who rolls to the basket after the screen, or
- pass to 1, who opens up to the ball after the screen.

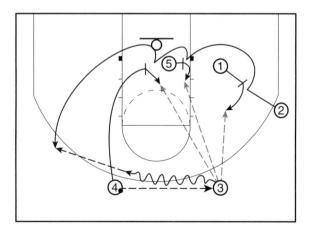

Figure 12.7   43 triple action: 3's passing choices.

24 Weak Dive

The set is similar to the previous ones, but now 2 and 4 are on the low-post areas above the blocks, with 2 the receiver in the "catch" area, 4 the receiver of the guard-to-guard pass, and 5 and 3 near the sidelines.

2 pops out over the three-point line and receives the inbounds pass from 1; 4 pops out over the three-point line (figure 12.8). After the pass to 2, 1 enters the court and replaces 4.

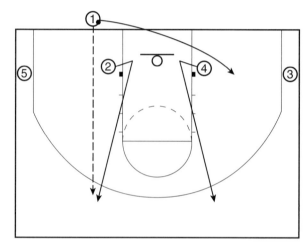

Figure 12.8   24 weak dive: the set and the start of the play with 1, who passes to 2.

2 swings the ball to 4; 5 sets a flare screen for 2. On the pass over the top from 4 to 2, 4 dives to the basket to receive the ball from 2. 2 can also pass to 5, who, after the screen, rolls to the free-throw area (figure 12.9).

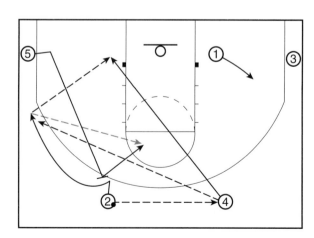

Figure 12.9   24 weak dive: the passing choices of 2.

Stack Plays

One common offensive set in the NBA is the stack, in which two or three players are lined up in a straight line, either perpendicular or parallel to the sideline. This special set is often used and recommended for out-of-bounds plays. Here is a series of plays that start from this formation and have different solutions.

Stack Regular

1 is the inbounder; 5, 4, and 3 line up in the stack formation on the left side of the court parallel to the sideline; 2 is at the top of the key. 3 curls around 4 and 5, rubbing off 5's shoulder, and goes to the opposite corner, outside of the arc of the three-point line. As soon as 3 curls around 5, 2 fakes a cut to the middle of the lane and then uses the double screen of 4 and 5 to go to the midpoint outside the lane (figure 12.10). 1 has the following choices:

- pass to 2 on the curl,
- pass to 3 in the opposite corner, or
- pass to 4 or 5, who roll to the basket in opposite directions after setting the double screen.

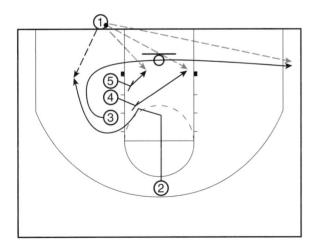

Figure 12.10   Stack regular: the set, start, and passing choices of 1.

Option. If 2 receives the ball and doesn't have a shot, 5 goes to the low-post area opposite of the stack; 4 plays pick-and-roll with 2; 1 enters the court, rubs off 5's shoulder, and goes outside the arc of the three-point line (figure 12.11). 2 now has the following choices:

- shoot, using the pick of 4, or drive to the lane;
- pass to 4, who after the screen rolls to the basket;
- pass to 1;
- pass to 3 in the corner; or
- pass to 5, who ducks into the lane.

If 1 receives the ball, he has these options:

- shoot,
- pass to 5 in the low post, or
- pass to 3 in the deep corner.

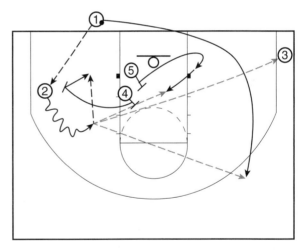

Figure 12.11   Stack regular option: the shooting and passing choices of 2.

Stack Special 1

Now let's look at some options to the regular stack. As said before, on every play a coach must have options based on the reactions of the defenders. The initial set here is the same as described for the stack regular: 1 is the inbounder; 5, 4, and 3 form the stack; and 2 is at the top of the key. After 3's curl, 5 screens for 4, 4 pops out, and then 5 screens again, this time for 2, and rolls to the basket (figure 12.12).

1 has the following choices:

- pass to 3 on the curl;
- pass to 4, who has popped out to the corner;
- pass to 2, who has cut into the lane; or
- pass to 5, who has rolled to the basket after the screen.

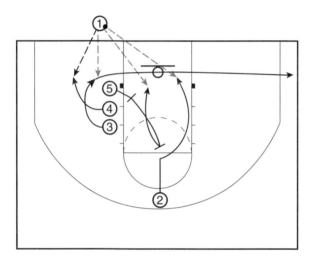

Figure 12.12   Stack special 1: the passing choices of 1.

Stack Special 2

Starting from the same set as just described, this time 3 doesn't curl around the stack but pops out to receive the ball from 1. 1 might instead pass the ball to 5, who's rolling to the basket after the screen (figure 12.13).

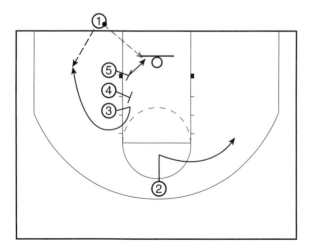

Figure 12.13   Stack special 2: 3 pops out to receive the ball from 1, who might instead pass to 5.

Stack Special 3

The starting set is the same as before. Here 3 doesn't cut into the lane. Rather, 3 and 5 pinch in and screen for 4, who pops out to the corner to receive the ball from 1. 1 might instead pass to 5 or 3, who roll to the basket in opposite directions (figure 12.14).

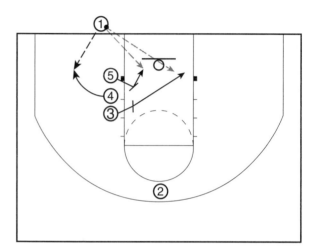

Figure 12.14   Stack special 3: 3 and 5 double-screen for 4.

Golden State

In this play we still form a stack but opposite to the ball and with different players. 1 is always the inbounder; 4, 2, and 3 set a stack formation on the right side of the court; and 5 is on the left low post, facing the ball.

2 pops out of the stack to the corner, while 4 and 3 squeeze the defenders, forming a double pick. 1 passes the ball right away to 2 for a three-point shot, or to 4, who rolls to the basket after the screen (figure 12.15). 1 can instead pass to 5, who's cutting to the basket, or to 3, who's rolling opposite to 4.

Option. With a few seconds left on the clock, after the inbounds pass directly to 5, 1 enters the court and cuts off 5 after faking away. 5 passes the ball back to 1 for a quick shot (figure 12.16).

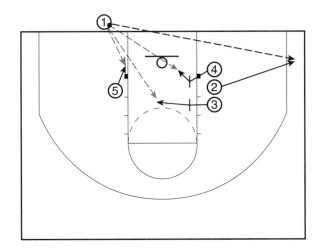

Figure 12.15   Golden State: the passing choices of 1.

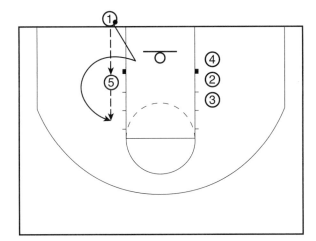

Figure 12.16   Golden State option: a quick action for the inbounder (1).

Indiana

I call this play Indiana because when I was assistant coach with the Indiana Pacers, we ran this set with a high rate of efficiency for Reggie Miller or Jalen Rose. You might recall Miller as one of the best outside shooters ever to play in the NBA.

Start in a flat formation on the baseline. 1 makes the inbounds pass; 5 is at the low post; 4 is at the low-post position opposite to 5; 2 is under the basket; and 3 is in the opposite deep corner on the same side as 4.

2 comes out of the lane using the screen of 5, goes to the deep corner, and receives

the ball from 1. After the pass to 2, 1 enters the court, is screened by 5, goes high, and receives the ball from 2 for a shot (figure 12.17). 2 can also pass to 5, who has rolled to the basket after setting the screen for 2.

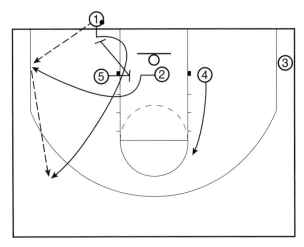

Figure 12.17   Indiana: a play for a good outside shooter.

On the pass from 1 to 2, 4 goes out of the lane opposite to the ball and screens down for 3 in the corner. 1 can pass to 3, who comes off the screen of 4, or to 4, who rolls to the basket after the screen (figure 12.18). After we ran this play a few times, we were able to give the ball right away to 3 (or to 2 in the corner) because all the defenders jammed the three-second lane (figure 12.19).

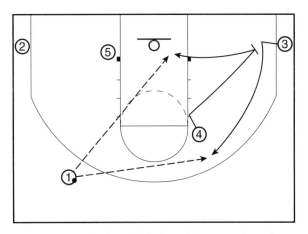

Figure 12.18   Indiana: If 1, 2, and 5 are not free, 1 can pass to 3 or 4 after a pick-and-roll.

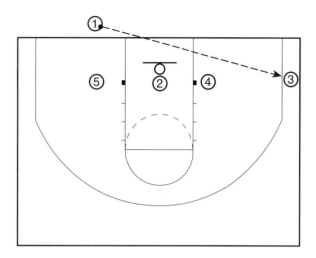

Figure 12.19   After you have run this play a few times, 1 can pass directly to 3 because the defense jams the lane.

New York

In this play, 3 is the inbounder, 5 is at the low post, 2 is in the opposite low-post position, 4 is at the corner of the free-throw area on the same side as 5, and 1 is set up above the three-second lane, making himself available as a safety. 2 screens for 4, and then 5 screens 2 in screen-the-screener action (figure 12.20). 3 has the following choices:

- pass to 4, who is screened for by 2;
- pass to 2, who cuts to the strong-side corner off the screen of 5; or
- pass to 5, who rolls to the basket after screening for 2.

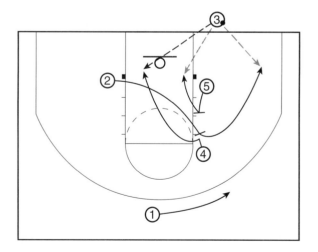

Figure 12.20   New York: the passing choices of 3.

After he has received the screen from 2 and can't receive the ball, 4 goes down and screens for 3, who, after the inbounds pass to 2, has entered the court. 2 passes to 1; 1 passes to 3, who comes off the screen of 4 (figure 12.21). 3 can then pass back to 4, who is rolling to the basket after the screen.

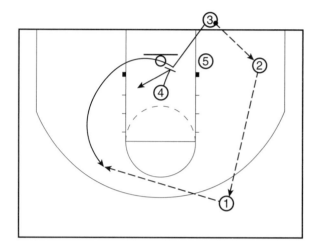

Figure 12.21   New York: if nobody is open, 4 screens for 3.

I remember a game when I was on the bench with the New York Knicks. We were down by three points at the end of the game, and we called this play (though it had a different name then). 1 was completely free at the top of the key, and Hubie Brown, our head coach, yelled to pass directly to 1 for a three-point shot. That tied the game. In fact, all the defenders, recognizing the play, were so worried about jamming the lane that they failed to cover 1.

25

This play is run for 2, the shooting guard, and 5, the center. 1 is the inbounder; 2, the best scorer, is under the basket; 3 is at the midpoint of the three-second lane; 5 is at the top of the lane, inside the three-point line; and 4 is outside the lane on the right side.

2 screens for 5, who cuts to the basket (the big men are not accustomed to being screened, so this move can surprise them).

On this type of screen, very seldom is there a switch because a smaller player cannot guard a big man, so 5 is left open.

3 pops out to the three-point line in the corner. 2, after setting the screen for 5, pops out on the ball side (figure 12.22). 1 has the following choices:

- pass to 5, who cuts off the screen of 2;
- pass to 2, who pops out after the screen;
- pass to 3, if his defender helps out on 5; or
- pass to 4, who has spotted up on the other side of the court.

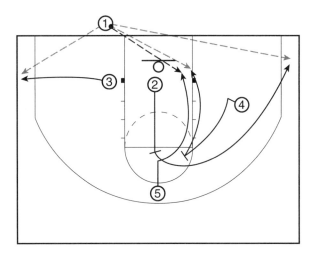

Figure 12.23   25 option: screen-the-screener action and the passing choices of 1.

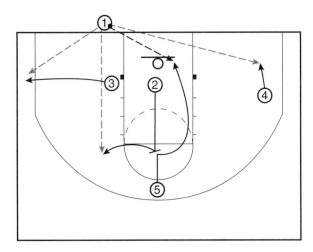

Figure 12.22   25: the passing choices of 1.

Option. The set is the same as just described, but on this option, while 3 pops out in the corner, 2, after setting the screen for 5, receives a screen from 4 (screen-the-screener action) and then pops out at the three-point line. After the screen, 4 rolls to the basket (figure 12.23).

1 has the following choices:

- pass to 5, who cuts off the screen of 2;
- pass to 2, who receives the screen from 4 and then pops out;
- pass to 3, who pops out in the corner; or
- pass to 4, who is rolling to the basket after setting the screen for 2.

Now I would like to show two inbounds plays particularly designed for the big men: 4, the power forward, and 5, the center.

54

3 sets up on the low post near the baseline on the same side as 1, the inbounder; 4 is at the corner of the free-throw area on the ball side; 5 is in the low-post area, opposite to 3; and 2 is set up outside the three-point line, opposite the ball.

3 pops out in the corner to take away the help; 5 makes a diagonal screen for 4, who cuts into the lane; 5 rolls to the basket after the screen; and 2 spots up on the ball side (figure 12.24). 1 has the following choices:

- pass to 4, who cuts off the screen of 5;
- pass to 5, who rolls to the basket after setting the screen for 4;
- pass to 3, if 3's defender helps on the roll of 5; or
- pass to 2, who spots up for a three-point shot.

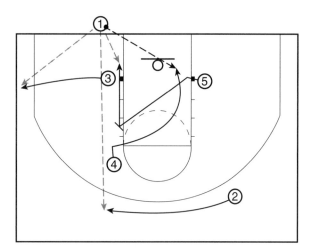

Figure 12.24   54: a play for the big men.

Quick 2

The action and the set are similar to the previous drill but this time involve mainly the guard (2) and the center (5). 1 is the inbounder; 4 is at the low post on the left side of the three-second lane, on the same side as the ball; 5 is on the low post on the right side of the three-second lane; 2 is at the corner of the free-throw area, facing the ball; and 3 is outside the arc of the three-point line. 5 screens diagonally for 2 and pops out, while 4 pops out of the low post and goes to the corner (figure 12.25). 1 has the following choices:

- pass to 2, who rubs off the screen of 5;

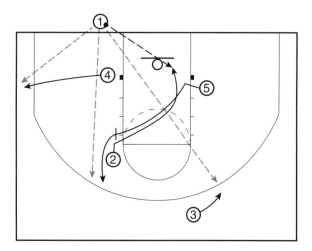

Figure 12.25   Quick 2: a play run for 2, and the passing choices of 1.

- pass to 5, who, after the screen for 2, pops out;
- pass to 4, if 4's defender helps on 2's cut; or
- pass to 3, who spots up for a three-point shot.

Baseline Out of Bounds vs. Zone or Combination Defenses

1 is the inbounder; 5, 4, and 3 form a stack parallel to the sideline near the lane on the ball side; and 2 spots up in the opposite corner for a potential direct pass. 5 and 4 cut into the open gaps of the zone while 3 cuts to the open area in the middle of the three-second lane. The cuts of 5, 4, and 3 shrink the zone defense, which enables 1 to make a direct pass to 2 in the corner (figure 12.26).

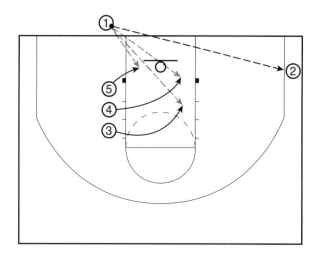

Figure 12.26   A play vs. zone or combination defenses.

SIDELINE OUT-OF-BOUNDS PLAYS

Let's now look at some sideline out-of-bounds plays, another basic aspect of the game that every coach at every level must be ready to face—but especially in the NBA, where many games are won or lost by 1 or 2 points.

End of the Game or Quarter Plays

The following plays are used on the sideline and when there are few seconds left on the clock at the end of the game or a quarter. This situation can give a definite advantage to the team on offense, because the opposing players are not accustomed to facing plays that are not run throughout the course of the game, and a basket scored on one of these plays can be crucial at the final buzzer.

Winner

Option 1. 3 is the inbounder; 5 is at the low post, ball side; 1 is outside the three-point line; 4 is at the elbow opposite the ball; and 2 is opposite to 5 and outside the lane. The easiest option is a direct pass to 5 for a quick shot (figure 12.27). If 5 receives the ball but can't shoot, 3 steps inbounds to receive a pass back from 5 for a three-point shot (assuming you need a three-pointer to win the game) (figure 12.28).

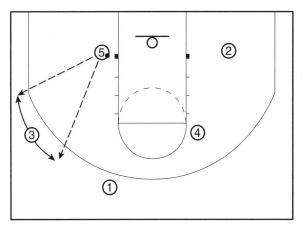

Figure 12.28 Winner, option 1: a pass back from 5 to 3.

Option 2. 3 has the option to pass the ball to 2, who cuts into the lane, gets a screen from 5, goes out past the three-point line (assuming you need the three-pointer), and shoots. If you need a two-point shot, 3 can pass to 1, who is screened by 4, or to 5, who rolls to the basket (figure 12.29).

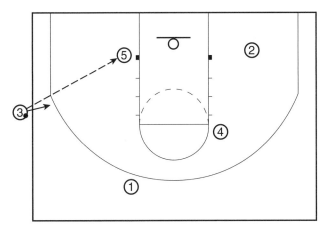

Figure 12.27 Winner, option 1: a quick pass to the low post.

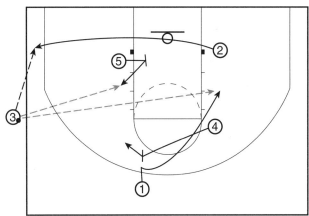

Figure 12.29 Winner, option 2: The play can also be run with a baseline pick-and-roll and a side screen at the top of the key.

Option 3. The play is run as before, but this time after setting the screen for 2, 5 rolls to the ball and receives the inbounds pass from 3 (figure 12.30). Right after the pass, 3 steps inbounds and receives a screen from 4, and 5 passes the ball to 3 for a three-point shot (figure 12.31).

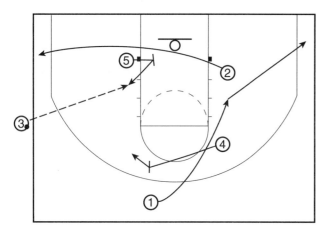

Figure 12.30 Winner, option 3: The play is run as before, but 5 receives the inbounds pass after setting the screen for 2.

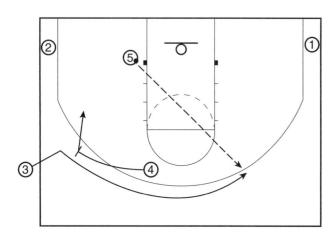

Figure 12.31 Winner, option 3: 4 screens for 3, and 3 receives from 5.

Option 4. 4 screens for 1, who goes to the corner, and 4, immediately after the screen, cuts to the ball and receives from 3, while 2 cuts to the other side of the court and is screened by 5 (figure 12.32). 5 can then roll to the basket. 3 passes to 4 and cuts off him; 4 hands the ball off to 3, who drives to the basket, looking to score or to kick the ball off to 5 on the low post, or to 1 in the corner (figure 12.33).

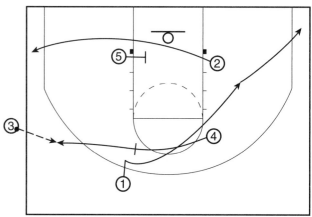

Figure 12.32 Winner, option 4: After the screen for 1, 4 flashes to the ball to receive a pass from 3.

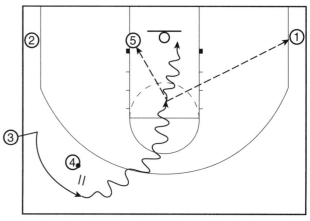

Figure 12.33 Winner, option 4: a hand-off pass from 4 to 3, who drives to the basket.

Option 5. 4 screens for 1, who goes to the corner away from the ball. 4, immediately after the screen, cuts to the ball (figure 12.34). 3 passes the ball to 4, who hands the ball off to 3; 3 passes the ball to 1 in the corner, and 1 passes to 2, who receives a screen from 5 and cuts into the lane (figure 12.35).

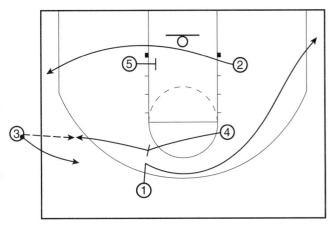

Figure 12.34 Winner, option 5: same start as option 4.

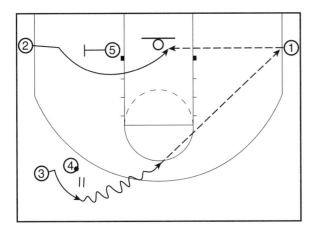

Figure 12.35 Winner, option 5: 2 receives another screen from 5, then cuts into the lane to receive the ball from 1.

Hook

The following plays were created by Chuck Daly, who won two NBA championships as coach of the Pistons. He was also coach of the original Dream Team, which won the 1992 Olympic Games. This was one of his favorite sideline out-of-bounds plays when

he needed a basket at crunch time. 3 is the inbounder; 4 and 5 set up outside of the free-throw elbows; 1 is near 4 on the ball side; and 2 is under the basket. 4 screens for 1, and 1 cuts off the screen and goes to the deep corner, ball side. At the same time as 4's screen for 1, 5 screens for 2, trying to set the pick at a certain angle. 2 comes out to the three-point line. As soon as 1 cuts off the screen, 4 pops out to receive the ball from 3. 4 passes to 2, who can shoot a two- or three-point shot. If 2 can't shoot, he passes the ball to 5, who has frozen his defender under the basket after setting the screen for 2 (figure 12.36).

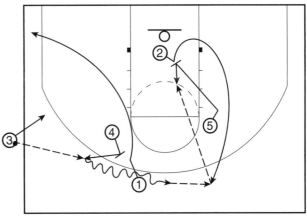

Figure 12.36 Hook: 4 pick-and-rolls with 1, who then goes in the corner; 4 pops out and receives the ball from 3, while 5 screens for 2. 2 can shoot or pass to 5, who has rolled to the basket.

X

4 is the inbounder; 3 and 2 are set up outside of the three-point line; 5 is at the top of the key; and 1 is under the basket. 3 and 2 cut off 5; 2 sets up at the low-post position, ball side, and 3 goes to the opposite corner (figure 12.37). Right after the cuts of 3 and 2, 5 turns and screens down for 1, who comes up and receives the ball from 4. After the screen, 5 cuts back to the ball as a safety valve in case 4 can't pass to 1. Right after 1 has received the ball from 4, 4 and 5 start to move to set a double pick inside the three-point line (figure 12.38).

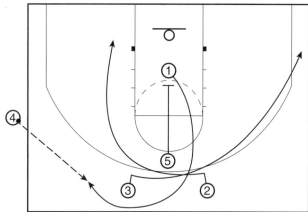

Figure 12.37 The X: 2 and 3 cut around 5, who then screens for 1, who receives from 4.

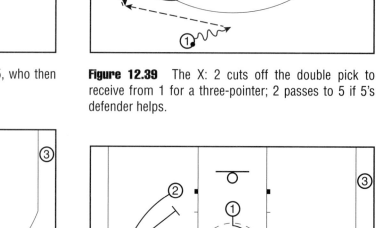

Figure 12.39 The X: 2 cuts off the double pick to receive from 1 for a three-pointer; 2 passes to 5 if 5's defender helps.

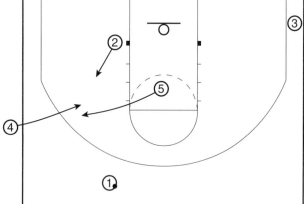

Figure 12.38 The X: After the inbounds pass, 4 and 5 start to move to set a double pick.

Figure 12.40 The X: If 1 can't receive the ball, 5 pops out after the screen, receives the ball from 4, who then screens for 2, who receives the pass from 5.

4 and 5 set a double screen for 2, who receives from 1 for a three-point shot. If 5's defender helps out on 2, 5 cuts to the corner to receive the ball and shoot a three-pointer (figure 12.39). Naturally, not all teams have a post and a power forward able to shoot from the three-point range, so change the role of your players as necessary. If your 5 is not a good three-point shooter, have your 4 set the down screen for 1 instead of 5. If you don't have a 4 or 5 that can shoot from the three-point arc, have a small forward inbound the ball. If 1 is denied the ball, 4 passes to 5, who has popped out after the screen, and then screens down for 2, who receives the ball from 5 to shoot (figure 12.40).

Line

3 is the inbounder; 5, 4, 2, and 1 are set in a straight line parallel to the baseline at the free-throw line. 1 cuts off 2, 4, and 5, looking for a pass from 3, but 1 is rarely open. After the cut, 1 goes to the deep corner on the weak side. After 1's cut, 2 brings his defender down into the lane and then cuts back off the double screen set by 4 and 5, looking for a pass from 3 (figure 12.41). If 5's defender shows to help on 2's cut, 5 cuts to the basket to receive the ball and shoot a layup (figure 12.42).

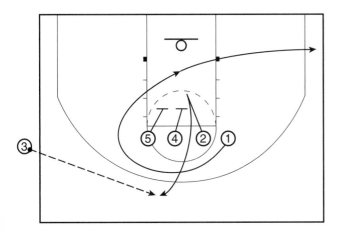

Figure 12.41   Line: 1 cuts off 2, 4, and 5 and, if he doesn't receive the ball, goes to the corner; 2 steps into the lane and then cuts back off the double screen of 4 and 5 and receives from 3.

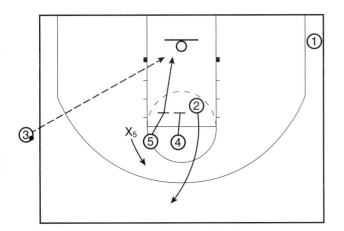

Figure 12.42   Line: If 5's defender helps on 2, 5 slips to the basket to receive from 3.

If the ball is inbounded by 3 to the deep corner, you can still run this play. The only thing that changes is the angle of the line, which will be at about 45 degrees to the corner on the ball side and is formed by four players. With 5, 4, 2, and 1 lined up in this order, 1 cuts around 2, 4, and 5, looking for a pass from 3 (figure 12.43).

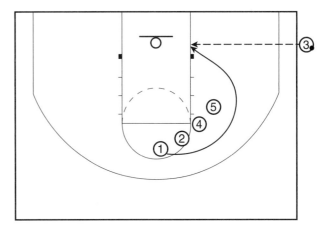

Figure 12.43   Line: The ball is inbounded to the deep corner; 1, 2, 4, and 5 set up in a 45-degree line.

If 1 doesn't receive the ball, he goes to the weak-side corner. The second option is the pass to 2, who, after having brought his defender down into the lane, cuts off the double screen set by 4 and 5 (figure 12.44). Finally, 3 can also pass to 5, who rolls to the basket if his defender steps out to help on 2, or 3 can pass to 4, who pops out after setting the screen for 2 (figure 12.45).

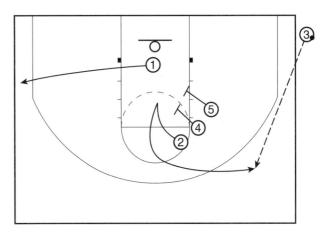

Figure 12.44   Line: 2 steps into the lane and then cuts back off the double screen set by 4 and 5.

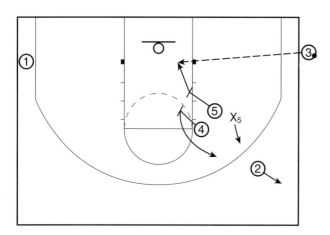

Figure 12.45   Line: If 5's defender helps on 2, 5 slips to the basket to receive from 3.

C

This is another play for when you need a basket late in the game. 3 is the inbounder; 1 and 2 are at the low-post positions; and 5 and 4 are at the elbows of the free-throw area, 5 on the ball side and 4 on the other side in a box set. 2 clears out to the opposite corner; 5 screens down for 1, who cuts off the screen and out to the three-point line; 5 rolls to the ball and receives from 3. At the same time, 4 screens for 1, who receives the ball from 5 for a three-point shot or a drive to the basket (figure 12.46).

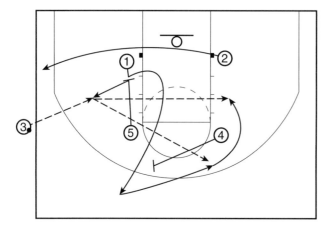

Figure 12.46   The C: 3 passes to 5 on the pick-and-roll; 5 passes to 1, who cuts off 4's screen.

Corner

3 inbounds the ball from the deep corner, always starting from a box set—this time with 1 on the ball side and 2 on the weak side. 2 clears out to the corner; 1 sets a diagonal back screen on 5's defender; and 4 sets a screen on 1's defender (screen-the-screener action). 3 can pass the ball to 1 or 5 (figure 12.47).

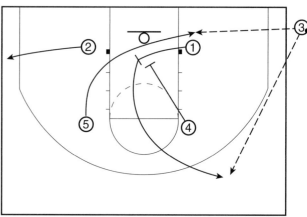

Figure 12.47   Corner: 1 sets a diagonal screen for 5 and then receives a screen from 4 in screen-the-screener action.

Argentina

This play was not taken from any NBA team playbook, but other NBA coaches and I had the chance to watch it at the 2002 FIBA World Championship in Indianapolis. We were impressed. 3 is the inbounder; 1 is on the weak side; 4 and 2 are at the low post spots; and 5 is on the high post, ball side. 2 back-screens for 5, is screened for by 4, and goes out to the three-point line. 3 passes the ball to 2 for the three-pointer (figure 12.48).

San Antonio

I watched the San Antonio Spurs run this play to win a game. 1 is at the low post, ball side; 5 is out of the lane; and 4 is at the elbow

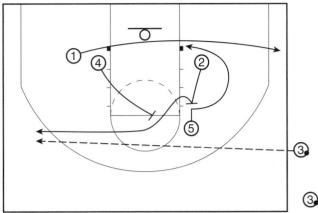

Figure 12.48 Argentina: 2 back-screens for 5 and is then screened for by 4 in screen-the-screener action; 2 receives the pass from 3 for the three-point shot.

of the free-throw area on the same side as 5. 4 and 5 make a stagger screen for 2, who cuts out to the three-point line. 3 can pass to 2 for a wide-open shot. If 5's defender helps out, 5 rolls to the basket to receive from 3 and shoot (figure 12.49).

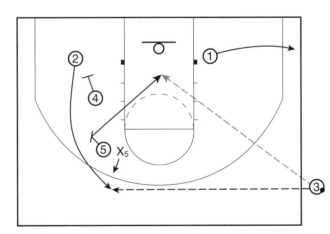

Figure 12.49 San Antonio: 4 and 5 set a stagger screen for 2, who receives from 3; or 3 can pass to 5, who slips to the basket if his defender helps on 2.

Short Clock (1 or 2 Seconds Remaining)

3 is the inbounder, 1 is at the low post, 2 is under the basket, and 5 and 4 are at the free-throw line. 5 and 4 set a double screen in the lane for 2, who cuts high out to the three-point line; 1 pops out to the corner,

ball side. Right after setting the double screen, 5 rolls to receive from 3 and shoots under the basket (figure 12.50).

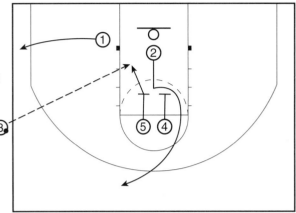

Figure 12.50 Short clock: 4 and 5 set a double screen for 2; 5 slips to the basket to receive from 3.

Short Clock 2

1 is at the low post, ball side; 5 is on the weak-side low post; 4 is at the elbow of the free-throw area; and 2 is outside the three-point line. This action all occurs at once: 1 cuts to the ball; 4 and 2 make V cuts to the ball; 5 cuts first to the free-throw line and then backdoor to the basket; and 3 makes a high lead pass at the rim to 5 (figure 12.51). The 5 player must be tall and able to catch a tough pass.

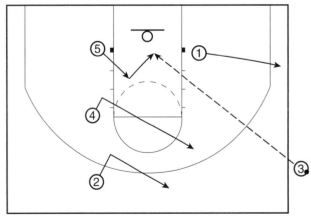

Figure 12.51 Short clock 2: 2 and 4 V-cut to the ball; 5 fakes a cut to the ball and runs a backdoor cut to the basket immediately after to receive a pass from 3.

THREE-QUARTER COURT SIDELINE OUT-OF-BOUNDS PLAYS

Following are two plays to run against a three-quarter press, one of the many defensive situations an NBA team, but also a team at the high school or college level, could face and must be able to beat.

Line Play vs. Three-Quarter Court Pressure

3 is the inbounder; 1, 2, 4, and 5 form a line outside the lane parallel to the baseline. 3 calls the name of one of his teammates (2, in this case), who fakes to cut high but then sprints to the basket to receive a long pass from 3 to shoot the layup (figure 12.52).

X Play vs. Three-Quarter Court Pressure

3 is the inbounder; 4 and 2 set up outside the three-point line; 5 is in the midcourt; and 1 is at the other half-court near the three-point line. 4 and 2 cut around 5 and sprint to opposite corners. Right after 4 and 2 are past him, 5 screens down for 1, who comes high. 3 can pass to 4 or 2 (figure 12.53). After the screen, 5 rolls back to the ball. 3 can also pass to 5 or 1.

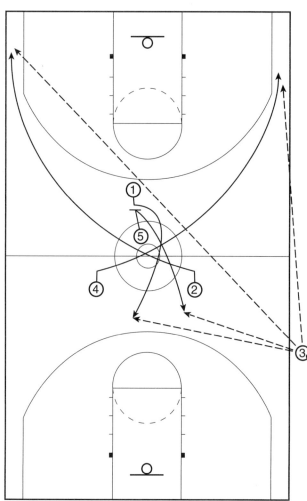

Figure 12.53 X vs. three-quarter court pressure: 4 and 2 cut around 5 and sprint to the three-point line; 5 screens for 1, then rolls back to the ball.

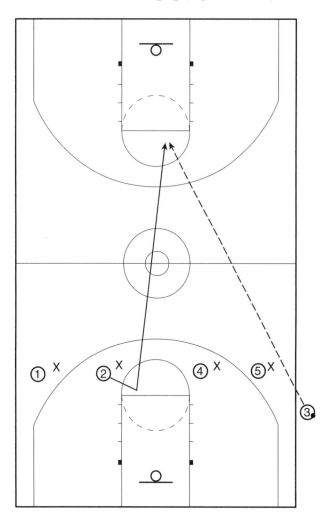

Figure 12.52 Line vs. three-quarter court pressure: 3 calls the name of 2, who fakes a cut high and then sprints down the court to receive the ball from 3.

FINAL POINTS

Depending on personnel and game situations, a coach can change the inbounder and the receiver of the passes. For example, if his best three-point shooter is a small forward (3), he can designate another player as the inbounder and 3 as the receiver of the pass for the shot. In short, the coach adapts the inbounds play to the skills of his players.

During my career I noticed a common mistake coaches make, so I'll share it with you by way of closing remarks: Don't take for granted that any play you watch and then adopt for your team will work as well for you as for the team you first saw use it. Very few coaches prove to be basketball geniuses, and while you can benefit from taking some ideas from others, remember that you must also be intelligent enough to evaluate whether certain plays really fit the skills of your players.

One final comment: Don't complicate your life and the lives of your players. Using strange and difficult inbounds plays is usually not wise for several reasons. Fatigue, stress, crowd noise, game momentum, and, above all, your opponents can all affect a play's dynamic, and when all these factors come together, as they often do, the last thing you need is to try something complicated. Sometimes the KISS rule (keep it simple, stupid) should override all others.

chapter 13

Last-Second Scoring Plays

Dave Wohl

In any NBA season, fewer than 25 percent of all teams will have an average winning or losing margin greater than 6 points, and anywhere between 20 and 40 percent of a team's games will be decided by that number of points or less. Think about that—your team's winning or losing margin can often come down to a last-second three-pointer to end each of the two halves, or three two-point field goals (or some combination of field goals and defensive stops) at the end of any of the four quarters.

In short, close games mean golden opportunities—chances to make a significant difference in a season's success simply by consistently converting before the buzzer. And last-second conversions become even more important in the postseason, when games tend to be even closer and more competitive.

Recall that in the 1994 Finals, no margin in the entire seven-game series between the Rockets and Knicks was greater than 10 points. Houston won the series four games to three, but the result might well have been reversed had John Starks been able to get an open three-pointer off before the final buzzer sounded in game six. (Starks' attempt was blocked by Hakeem Olajuwon.) More recently, in Cleveland's 4-2 Eastern Conference series victory over Detroit in 2007, only the final game was decided by a margin greater than 6 points, and three games were decided by 3 points or less.

Whether a title contender or a squad simply seeking to earn a postseason berth,

One of the rare players who can take over and deliver in the final seconds, LeBron James hits a game-winning buzzer beater from the arc over Kobe Bryant.

every team needs to be able to execute plays that can beat the clock. This chapter provides both the key principles for developing last-second plays as well as detailed diagrams and descriptions for executing them. When taught well and performed properly, these plays are proven game winners.

PRINCIPLES OF GAME-WINNING SHOTS

You might be of the opinion that the key to a successful last-second shot is to get the ball to Kobe Bryant, Dwyane Wade, or LeBron James and let him create a scoring opportunity. Well, most of us don't have the luxury of having such an elite player on our roster, and even if we did, what do we do when that player is injured, fouled out, or denied the ball by a great defender?

The point is, resting all your last-second scoring hopes on a supreme talent isn't much of a plan. Instead, keep these concepts in mind when devising your array of buzzer-beating plays:

• Keep things simple. Go with a play in which players can understand what they're trying to do in the heat of competition and under the pressure of a big game. The simpler, the better.

• Thousands of plays might look great on paper, but the ones with the fewest passes before a shot usually have a higher rate of success. The more passes, the more chances that something will go wrong.

• When talking to your team during a time-out, remain calm and controlled; your team will feed off your confidence and not get caught up in the frenzy of the moment. Make eye contact with each of your players as you diagram your play. This lets you know whether they are focused on the play or still caught up in the pressure of the game. Draw your plays a little slower than usual. Help your players to slow down and focus. Make sure everyone knows his role before leaving the time-out.

• Know the best lineup at the end of the game that can execute the winning play. This lineup might not be your five best players. In a last-second shot situation, you might need five good shooters on the floor one night and two terrific offensive rebounders the next night, if there's time for a tip-in off a missed shot.

• Know who you want to take the shot and who you want to make the inbounds pass. These are the two most important components involved in successful last-second shots. The coach has to know which of his players enjoys the pressure of a big shot and won't hesitate to take it, and who has the vision, passing skills, and coolness under fire to make the right inbounds pass. I have seen more plays fail because the player passing inbounds, afraid of making a mistake, held onto the ball too long or tried to pass too quickly and threw it right into a defender's hands.

• Know your players' strengths and weaknesses. Many players, even good players, don't really like pressure situations at the end of a game. Know which players thrive on pressure, and make sure they're in the game.

USING THE CLOCK

Teach your players to use the clock in game-winning situations. Unless they practice a lot for these types of plays, players often rush through a play, failing to execute, thinking time will run out on them. The result is usually unsuccessful.

One method of explaining the clock to players is to divide the remaining time into smaller and smaller segments and discuss what can be accomplished with fewer and fewer ticks left on the clock. Here are some examples:

• If you have 8 seconds left on the clock and the ball is going to be thrown inbounds from the sideline at your basket, you have time to set up a quick isolation for a drive and one more pass. Or you probably have time to make two quick passes before the last shot must be released to beat the buzzer.

- If the ball must be brought up full court in 8 seconds, your dynamic for getting the ball across half-court must change significantly.

- With 4 seconds left, a player might have time to take a dribble or two to get away from his defender, but if he does, there's probably no time left for an extra pass.

- When the clock is down to 2 seconds, the situation usually demands a "catch-and-shoot" type of player; the shooter should try to come off a screen to get free for a good look at the hoop on the inbounds catch.

- With one second or less left, the lob pass comes into play.

Once your team knows how to best use the time left on the clock, they'll know what they can and cannot do in any situation, and the clock becomes their friend and not their enemy.

ROLES AND PLAYERS

If you were writing up a recipe for success at game-winning shots, the ingredients might look something like this:

- One great individual scorer, either with size inside or athleticism outside, in order to create and make a tough shot.

- One terrific inbounds passer with great court vision, a keen sense of timing, and no fear.

Super three-point shooter Ray Allen fulfills his role perfectly by netting this game-winning jumper just before the buzzer.

- Two deadeye three-point shooters to spread the court.

- One great screener unafraid to put his body on a defender.

Mix these together, bake at high heat under the bright lights, and admire the result: a team that always hits the big shots when it counts.

FULL-COURT PLAY

On full-court plays, especially with no time-outs left, players must stay "on" the play and avoid getting creative unless they read a defensive mistake. The full-court play might be the most dramatic and difficult play when the clock's ticking because you need to bring the ball up from one side of the court to the other.

With 8 to 5 Seconds on the Clock

Here are the skills and roles of the players who should run the play and receive the ball for the final shot or drive to the basket with 8 to 5 seconds remaining on the clock:

- 5 and 4 are your screeners.
- 3 is your small forward with a good three-point shot.
- 2 is your player designated to catch the ball and shoot or drive to the basket.
- 1 is your ball handler.

1 pushes the ball hard on offense, 2 and 3 run on the wings near the sidelines, and 4 and 5 are the trailers but stay ahead of the ball. 2 makes a change of pace and direction, pops back, and catches the ball passed by 1 while 4 and 5 set a double screen (figure 13.1)

See figure 13.2. 2 drives around the corner of the double screen and looks to

- drive straight to the basket;
- pass to 3, if X3 helps;
- pass back to 4, who comes high off the double screen if X4 sinks into the three-second lane to help; or
- pass to 5, who has rolled to the basket after the double screen if X5 sinks into the three-second lane to help.

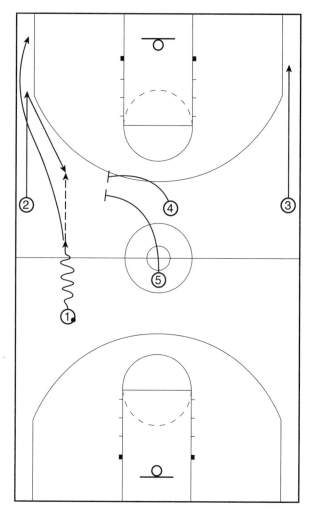

Figure 13.1   Full-court play with 8 to 5 seconds on the clock: 2 receives the ball; 4 and 5 double screen.

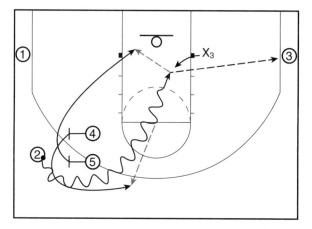

Figure 13.2   Full-court play with 8 to 5 seconds left on the clock: passing options for 2.

Half-Court Play

On special half-court last-second plays, your players need to be very quick in getting into proper position. If they fail to do so, the defense likely won't let them adapt and change their position; plus, they don't want to take the time.

With 7 to 5 Seconds on the Clock

Here are the skills and roles for players involved in running the play and receiving the ball for the final shot or drive to the basket with 7 to 5 seconds remaining on the clock:

- 5 and 4 are your screeners.
- 2 should be a great scorer.
- 1 should be a good shooter.

1 is the point guard, who brings the ball down the court; 5 is at the high post; 2 is at the low post on the left side of the three-second lane; 4 and 3 are in a stack on the right side.

3 cuts in the lane as if to go around a screen of 2, but 2 leaves early and cuts high after the down screen (also called "zipper") of 5. 1 passes to 2, while 3 goes to the corner and 4 goes to the elbow of the free-throw area (figure 13.3). 4 makes a back screen for 1, and 2 makes a skip pass to 1 (figure 13.4).

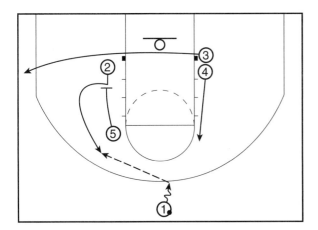

Figure 13.3 Half-court play with 7 to 5 seconds on the clock: first option for 2.

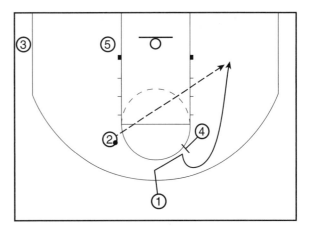

Figure 13.4 Half-court play with 7 to 5 seconds on the clock: second option for 1.

If 1 is not open, 2 plays pick-and-roll with 4 (figure 13.5). 2 can

- drive straight to the basket;
- make a jump shot;
- pass to 4, who has rolled to the basket or popped out, if he is a good three-point shooter;
- pass to 1 in the corner; or
- pass to 5, who has faked to come up and then cut to the basket.

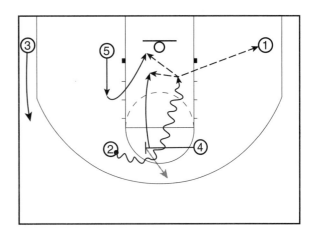

Figure 13.5 Half-court play with 7 to 5 seconds left on the clock: other passing options for 2.

SIDELINE INBOUNDS PLAYS

Players usually have a little more time to set up on the sideline inbounds play. The coach usually has a few seconds to call the play from the bench. But perfect execution, timing, and spacing are still vital to success.

With 8 to 1 Seconds on the Clock

Here are the skills and roles for players who run the play and receive the ball for the final shot or drive to the basket with 8 to 1 seconds remaining on the clock:

- 5 is your post player.
- 4 is your screener.
- 2 and 3 are designated to catch the ball and shoot on the run.
- 1 is the inbounder (or another 3, a small forward, can be the inbounder, who can make a tall pass if the defense puts a big man on the inbounds play).

3, 4, and 5 set a wall screen (vertical stack with three players) on the side of the ball; 2 is under the basket.

2 curls over the top of the screen, catches the ball, and shoots on the run (figure 13.6). 5 screens for 3, and 4 curls around 5 to screen again for 3 (stagger screen). If 2 is not open, 1, the inbounder, looks to give

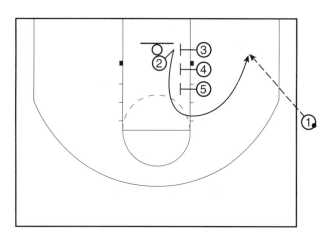

Figure 13.6 Sideline out-of-bounds play with 8 to 1 seconds on the clock—first option: the pass to 2.

the ball to 3 (figure 13.7). 5 keeps walking deep in the lane, and then opens to receive the ball right under the basket if 2 or 3 can't receive the ball (figure 13.8).

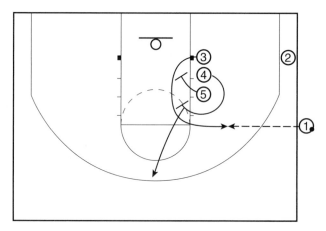

Figure 13.7 Sideline out-of-bounds play with 8 to 1 seconds on the clock—second option: the pass to 3.

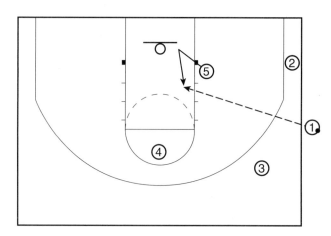

Figure 13.8 Sideline out-of-bounds play with 8 to 1 seconds on the clock—third option: the pass to 5.

With 5 to 3 Seconds on the Clock

Here are the skills and roles required of the players who run the play and receive the ball for the final shot or drive for a two-point basket with 5 to 3 seconds left on the clock:

- 2 and 3 are quality shooters.
- 4 is the inbounder and should also be a good shooter so that the defense must play up on him.
- 5 is the screener.

4 is the big inbounder, 5 is set up on the high post, and 3 is on the low post near the three-second lane; if 3 is covered by a tall defender, 1 and 2 set a horizontal stack on the ball side. 1 sprints over the top of 2 to the wing position, 2 sprints toward 3, and 5 goes to the low-post position, ready to set a screen (figure 13.9).

The defense often switches late in the game with defenders of the same size, so 2 breaks off 5's screen, leaving the defenders caught in between, and receives the ball from 4 (figure 13.10). If 2 is not open, 3 sprints to receive the pass from 4, and 4 sprints onto the court and plays pick-and-roll with 3, who comes off the screen for a quick shot (figure 13.11).

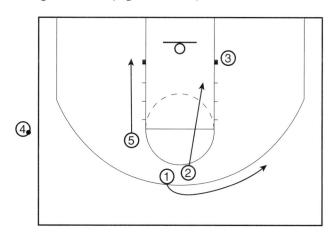

Figure 13.9 Sideline out-of-bounds play with 5 to 3 seconds on the clock: 1 sprints to the wing, 2 sprints toward 3, and 5 posts down low.

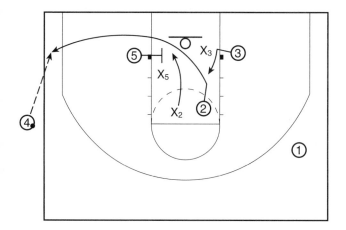

Figure 13.10 Sideline out-of-bounds play with 5 to 3 seconds on the clock: 5 screens for 2, who receives from 4.

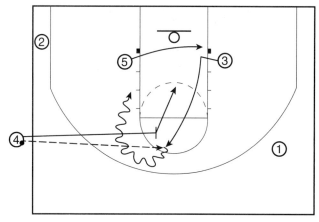

Figure 13.11 Sideline out-of-bounds play with 5 to 3 seconds left on the clock: 3 sprints outside, receives from 4, and plays pick-and-roll with him.

With 4 to 3 Seconds on the Clock

Here are the skills and roles required of the players who run the play and receive the ball for the final shot or drive for a two-point basket with 4 to 3 seconds left on the clock:

- 3 is an athletic player, able to catch and shoot on a lob pass.
- 5 is a good passer and shooter.
- 4 is the screener.
- 1 is a good passer.

3 is the inbounder; 4 is set up on the low corner near the baseline; 5 is at the high-post position at the corner of the free-throw lane; and 1 and 2 are near each other, facing 5.

1 slices off 5 to free him, and 3 passes the ball to 5. 4 comes up to flare-screen for 2, who runs wide and sets up in the low corner on the opposite side of the court (figure 13.12).

1 screens for 3, who runs onto the court, slashes to the hoop, and receives an over-the-top pass from 5. If 5 can't pass to 3, 1 curls around 5 and receives a quick dribble hand-off pass (figure 13.13). 1 looks for his own shot or can pass to 5, who, after the hand-off pass, has rolled to the basket opposite the drive of 1 (figure 13.14).

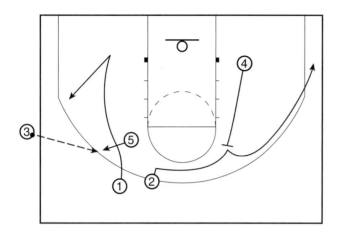

Figure 13.12 Sideline out-of-bounds play with 4 to 3 seconds on the clock: 1 cuts around 5, who flashes to the ball and receives from 3, while 4 screens for 2.

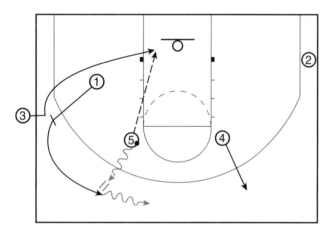

Figure 13.13 Sideline out-of-bounds play with 4 to 3 seconds on the clock: 5, after the screen of 1 for 3, can pass to 3 or make a hand-off pass to 1.

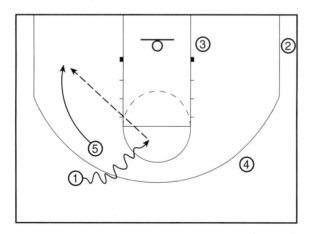

Figure 13.14 Sideline out-of-bounds play with 4 to 3 seconds on the clock: 1 can shoot, drive to the basket, or pass to 5.

With 3 Seconds on the Clock

Here are the skills and roles required of the players who run the play and receive the ball for the final shot or drive for a two-point basket with 3 seconds left on the clock:

- 4 and 5 are the screeners.
- 2 catches the ball and shoots.
- 3 is at the low-post position.

1 is the inbounder; 5 and 4 are at the corners of the free-throw area; and 2 and 3 form a vertical stack in the middle lane of the half-court. At the same time, 2 and 3 start to curl over 4, who takes a step out to screen. 2 stops right past 4 to screen 3's defender. 1 passes to 3 in the low post, while 5 takes a step toward 4 (figure 13.15). 4 and 5 run a stagger screen for 2, who comes back off the stagger screen. 1 passes to 2. If X5 helps out early on 2, 1 looks to pass to 5 on a roll to the basket (figure 13.16).

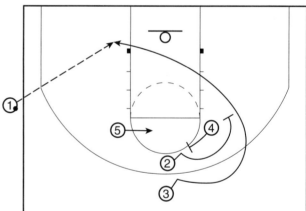

Figure 13.15 Sideline out-of-bounds play with 3 seconds on the clock: 2 and 3 curl around 4's screen, and 2 also screens for 3, who cuts and receives from 1.

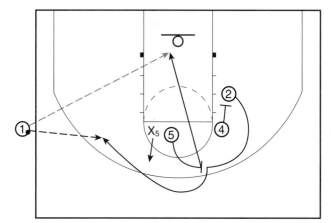

Figure 13.16   Sideline out-of-bounds play with 3 seconds on the clock: 2 comes off the stagger screen of 4 and 5 and receives from 1, who can also pass to 5 as he rolls to the basket.

With 3 to 1 Seconds on the Clock

Here are the skills and roles required of the players who run the play and receive the ball for the final shot or drive to the basket for a two-point or three-point basket with 3 to 1 seconds left on the clock:

- 2 is an athletic player.
- 3 is a solid passer with a three-point jump shot.
- 4 is a solid three-point shooter.

3 is the inbounder; 2 is set up on the low post on the ball side; 5 is on the high post at the corner of the free-throw lane on the ball side; 4 is in the middle of the central lane of the court; and 1 is at the low post on the opposite side of the ball. 1 cuts on the baseline around 2, and 3 has this first option to pass him the ball. Just before 1 gets to 2, 2 runs up, curls over 5, and goes to the basket to receive a lob pass from 3 (figure 13.17).

If 2 is covered, 4 comes to the ball, receives from 3, and then 3 runs onto the court for a hand-off pass and a quick shot or drive to the basket (figure 13.18). After the curl of 2 around 5, if X5 has helped on 2's cut, 5 dives to the low post. 3 passes to 1, and 1 passes to 5 (figure 13.19).

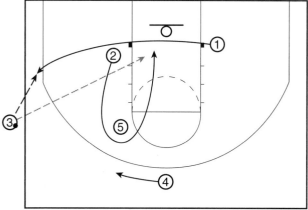

Figure 13.17   Sideline out-of-bounds play with 3 to 1 seconds on the clock: 3 can pass to 1 or to 2, who curls around 5.

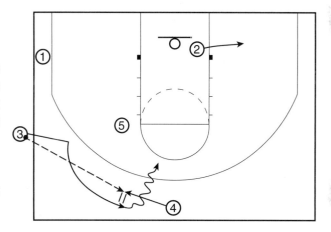

Figure 13.18   Sideline out-of-bounds play with 3 to 1 seconds on the clock: 3 can also pass to 4, receive the ball back from 4, and shoot or drive to the basket.

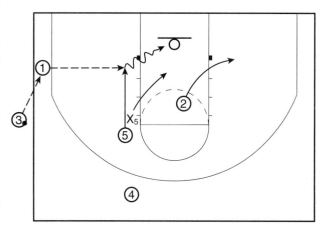

Figure 13.19   Sideline out-of-bounds play with 3 to 1 seconds left on the clock: 5 dives to the low post; 1 receives the ball and passes to 5.

With 2 Seconds on the Clock

Here are the skills and roles required of the players who run the play and receive the ball for the final shot or drive to the basket for a two-point or a three-point basket with 2 seconds left on the clock:

- 4 must be a solid passer, unafraid to throw the pass required on this play.
- 2 and 3 are good scorers.
- 5 is a solid screener.

4 is the inbounder; 1 is in the low-post position on the ball side; 3 is in the corner; 2 is outside the lane opposite the ball; and 5 is at the elbow of the free-throw lane opposite the ball. 2 and 3 can also be set up on opposite spots.

1 runs to the sideline on the corner; 2 and 5 turn and move toward 3, setting a stagger screen for him (figure 13.20). Just before 3 gets close to 2, 2 slips and cuts hard to the basket, and 4 makes a hard and crisp pass to 2. This play is based on perfect timing and can be successful because defenders X2 and X3 will usually try to switch their assigned offensive players, and 2 slips to the basket before the switch (figure 13.21).

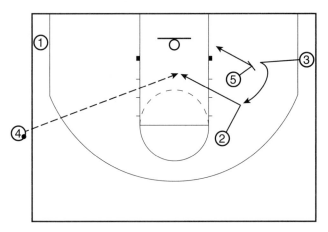

Figure 13.21 Sideline out-of-bounds play with 2 seconds left on the clock: Just before 3 gets close to 2, 2 slips to the basket to receive a pass from 4.

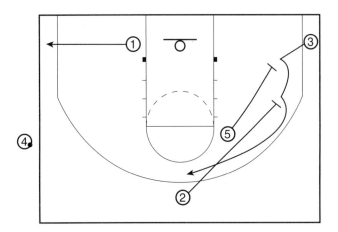

Figure 13.20 Sideline out-of-bounds play with 2 seconds on the clock: 2 and 5 make a couple of steps toward 3 for a stagger screen.

BASELINE OUT-OF-BOUNDS PLAYS

Because they're run with the ball near the basket, baseline out-of-bounds plays usually involve a lot of body contact. They require screeners to be tough and aggressive, though they must avoid pushing and shoving.

With the Need of a Three-Point Shot

For success in this play, the player who receives the ball for the three-point basket must be a good three-point shooter.

3 is the inbounder; 2 is set up at the free-throw area; and 4, 5, and 1 set a triple stack on the same side as the ball. 1 dives to the weak side, 4 curls over 5, and 5 follows 4 to set a stagger screen for 2 (figure 13.22). 2 brings his defender to the stagger screens of 4 and 5, and then goes to the corner to receive from 3. When 2 goes over 4, 4 turns and receives a screen (screen-the-screener action) from 5 (figure 13.23).

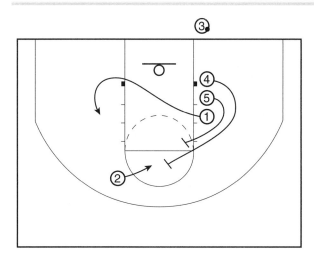

Figure 13.22   Baseline-out-of-bounds play for a three-point shot: 1 cuts to the weak side, 4 curls on 5, and they start to set a stagger screen for 2.

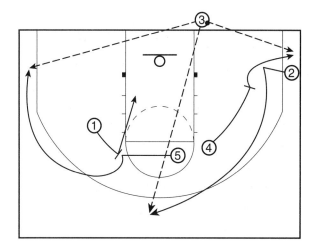

Figure 13.24   Baseline-out-of-bounds play for a three-point shot: 4 screens again for 2 and pops out; 1 screens for 5, who then pops out; and 3 has three passing options for a three-point shot.

After a Made Free Throw

As in every offensive action, spacing, the right angle of a cut, reading the defense, setting the screens, and crisp passes away from the defender are the keys for success of all these plays. But when we come to the last-second shot after a made free throw, two other factors come into play: blocking out for the defensive rebound and a very quick baseline out-of-bounds pass. Players need to run the whole court to get to the shot, which means they must be quick without being rushed.

With 5 to 6 Seconds on the Clock

Here are the skills and roles required of the players who run the play and receive the ball for the last-second shot after a free throw:

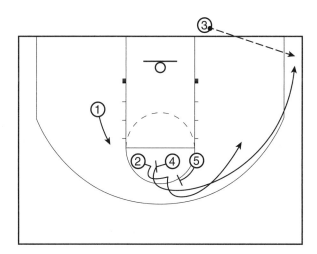

Figure 13.23   Baseline-out-of-bounds play for a three-point shot: 2 comes off the stagger screen; 4 turns and receives a screen from 5.

If 2 is not open, 4 continues his cut, screens for 2, and then pops out beyond the three-point line. 1 screens for 5, who also pops out beyond the three-point line. 1 then rolls to the basket after the back screen (figure 13.24). 3 can pass to 2, 4, or 5 for a three-point shot.

- 3 is a solid rebounder and makes the inbounds pass.
- 1 is the designated shooter or driver to the basket.
- 5 is a solid screener.

3, on the left block of the three-second lane, is the inbounder; 5 is already on the offensive half-court at the midpost position; 1 is in the right lane of the court outside the three-point line; 4 is on the block with 2, ready to go after the rebound.

2 blocks out the free-throw shooter and then sprints to the left side of the court, while 4 sprints to the midcourt. 1 sprints to the same side as 2, and then both of them sprint past each other to the right side of the court, with 2 going deep on the offensive half-court and 1 coming back off 4's screen. 3 passes to 1 on the run, and 1 dribbles fast to the basket (figure 13.25).

5 comes high to screen for 2. 1 passes to 2 early if he's open; if he's not, 1 receives a screen from 5, and then 5 rolls to the basket (figure 13.26). 1 can shoot, drive to the basket, pass to 2 on the drive, or pass to 5 on the roll.

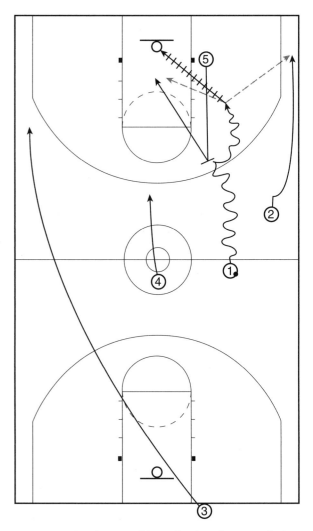

Figure 13.26 An out-of-bounds play after a made free throw: 5 sets a high pick for 1, who has several options.

FINAL POINTS

Sometimes luck seems to play a huge part in the success or failure of this type of shot. I've seen many situations in which a coach drew up a terrific play that got his best shooter open, but the shooter simply missed the shot. I've seen other games when the

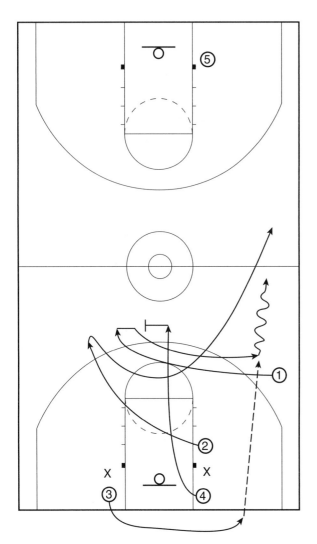

Figure 13.25 An out-of-bounds play after a made free throw: 2 and 1 sprint on the same side; 4 sprints and screens for 1, who receives from 3.

defense seemingly guarded the play perfectly, and the offensive player still managed to throw in an acrobatic no-look bank shot over two defenders for three points that closed out the game as the horn sounded.

Though it's nice to have luck on your side, last-second plays are usually success- ful because a coach has put a great deal of thought and preparation into what he wants to do in each situation. Through repetitions in practice, he imparts a confidence in his players that they can execute the play no matter what the defense does to try to stop them.

PART V

Individual and Team Defense

chapter 14

On-the-Ball Pressure

Mike Fratello

The phrase "defense wins champion-ships" applies to all levels, from high school through college to the pros. For our purposes in this chapter, defense means to aggressively attack an opponent's offense, harassing and disrupting its every move.

Playing defense requires being extremely active. It means generating pressure on the offense, *acting* rather than reacting, looking to force turnovers, trying to confuse the offense and keep them off balance, and not waiting for mistakes to occur but creating them through aggressive, disruptive pressure.

To establish a defensive foundation for his team, a coach must consistently preach, teach, and be firm on this basic aspect of basketball. Defense is not a play a coach invents during a time-out or as a desperation move—it is a *constant* practice after practice, game after game, and season after season.

RULES FOR BUILDING A DEFENSE

To build a defense, you want precise rules that are easy to understand. Establishing individual defensive rules strengthens the importance of defense. Here are my building blocks for a pressure defense:

• Force the dribbler to make as many turns as possible, blocking his complete view of the court and making him lose time. This disrupts the flow of the offense,

forces delays at the beginning of the play, and presents the defense chances to trap the ball handler.

• Don't give an easy path to the basket to the player with the ball; always stay between him and the basket. If the defensive player on the ball handler is beat, all other defenders must rotate to stop the drive, which can create easy shots for the opponents.

• Pressure the ball as long as it's in the hands of the offensive player; this means pressuring the dribble and also the pass. Pressuring the ball handler and contesting the pass means preventing the ball from getting inside the lane and taking away high-percentage shots.

• In general, force ball handlers to the sideline to block their view of the court and limit their passes to one direction. (Depending on the situation, you sometimes might want to force the ball handler to the middle.) If the defense keeps the ball on one side of the court, the ball handler stops or delays the quick reversal of the ball to the other side of the court. This is a great advantage because the reversal of the ball can create the problem of closeouts for the defenders on the weak side and rotation.

• Take away as many strengths of the opposing player as possible. Force the offensive player to shoot if he's a nonshooter, to dribble with his weak hand, or just to dribble if he's not a great ball handler. Basketball is a game of moves and countermoves; if you're clever enough to take away the most dangerous moves of your assigned offensive players, you've done half your job.

• Remember that a defender is responsible for one offensive player and a half: his own assigned offensive player and "half" of the player assigned to the teammate nearest him. Each defender must understand he's part of a defensive system, and his job is not only to stop his assigned offensive player but also to be part of a collective defense. The defender must always be ready to help, taking a charge whenever possible as well as blocking out and rotating as necessary.

FOUR FOUNDATIONS FOR BUILDING THE DEFENSIVE WALL

Playing defense is like building up a wall between the offense and the basket. To build the wall you start with four foundations:

mental skills, physical skills, technical skills, and communication.

Mental Skills

An offensive player must have skills such as passing, dribbling, and shooting. Playing defense is more a state of mind, but some individual and collective fundamentals are involved.

Any player—small or big, quick or slow—can play defense. He needs no particular physical assets but only these mental skills that any player can develop:

- Aggressiveness (but also control)
- Strong will to never give up
- Determination to give 100 percent
- Individual and collective pride and motivation
- A big heart
- Enthusiasm (which is contagious)

One big reason San Antonio has been the league's best team since 1999 is its emphasis on defense. Perennial All-Defensive Team selection Bruce Bowen typically draws the Spurs' opponent's offensive leader, whether he's 6-foot-11 or 6 foot tall.

Barry Gossage/NBAE/Getty Images Sport

- Court intelligence to help read and react to the offense
- The desire to help a teammate who's been beaten

As I've said, playing defense requires a total commitment from all players on the team. A coach must reach this goal by practicing all phases of defense: stance, foot movement, strong- and weak-side positioning, and rotations. Talk constantly, challenging and motivating your players to be the best they can be on defense. Set goals for each player as well as for the team. Goals give an exact vision of what you intend each player and the team to accomplish.

Individual Goals. Having all players, starters and reserves, keep a defensive goal in mind helps build both individual defensive pride and team pride. These are some of the defensive goals a coach can assign to a defender:

- Keep an assigned offensive player under his usual scoring average.
- Stop a great passer from recording his usual number of assists.
- Block out a great rebounder to reduce his offensive rebounds.

Team Goals. In addition to individual goals, also set team goals, which are important to motivate your team on defense. Here are some examples of team goals:

- Reduce the opponent's number of dribble penetrations.
- Reduce the number of assists.
- Take away as many passes inside the lane as possible.
- Minimize fast-break opportunities.

Talk about the importance of defense at the first team meeting and then throughout the season. Talk both to the team and to individuals, perhaps particularly to your point guards, who are your right-hand men on the court. Also meet with team captains, who tend to have a positive influence on the team.

When you correct players in practice, be positive. Tell them what to do right, not what they're doing wrong. Be sure to praise players when they perform techniques correctly.

Physical Skills

It's true that playing defense is a state of mind. It's also true that superb physical conditioning can enhance mental skills. When a player is on the defensive end of the court, he needs strength, stamina, and power to deal effectively with talented offensive players. This conditioning helps defensive players to sprint and recover in defensive transition, to pay the toll necessary in fighting through screens, to cope with all the bumping that occurs in the lane, to take charges and dive on the floor for loose balls, to rotate to help a teammate, and to block out a big, tough player. Without proper conditioning, the defender loses his mental toughness and is much easier to beat.

To attain superb physical conditioning, players must work on several areas, including

- flexibility, to improve performance and prevent injuries;
- core strength, to improve muscle balance, muscle movement, efficiency, and durability;
- agility, to be able to perform such demanding moves as changing direction and pace, repeated jumping, sprinting, cutting at various angles, and sliding while moving side to side and backward and forward; and
- speed, to be able to beat offensive players to spots and for recovering from rotations back or close up to their own men.

Preparing players for the tough demands of a long basketball season is the job of the strength and conditioning coach, an essential member of the coaching staff at any level of the game. This coach must work on individual programs appropriate to the physical and body characteristics of each player.

Technical Skills

Whenever you are building something, you need to start with a foundation, laying the first brick on the ground. On defense, the first brick is the coverage of the player on the ball, usually made by your point guard, the first line of your team's defense.

If you watch players like Chauncey Billups or Tony Parker, you see perfect examples of how to pressure the offensive player with the ball. The primary technical skills for pressuring individually on the ball are the defensive stance, step-and-slide moves, the close out, and stealing the ball.

Chauncey Billups knows that good defense starts with a balanced stance that allows him to move quickly in any direction.

Defensive Stance

Just as an offensive player must assume a correct basic triple-threat position as soon as he receives the ball, the defender must start in a proper defensive stance. Balance is key on all offensive moves with or without the ball, and the same is true on defense. Let's examine the details.

Foot Position. To establish a good base, place one foot forward and the other back, about shoulder-width apart. From here, you can quickly slide side to side or back and forth and can move either foot forward or back. Feet should be no more than shoulder-width apart to prevent loss of quickness. The lead foot is ahead of the back foot, and the toes of the back foot are aligned with the ball of the lead foot.

This foot positioning allows good balance, both laterally and back and forth. Which foot should be forward? It depends on the defensive philosophy of the coach. If a coach wants to funnel the dribbler to the middle of the floor, the defender keeps the foot nearest the sideline forward; if he wants to push the dribbler to the baseline, the defender keeps the foot farthest from the sideline forward (figure 14.1).

There's often debate over where to place body weight. Many coaches say body weight should be on the balls of the feet; others dis-

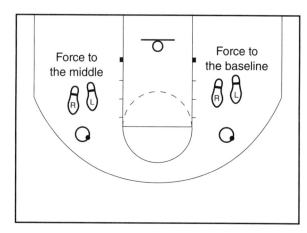

Figure 14.1 Foot position to funnel the dribbler to the middle of the floor or to push him to the baseline.

agree. In my view, players should do what's most comfortable. Whether they put their weight on the balls of their feet or keep their feet planted, it's all the same to me. All I ask is that their positioning doesn't hinder their defensive sliding ability or quickness.

The key is how quickly players can move their feet. They must move with what I call a "step and slide" technique, which involves moving in a sequence of steps and slides—not bringing the feet together or crossing them. If they bring together or cross their feet, balance and quickness are affected, as is the ability to change direction quickly. They must lead with the foot closest to the direction of the dribbler. Here's the pattern: right dribble, left foot lead step, right foot slide; left dribble, right foot lead step, left foot slide.

Leg Position. Bent knees make for quicker defenders. The knees should be bent as far as comfort allows. In most cases, we like our players to appear as if they're trying to sit on a chair.

Trunk Position. The trunk should be slightly bent forward, but not too much. The primary bend should be at the knees, not the trunk. Too much bend at the trunk causes a loss of balance.

Hand Position. The role of the hands in the defensive stance is crucial. I teach defenders to raise the hand on the same side as the forward foot. The hand corresponding to the back foot (the back hand) is placed on the side to take away the passing lanes. This hand is constantly tracing the ball, trying to get a piece of it. The defender stays half a man away from the ball, with his nose on the ball.

Once the ball has been picked up and the offensive player can't dribble anymore, the defender swings up the back hand and mirrors the ball, tracing the ball's movements with hands crossed at the wrists, chesting up to the offensive player and aggressively pressuring him, trying to deflect the ball, taking away the passing lanes, and restricting the view of the offensive player by forcing him to turn his shoulders away from where he wants to pass.

Chest Position. This is an important point. I tell players that when pressuring the opponent with the ball, they must always have their chest in front of them. When they're in the middle of the court, on the wing, or in the deep corner, they should be in a direct line between the offensive player and the basket, with the chest always fronting the offensive player (figure 14.2).

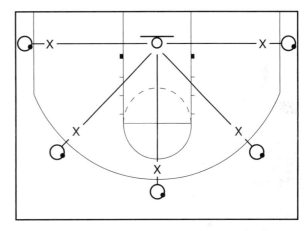

Figure 14.2   The chest of the defender on the ball must always be in a direct line between the offensive player and the basket.

When pressuring the ball, never assume a fencer or boxer stance. Athletes in these sports turn sideways, reducing exposure of the target to the opponent to avoid being hit. If a defender turns too much, he offers the ball handler a straight-line drive to the basket—a drive we want to avoid because it disrupts the entire defense.

Step-and-Slide Moves

As mentioned, when pressuring an offensive player dribbling upcourt, the defensive player moves with alternating steps and slides. The initial step-and-slide technique must take into account the speed and quickness of the offensive player as well as that of the defensive player. The quicker the defender is than the offensive player, the closer he can get up on the ball initially. The slower the defender, the farther away he needs to start.

Side to Side. This technique is used when the defender is quicker than the offensive player or the defender is trying to impede all progress of the ball, taking away all angles to the ball handler. It is the basic step-and-slide technique described earlier. Lead with the foot closest to the direction of the dribbler, keeping feet spread apart and moving them as quickly as possible. Try to anticipate which direction the ball handler is trying to take; then beat him to the spot and take it away, forcing the ball to change direction and repeating the process in the other direction.

Retreat Step Slide. This technique is used when the defender encounters a quick and clever ball handler or when the coach wants to force the offense to take time off the clock under pressure. The retreat step helps keep the ball in front of a slower defender. The defender takes his first step slide movements in retreat, giving ground and letting the ball come to him. This technique ensures that the ball remains in front of the defender and is not designed to force a change in direction of the ball.

Drop Step. Use the drop step in a step and slide to change directions quickly. As the defender is stepping with his left foot and sliding with his right foot, he cuts off the direction of the ball and forces it to change direction.

On the drop step, plant the outside foot and push off and change direction with the ball. Drop the inside foot and open up to avoid contact with the offensive player, retreating until you can get in front of the ball and gain control again.

Crossover Step. When executing the step-and-slide technique and losing ground to the offensive player, stay low and execute a crossover step to turn and then run to catch up with the ball. Sometimes you might need to take two or three running, or crossover,

steps to catch up to the ball. Once back in front of the ball, revert to the step-and-slide technique.

Closing Out

One of the most important techniques in pressuring the ball is the closeout, which is used in simple help-and-recover situations, when rotating out of double teams on the post, when rotating out of traps in pick-and-rolls, after offensive rebounds, or when chasing loose balls. All these situations require a defender to close out on his man.

The closeout technique is about quickness, balance, and control. When closing out, you must recover quickly and get close enough to take away initial shots while also preventing drives to the basket. You must move quickly, maintain control, and stay low. You want to be able to challenge a three-point shot while also being prepared for a drive to the basket. As you get close to the offensive player, run in short, choppy steps so that you're ready for a quick drive to the basket and can maintain balance when challenging a shot. If you're standing upright or are off balance, you'll tend to lunge at the shooter, who will fake and drive easily to the basket.

Stealing the Ball

Pressuring the ball means trying to create turnovers and force the offense into mistakes. It also means trying to steal the ball.

There's no special technique to teach here because some players have the instincts to know when to go for the steal and some don't. Ball steals are based on timing and gambling, but keep the gambling to a minimum. If you go for the steal and miss, the dribbler gets inside the defensive gut and puts the defense at a disadvantage. A missed steal can force defensive rotations and cause mismatches, such as guards defending and blocking out big men, and big men getting into foul trouble because they're guarding smaller players—all serious problems for the defense.

Communication

Communication among defenders is extremely important. We created a defensive terminology that we use all the time, both in practice and games. Consistent terminology helps defenders move in a synchronized way; it alerts teammates that a screen is coming, where help is needed on the court, and how to play the pick-and-roll.

Here are some examples of the terminology we use:

- When we want to double team the ball handler on a pick-and-roll, we say "Blitz!"

- When we want to change defensive assignments as offensive players cross, we say "Switch!"

- When a defender gets over, under, or through a screen, we say "Over," "Under," or "Through!"

- In pick-and-roll situations, when the defensive player guarding the screener can't stay attached to his man (usually in quick-hitting screens in transition) or when one offensive player sets a screen across, before that player goes and sets the screen, we say "Track!"

I want to add a quick note about tracking. The rule is that when a defender can't stay attached to his man, he'll take a defensive stance with chest facing the half-court, feet sliding sideline to sideline, trying to keep the ball in front of him until the original ball defender can recover. He doesn't trap or show but just tries to contain the ball. Tracking is a passive technique. It prevents quick splits by guards coming off the pick-and-roll.

TIPS ON SPECIAL INDIVIDUAL DEFENSE

Mainly in the NBA, but also at the high school or college levels, teams often face the problem of how to defend in special situations, such as against a great penetrator, a great shooter, or a player with a signature move. When trying to defend a player with special offensive skills, there's always a trade-off. You need to determine how the player can hurt you most. If he's dangerous in several areas, don't expect to shut him down completely, but try to minimize his options so that he can't beat you by himself.

Let's looks at some guidelines for defending players with unusually strong offensive skills.

A Great Penetrator

When defending a great penetrator, you want to give yourself enough space without giving him too much space. There might be a very thin line between too much space and not quite enough, but you want to find that line. If the penetrator also has a good pull-up jump shot, you'll want to play him a little closer but not so close that he can get by you. Most coaches choose to give up the perimeter shot rather than the penetration because penetration hurts the interior of the defense, creates foul trouble, and allows wide-open shots to be created when defenders help on the penetration.

A Great Shooter

You defend a great shooter by relentlessly dogging him to restrict his opportunities to touch the ball. You always want to be close enough to touch him when he catches the ball, before he has a chance to put up a shot.

Once the shooter catches the ball, don't go for ball fakes; crowd him and force him to put the ball on the floor. Don't let him get a good look at the basket. If he goes up for a shot, get an extended hand to the ball to challenge the shot. If you're smaller than the shooter or if you have quick hands, try to strip the ball from his hands before he can get the ball into shooting position. Always force him to shoot with his weaker hand and from the direction he least prefers.

A Player With a Signature Move

Great players like Kobe Bryant, Tracy McGrady, Kevin Garnett, LeBron James, and Dwyane Wade have signature moves that make them dangerous on offense. When possible, watch film of such players to understand their tendencies. Study pre-game scouting reports to develop a defensive strategy. A player might be weaker from one side than the other. You must learn his signature move and try to take it away from him as often as you can. If you take it away, he might find another way to score, but don't get discouraged. Continue to focus on his most dangerous move. Team defense plays a big part in this. No single defender can guard these great players.

DRILLS FOR PRESSURING THE BALL

To pressure the ball, a player must have the desire and will to stop his offensive player, but he must also possess the proper defensive skills and techniques. These are only some of the many drills that can help to build a pressuring defense on the ball.

Zigzag

We use all four corners of the court for this drill. Big men play with big men, and the small with the small. You can run the drill on each half of the court or on the full court, depending on how many players are involved. The drill has four parts.

1. Players line up on the baseline at the right corner. Player 1 jumps onto the court facing the baseline, his back to the court and his hands together behind his back. He steps and slides, stepping with the left foot and sliding with the right foot, along the baseline from the right corner to the left corner. He then places his left foot at the intersection of the baseline with the sideline, drop-steps his right foot, changes direction, and then steps

and slides with his right foot stepping and left foot sliding. When he reaches the free-throw line extended, he plants his right foot, drop-steps with his left foot, pushes with his right foot, and steps and slides with his left foot. He now steps and slides to the other free-throw line extension, drop-steps again, and then steps and slides until he reaches the intersection of the sideline and baseline. He then steps and slides along the entire baseline and repeats the same moves as he returns to the starting point on the other side of the court (figure 14.3). Once player 1 has reached the midpoint of the baseline, player 2 enters the court to begin the drill.

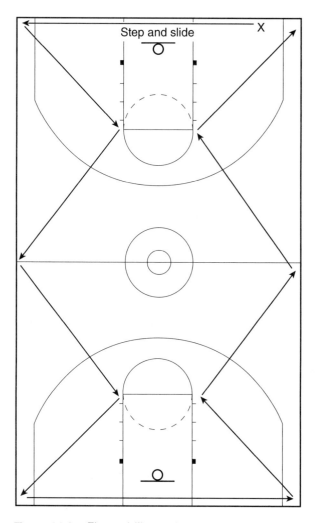

Figure 14.3 Zigzag drill: part 1.

2. Players line up outside the baseline in one corner. This part of the drill starts with two players, one on offense, with the ball, and one on defense. The offensive player dribbles hard to the lane while the defensive player steps and slides to cut the dribbler off. The offensive player reverses the dribble and dribbles hard to the sideline, while the defensive player steps and slides to cut off the sideline. The offensive player continually dribbles to the lane and to the sideline while the defensive player continually slides and steps and cuts the dribbler off from the lane and from the baseline (figure 14.4).

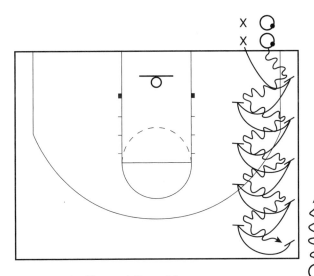

Figure 14.4   Zigzag drill: part 2.

This part of the drill ends at the half-court, where the two players exchange roles. They then return to the baseline in the same way as described.

3. The start is the same as the second part of the drill, but now the dribbler takes two hard dribbles and picks the ball up. The defensive player raises his hands, with wrists crossed, to jam and mirror the ball to prevent the pass.

The dribbler picks up the ball three or four times, and each time the defensive player jams the ball. The two players then exchange roles.

4. The offensive player now plays normally, trying to beat the defensive player to half-court, while the defensive player steps and slides and cuts the dribbler off as in a game situation. At the half-court line the two players exchange roles.

Five-Second Drill

Players are paired, with defenders inside the court and offensive players outside the court. We run this play on the half-court, using the two half-court sidelines, the baseline, and the half-court line (but you can use any line on the court).

The defender with the ball passes to the offensive player, who makes two hard dribbles, picks up the ball, and raises it over his head. The defender steps and slides to guard the two dribbles and, when the offensive player picks up the ball, jams the ball with the same technique as described in the previous drill (figure 14.5).

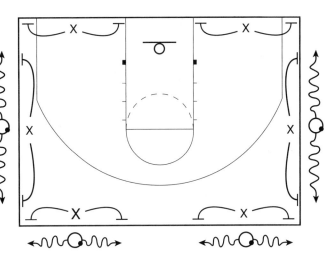

Figure 14.5   Five-second drill: the defender steps and slides and then jams the ball.

The ball handler dribbles back and forth from where he started the drill, and then the two exchange roles. This is a very short but intense drill; we emphasize the technique of jamming the dribbler.

One-on-One

Six players line up on the baseline; the coach has the ball on the wing. At the call of the coach, the six players run onto the court. The first player is on offense, the second on defense, and so on; the three pairs set up on the two wings and in the middle of the court.

The coach passes the ball to one of the offensive players, who can go to the basket with only two dribbles or pass the ball to one of the teammates (figure 14.6). The drill ends only with a score or if the defense recovers the ball. If the offense makes more than two dribbles, the ball goes to the defense, and the defense goes on offense.

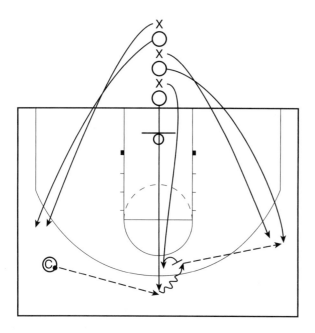

Figure 14.6 One-on-one drill.

Closeout

A coach has the ball in the middle of the court. Two offensive players are set up at the wing positions, and a defender is in the middle of the three-second lane. The coach passes the ball to one of the offensive players, who drives to the baseline. The defender closes out, slides, and cuts off the path to the baseline, hitting the dribbler with his chest (not pushing him with his hands). At

this time, the offensive player passes the ball back to the coach, who reverses the ball to the other offensive player, who drives to the baseline. The defender must recover, close out, and cut off the path to the baseline, while the offensive player can only drive, not shoot (figure 14.7).

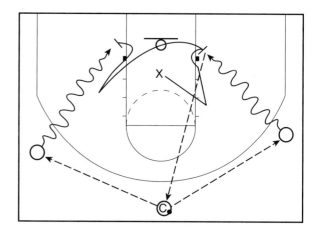

Figure 14.7 Closeout drill.

Two-on-Two Help-and-Recover

The ball is in the wing area or at the top of the lane in the hands of 1, while 2 is on the opposite wing. X1 covers 1; X2 helps and recovers on the baseline. 1 drives to the baseline or into the lane. As soon as 1 drives, 2 slides to the corner to receive the pass. X1 and X2 must communicate and not let the ball go to the baseline (figure 14.8).

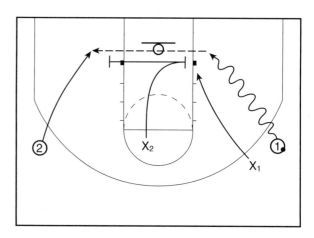

Figure 14.8 Two-on-two help-and-recover drill.

Three-on-Three Help-and-Recover

The drill starts with offensive players 1, 2, and 3 on both wings and at the top of the key. The ball can start at any position on the court—top of the key or either wing (in the figure, the ball starts on the right wing). X1 guards 1 and forces him to drive to the baseline. X3 rotates off 3 and cuts off 1's baseline drive. X2 rotates off 2 and picks up 3 on the baseline. X1 rotates off the baseline back to 2 at the top of the key (figure 14.9). The play is live and doesn't end until the ball is secured by the defense or the offense scores a basket.

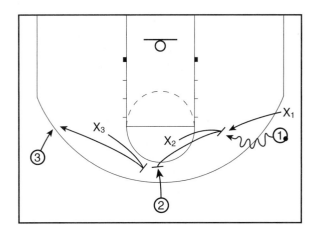

Figure 14.10   Help-and-recover drill.

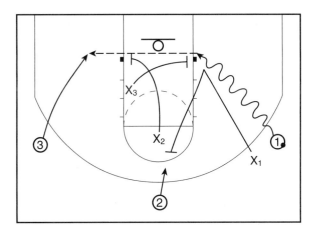

Figure 14.9   Three-on-three help-and-recover drill.

Out of the same set, the ball can be forced to the middle of the court to work on the help-and-recover and full rotation. The help-and-recover happens when the closest defensive player to the ball stunts to help take away middle penetration and recovers to his own offensive player. That is, X2 steps in to help stop the penetration by 1 and recovers to 2; X1 stays with 1; X3 is in a position to help X2 on 2's penetration and then recovers to 3 (figure 14.10).

The full rotation occurs when the next closest defender rotates off his offensive man and traps the ball on penetration. The next defensive player then rotates to cover for that defensive player by picking up his open man (that is, 1 penetrates to the middle

of the court, X2 traps the ball, X3 rotates to 2, and X1 rotates to 3) (figure 14.11).

These drills are designed to help with communication and quick reaction in help-and-recover and full-rotation situations. At the end of the drill, the offense goes off and the defense goes to offense. A new defense comes on the court. (Always send the next three players in on defense, not offense.) You can make the drill competitive by keeping score.

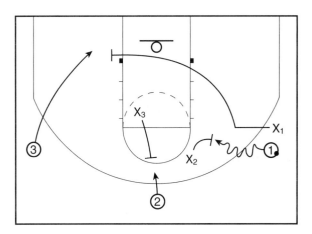

Figure 14.11   Help-and-recover drill: full rotation.

FINAL POINTS

As coach, you can decide to play any type of defense you choose—half-court or full-court man-to-man, zone, or matchup—based on the rules at your level of play and your philosophy of the game. But no matter what defense you play, if you want to be aggressive, the most important step is to pressure the offensive player with the ball. If the ball is easily passed around the perimeter, gets easily inside to the low-post area, or is quickly reversed, your defense won't be at all effective. Pressuring the ball is the key to any type of defensive set and is by far the most important aspect of this phase of the game.

chapter 15

Full-Court Pressure

Jim O'Brien

The full-court press can be a terrific weapon at any level of basketball. There have been some great teams that have used the press impressively. Some teams use it every once in a while, and others have total commitment to an all-game harassing style of play. Many coaches are somewhere in the middle, using the press off and on during a game to suit their purpose or the game's situation. With experience, coaches who put on the press and take it off at different times of the game are able to dictate the tempo they feel is advantageous to their team.

A total commitment to pressuring all game is certainly not for every coach, but those who embrace this style of play are no fun to play against because they never give their opponents a moment's rest. Most players love to play this aggressive style of defense, and fans really enjoy watching pressure basketball.

I was introduced to pressure basketball at a young age in Philadelphia at Roman Catholic under Speedy Morris. Jack Ramsay had a strong influence on my approach to defense, too, with his full-court 1-2-1-1 zone press, which dramatically impacted how basketball was played in the East during the 1960s and '70s. His book, *Pressure Basketball,* remains one of the finest books on defense ever written. As an assistant coach at the University of Oregon for five years, I had the chance to observe Ralph Miller of Oregon State University. Ralph's teams used pressure all over the court and often ranked among the top defensive squads in the country.

When I joined the New York Knicks and Rick Pitino in 1986, I observed a coach who brought full-court pressure to another level, making the Knicks a contender with a very aggressive brand of pressure basketball. A decade later, when Rick asked me to be on his staff at the University of Kentucky, I witnessed the best pressing team I have ever watched. The 1996 Kentucky team pressed the entire game, held opponents under 40 percent shooting from the floor, and won the national championship.

The potential effectiveness of an attacking defensive style has only been confirmed in all my head coaching jobs at Wheeling Jesuit University in West Virginia and Dayton University, and with the Boston Celtics, Philadelphia 76ers, and Indiana Pacers. And it is with those experiences and evidence in mind that I present the following information on full-court defense.

MATCHUP PRESS

The matchup press starts with a zone concept and quickly switches to man-to-man when the ball is thrown inbounds. This press seeks to force a high tempo and concede no passes except for those that take a team backward. This defense attempts to pressure the ball handler into an uncontrolled speed dribble and then to trap him.

Doug Pensinger/Staff/Getty Images Sport

Very successful applications of high-pressure, full-court defense throughout my career, including a stint at Kentucky in which our press was the key to winning a national title, have made me a believer.

The full-court matchup press works best when a coach is fully committed to it and practices it hard every day. The best way to begin is for everyone to understand that your team must be extremely well conditioned. Your conditioning must be a weapon in itself. In most cases you don't enter a season with the most talent in your conference or league. If you're at the high school or college level, once the season starts you have the players that you'll have all season,

and you must work with what you've got. At this point you can only do so much. You can work with your players to improve their individual skills and drill your team to execute your plan, but your talent to a large extent is set. However, one thing you can do with any team, no matter its talent level, is ensure you have the best-conditioned players on the floor on any given night.

Ask your players if they think they can become the best-conditioned team in your conference. Of course they'll say yes. Everyone wants the best chance of success for the team. Now it's imperative that you drive them to meet this objective. When they tire and want to stop, remind them that they set the goal—you're just helping them get there. There's no better confidence booster than to know every time you set foot on the court that you're better conditioned than your opponent.

BLACK AND WHITE PRESSES

For each of these styles of press, I'll explain the entire press first and then break it down into segments later in the chapter. This is the same way we teach the press from day one. You'll note that the difference between the black press and the white press is small—the white press pressures the inbounder, whereas the black press does not.

White Press

There are many ways to adjust the white press, but for now I want to explain the all-out full-blown press that denies the inbounds pass and looks to force a high tempo (figure 15.1).

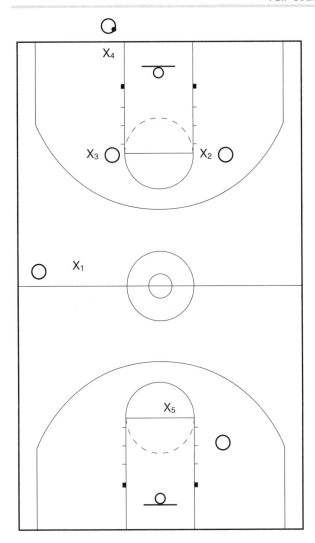

Figure 15.1   The white press pressures the inbounder.

On the inbounds play, I like to put

- our most mobile big man at the front of the press (X4);
- our most athletic wing man on the left side (X3);
- our other wing on the right side (X2);
- our point guard near the half-court line (X1); and
- our other big man back (X5).

Note that these spots are just areas of the court where your defenders will generally find someone to match up against immediately after you score. The alignment of your players is ultimately determined by the opponent's press offense. Each of your

players is matched to a player in his area and does not concede the inbounds pass.

The defender on the ball, X4, must be directly in front of the inbounder and seek to deflect the inbounds pass. If the inbounder runs the baseline, X4 shadows him until the pass is made. We prefer him to have his feet almost on the line—to the point the referee might warn him he's too close to the inbounder.

The wings, X3 and X2, are shoulder to shoulder with the players they're guarding. They must maintain vision of the inbounder and play their offensive player in much the same way a defensive back guards a receiver in football, staying squared to the quarterback and reading the passer's intent.

X3 in particular reads where his player is lining up in the press offense. If the offensive player—usually the point guard—is directly in front of the passer, X3 wants to stay on the side closest to the left sideline.

X2 lines up next to his man and is generally on the offensive man's left shoulder. If the offensive player is further away, X2 can allow some space until the inbounder turns to look at X2's player, and then X2 must close the gap.

No defensive player wants to allow the ball to enter the court in his area. All defenders position themselves in order to see both the passer and the player they're guarding.

X1 picks up the player closest to half-court on ball side; X5 picks up the remaining opponent, wherever he might be.

Black Press

As mentioned, the difference between the white press and the black press is how players begin the press on the inbounds play. In the black press, instead of pressuring the inbounder, X4 is off the ball and behind the front line of the press (behind X2 and X3). His job is to support X3 and X2 and make it more difficult for the opponent to inbound the ball. In many cases, X3 will be picking up the opponent's point guard, 1, on the left side, and X4 will be shading this area (figure

15.2). As in the white press, if the inbounder runs the baseline, X4 goes with him to the other side to make it difficult for the passer to inbound the ball (figure 15.3).

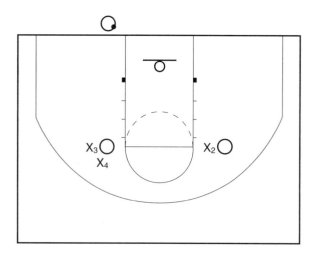

Figure 15.2 The black press puts no pressure on the inbounder; X4 stays behind the defensive front line.

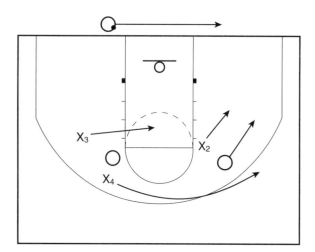

Figure 15.3 If the inbounds passer runs the baseline, X4 goes with him to the other side.

Using Both Presses

Generally speaking, we use the white press when we score a basket inside the paint. We use the black press when we make a perimeter shot. We've found that this method confuses teams, at least at first. We also generally use the black press on dead-ball

situations, when the opponent has the ball on the baseline with a chance to set up its offense while the referee handles the ball. We believe we're more vulnerable to the deep pass in these situations.

Denying the Inbounds Pass

All players play with their hands no lower than their shoulders. We believe the best position of the hands and arms is elbows bent and close to the body like a boxer, with hands close to the shoulders and thumbs pointing at the shoulders. This positioning allows for quickest movement of the hands in deflecting the ball. Again, we don't want any pass conceded; the man guarding the ball always believes he can deflect the next pass. The player guarding the receiver of the pass also believes he can intercept or deflect every pass.

If any two offensive players come together prior to the inbounds pass and cross one another, their defenders automatically switch (figure 15.4). If the offensive player guarded by X3 (or X2) leaves his area and goes beyond the top of the key extended, he is released, and X3 (or X2) moves to the middle and searches for a new player coming into the area (figure 15.5).

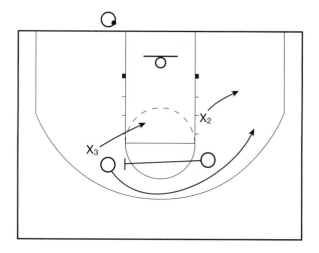

Figure 15.4 When two offensive players come together prior to the inbounds pass and cross one another, their defenders switch automatically.

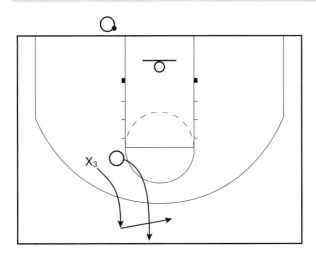

Figure 15.5 When an offensive player leaves X3's (or X2's) defensive area and goes beyond the top of the key, X3 (or X2) runs to the middle to find a new player entering the area.

Matching Up on the Inbounds Pass

Once the ball is thrown inbounds, all defenders immediately match up with the offensive man closest to them. The only exception is in the white press when the ball is passed into the "coffin" corner—the corner near the baseline. If this happens, X4 immediately traps the ball handler (figure 15.6).

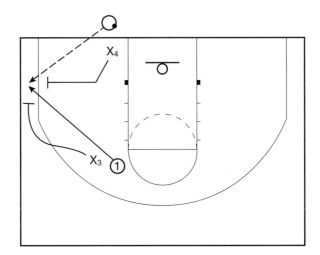

Figure 15.6 If the ball is passed into the corner near the baseline, X4 immediately traps the ball handler.

In the white press, if the ball is passed to any area other than the coffin corner, X4 drops below the ball line (figure 15.7), which is the imaginary line drawn through the ball

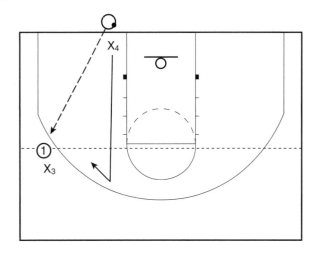

Figure 15.7 If the ball is passed into any area other than the coffin corner, X4 drops below the ball line.

from sideline to sideline. In the black press X4 is in this position anyway. In either case, X4 matches up with the player who has thrown the ball inbounds.

Because nearly every press offense looks to attack the pressure defense with a pass to the middle, it's important for the defense to take any middle pass away behind the front line (figure 15.8). As the ball is in the air on the inbounds pass, all weak-side defenders move to the middle of the court to prevent the lethal middle pass.

Notice that although X2 has sprinted to the middle, he's still responsible for 2, who

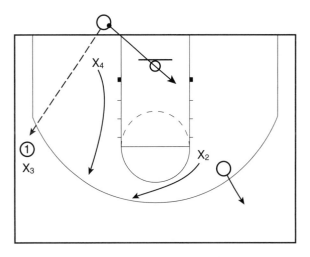

Figure 15.8 On both types of press, X4 matches up with the player who has inbounded the ball, preventing a pass to the middle of the floor.

is his matchup. A general rule is this: If the second pass is allowed to be completed to the middle of the court behind the front line, the press is off and the defense retreats into its half-court defense. For any pass thrown backward, the press remains on. The press is happy to allow any pass that takes the offense backward.

Ball Pressure

Once the ball is passed, the player with the ball is pressured hard. Any advance

pass must be denied, and the ball handler must be pressured to dribble the ball. This pressure on the ball is the key to the press. Whoever is guarding the ball must make it uncomfortable for the offensive player. The goal is to force the player with the ball into a speed dribble in which he's likely to lose control. This can happen only with extreme pressure on the ball and denial of all passes up the court. Later we'll look at drills that work on pressuring the ball.

The defender on the ball does not force the dribbler to the sideline. Forcing the ball handler up the sideline reduces the type of pressure we want to exert. We don't want to influence the ball—we want to pressure the ball! Ball pressure should force the dribbler into a fast tempo without allowing him to blow by you.

Trapping the Speed Dribble

Once the ball handler is pressured into the speed dribble, he's trapped by the closest defender in the direction of the dribble (figure 15.9).

The player trapping the ball wants to trap the ball handler in a controlled manner, similar to a defender closing out on an offensive player in the half-court. The defender guarding the ball wants to be as close to the ball handler as possible as the ball enters the trap area. In figure 15.9, X3 and X1 trap the ball.

As you teach this press, make your team understand the difference between a controlled dribble and a speed dribble. The more your pressure has forced the ball handler into an uncontrolled dribble, the better chance you have of turning

Gary Dineen/NBAE/Getty Images Sport

Effective traps are essential in any pressure defense. Here the two defenders have caused the point guard to turn completely away from his basket and teammates, disrupting the offense and perhaps setting the stage for a turnover.

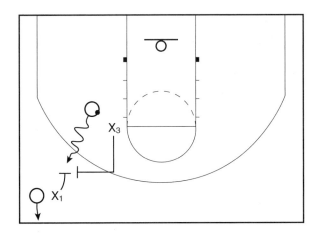

Figure 15.9 If the ball handler speed dribbles, he's trapped by the closest defender in the direction of the dribble.

him over. You don't want to trap a player who's under control and can easily change direction or pass the ball. In your drill work, teach your players that the speed dribble triggers the trap.

Rotations on the Trap

Coaches teaching the press for the first time sometimes focus too much on rotations. We've always thought that rotations after a trap are mostly instinctive and evident to players. Overburdening players with strict rules of rotation hinders their ability to react quickly.

In figure 15.10, X3 and X1 have trapped the ball. Who rotates to 2, whom X1 has left to trap the ball?

Either X2 or X5 could rotate to 2. We want to teach aggressiveness and let our players react. Whoever rotates wants to be thinking of a steal.

If X5 rotates up to 2, X2 protects back. If X2 rotates to 2, X5 stays in the basket area. In either case, the key defender is X4, who has middle responsibility to take away the pass to the gut. X5 has rotated up, X2 is protecting back, and X4 has middle responsibility (figure 15.11). The only pass undenied is the pass backward. Note that all defenders are staying below the ball line.

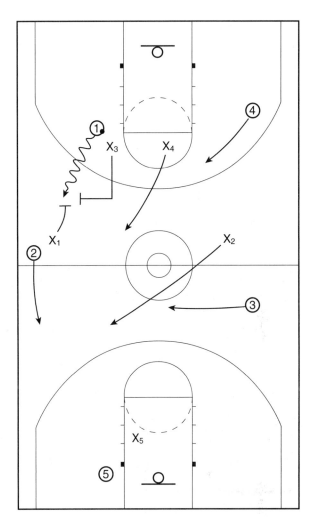

Figure 15.10 Rotation on the trap.

Alternatives to the Trap

Trapping good teams is difficult. In such cases, instead of trapping, try to turn your opponents over by forcing them into an out-of-control tempo. Teach your team to pressure the ball to force opponents to speed up the dribble. This is best done via one-on-one defensive drills, without fouling but ensuring the ball can't be advanced upcourt on a pass.

Ball handlers at times will beat your defenders and blow by them on the dribble. You don't want this to happen, but you can turn this situation to a possible advantage by training your players to sprint after the dribbler and try to tip the ball from behind

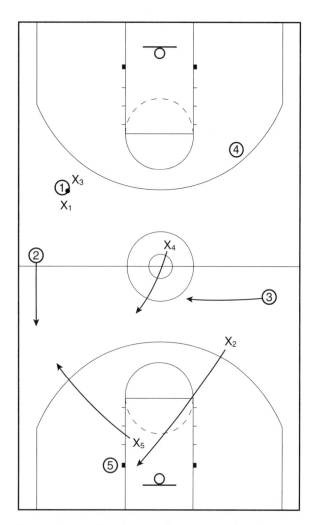

Figure 15.11 Rotations on the press—either X2 or X5 can rotate. If X5 rotates, X2 covers the basket.

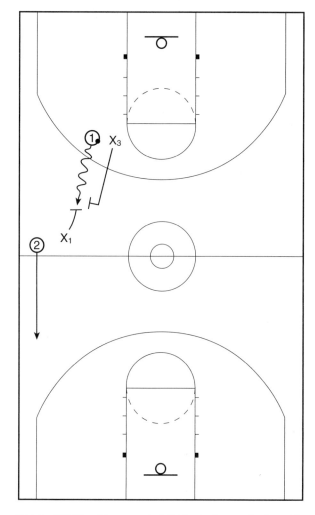

Figure 15.12 The speed dribbler is trapped when his defender maintains a close guarding position alongside him.

(back-tip). When a player who is dribbling fast must suddenly slow down as he confronts a defender upcourt, he's often susceptible to the back-tip from a defender who has come up quickly from behind.

The Decision to Trap or Level

The decision to trap or level is probably the most important decision in the press. Every player must have the discipline to know when to trap and when to level the speed dribbler.

The speed dribble is trapped when the defender can force the speed, or uncontrolled, dribble and maintain a close guarding position alongside the ball handler. In figure 15.12, X1 would trap 1.

When trapping, the defender stays low and chops his feet in a closeout position, with hands high enough to prevent a bullet pass over his head. The trap should occur on the imaginary line between 2 and 1. Again, the trap is triggered only by a speed dribble and when the defender can stay in close proximity to the dribbler.

As X3 pressures 1 into a speed dribble, he'll sometimes be beaten and won't be able to stay on 1's hip. In such a case, X3 may be trailing 1. If this occurs, X1 attempts to "level" the ball handler by faking at him back and forth in an attempt to slow him down or force him to take a sideways dribble (figure 15.13). As this is happening, X3, in

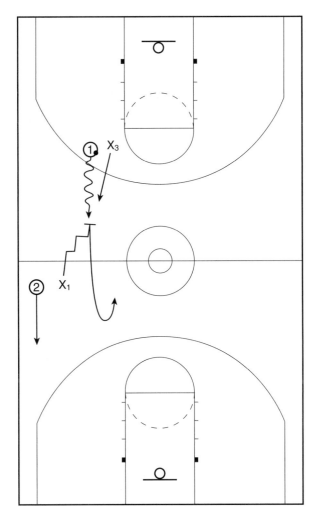

Figure 15.13   If X3 is trailing the ball handler, X1 fakes to slow the ball handler down or to force him to take a sideways dribble; meanwhile, X3 recovers to tip the ball from behind.

full sprint, is trying to back-tip the dribble. Intense back-tipping can force a turnover by the best of ball handlers.

DRILLS FOR THE FULL-COURT PRESS

When you want to teach an offensive play, you need to break it down into different parts and then practice each segment of the play. The same must be done with any type of defense. The players must see the big picture and then work on the parts. Following are drills I use for building our full-court pressure.

One-on-One

The court is split down the middle from basket to basket, and only one side of the court is used. We usually run this drill simultaneously at both ends of the court. A coach inbounds the ball into the shaded area in figure 15.14.

This drill works on disallowing the ball to be inbounded in front of the defender. Once the ball is inbounded, we work on pressuring the ball handler into a speed dribble, while remaining in contact with the dribbler. If the dribbler blows by the defender, the drill's focus is now on

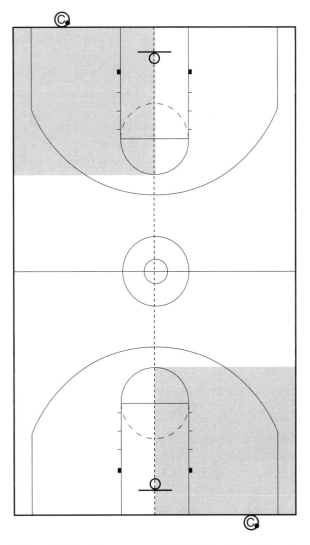

Figure 15.14   One-on-one drill: Disallow the inbounds pass in front of the defender, and then force the ball handler into a speed dribble.

sprinting in an attempt to back-tip the ball away from the dribbler.

The ball can be passed only to the offensive player on one side of the court and from the top of the key extended to the baseline from where the ball is being inbounded.

We start the drill with the offensive player directly above the coach inbounding the ball. The defender lines up on the sideline side, facing the coach. The defender is in contact with the offensive player with his hip and his elbow (figure 15.15).

Because the area is limited, the defensive player can be very aggressive in preventing the ball from being caught. At the beginning of the season, we make the defender aware that this denial must happen with vision of the inbounder and without fouling the offensive player.

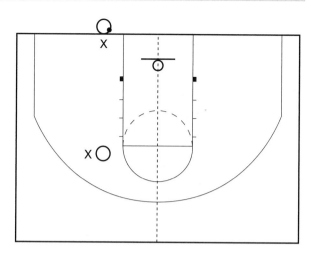

Figure 15.16 Two-on-two drill: The inbounder is covered by a defender.

figure 15.17). Either way, the emphasis is on denying the inbounds pass. We're always emphasizing trying to deflect a pass with the hopes of turning our opponent over.

If the ball is inbounded successfully, we play live two-on-two basketball. We're looking to force the speed dribble and get a trap. We don't worry that we're trapping and leaving a man open. This forces defenders to try to get a piece of the pass. If the pass is completed after the trap, defenders sprint out of the trap and try to back-tip the ball handler, who has a breakaway opportunity.

In these drills, because of the limited space on one side of the court, it should be very difficult to get the ball inbounds against

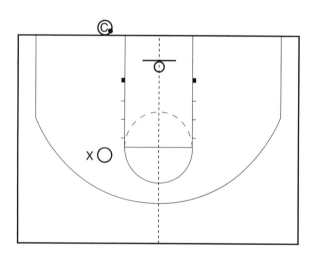

Figure 15.15 One-on-one drill: The defender lines up on the sideline side in physical contact with the offensive player.

Two-on-Two

This drill is similar to the one-on-one drill. It's done on one side of the court, with the line from basket to basket being an imaginary out-of-bounds line. The inbounder, however, is now a player. We run this drill in two ways. First, the inbounder is guarded by a defender (white press; figure 15.16).

Second, the defender is in the off position, not guarding the inbounder (black press;

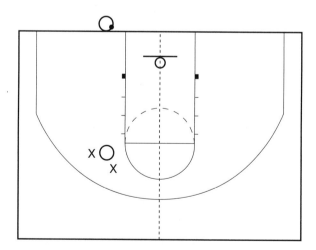

Figure 15.17 Two-on-two drill: Here the inbounder is not covered by a defender.

either press. This builds confidence in your players at the front of your press.

Three-on-Three

In this drill we open up the entire court and don't limit where the ball can be inbounded. Again, defenders can line up in either the white press or the black press. As always, in the white press alignment, the inbounder is covered (figure 15.18); in the black press, the inbounder is not guarded (figure 15.19).

We start the drill by designating which press we're in and then play it live until the ball is dead. This is a key drill in helping your defense develop new concepts. As players are allowed to play live three on three

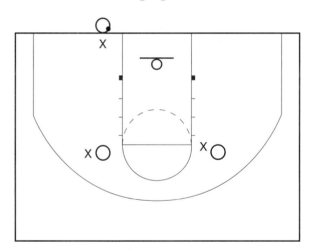

Figure 15.18 Three-on-three drill: white press alignment.

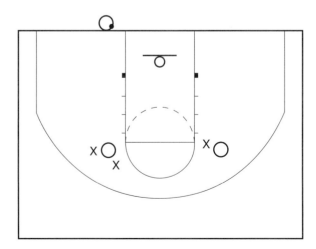

Figure 15.19 Three-on-three drill: black press alignment.

on a full court, they must learn to recognize which press to use depending on how the three players on offense have scored (near the basket or from the perimeter). The drill also promotes aggressiveness in denying the inbounds pass, especially when defenders are in the black press alignment. Your players quickly learn the necessity of keeping the ball in vision and how to read and react to various situations.

4–4–4

The 4–4–4 drill is a very good offensive and defensive drill that we use every day. Break the team up into three teams of four: team A, team B, and team C. The alignment to begin the drill is shown in figure 15.20.

Team A starts with the ball in the backcourt at the top of the key. It's attacking team B, who has two defenders guarding the basket in tandem. The other two players on

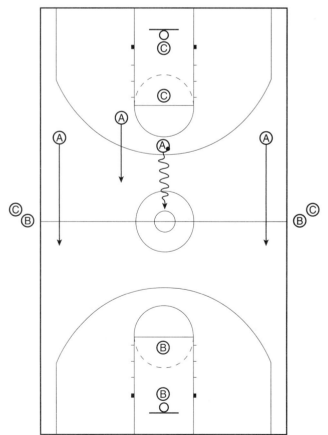

Figure 15.20 The 4–4–4 drill: initial alignment.

team B are at the intersection of the center line and the sideline, one on each side of the court. The defenders at half-court can't enter the action until the ball is passed or dribbled over the center line. When the ball passes the midcourt line, the two trailing defenders must touch the center circle before they can defend.

The drill is run live. If team A misses the shot, team B rebounds the ball and fast-breaks against team C, who has two defenders in tandem at the other end and two players out of bounds at half-court. The same rules apply to the defensive team regarding when the two trailers can become involved.

If team A scores with original possession, it immediately presses team B with either the white press or black press, depending on whether it scored in the lane or on a jump shot.

Team A can defend team B only to half-court, where team C takes over. Because of this rule, team A can be extremely aggressive in its press.

If team B beats the press, team C defends it as it attacks, with the two players on C coming in to touch the center line when team B crosses half-court with the ball. Team A then puts two defenders at half-court out of bounds and two others in a tandem, ready to protect the basket it just attacked.

We generally run this drill live to a certain score and allow the winner of the contest a water break while the losers run.

This can be a wild drill at times, and the coaching staff must be diligent in striking a balance of nonstop aggressiveness and teaching the rules of the press.

FINAL POINTS

A common mistake among coaches who use a full-press defense is to get discouraged and change it after the opponent has scored one or two easy baskets. Don't be swayed by this negative side of the full-court press. Every defense has weaknesses. That you'll give up an easy basket here and there is the negative side you must accept if you decide to adopt a full-court pressure defense. Of course, your reason for adopting this defense is that you see more positives to it than negatives. You need to trust your defensive philosophy if you want to sell it fully to your players.

Finally, considering our subject in this chapter, it's fitting to end with a few final words on conditioning. To run this defense, your players must be able to run at full speed for an entire game. They need to be in better shape than your opponents. On top of this, they must also have great defensive conditioning. That is, they must be able to play long periods with their knees bent so they can make quick defensive slides and close out their rotations. You can't run an effective full-court press if your players lack defensive conditioning.

chapter 16

Defensive Strategies

Del Harris

There are three phases to consider in planning defensive strategies as you prepare your team for confident team play on the defensive end: pregame strategy, in-game adjustments, and late-game adjustments.

We can't address each of these phases in depth in one chapter, but we will provide an overview in the hopes of stimulating you to think more deeply about these issues of vital importance to winning basketball.

PREGAME PLAN

First, you must determine if your primary defense will be man-to-man or zone. No matter which you choose, I recommend teaching the other as well so that your team can switch to its secondary defense when you think it's called for. Of course you'll also want to teach a couple of presses. Although many successful coaches have decided to live or die with one chosen defense, we believe (to use a baseball expression) that you need more than one pitch once you have advanced to the highest levels of competition. On the other hand, one fools himself if he thinks he can be *equally* successful with several defenses.

Use one defense as your bread and butter, and reserve the other for special occasions. When I was in Dallas, our use of multiple defenses over the years was predicated on two factors:

1. You have to play against various defenses in games, so you need to practice playing against them to be prepared. It does little good to practice against a defense that's not effective, that doesn't understand what's supposed to happen in its particular form. Thus, you need to teach something about man-to-man, zones, and presses in order to have an effective offensive practice against each.

2. Once your team learns to use each of the major styles of defense reasonably well, you might as well try your secondary defense occasionally, such as when things aren't going well for the primary defense against a particular opponent. Changes of pace can upset your opponent's flow just long enough to allow your team to get back into position to win the game.

Matchups

We'll assume that the basic defense preferred by most good teams is man-to-man because that's the case about 90 percent of the time. Other defenses tend to be used when the lack of talent, depth, or athleticism disallows success in one-on-one confrontations. And that's quite an acceptable decision for the coach to make. Certainly zone adjustments helped the Mavericks win a lot of games over the years.

Within a basic man-to-man defense there are several items of strategy to consider, and the first of these is matchups. While it's easy to match centers with centers, point guards with point guards, and so on, that's not always the best strategy. The advantages to that method are in its simplicity and during in-transition defense, when it's often easier to be matched up than cross-matched. That said, cross-matching is not an insurmountable obstacle and often has advantages. Ideally, you'll have a perimeter defensive stopper on your team with enough versatility to guard two or even three positions. You can put this player on your opponent's best perimeter player immediately, or you might decide to switch him over if the player gets on a roll, or you might wait until the last quarter to switch him to save him from foul trouble.

Small, quick point guards can pose problems for many teams, and the normal response is to put small defenders on them to match them speed for speed. But if the opponent is quicker still, the matchup might be an exercise in futility. In such a case, try putting a taller man on the guard and have him leave enough space to contain him but still challenge his shot with his greater length.

Powerful big players can also be problematic to guard if your bigs are weaker or slower than theirs—though occasionally you can win a matchup for a while with a smaller, quicker player on their big one. Eddie Najera, at 6-foot-7, for example, was instrumental in stopping the great Yao Ming just long enough to get us a victory in a big game. Najera used his quickness to deny Ming the ball and to gain great position to hold him off the board in that game.

Playing a small on a big won't work every time, but on some nights you need to try something unusual to win the game at hand. You can worry about another strategy once the current one fails. And it's true that most big players don't like to have the smaller ants under them, banging on their knees, fronting them, and outrunning them to their favorite spots. Also, playing small and fronting on their big man might give your own big man time to help out when the opponent tries to lob over your small man's head.

There are many ways that cross-matching can confuse your opponent just long enough

Glenn James/NBAE/Getty Images Sport

Assigned a player nearly a foot taller, Eduardo Najera was up to the challenge of Yao Ming on this particular night. Such cross-matches can be the best solution to an opponent's apparent offensive advantage in a given game.

to throw the momentum of a game in your favor, and sometimes that's all you need for the win.

Pressure Defense Adjustments

Another game plan decision is how, when, and where to apply the press. A full-court press can be used to advantage in many situations, and sometimes for totally opposite reasons. For example, you can play full-court pressure man-to-man to disrupt timing, wear a thin opponent down, gear up your own aggressiveness, or speed up a game. On the other hand, you can run a softer position press to slow an opponent down.

When a good ball handler is able to push the ball up the floor against you too easily, a full-court man-to-man or zone press can trap him and get the ball out of his hands. Once he has passed the ball out of the trap, his main defender should try to deny him from getting it back. For that matter, you might try to deny him the ball on the initial inbounds play by playing his defender behind him while the defender of the inbounds player plays in front of him, forcing another player to receive the ball. Once the ball is passed in, the trap is released, but the original defender tries to deny their good ball handler the ball as long as possible.

As mentioned, the irony of pressing is that a team can employ a press such as a 2-2-1 that can either slow down *or* speed up an opponent's play. And it's easier to get into the 2-2-1 after scores or even after some rebounds than many coaches think, especially if you practice it. A team that's trying to slow an opponent or slow a game's tempo can get into the 2-2-1 quickly at the three-quarter court and be selective in its trapping, while still being sure to set a few traps to keep the opponent off balance. This is usually a one-trap-only situation, and then you'll fall back into a half-court man-to-man or zone (zones tend to slow teams better than man-to-man).

If you want to increase tempo, you can be aggressive enough to trap initially and then continue to trap as the ball is advanced downcourt. When I was a young coach at Earlham College (1965-74), we used the full-court press considerably with a team that finished sixth in the NAIA in scoring at over 101 points per game (out of 700 schools in those days). With a different set of players a few years later, our team pressed with a different purpose and finished sixth in

fewest points allowed. Both teams used a lot of pressing, but the styles and results were entirely opposite.

Pick-and-Roll Strategy

Further, in pregame strategy you must decide how to play against your opponent's key plays. For instance, when playing a pick-and-roll team (as is quite prevalent in the NBA and increasingly so in top Division I NCAA schools), you'll need to determine how to defend in the five areas in which pick-and-roll attacks are initiated: the top of the key, the wing, the high wing (the area between the top of the key and free-throw line extended), and the elbows of the free-throw lane.

While pick-and-rolls along the sideline angles may be covered in the same way (or not, depending on the coach's decision), the top and elbows generally require different techniques if you want to be successful. (There are even variations within these basic five angles that we can't go into here.)

There are many types of coverage to choose from when determining your pick-and-roll strategy, but we suggest having one way that you become best at and then also a plan B to revert to when plan A isn't working.

In the NBA, teams often employ four or five different techniques for certain situations, but the best defensive teams have a basic choice and then a counter or two at most, knowing that most opponents won't be proficient in stopping too many techniques. Again, the principle applied here is that you can't do a great job at any one thing in basketball if you try to do too many things. Following are standard choices in pick-and-roll coverage.

Help-and-recover. Some coaches call this hedging or showing. The idea is that the defender on the pick player helps the defender on the ball at a prescribed angle to negotiate (defeat) the screen, and then each defender recovers to his own original

Jennifer Pottheiser/NBAE/Getty Images Sport

Every coach and team needs to establish preferred ways to handle screens. Here, because of the location on the floor and orientation of the ball handler, the defense appears prepared to offer the picked player soft help until he can recover.

man (ideally). There are many variations of this:

• *Hard help.* Here the helper is right up on the picker as the pick is set in order to jump quickly out at a hard angle (90 degrees facing the sideline) in the path of the ball handler. This prevents the ball handler from "turning the corner" over the pick and getting into the middle of the defense. It forces the ball handler to break his angle of attack or to charge into the defender. Of course, this allows his defender space and timing to go under the defensive helper but over the player setting the pick to reengage the ball handler. The

helper then recovers back to the picker, unless he gets too extended and someone has to pick him up, in which case he rotates to the paint to find an open offensive player. In this "hard" help method, the helper might be told to stay with the ball handler until his teammate recovers, until the ball handler passes, or for a certain number of steps, ranging from zero to three.

These are strategic decisions based on the abilities of the opponents and how they attempt to score on their pick-and-roll action—by rolling, popping, or having the ball handler shoot or else penetrate and swing the ball to the weak side to shooters or to a post player.

• *Soft help.* The helper might help at a much softer angle (45 degrees or less), attempting to jam up the middle with his coverage. "Covering the turn" means that the defender on the picker will drop back roughly in line with the "box" along the strong-side foul lane and give a sort of zone coverage to the ball handler and the foul lane. The defender on the ball must continue a hard pursuit over the pick. This method is less aggressive but prevents splits and tends to offer the jump shot more than the roll or penetration for teams that are strong in that area.

In any coverage, the defender on the ball might be told to go over or under the man setting the pick on him. That decision is made based on two factors: the distance the pick is set on the floor and the ability of the ball handler to shoot behind the screen relative to his skill at penetration. We prefer to go under the picks set far out on the floor and against poor shooters, and we prefer to go over on closer setups and against good shooters. Again, these are strategies that scouting or time-out adjustments must address.

Trap. A more aggressive coverage is to trap the ball handler with the defender of the picker. The most aggressive is for the defender of the picker to trap the ball handler before the pick is actually set, but the more common way is to trap just as the ball handler is coming over the pick. Naturally, with either form of this aggressiveness comes some risk. A rotation is necessary if the ball handler is able to pass the ball to the picker quickly on a pop or roll, with the lowest defender near the goal rotating to him. X5 jumps out to trap 1, and X4 rotates over to pick up 5 as he sees the ball in the air from 1 to 5. X5 rotates opposite the pass into the paint and picks up the open man, normally 4, although X3 has to help until X5 can get there. Sometimes X5 is late, making it necessary for him to cover 3 on the weak side (figure 16.1).

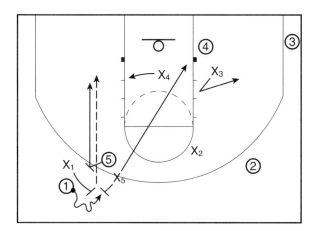

Figure 16.1 Pick-and-roll coverage: trap and rotation.

Switching. This method is the easiest form of help-and-recover and is used most often when equal-sized players are involved in the pick-and-roll. However, late in the game, most NBA teams will use the switch with four or even all five defenders to prevent a quick easy shot, especially a three-pointer.

Note that switching is a critical strategy when protecting a lead late in the game. It's also a good strategy at any time in the game when the possession clock is down

to seven seconds. The open shots kill you, especially the threes. Mismatches caused by switching are far less dangerous than giving up an open shot to a good shooter. Teach players to pass off mismatches quickly, or drill them on how to trap out of mismatches when they occur. That is, a big player must automatically trap down for a small teammate being posted by a big post, as X4 does in figure 16.2.

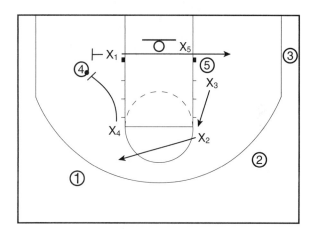

Figure 16.2 Pick-and-roll coverage: switching.

A small player must rotate over to replace a bigger teammate stuck out on the perimeter defending a quick-penetrating, smaller player caused by a switch or emergency coverage, as X3 does for X5. The mismatched man rotates off to the weak side and picks up an open man. X2 rotates to 3, and X1 picks up 2 (figure 16.3).

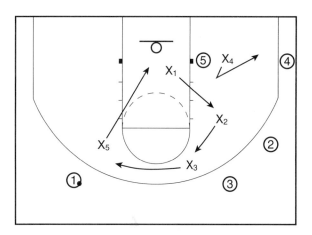

Figure 16.3 Pick-and-roll coverage: A small player rotates over to replace a bigger teammate.

Overplaying down to the baseline. Another often-employed technique is to push the ball handler down toward the baseline. To do this, the defender on the picker must immediately call out the signal for the coverage (usually a color, or simply "Down!") as he sees the pick about to be set. He then assumes a position two to three steps below the picker in the direction that the ball defender must push the ball, and the defender on the ball must overplay severly, pushing the ball handler "down" toward the baseline and into the defender on the picker (figure 16.4). This play usually occurs on wing and corner coverage.

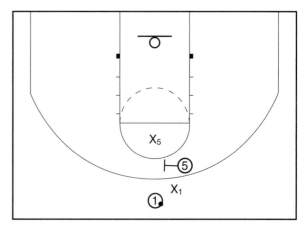

Figure 16.5 Pick-and-roll coverage: the picker's defender calls "Down right!" or "Down left!"

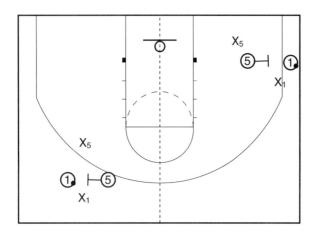

Figure 16.4 Pick-and-roll coverage: overplaying down to the baseline.

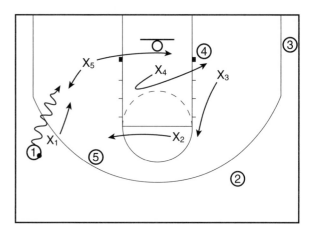

Figure 16.6 Pick-and-roll coverage: In either case, X1 maintains contact with the ball handler.

The down play can be used on the top as well, but it's less safe there. The defender on the picker calls "Down right!" or "Down left!" depending on which way he wants the defender to send the ball handler. The ball defender then gets into a position on the high side to push the ball handler down toward the defender on the picker (figure 16.5).

In either case X1 must maintain contact with the ball handler to keep him from splitting quickly between himself and X5. On the sideline pick-and-roll, you must decide if you want to have X5 recover back to 5 on a pass to him, or to have a player rotate to 5 (figure 16.6). X2 rotates to 5 because the game plan dictated that 5 was a great shooter from 15 to 17 feet out. X4 rotated to 5 on the roll because X5 didn't get back to 5. The defender (X5) then rotates across

to the weak side to pick up an open man, in this case 4 (figure 16.7). The same decisions must be made on the coverage of the top-angle pick-and-roll.

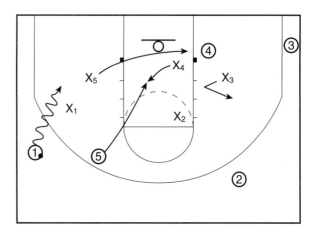

Figure 16.7 Pick-and-roll coverage: X4 rotates to 5 if X5 doesn't get back to 5.

Defensive Strategy Against the Post-Up

Another pregame decision concerns how to best defend the posts. Against teams that dominate with one or more low-post threats, it might be best to stay man to man and give help to the defenders in the low post either when a player catches the ball or when he penetrates toward the free-throw lane. Or it might be preferable to try to front some or all of the players in the low-post area and come to help from the weak side during the air time of the lob pass inside. Another option is to trap a particular player in the post, only to dig back and bother others in the post until they get the ball into an extremely deep position. Yet another possibility is to zone up against a strong low-post team. How to execute the traps and rotations is not the subject here. But your team must be equally prepared to cover the low post as it is to cover the pick-and-roll game.

Isolated Player Strategy

Some teams have one or two good one-on-one players whom they try to isolate in one-on-one attacks. If you're the coach, you must decide if you're willing to go one on one with the player, to trap from the top, or to push the player to the baseline to set a trap there. In figure 16.8, X2 is influencing the ball to the middle, and X1 is coming to

trap 2 in the isolation. The defenders X3 and X4 rotate accordingly.

In figure 16.9, the ball is being shaded to the baseline; X5 steps out to trap while the defense rotates behind X5, with X4 fronting 5 and X3 V-cutting back to cover 4.

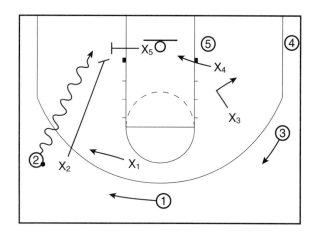

Figure 16.9 Isolated player strategy, option 2: Force the ball handler to the baseline; X5 traps with X2, while the other defenders rotate.

It's also possible to shift into a zone defense, usually a 2-3, when a player is isolated to be in a position to give help. Players simply fill in the four zone spots around the defender on the ball, ready to give help or to trap on penetration. Figure 16.10 shows players filling in around X2 on the isolated player (2) and forming the 2-3 zone. Naturally, this shift to the zone must be planned for and a verbal signal given on the court.

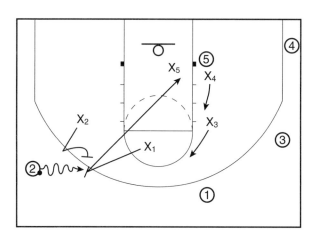

Figure 16.8 Isolated player strategy, option 1: forcing the ball to the middle and trapping.

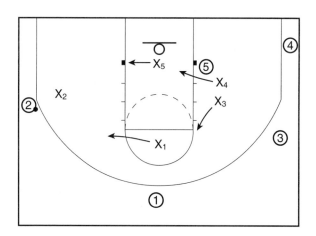

Figure 16.10 Isolated player strategy, option 3: Play a 2-3 zone.

Clarifying the Switching Concepts

It's important that a team understand what the strategy in general is relative to rules for switching in the man-to-man defense. Some coaches prefer never to switch, some allow emergency switching when a man is beaten, and others prefer to switch quite readily, whenever the situation allows. Coaches have won championships with each of these techniques (and other variations as well). There's no one answer on this issue. What's of utmost importance is to drill your team on the strategy that's selected, commit to the strategy, and ensure consistent communication so that doubt is eliminated when potential switches arise. Such preparation requires concerted practice time.

Setting Strategy Against the Opponent's Key Play Actions

To conclude this section: It's important not only to get the matchups right and to have a system to cover the general offensive situations that will arise, such as pick-and-rolls, post-ups, isolations, and so on, but you must also look at the two to five or so key plays that an opponent employs in its offensive schemes and clarify how you want your defense to adjust to help minimize these plays. Your team won't be able to study every play a team uses (some NBA teams use more than 60), but there will always be some key actions that the opponent does best, and your defense must prepare for those. Your game plan might involve trapping, switching, or overplaying to make the opponent's execution more difficult.

Don't fail to be prepared for an opponent's out-of-bounds plays. An assistant coach should have a diagram of the key out-of-bounds plays an opponent has used in close, late-game situations. Equally important is to have general concepts of how the team will defend out-of-bounds plays, be they from the side, under their own basket, or at the full court.

Sideline out of bounds. Our basic plan with the Mavericks in this situation was to prevent two particular passes: the direct pass from out of bounds into the low post, and the pass down to the strong-side corner (which sets up either a quick drop pass to the low post or a three-point shot). Figure 16.11 shows X3 (who needs to have active hands) playing in the passing lane to the corner and X5 in denial on 5.

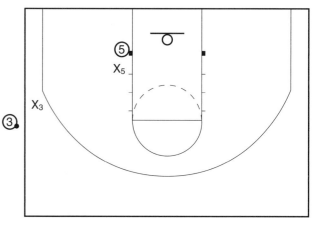

Figure 16.11 Sideline out-of-bounds: no pass to the strong-side corner or to the low post.

We have used our advantage in numbers for our side out-of-bounds defensive plays to dictate some trick coverage:

- We can call a shift to zone.
- We can call for a trap to be made on the first pass below the foul line.
- We can call for a trap to be made when the ball is passed to the weak side.
- We can call for switching certain players or all players, and so on.

The advantage to tricking up on the defense in this situation after a time-out is that the opponent will normally have set a play, and you want to make it hard for him to run the play easily. It is dangerous to trap the first pass in, particularly if the inbounds passer is a good shooter. After passing the ball, he's a dangerous man as either a step-in shooter or a slice cutter. A technique we've often used is to pressure the inbounds man toward the baseline side for two, or even three, counts and then jump off to face the other four players inbounds to try to deny the pass to the first man who becomes open. The defender must quickly get back to his own man, however, if the ball is passed in. Other times we've told the defender on the ball out of bounds to check the ball two counts and then quickly find the one opposing player we don't want to get the ball, such as a Kobe Bryant type. Again, that defender must get back quickly to the passer once he does this.

Note that some teams prefer to pressure the passer with a man (or even with two men) the entire five seconds. This is most effective when one or two seconds remain and the lob is the most likely scenario. Then, putting a taller player with active hands on the ball out of bounds is necessary.

Baseline out of bounds. Our general coverage is man-to-man, and we emphasize trying to prevent two easy looks here as well—the direct pass under the goal and the easy catch-and-shoot in the strong-side corner, where most passes are made. We also have zoned up against the end out but find it to be more risky against great players. Still, in high school and college, the zone can be effective, but the better the skill of players at any level, the more risky the zone under the goal becomes. A mistake can permit a quick layup if the offense overloads the baseline or draws the middle man and cuts a player into an opening.

To help keep the ball from coming inbounds right under the goal, we play man-to-man and have the man on the ball out of bounds move to an angle off the ball and toward the basket. He'll stand in such a way as to see both the ball and what's going on behind him toward the goal (figure 16.12). He must have active hands. In this position he can also usually prevent an easy weak-side pass to the corner.

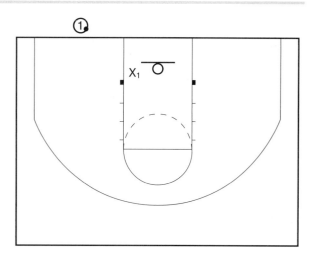

Figure 16.12 Baseline out of bounds: no pass under the rim or to the weak-side corner.

To prevent the easy strong-side corner catch-and-shoot, we have some choices of strategy:

- We might just have our players body up and play their own men, switching only in an emergency.

- We might put a smaller player on the outside of a stack or pick and one in the lane area and have them switch. The man on the outside won't go through with the first cutter, passing him off and getting back to cover the corner area (figure 16.13).

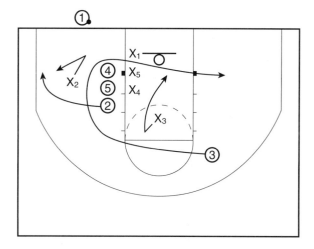

Figure 16.13 Baseline out of bounds, option 1: Put a smaller defender outside the stack and another one in the lane, then switch.

Some teams will have the defender on the ball out of bounds check the middle of the lane and then switch out to the corner to cover there. The player in the lane (X3) will switch into X1's position, but that's all predetermined or communicated by X3 and X1 (figure 16.14). While this maneuver can be effective if not overdone, it's also risky.

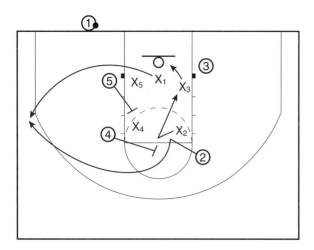

Figure 16.14 Baseline out of bounds, option 2: Put a defender in the middle of the lane, then switch out to the corner.

Full-court out of bounds. Over the course of a game, a team's philosophy of pressure defense will dictate how this situation is played. It can vary in a myriad of ways. But when there are short seconds left in a period, regardless of whether a team prefers a full-court man or zone press or a half-court defense, we recommend having the defender of the inbounds player back up to the half-court area to play "centerfield." He'll watch the ball and follow the long pass to help the defender on that man contain the man and prevent a shot. If a short inbounds pass is made first, he won't go for that but will wait to see where the next long pass is made and then go to it on air time to double team. Or, if the receiver tries to drive the ball upcourt for a quick penetration and shot, he'll give help to stop that.

Alternatively, some teams like to pressure the man out of bounds to bother his vision and pressure the pass; though that's quite defensible as a strategy, we prefer the centerfield method.

IN-GAME ADJUSTMENTS

The three most important strategic elements to monitor during the flow of the game are momentum, game pace, and matchup changes. As the coach reads these, he'll be led to make or not to make strategic adjustments. Let's address these situations one at a time.

Momentum

Much of the game should be dictated by momentum, which can be described as having three phases: positive, negative, and zero, which means up for grabs. We like to avoid making changes when we have a positive flow. We stick with our lineup and our coverages and avoid calling time-outs. When there's zero momentum, we might try to stimulate the game with a play call, a key substitution, or a defensive adjustment. When momentum is negative, we're definitely on alert to make a change in our matchups, our lineup, or either our offensive or defensive scheme. In general, defensive adjustments tend to be more effective in changing momentum. A change from man to zone or vice versa, to a type of press, to trapping a key player, or some other defensive change can potentially bother the opponent's offense while stimulating ours. Even when momentum is negative, we usually resist giving up entirely on what we're doing. A subtle adjustment can be easier to make and less confusing to the team while still getting the job done on the opponent. Don't let panic be your guide, but also don't be too stubborn to adjust.

Pace

Most teams find a pace in which they tend to play better, and then they stick with it—

though the opponent might like that same pace and be better at it, which is never a pleasant discovery. You can determine your team's best pace by keeping track of the possessions over a period of time, starting with practice scrimmages, to see how your team plays with more and less possessions per period of play. Averaging over 1.75 possessions per minute marks a faster pace, and less than that indicates a slower pace (at least in our unscientific but experienced opinion). In scoring this way, a possession doesn't end until a team has given the ball over to the opponent. That is, in this system, a ball that's knocked out of bounds by the opponent is still regarded as the same possession, as is an offensive rebound. It's our ball until it's theirs, basically, is the way we keep the chart.

Determining Momentum and Pace Strategically During the Game

We've found it's best not to trust "feel" for momentum and pace unequivocally. The best way to assess momentum and pace is to use a possession chart that includes multiple bits of information, depending on how in depth you want your stats man to go. He can note various details, including how each possession was attained and how it was lost, who took the shot, who rebounded or stole it or turned it over, what play action was used, and more, if so assigned. But the key elements of the chart are momentum and pace. Tables 16.1 and 16.2 show two ways the chart can be kept. Table 16.1 is the simple chart, and table 16.2 is an example

of making your chart more complex and informative.

Your chart gives concrete evidence of the pace of the game. Have your chart keeper simply circle the possession if a score occurs, or put an X through the possession number if no score occurs. Have a chart for each period in the game. This kind of charting might seem elementary, but a closer look at what you get out of it gives the system credibility. Knowing the pace of the game can be of significant help. For instance, if you're a team that prefers to run the ball and get volume shots, you'll want to know halfway through the period the number of possessions you've had. If you want to average somewhat over two possessions per minute, eight possessions after five or six minutes is not your pace. Conversely, if you want to keep your opponent from getting into a full-court game, that number of possessions might be just what you want for your half-court pace that night. If you're not doing well in a slow-paced game, you can attempt to speed up the pace with either an offensive or defensive adjustment. And, of course, if the fast pace is not working, you can try to slow it down.

The chart keeper should inform the coach or an assistant whenever the team fails to score on four possessions in succession or when the opponent has scored on four possessions in a row (this number is somewhat arbitrary; you might prefer three). The chart keeper's marks tell you what you need to know about momentum. You might or might not call a time-out or make a change when first given this information, but if negative

Table 16.1 Simple Possession Chart

OUR TEAM																				
1	2	3	4	5	6	7	8	9	10	11	12	13	14	15	16	17	18	19	20	21
THEIR TEAM																				
1	2	3	4	5	6	7	8	9	10	11	12	13	14	15	16	17	18	19	20	21

momentum persists, you have good reason to make some kind of adjustment.

As a head coach, I have often asked my stats man, "How many times have we had the ball?" People near the bench probably wonder what difference that makes, but to a coach it might mean the difference between making a change or not.

Table 16.2 shows a more complex system of charting. This chart is virtually a summary of the game. The table informs us that we got the ball off the jump ball (jb), and player 14 took the shot (if he scored, his number is circled; if he missed, it's not). The play we used was the 3 up, and the shot came in the low post. If 14 is circled and the comment is "lob pass," we assume that player 5 assisted (Ast.). We then got our second possession via a steal by our player 5 (st-5). However, we lost the ball because 44 traveled (tr-44) on the fast break. The third possession came as a result of the opposing team's number 13 scoring (fg-13). Player 20 shot and missed but scored on his own offensive rebound (orb-20).

This chart gives you an idea of some of the details that can be included by a good stats man, if so desired. When I coached at Earlham College many years ago, I had a manager named John Shiffert who could script virtually an entire game. He has gone on to be a successful public relations director and author. When I coached high school

basketball, a friend who was a car dealer managed this chart for me, so you don't have to be a coach to do this.

Matchup Changes

Obviously, one strategy a coach can choose is to change his matchups when the original choices are not effective. Sometimes a change to a "small ball" lineup can be effective to increase the tempo and the pressure on defense in the game. At other times a switch to "big ball," or the post-up game, can be effective. Maybe one lineup is better with a zone and another better for a press, and so on. Again, sometimes going small on a big man works well; or going big on a small player can at times be a solution because you force him to shoot over the longer defensive hand.

Other Tools to Help Determine In-Game Adjustments

I don't think that statistics are *the* tool a coach should use to run a game or to evaluate teams or individuals, but they certainly are one of the tools you can use intelligently. This being the case, we like good chart keeping during the game. The chart information is given to an assistant coach at each timeout and plays a big part in our halftime evaluation. The information most helpful

Table 16.2 Complex Possession Chart

	HBO	FGA-FG	FTA-FT	HBL	Play action	Ast.	FB	SEC	Comments
1	jb	14			3 up, low post	5			lob pass
2	st-5			tr-44					
3	fg-13	20-20			4 down			orb-20	
4									

Key: HBO—how ball was obtained; FGA-FG—a space to record the number of the player who shot the ball; circle it if he scores. FTA-FT—free throws made and missed; HBL—how the ball was lost (unnecessary to note after a score of ours); play action—record the play call that was used, if any; ast.—assist and the player's number; FB tells us if we got a fast break and SEC tells us if it was a secondary break action; comments—comments on any action, good or bad, that we may want to mention or edit; can also be used to give the time and score or to note any defensive changes or substitutions by either team. You can make your own abbreviation system to fit what you need to know.

to our team, in addition to the possessions chart, is the following:

• *Pick-and-roll chart.* We want to know how we're doing on defense against their pick-and-rolls and how successful we are in using this play action ourselves. We break it down to indicate the participants in the play and the location of the pick—top, wing, corner, elbow, and the high-wing area. We also keep track of transition pick-and-rolls set on the move. We want to keep the scoring ratio below one point per possession on defense. If we're not doing that, we change our coverage or put in a different player.

• *Man-to-man versus zone chart.* We want to know how many possessions we've used in our different defenses and how many points we've given up on each. We also include variations such as pressing defenses and combination defenses that we might use, such as box and one, triangle and two, or switching from man to zone during a possession or, conversely, from zone to man during a particular play action.

• *Low-post defense chart.* We want to know how many times we've allowed the ball into the low post and what's happened. We chart whether we've trapped, dug, or played it one on one and how many points have been given up on each attempt. The results determine whether we increase or decrease our tactics in the post.

• *Fast-break game.* We keep close track of how our transition defense is holding up. We also want to know whether we're getting our share of fast breaks and what percentage we're converting.

• *Penetration game.* We're quite concerned about how many penetrations we're allowing off the dribble in the front court. If we're giving up too many, we might soften our man-to-man defense or go to a zone for a time, though that defense might allow penetration as well. If a particular player is having trouble, we might sub him out or perhaps try to trap the player who's beating our guys one on one.

Many other details can be tracked, but these are the main ones we want to see; they indicate to us that a strategic move might be in order to begin the second half or during the flow of the game.

Using Combination and Alternating Defenses

While we can't show the dynamics of the techniques involved here in this chapter, the flow of a game can often be changed in your favor by deviating some from your standard defenses. We don't suggest trying anything too unusual when you can overpower a team with your basic system. Such defensive tactics are more suited to the underdog role. But sometimes your team, especially if you're at the high school or college level, is put into situations in which your normal bag of tricks just isn't enough to produce a victory. Many an upset has been staged by teams applying some of the following strategic defensive moves:

• *Box-and-one defense* is used in a 2-2 or a 1-2-1 zone formation for chasing a particularly dominant player, with one man who's trying to prevent that player from getting the ball. When coaching college ball in the late '60s and early '70s, I used a "matchbox-and-one" defense that complemented our matchup zone and our man-to-man defenses. The four men in the box used matchup rules to stay matched to the other four players, while we chased the hot man with one player.

• *Triangle-and-two defense* is a variation of the box and one that uses two chasers in the man-to-man.

• *Zone to man adjustment* is a technique in which a team shows a zone defense and then shifts into a man-to-man on a particular key, such as when the ball goes to the high post, when the ball is swung from the first side to the wing area on the second side, or when the ball is passed to the corner. The advantage here is that the team may stay with its zone attack against your man to man, and most zone attacks are much easier to cover than man-to-man sets.

• *Man to zone* is an adjustment that reverses the one just described and is used when an opponent is having success with a certain man-to-man action. Here, when the ball goes to a predetermined spot or player, the team shifts into a zone. This adjustment can be effective against certain pick-and-roll combinations, especially against a player who's a good isolation one-on-one attacker. It's also useful against some low-post attacks.

• *Alternating defenses* keeps opponents guessing and perhaps disrupts an offense that's clicking a little too efficiently. We've had success at confusing opponents by changing defenses in various ways other than during time-outs. For instance, we've played man-to-man when the ball comes across the half-court (in a non-fast-break situation) depending on which side of the floor we're on—the right side might be man-to-man and the left side a zone. We've also changed from zone to man-to-man when the ball swings to the weak-side wing or when it's passed to certain areas or certain players. We've changed our defense based on whether we scored on our last possession or whether our score ended in an even or odd number. Remember that these kinds of tactics are reserved mainly for an underdog team or for situations when your team is behind and your normal stuff is not working. These are not ways a good team will start a game but are tactical adjustments only.

LATE-GAME ADJUSTMENTS

You'll generally want to plan your late-game strategies well in advance to avoid coming up with something desperate and ill-advised when you're under pressure at the end of a big game. Here are some late-game considerations you might want to mull over from the security of your office rather than in the heat of the moment:

• *When to foul when trailing late in the game.* The lower the level of competition, the sooner a team should try to stop the clock by fouling. That said, a wise coach also teaches how to foul while going for the ball in an aggressive defense. Sometimes the referee will swallow the whistle when a team is aggressive and is forging a comeback; you might get a steal or turnover without having the foul called. In any case, the lower the level, the less likely teams are to make their pressure free throws. If the opponent's stats are available to your team, you should always know who the best and worst foul shooters are. In the NBA, our teams have made some news with the "Hack-a-Shaq" approach of fouling Shaquille O'Neal and other poor foul shooters intentionally to force them to score via the free throw rather than the dunk.

Of course, a primary factor to consider in this situation is the number of points you're behind. By the time your team is in these situations, you should have made decisions on when to start fouling with a 10-plus point deficit, a 7- to 9-point deficit, and a 6- to 1-point deficit. The larger the deficit, the sooner the fouls must start to stop the clock and lengthen the game. A deficit in the 6- to 1-point range is a one- or two-possession game with far different considerations for fouling than you'll have with larger deficits. The time remaining in which you choose to foul will depend on the level of competition and their ability to shoot free throws. The important thing is to have a formula ahead of time. In the NBA, we like to foul at three minutes with a deficit of 10 points or more and at the 90-second mark with a 9- to 7-point spread. We foul with 30 seconds or less in a two-possession game. In every situation we try to steal the inbounds pass before fouling.

• *When to foul with a three-point lead.* Many people argue the pros and cons of fouling late in a game with a three-point lead to send your opponent to the free-throw line instead of risking its scoring on a three-pointer to tie the game. When I was at Dallas, we had owner Mark Cuban's favorite stats genius figure this problem out over a cross section of many games. According to him, the odds favor you (though not by a lot) to foul with 6 or fewer seconds remaining, even if the opponent makes 90 percent of his free throws. Before getting this information, our tendency had always been to foul at 5 seconds or less, and that had been effective for us. Whatever your decision on this matter, figure it out ahead of time and have your players practice it.

• *Switching to defend the three-point line.* In protecting a lead late in the game, it becomes even more important to protect against the three-point shot. When the opponent needs a three-pointer in the waning seconds, good switching techniques are vital. Put in a lineup that can switch readily, taking out a bigger, slower player or a poor defender. You have the game won if you can stop the shot. But it's important to remind your players not to perform the normal defensive maneuver of dropping back to help on penetration or to trap in the low post or foul a shooter. The natural tendency to drop to the level of penetration allows the opportunity for penetration followed by a pass out to a three-point shooter for a nice rhythm-up catch-and-shoot. Resisting this natural urge takes some discipline and repetitions in practice.

There are three plays that tend to beat a defense that's trying to hold onto its lead late in a game:

- the three-pointer, which gives the quickest route to the opponent;
- the quick two-point score that takes little time off the clock; and
- the offensive rebound put-back, which is the single play that decides most 1- or 2-point games.

A team trailing by 5 points with a minute or less to go and a chance for two possessions will often try to get the quick 2 points

first and then go for the three-pointer later, knowing that if they miss on the lower-percentage three-pointer first and then foul, two more points for the opponent makes it a three-possession game. Thus, although you must tell your players to be ready to switch out to three-point shooters and to switch all switchables in pick situations, they must still be in containment mode, defending the ball against the quick score, and must be reminded to block out to prevent giving up the rebound that leads to the second shot.

Many a game has been lost, even despite good defense, because the opponent had nothing to lose and crashed the board with all players for a second shot. Naturally, in a 2-point game, the chance for a tie is obvious. But if the rebounder is fouled or if he can pass it out deep to a player standing behind the three-point line, the game can still be lost. And the careless foul of a two- or three-point shooter can be a game-breaker as well.

When an opponent needs a three-point basket to tie with short seconds remaining, all defenders must play on the top side of their assignments (figure 16.15) and prevent the pass to the strong-side corner. Your team should drill this situation—and we have some suggestions for doing so in the drill section that follows.

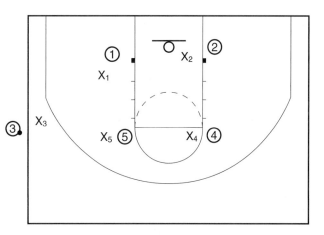

Figure 16.15 Late-game adjustments versus a three-point shot: All five defenders must play on the top side of their offensive players.

Players will switch out on picks, but they must communicate. A strategy to use—but try it in practice first—is to have all five players line up in an arc above the three-point line, as shown in figure 16.16.

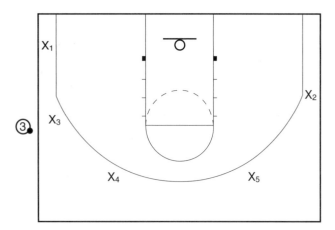

Figure 16.16   Late-game adjustment versus a three-point shot: All five defenders line up in an arc above the three-point line.

Remember that it's only the three-point shot that ties you, and that you have the option to foul with under 6 seconds, but the foul must come in a situation in which the player can't go into a quick shooting motion and get three free throws or, much worse, a chance for a four-point play.

DRILLS FOR STRATEGIES

If you're going to be successful in winning close games, you must drill your players so they're accustomed to playing in strategic pressure situations. Below is a list of some of our techniques for teaching. Use this abbreviated list to set up your own extended program.

• *Play a game or series of three games to three baskets from the various out-of-bounds positions*—side out, end out, full court, three-quarter court, and in the corners of the front court along the baseline. Change the time on the clock in these games from 20 to 10 to 5 to1 seconds remaining. In this drill every change of possession starts an out-of-bounds play.

• *Two-minute game.* Just as football players have done for years, basketball players can benefit from playing two-minute games. These can be structured in various ways. You can play as you would a regular game, puting a score on the board and playing the game out. Or you can try a variation we like: Let the situation stay the same for the entire two minutes. That is, the defense is always 2 points behind, for example, regardless of which team is on defense. This way, each time possession changes, the team with the ball will be playing to protect a 2-point lead and the team on defense will be playing to catch up. The only change in the situation is that the time will continue to decrease. By playing this way, you can work on how to play when your team is 2 points ahead *and* 2 points behind. Of course, you'll want to vary the situation from one practice to the next. Play two-minute games with a tied score, with the team 3 points up/behind, 1 point up/behind, 5 points up/behind, and so on.

• *Seven- or nine-possession game.* We will have already drilled the offense playing against no defense on some play actions to perform in these situations, so now it's up to the defense in this drill. Each team keeps the ball for either seven or nine possessions. The possessions go like this:

Full-court inbounds play versus a man-to-man press.

Full-court inbounds play going back the other way versus a zone press.

Three-quarter court inbounds play versus either a man defense or a zone going the other way.

Front-court side inbounds play versus man-to-man.

End inbounds play on the same end versus man-to-man.

Set play versus man-to-man with a need to score.

Set play versus zone with a need to score.

You can add two more possessions if you prefer, such as side and end inbounds plays versus the zone, a half-court inbounds play needing the three-pointer, or an inbounds plays with only 5 seconds on the clock, and so on.

• *Three-possession offense-defense-offense game (O-D-O).* The coach determines the score and the time situation. One team starts a possession wherever the coach instructs: full court, side, or end out of bounds, or from a rebound or steal. The offense gets a point if it scores, and the defense gets a point if it gets a stop. Either way, the ball goes to the other team, and it goes to the other end in the same situation with the same scoring opportunities. The original offensive team then advances the ball for the third possession under the same conditions. After three possessions there is a winner, with a score of either 2-1 or 3-0. The winning team gets the ball to begin the next game, and the coach picks a new situation.

• *Set up a series of 1-, 2-, 3-, 4-, and 5-point situations.* Some of the basic situations in a series would look like this:

> 1 point behind and opponent shooting two free throws.
>
> 1 point behind and opponent's ball out on the side.

1 point ahead and opponent's ball under the goal.

1 point ahead and opponent's ball out at full court.

• *Do the same with 2-, 3-, 4-, and 5-point deficits.* Now the offense is in the opposite situation, playing with a lead. Change the time on the clock to anything from one minute down to a few seconds.

• *Draw cards describing various situations.* We have printed up 100 game situations on cards and will mix up our late-game drills by having a player pick a card and having the team play out the situation described. The player who has picked the card might even be the coach of his team and tell it what to do, as will the "coach" of the other team, who will pick a card also. See which team is able to succeed in the two possessions drawn up and then discuss what went right and wrong.

The main goal is to use a variety of strategic defensive situations and to work on them as often as possible in practice. Coach Jim Calhoun of the University of Connecticut drills nine of them per practice, and his teams are always prepared.

PART VI

Coaching Essentials

chapter 17

Productive Practices

Lawrence Frank

There's an old adage in basketball: "The will to win is meaningless without the will to prepare to win." To perform at a high level over a long season, a team must be committed to invest the time and effort required to develop good practice habits.

Preparation is more than just practice. Player development that occurs before and after practice sessions; film sessions; strength and conditioning sessions; individual meetings with players; meetings with the coaching staff, individually and collectively; and networking with other coaches to learn new plays and stay abreast of current developments in the game are also part of preparation.

Every member of your team, including the coaching staff, must be willing to pay the price to get the team prepared to excel. Otherwise, excellence won't happen; it's that simple. It's easy to be motivated on game day, but if your players and staff aren't motivated to commit themselves during practice and other preparation sessions, game day won't go the way your team wants it to go. It's during games that you most rely on the training and preparation.

PHILOSOPHY AND PLAN

A team needs to have both a philosophy and a plan, and all members of the team need to buy into both. Your philosophy is the basis of your plan. You implement your plan during detailed practice preparation. Never practice just to practice. Have a goal in mind. A goal early in the season is to get all players clear on your basketball philosophy. Once they understand what you're trying to accomplish and how you're going to implement your plans, they can start to make it happen on the court. Enthusiasm is contagious, so get enthused about your plan for the team and for the season. Your players will follow your lead.

MASTER CALENDAR

The first thing our staff does is put together a master calendar outlining the entire season. We label practice days, game days, and off days. We list the skills we want to work on and the objectives we want to achieve each day, week, and month.

Included in these objectives are areas related to individual player development, team development (offense and defense), special situations, and our message of the day. Once we have constructed a master schedule, we start scripting our individual practices. We want every practice to have a purpose. After developing a comprehensive plan, we start prioritizing and allocating the appropriate amount of time to develop our team.

On our staff we are firm believers in having a detailed practice plan every time we're on the floor with the players. I was fortunate to have learned from one of the best coaches in the history of the game, coach Bob Knight. He taught me that preparation, discipline, and organization are keys to success. Whether we're in training camp or a midseason shoot-around, we have a detailed minute-by-minute plan of exactly what we want to accomplish (see figure 17.1). Our plan helps us stay organized, helps our coaches and players be prepared for each segment of practice, and keeps practices moving at an efficient and intense pace.

Before every practice, we meet as a staff to prepare our practice plan. As the head coach, I come to the meeting with a pretty good idea of what I want to get done that day, but I feel it's important to get input from my staff and to adjust my plans as necessary. We all value each other's opinion and, even if we differ in the meeting room, we're always united on the court.

PRACTICE REPETITION AND CONSISTENCY IN THE GAME

We've found that to have great execution we must practice the same things over and over. We try to teach and emphasize both the physical and mental skills we want to see repeated in the game during our practice sessions. We believe that every drill must have a purpose and that what you practice must translate to games. If you're a running, pressing, up-tempo team, you're going to have high-energy practices in which you run the team up and down the court without much rest. You can't practice one way and expect to play another.

Your players repeat in the games what you demand from them in practice. If you want your team to be persistent and tough-minded, find a way to instill these traits in practice. If practices are loose and free flowing, your players will probably play the same way in games. If your practices are detailed and precise, your players will probably carry that into games as well.

TEACHING METHODS

We use numerous teaching methods to get our points across in practice. We are believers in the part–whole method in which we break down and isolate specific skills, then build the whole back up. Whether it's the head coach leading five-on-five drills or an assistant coach working individually with a player in breakdown drills, our primary goal is to get our players to understand and perform correctly the actions we want to see repeated in games. We use different means to achieve this goal. Sometimes we show players the desired objective on film; other times they might need to watch a teammate perform the task. For some players, it takes an assistant coach to pull them aside and talk with them individually, but we have found the best way to learn is to have them participate and execute the desired skill.

PRACTICE COMPONENTS

We practice according to our predetermined plan, but we allow some flexibility to account for unexpected changes or to fit our players better. Keep in mind that there's a fine line between long, demanding practices and overtraining. You need to read your team and allow recovery time as necessary. We believe it's important to pace your team during the course of the season. We want to have a high level of intensity but also to have our players fresh and ready to play at game time. Sometimes a crisp 90-minute practice is more effective than a grueling three-hour session. Assess your plan throughout the season and makes changes as necessary. In the next session we discuss the main segments of our practice and factors that affect how we run them.

Practice Rules

We have some basic practice rules. We require everyone (coaches included) to tuck in their shirts and drawstrings. Regardless of whether it's the start of training camp or four months into the season, we start every practice by coming together as a team at midcourt. Our players sprint to the

Sample Practice Plan

Practice 24	**November 7, 2007**	**Time: 10:00 a.m. to 1:00 p.m.**

9:30-10:00   Prepractice skill development

10:00-10:15   Huddle, talk, walk-through

         1. Message of the day

         2. Foul to give rules

         3. End of quarter execution

         4. Post offense (spacing) (cuts off feed)

         5. Intro open set

10:15-10:35   Stretch/warm-up/closeouts

10:35-10:45   Shooting (three men/two balls); shots off the move

10:45-11:00   5-0 rehearsal offense

         1. Get to the second side

         2. Post-up plays: rub, chin/fo power, chin LA, 45

         3. P/R plays: fist out swing, chin/fo to 15, elbow get

         4. Catch-and-shoot: rub chase, chin thru twist, thumb

11:00-11:10   Transition defense: 5-on-5 change drill

         1. 1 and 2 sprint back on rhythm of the shot

         2. Load to the ball

         3. Point and talk

11:10-11:15   Green drill

11:15-11:30   Shell/defensive game

         1. Defend flares to rescreens

         2. Defend flex action

         3. Defend side P/R to step-up

11:30-11:45   5-on-5 offensive execution

         1. Post-up plays

         2. Run-out pick-and-roll plays

         3. 2nd side

         4. Drive and kick/spacing

11:45-12:00   Work vs. 2-3 zone with conversion

         1. Sets: chin opposite, thumb up 32/23

         2. Attack middle and short corners

         3. Dribble penetrate the gaps

12:00-12:15   Position skill work

         1. Guards: P/R recognition, pinch post

         2. Forwards: logo moves

         3. Centers: post moves

12:15-12:25   Free throws

12:25-12:30   Huddle/postpractice comments

12:30-1:00   5-on-0 half-court offensive review

Figure 17.1   Sample practice plan.

huddle and start clapping. We line up in a circle formation and don't allow anyone to hide behind teammates. We like to bring our players together to quickly talk about what's going on both inside and outside of basketball.

Whether it's somebody's birthday or we have a new father on the team, it's good for the camaraderie of the team to come together and learn about each other. With all the practices, meetings, trips, and games, we end up spending more time with each other during the season than we do with our own families, so it's important to us that we encourage a feeling of unity.

If you're at the pro or college level, or even in high school, you might have a foreign player who is homesick, or another player might just be going through a tough time in his life. Sometimes just coming together as a team, as a family, and laughing or smiling is all it takes to pick someone up.

Once the fun has been had, we begin to discuss the previous day's results. In training camp, we talk about the previous day's practice; during the season, we discuss the previous night's game. We feel it's important that our players understand why we won or why we lost. Regardless of the outcome, we talk about what we did well and what we need to do to improve. We try to point out positive performances and efforts, the things we want to see repeated. This prepractice meeting is kept brief so that we can get right into practice.

Practice Format

We believe we should have a format to our practices. It doesn't have to be the same every day. Some coaches like to have the same routine; others try to avoid monotony. Read your team to determine what works best for you.

Before our team practice begins, we have prepractice skill-development work with selected players. We might work with certain players individually, in small groups, or as an entire group. Daily skill work is important to us.

After prepractice work, we like to start our practices differently from some other teams. Many coaches prefer to get their guys loose or stretch them out first. We begin each day with a teaching segment before the players get stretched. This segment is simply a talk- or walk-through of any skill, concept, or play set that we want to introduce, review, or improve. In training camp, we use this segment to implement our basic offensive and defensive packages, special situations, and drills.

We've found that if we walk through and teach things slowly at the beginning, practice flows smoothly once we get the players moving. For example, if our side pick-and-roll defense was poor the night before, we'll walk through our adjustments at the beginning of practice. This way, when we get to the side pick-and-roll defensive segment of practice, we don't have to stop for review. The players already understand what we need to improve, so we can give them a quick reminder and get right into the drill. At one point or another, we talk or walk through everything we'll work on in practice. From new drills to end-of-game defense to press offense, we teach it at the beginning of practice and drill it once the contact part of practice has begun.

Warm-Up Routine

After our teaching segment, we devote the next 20 minutes of practice to getting our players physically ready to practice. Rich Dalatri, our outstanding strength and conditioning coach, puts our players through a series of movement and stretching techniques to prepare them to hit the floor running for practice. Rich uses several techniques, including Pilates, yoga, stationary bikes, and kinetic stretching exercises to get players ready for practice. The last 5 minutes of his warm-up include some type of closeout or stance drill.

Practice With the Ball

Once players are warmed up and stretched, we usually begin practice with some sort of three-man, two-ball shooting drill. We want our players to shoot game shots at game speed and game rhythm. We mix up the shooting drills throughout the season. After shooting, we rehearse our offense in a 5-on-0 full-court format. We want our players to flow into our offense and pay attention to detail. We emphasize timing, spacing, setups, hard cuts, proper angles on screens, and passing the ball on time and on target.

We want our players constantly running through our plays, which we believe helps our offensive flow during games. Not only do the players get to their spots quicker, which gets us into our sets quicker, but they get a better understanding of what options we're looking for in each play as well.

In our 5-on-0 rehearsal segments, we like to not only give them a play call but to also give them the exact option we're looking to get out of that particular play. We take a couple of plays and have them explore all the options within that set. We'll also incorporate dribble penetration at the end of the play instead of always taking a catch-and-shoot jumper. For example, if we call a side pick-and-roll play, we don't always need to rehearse the ball handler coming off the screen for a jump shot. We want to incorporate as many offensive concepts as we can. We might tell the ball handler to "pass ahead and get into a drive-and-kick game on the second side of the floor." Now we're not only rehearsing our offensive sets but incorporating our drive-and-kick principles as well.

Improving Shooting Skills

Shooting is important enough to us that we have a full-time shooting coach whose sole purpose is to work with players on shooting mechanics. He works daily with players both before and after practice, focusing on technique and often using film breakdowns to help them with their mechanics.

Pace and Flow of Practice

As mentioned earlier, we like to run an up-tempo, fast-paced practice (though we also try to be flexible enough to slow down to emphasize teaching points as necessary). Once players get loose, we want to keep them loose. There are no breaks between drills. One drill flows immediately into the next. We require our players to sprint from drill to drill. If we're working as a team on the half-court, when we move to the next drill we sprint to the other end of the floor.

As a time-saver, we give every drill or segment of practice a unique name. This way when we repeat the drill the next day, we don't need to explain it again. We just call it by its name, and the players jump into it.

Flexibility in the Practice Plan

Our master practice calendar helps us pace our team throughout the season. For instance, we know that over a long season every practice can't be three hours long. We try to combine a live-in-the-moment mentality with a big-picture view regarding how long we want to practice the last third of the season. As the season progresses, we try to take into account the number of minutes certain players have played the night before. Instead of practicing long, we might have a shorter but more intense practice.

As is true for most teams, not all our roster players play heavy minutes in games. This being the case, some players don't get the same workout during games as other players do. We keep this in mind when planning our practices and have our bench players play some additional three on three or work extra time on individual skills. Otherwise, they'll coast through the shortened practices and their progress might slide. We want to have a concrete plan for each player's

Jesse D. Garrabrant/NBAE/Getty Images Sport

Even veteran pros like Jason Kidd benefit from individual shooting technique instruction and practice.

development. All bench players who don't play regular minutes must have the same preparation mentality as they would were they regulars in the rotation. They must always be ready to contribute when their opportunity arises.

ROLE OF ASSISTANT COACHES

We're fortunate to have an outstanding coaching staff. Our assistant coaches do an excellent job and are a big reason for our success. Each member of our staff understands his role and responsibilities. Each one has designed a detailed teaching plan for developing the players assigned to his area of responsibility.

Not only are our assistant coaches excellent teachers, but they also have a good sense of the pulse of the team. They spend enough time with players to gain their trust. They have insight into the players' states of mind. As a result, their help in planning or tweaking a practice comes in handy. For instance, an assistant might remind me that the guys have been working hard, giving great effort, and could use a slightly shorter practice. Because of their relationships and interactions with our players, our assistants can anticipate problems and nip them in the bud before they turn serious.

Our assistants spend a great deal of time working individually with players. Because the NBA season is quite long, it's vital that our players continue to improve throughout the season. Whether it's working on pick-and-roll recognition, post moves, shooting, on-ball defense, or ball handling, the assistant coaches are at the forefront of our player-development program.

PRACTICE DRILLS

Drills are an integral part of our practices. We want to make sure what we expect from our players in games is what we emphasize in practice, and we place this emphasis through drills. Like most coaches, we believe that drilling is the best way to make things become automatic in games. We'll look now at some of our favorite drills that we run regularly in practice.

Defensive Drills

At the core of our practices are our defensive breakdown segments. We place a great deal of importance on team defense. Every day we try to work on transition defense, post

Assistant coaches add great value to practice sessions, from providing player instruction to ensuring that drills are conducted crisply and properly.

Nathaniel S. Butler/NBAE/Getty Images Sport

defense, pick-and-roll defense, individual on-ball defense, defending baseline screens, closing out, blocking out, and rebounding.

One of the core defensive drills we run every day might be familiar to you. It's called the shell drill. We start with basic positioning and then build from there. From day one, our players understand that we want to take away the middle of the floor, protect our three-second lane, contest shots, and block out and rebound. We incorporate every action we must defend over the course of the season into our shell drill. We also drill our pick-and-roll defense; here, the defense must guard multiple pick-and-rolls within the same possession.

Closeout 1

X1 starts on the left block, sprints to the right corner of the free-throw lane, and closes out, not giving up the middle of the court. He then slides down the lane to the right block, sprints to the left corner of the free-throw lane to close out, again not giving up the middle of the court, and then makes defensive slides to the same position from where he started (figure 17.2). This equals one trip. Each player goes three times.

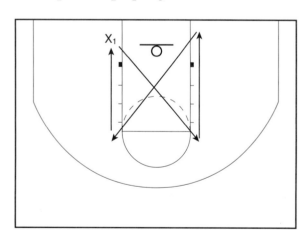

Figure 17.2   Closeout 1 drill.

Closeout 2

X1 starts in the left corner with his back to the basket; he's holding a medicine ball. He defensive slides to the first cone just outside the left corner of the free-throw lane. When

he gets there, he drops the medicine ball and then slides to the cone directly under the rim. There he picks up another medicine ball and defensive slides to the cone outside the right corner of the free-throw lane. When he gets there, he drops the medicine ball and defensive slides to the cone in the right corner (figure 17.3). This equals one trip. Go three times. Two coaches pick up the balls when X1 drops them and return them to the baseline for the next cycle. Players need to stay in a stance. Don't let their feet come together. Slides should be short, quick, and low.

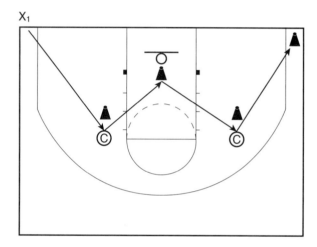

Figure 17.3   Closeout 2 drill.

Shell Shooting

In our shell drill, we have three teams of four players (with substitutes, if necessary), but instead of having one team off the floor waiting, we send them to the other end of the floor to do shooting drills with a coach. We call this our shell shooting segment of practice. We learned this drill format from coach Dean Smith. By having the third team in an organized shooting segment, there's no dead time for any group and they don't get a break. Teams rotate from offense to defense to the other end of the floor for shooting. The first time through, each segment lasts six minutes. The second time through lasts four minutes. Each group ends up going twice on offense, twice on defense, and twice to the other end for shooting. This takes 30 minutes. On half the court we play a shell four on four; on the other side we shoot with a line of shooters, one passer, and one rebounder (figure 17.4).

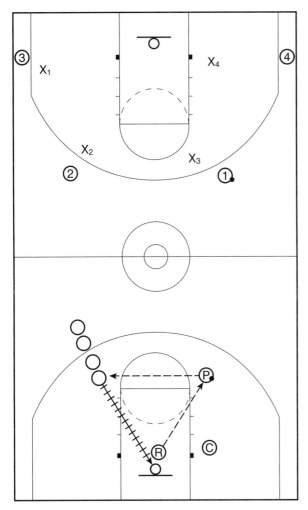

Figure 17.4　Shell shooting drill.

Green

Green is our color command for fronting the low post. We start out playing four on four at the typical shell spots. We have two guards line up with the pro lane line and two forwards at the free-throw line extended outside the three-point line.

As the ball is passed from guard to guard, the defenders shift to their corresponding help positions, as in a typical shell drill. What's different here is that when the ball is passed from guard to forward, the guard who didn't pass the ball slice cuts to the ball-side post. His defender must jump to the ball,

defend the cut, and then get to a "green." As the guard is getting to a green, the weak-side forward gets to what we call a tag position. He must be in the three-second lane to prevent the lob pass versus the front.

If necessary, the weak-side forward comes all the way over and tags the offensive player posting up to make sure that he's not called for a defensive three seconds. The defender on the ball must apply good ball pressure using the nearest hand to trace the ball to limit the vision of the passer. The defender at the top, closest to the ball, gives elbow protection and is ready to help if the ball handler drives to the middle. As the ball is reversed to the opposite side of the floor, the offensive players rotate out and fill their spots.

The drill now repeats on the other side of the floor so that defensive players are in different spots. It works out that all four defensive players can both get to a green and tag the post. 1 and 2 are lined up outside the pro lane. 3 and 4 are lined up at the corners. 1 starts with the ball. X2 is on the help side near the free-throw area; X3 is splitting the difference. 1 passes to 4, and 2 cuts to the box. X2 gets to a green; X3 tags the player who's going to the low post. X2 is now yelling "Green! Green! Green!" with hands high and butt low. X4 is in a hard, no-middle stance, pressuring the ball to discourage the post pass. X3 is in good help position, yelling "Tag! Tag! Tag!" and using all three seconds (figure 17.5).

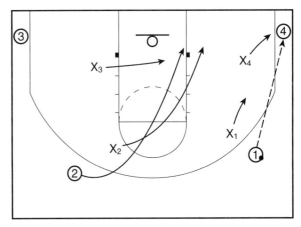

Figure 17.5　Green drill: the guard-to-forward pass; the weak-side guard cuts to the low post, who is covered in front.

After 4 holds the ball for a count to let X2 green, 4 passes to 1. (3 doesn't slide up until 4 passes back up top.) On this pass, X3 now gets near the free-throw area, 2 fills the weak-side corner, and X2 splits the difference (figure 17.6). 1 swings the ball to 3, who swings it to 2 in the corner.

1 now slice cuts to the post, and the drill is repeated. It works out that everyone gets to defend the slice into the post (figure 17.7).

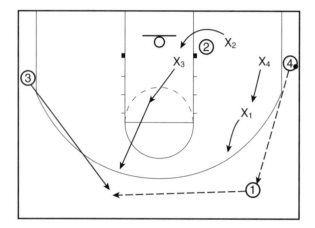

Figure 17.6 Green drill: ball reversal from the wing to the guard to the weak-side guard, who's covered in front.

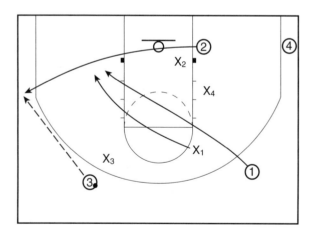

Figure 17.7 Green drill: The weak-side guard slice cuts to the low post, and the drill is repeated.

Five-on-Four Scramble

Four defenders get into a diamond set versus five offensive players in a three-players-out and two-players-in formation. The offense gets only five passes and three dribbles before it has to shoot. It has the advantage, so it should be able to get a good shot quickly. Defensively, we're working on challenging shots, rotating to open men, and protecting the three-second lane. The defense has only four players in a diamond at the start, but it does have one guy at the opposite end of the floor (figure 17.8). As soon as the offense scores or the defense comes up with the ball, the fifth man is in play and can be passed the ball. This forces 1 and 2 to get back as soon as possible. Now you play five on five at that end, then come back and play five on five at the end where you started, and then stop. Tell the defense to keep coming.

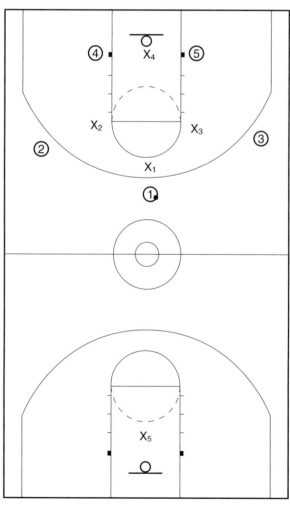

Figure 17.8 Five-on-four scramble drill.

Five-on-Five Change

Offense plays five on five live until the coach yells "Change!" The offense then drops the ball and sprints back on defense. The offense can't guard the same player as before. Defense now goes to offense and looks to score. As soon as the offense picks the ball, it must throw it ahead to a coach at the hashmark (the line at the extension of the three-point arc) on the other end (figure 17.9). This forces the defense to get back quicker and get to the level of the ball.

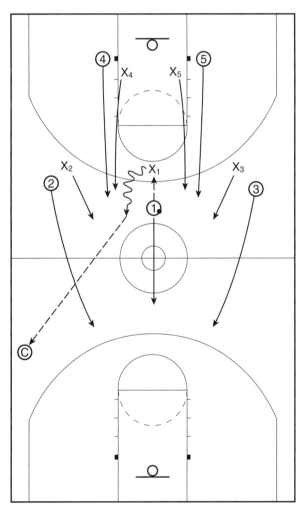

Figure 17.9 Five-on-five change drill.

Two-on-Two Help-and-Recover

1 starts with the ball at the top of the key. 2 is outside the corner of the three-second lane, and the coach is on the opposite wing. 1

passes to the coach and sprints to the ball-side corner of the free-throw lane; 2 moves toward the three-second lane. When the coach passes back to 1, X2 closes out and X1 helps the helper. 1 then drives hard to the right elbow. X2 helps and recovers back to 2 on 1's pass out to 2 (figure 17.10). Play live.

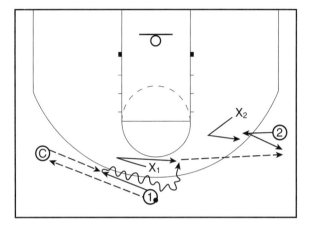

Figure 17.10 Help-and-recover drill.

Two-on-Two Help-and-Recover, Middle Drive

1 starts with the ball at the top of the key. 2 is outside the corner of the three-second lane. 1 passes to the coach and sprints to the ball-side corner of the free-throw lane; 2 moves toward the three-second lane. When the coach passes back to 1, X1 closes out and X2 helps the helper. 1 then swings the ball to 2, who drives hard to the middle. X1 helps and recovers back to 1 (figure 17.11). Play live.

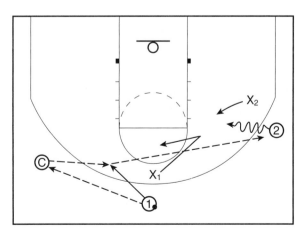

Figure 17.11 Help-and-recover, middle-drive drill.

Offensive Drills

One of the main actions to watch on the offense of an NBA team is the drive of the ball handler and the kickoff pass to an open teammate. This technique must be mastered by perimeter players through practice and more practice. In fact, this action involves not only the ball handler but also the team-mates on the floor, who must be able to move to the proper spots of the floor and create space to offer the driving teammate the passing lane. We run different drills with different situations that our players might face during a game, always followed by a shot taken by the player who receives the ball.

Drive-and-Kick Series (Three Out, Two In)

Middle drive. Three players set out, and two players set in. 1 attacks the three-second lane to either side, kicks the ball to 3, and continues to the corner on the ball side. 3 now drives to the middle and hits 2 slid-ing up. 3 follows his pass to fill that corner (figure 17.12). 2 now drives to the middle and makes a play. Players must take at least two dribbles and get two feet in the three-second lane. 4 and 5 flatten out to the baseline. Finish with a shot from anyone you want. Practice on both sides and with guards starting in different spots.

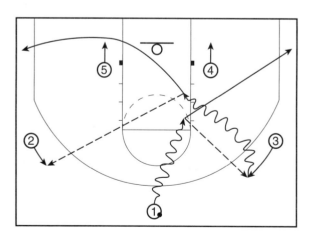

Figure 17.12 The drive-and-kick series: the middle drive.

Baseline drive (peel). 1 passes to 3, who drives hard to the baseline. 4 "peels up" to the elbow of the free-throw line, always seeing the ball. 5 cuts until he "finds the dots" in the middle of the three-second lane. 2 drifts to the baseline. 1 drifts off to the elbow on the weak side. 3 passes to 4 (figure 17.13).

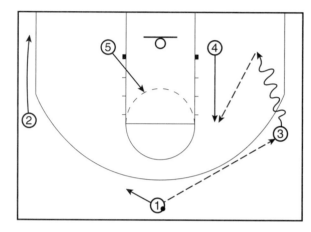

Figure 17.13 The drive-and-kick series: the baseline drive (peel).

Baseline drive (find big at the dots). 1 passes to 3, who drives hard to the base-line. 4 peels up to the corner of the free-throw lane, always seeing the ball. 5 finds the dots in the middle of the three-second lane. 2 drifts to the baseline. 1 drifts off to the elbow on the weak side. 3 passes to 5 (figure 17.14).

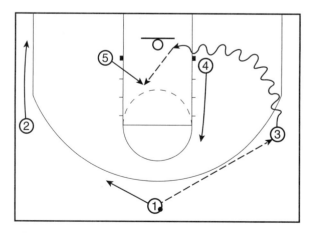

Figure 17.14 The drive-and-kick series: the baseline drive (find big at the dots).

Baseline drive (baseline drift). 1 passes to 3, who drives it hard to the baseline. 4 peels up to the elbow of the free-throw area, always seeing the ball. 5 finds the dots in the middle of the three-second lane. 2 drifts to the baseline. 1 drifts off to the elbow on the weak side. 3 passes to 2 (figure 17.15).

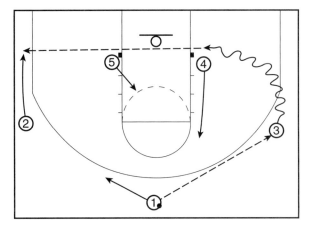

Figure 17.15   The drive-and-kick series: the baseline drive (baseline drift).

Baseline drive (skip it, second drive, and kick). 1 passes the ball to 3, who drives hard to the baseline. 4 peels up to the elbow, always seeing the ball. 5 finds the dots in the middle of the three-second lane. 2 drifts to the baseline. 1 drifts off to the elbow on the weak side. 3 finds 1 on the skip pass; 1 drives hard away from where the defense is loaded up, draws X2 away, and then hits 2 for an open jump shot (figure 17.16).

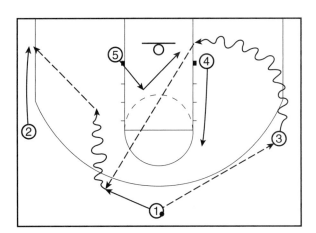

Figure 17.16   The drive-and-kick series: the baseline drive (skip it, second drive, and kick).

55-Second Shooting

Three players are involved in this drill: a shooter, a rebounder, and a passer with two balls. 1 comes hard to the wing for a catch-and-shoot jumper, planting on his inside pivot foot (he takes a one-two step into the catch). 1 then fades hard to the corner for a second shot (figure 17.17). Repeat for 55 seconds. Give five seconds to rotate shooter to rebounder, rebounder to passer, and passer to shooter.

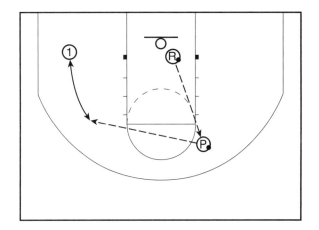

Figure 17.17   55-second shooting drill.

FINAL POINTS

You know by now that success starts with preparation. What you do every day in practice determines how you'll perform in games. The greater attention you give to detail, the better chance your team will execute come game day. We believe in making the most of every minute of practice, which means a lot of organization up front. If you don't use a master calendar, find another way to get organized. This will save you from wasting time and help you get the most out of your players. There are many different ways to be successful in this game, but most of them start with a plan.

chapter 18

Game Preparation

Mike Dunleavy and Jim Eyen

In the NBA, you have incredible talent on every team, from the starting five to the players sitting on the bench. On a given night, any team can beat another. To compete at this upper echelon of basketball you must look for and use any and every advantage. Games are frequently decided in the final seconds. In fact, the average point differential of a NBA game is plus or minus 4 points. Consequently, an area we place a great deal of importance on is game preparation. In this chapter we will give an overview of our scouting program and the responsibilities of our staff. We'll detail the role of the advance scout, the preparation of our game plan, and our use of video and technology. We'll then describe what we do in practices on the days leading up to a game. In addition, we'll look at our game day, pregame, and postgame routines. By the end of the chapter, you'll have added insight into the logistics and thought processes that go into game preparation.

At the professional level, talent and skill are foremost in the quest for success, but preparation can be a great equalizer. A coach's goal in his preparation is to maximize the talent on his team and minimize the effect of the opponent's talent. Technology and available resources enable us to compile a great deal of information on a prospective opponent. The key is to convey to the players the correct amount of information—a dose that can be absorbed in the short amount of time that an NBA team has to prepare for

each upcoming game. As a coach, you tend to feel that the more information you have, the better. As a player, you want only the information that can help your performance without creating confusion. Preparation time in the NBA can vary from a few hours to a few days. Each team is at the mercy of the schedule. Coaches always feel they could use more time to prepare than is available. However, unlimited preparation is not the nature of our league. But with the average point differential so minimal, never underestimate how detail and efficient preparation can affect outcome.

ADVANCE SCOUTING

In this age of video technology, some argue that actual on-site scouting should be replaced by watching games on video. We disagree. There's no substitute for observing a team's live performance. We prefer to scout an opponent as close to the date of our game as possible. Generally, our scout sees an opponent twice, including its last game prior to playing us. As we progress into the season, when an upcoming opponent is a team we've already played, we'll often scout the opponent only one additional time. That decision might change depending on how much earlier we played the team or how important the game is to our season. We employ two scouts—one on the East Coast and one on the West—who travel many miles throughout the season, often seeing games several nights in a row in a different city each night. At times they'll travel with the team as the schedule allows, but typically they're a city ahead of us. Scouting can be a thankless job, but many coaches have come up through these ranks and understand the rigors and greatly value the contribution of the scouts to game preparation.

First and foremost, our scouts try to obtain the play calls of the opponent, recording them on a worksheet such as that shown in figure 18.1. In baseball, much energy is expended trying to steal signs because it's a great advantage to know in advance when a base runner is going to steal or a hitter is going to bunt. Similarly, in basketball, it's advantageous to know what a team is going to run as soon as you hear the call (or see the signal) from the coach or a player. A call, of course, is the way a coach (sometimes through a player) communicates his intentions to his team. For example, when we want to get the ball in the post to Cuttino Mobley (our 2 man), the point guard calls out "2 down" or shows two fingers pointing down and the team executes accordingly.

Some coaches go to great lengths to hide or disguise their calls, whereas others apparently couldn't care less if they're stolen. Some coaches bark out fake calls, and others give two or more signs in an attempt to throw off the opponent. It is the job of the scout to differentiate what is real or fake, a job that's not easy to do. Quality scouts have the ability to watch the coach and simultaneously see the point guard. If the calls are verbal, he must listen acutely. Often because of arena noise and distance from the court, a scout must resort to one of his most valuable acquired skills: the ability to read lips. Frequently, a scout can note a call but might miss viewing part or all of the play. In such cases, he'll write down the time on the clock and then go back and review the game film to determine what play was being run with a particular call.

The ability to be resourceful and anticipate when, where, and how calls are made is an irreplaceable asset for a scout to possess. Obtaining calls is not something that can be accomplished through watching video unless the camera happens to catch a coach or player at just the right moment. This is one reason a scout needs to see the game in person. Other advantages to attending live games include the opportunity to witness bench behavior, body language of the players, interaction among players and coaches, and play action away from the ball. Sometimes these off-camera glimpses of an opponent lend insight into the overall state of the team.

SCOUTING REPORT

A report is compiled for each game scouted. The depth and breadth of a written scouting report is based solely on the philosophy of the head coach. Some coaches feel the need to include every detail of the opponent in the report; others desire only the basic tendencies. Our needs and the reporting format we use fall somewhere in the middle based on years of refining and working with several teams. Although we might present only certain tendencies to the players as we prepare, we do prefer to have more information rather than less. The report consists of three sections:

- Defensive tendencies
- Offensive tendencies
- Actual play sets

The defensive tendencies include ways in which a particular team attacks defensively: full-court presses, half-court traps, zone defenses, pick-and-roll schemes, and so on. All teams employ these tactics, but most teams have defenses they use more than others, particularly in certain situations. This is the information we like to know. For example, if a particular team shows a strong tendency to trap all pick-and-rolls that are set on the wing, it's useful for us to know that as we prepare in practice.

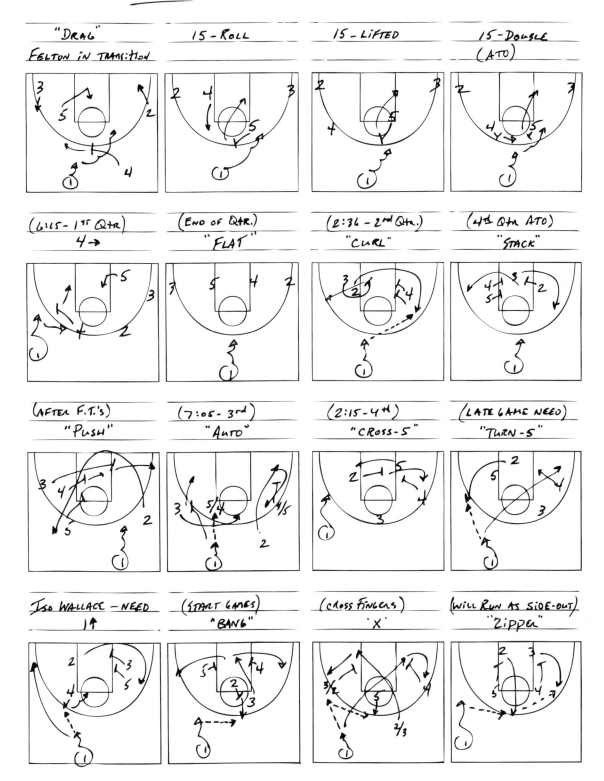

Figure 18.1 Scout's worksheet.

As for offensive tendencies, we want to know if an opponent runs a motion offense or more isolation. What type of pick-and-roll does it run? How effective is its low-post game? Again, although most teams have a certain level of expertise in many or all of these areas, we look for particular strengths, weaknesses, and definitive tendencies. For example, if we're able to anticipate certain plays or actions, particularly in late-game situations, this can greatly benefit our defensive preparation.

You can never be certain of an opponent's game plan, but it's crucial to familiarize yourself with the team's dominant tendencies. For example, if we know our impending opponent is an up-tempo, fast-breaking team, we'll spend time in practice on floor balance and transition defense. Similarly, if a team's offense consists primarily of pick-and-rolls, then obviously our practice time will focus more on pick-and-roll coverages and schemes.

The final category of the report consists of the opponent's play sets. This is the most detailed section, and specifics are important. The number of plays each team runs varies greatly. Some coaches have a large playbook but use only a few main sets. Other coaches will rotate their main sets over the course of the season and keep you guessing as to what plays you'll see. But, again, we focus on tendencies, and teams often will use specific plays in certain situations.

VIDEO AND OTHER TECHNOLOGY

The video coordinator and his staff are crucial to our overall game-plan preparation. Countless hours are involved in recording games, logging the film, and establishing breakdowns. At the end of the day, the video personnel are as versed on the opponent as the scouts or coaches are.

The breakdown of game film is a long-standing practice in all sports. Coaches need to view games of opponents and of their own team throughout the course of the season. The advent of digital technology has changed the methods and applications. Actual games are no longer recorded on film or video, although we continue to refer to them as such. We view games and breakdowns in digital form either on our laptop computers or from a DVD. This is more efficient and flexible when viewing alone or when presenting to the team. Through the use of special editing software, we can, in an instant, pull up specific points of a game. The edits can range from full-game mode to offense only, from pick-and-rolls to isolation of individuals. The ability to customize the game film to focus on a desired area of emphasis is a valuable coaching tool.

What are "breakdowns" and "edits"? Each game is broken down (by our video staff) into individual plays. Each play is broken down into categories such as offense, defense, particular play sets, turnovers, offensive rebounds, and so on. Once the game has been logged into the computer program, we can pull out whatever we want to see from the game. For example, when we're preparing to play the Phoenix Suns, an edit is produced that shows all the Suns' recent pick-and-rolls with Steve Nash. We can view this as coaches, show it to the team, or view it individually with the one or more players who will defend Nash. Video is a teaching tool with numerous applications.

We begin showing the team film of our upcoming opponent prior to our practice the preceding day. Usually this consists of a 20- to 25-play edit of the opponent's play sets lasting approximately 10 to 15 minutes. After viewing a sample of the offense and a quick discussion of the team's tendencies, we then move onto the practice floor.

On the morning of a game day, prior to our pregame walk-through and shoot-around, the team views another edit. This edit is divided into five categories:

- the opponent's transition offense,
- set offense,

- side out-of-bounds plays,
- baseline out-of-bounds plays, and
- an example of the opponent's defense.

Prior to the actual game, the team receives one more 10- to 15-minute dose of the opponent. This edit includes more clips of its recent games but with an added emphasis on our last game versus this team. For example, versus Phoenix, the edit will include a series of examples of our defense versus Nash in pick-and-rolls or our double team against Amare Stoudemire. The edit will also include clips of Phoenix defending our offense, in particular Chris Kaman in the post or a zone trap they might surprise us with after a timeout.

After the game, complete copies and breakdowns are provided to coaches and players. In our postgame analysis, we refer to film often while addressing the team and on an individual basis. Film is an important ingredient to many postgame discussions, particularly when there's a difference of opinion regarding a situation. As the saying goes, "The film doesn't lie."

With detailed scouting reports, statistics, and video right at our fingertips in the office, on the road, or at home, computer technology has made game preparation more convenient and efficient.

GAME PLAN

As a coach, the first order of business in preparing for an upcoming opponent is to compile as much information as is available. We rely on our scouts and video staff to assist in this area. Routinely, this process begins long before the upcoming game. In fact, the team might be playing one or two games versus other opponents while one of the assistant coaches begins preparation for a more distant game.

Our game-plan system operates by dividing all 29 opponents in the league among the three assistant coaches. Each coach has a responsibility to become an expert on his teams. As a game approaches, he must view previous games, compile scouting reports, and begin to analyze statistical information. This type of preliminary work can be a juggling process in which you're practicing to play one team while you're in preliminary preparation for another. This is the nature of the NBA schedule; when one game concludes, you must be ready to prepare for the next. In our system, the onus is on the assistant coaches to meet those needs, thereby allowing the head coach and the team to move forward immediately in preparation for the next scheduled game. All available information—scouting reports, film (edits and game copies), and the suggested game plan—must be ready and available for the staff when the preceding game is over. An example of a suggested game plan is shown in figure 18.2.

After experimenting with other systems, we've found this method to be the most effective. Although each assistant coach is involved in the preparation for every game, there's value in having one coach accountable for each team. Over the course of the season, you become familiar with your assigned teams, and this additional insight and expertise can be advantageous.

Statistical information is a foundation for many of our decisions. An opponent's cumulative stats (which include field-goal percentages, free-throw percentages, rebounding averages, turnovers, and so on) clearly depict its strengths and weaknesses.

It's the purely objective part of the equation that formulates the game plan. For example, before we decide to double team the opponent's best player in the post, we need to know the three-point accuracy of their remaining shooters or we might pay a steep price when they get open shots off our double teams.

To analyze an opponent's most recent play, we also use five-game stats; the information included is the same as for season cumulative stats, but only for the most recent five games (tables 18.1 and 18.2).

In addition, we analyze individual stats, both cumulative and five-game. This gives us an indication of who's hot and who's not and any other trends. For example, if one player has a high number of turnovers, we might perceive him as turnover prone and be more apt to apply defensive pressure when guarding him; or if a player has made his last 10 three-point shots, we undoubtedly will pay him more attention on the perimeter than usual. Again, statistics do not always tell the entire story, but they are certainly an integral part of the equation.

Along with the scouting report, film, and statistical information, the assistant coaches also submit a suggested game plan. This plan is the basis on which the coaching staff makes their decisions regarding defensive matchups, coverages, and the overall defensive scheme. We discuss as a staff the questions at hand and, after viewing film, practicing (if schedule and time permit), and more discussion, the end result becomes the final game plan.

GAME-DAY PREPARATION

The majority of our games are played at 7:30 p.m. Routinely, our game day starts with an 8:30 a.m. coaches' meeting, followed by a film session with the team, a walk-through on the court, and a shooting session. The coaches' meeting begins with a conversation regarding the latest information on our opponent (injuries, updated stats, rumors, and the like). Next, we view the most recent film of the opponent and discuss the defensive coverages we'll use against particular plays, preview the film edit that will be shown to the team, and finalize the defensive matchups and coverages we'll use that night. We also review the opponent's depth chart (players available at each position), thus anticipating the substitution pattern and how it may affect our rotation. Our trainer drops in and provides a brief injury report on our players and the status of any lingering issues. We then put aside our defensive concerns and discuss how they might defend us and what we can do to attack their schemes, traps, and coverages.

The players' film session begins with a synopsis of the opponents and their tendencies. We elaborate on their strengths and weaknesses as a team and individually. We announce our starters for the game along with the defensive matchups. We encourage input and interaction from the players regarding any insight, questions, or suggestions regarding anticipated coverages. After viewing the 15- to 20-minute film edit, we entertain any additional questions and then move onto the court.

SUGGESTED GAME PLAN

vs. CHARLOTTE   Date: 3-16-07

1 BASIC DEFENSE

A. Transition Defense starts w/ Floor Balance / Vision
B. Track Ball (Felton) in open court / Fan out
C. Deny dribble penetration - contain first, then contest
D. Control boards - long shots = long rebounds

5	KAMAN	vs	VOSKUHL
4	BRAND	vs	WALLACE
3	Maggette	vs	ANDERSON
2	MOBLEY	vs	CARROLL
1	HART	vs	FELTON

2 LOW POST DEFENSE 2X From Top or Weakside / Front

A. WALLACE = 2X vs 1st Bounce   w/ opportunity
B. MAY = Read / BLUE vs Deep Catch
C. BREZEC = BLUE - Likes to Face up
D. VOSKUHL > WHITE
E. HOLLINS

SHOOTERS

CARROL
MORRISON
HERRMANN
WALLACE
FELTON / ANDERSON

3 PT. SHOOTERS	ROTATE TO	STUNT TO	POOR FT SHOOTERS
CARROLL 41%	3 pt. Shooters -	NON - SHOOTERS -	E. WILLIAMS 57%
HERRMANN 40%	Full Rotation vs.	use of stunts	HOLLINS 59%
FELTON 34%	Same size	vs. Range shots	BREZEC 61%
MORRISON 34%	+ WALLACE	& flow of game	
ANDERSON 32%			

3 PICK/ROLLS   QUICKS   Anticipate & Talk = Brown

A. WING	B. TOP	C. ELBOW	D. CORNER
GREEN -	GOLD -	GOLD -	BROWN -
Under w/ opportunity	Anticipate Flat	Alert for	Slip / Roll
vs. NON-SHOOTERS	Pick from	slip	To LOB
	1-4 set		

FELTON, McInnis will
crossover to baseline

4 1-1 ICES

A. WALLACE - from top & wing - strong Rt. / will spin
B. FELTON - Explosive / Excellent crossover / 1-4 flat
C. McInnis - Strong Rt. / will spin into push shot
D. CARROLL - Range jumper - No space

NOTES

OKAFOR = OUT w/ KNEE

MAY, KNIGHT =
   QUESTIONABLE / DOUBTFUL

* CHARLOTTE HAS WON
  2 games in Row - LAST
  LOSS in O.T. @ PHOENIX
* WILL PLAY "SMALL" @
    4 SPOT
* PREPARE FOR ZONE DEFENSE

OPPONENT DEPTH CHART

1	2	3	4	5
FELTON	CARROLL	ANDERSON	WALLACE	VOSKUHL
McINNIS	(ANDERSON)	MORRISON	MAY	BREZEC
KNIGHT		← HERRMANN →		HOLLINS

Figure 18.2   Suggested game plan.

Table 18.1 Charlotte Per Game Averages, Last Five Games

Player	Games	Time per game	FGM	FGA	FGM avg.	FGA avg.	FG%	3PM	3PA	3P%	FTM
Wallace	5	39:09:36	38	81	7.6	16.2	46.9	6	11	54.5	30
Felton	5	32:44:12	29	71	5.8	14.2	40.8	8	24	33.3	20
May	3	27:24:00	20	35	6.7	11.7	57.1	2	2	100.0	5
Carroll	5	26:45:00	20	42	4.0	8.4	47.6	9	19	47.4	13
Anderson	5	25:44:24	19	36	3.8	7.2	52.8	9	17	52.9	9
Morrison	5	23:48:24	18	49	3.6	9.8	36.7	5	16	31.3	3
Knight	4	20:57:30	10	25	2.5	6.3	40.0	0	2	0.0	8
Voskuhl	5	26:00:00	15	29	3.0	5.8	51.7	0	0	0.0	4
Hermann	3	9:55:20	7	9	2.3	3.0	77.8	4	4	100.0	2
Brezec	5	16:45:48	15	28	3.0	5.6	53.6	0	0	0.0	3
Williams	1	7:41:00	2	3	2.0	3.0	66.7	0	0	0.0	0
Hollins	2	10:09:00	2	3	1.0	1.5	66.7	0	0	0.0	2
McInnis	3	15:29:20	3	9	1.0	3.0	33.3	0	0	0.0	0
Okafor	0	0:00:00	0	0	0.0	0.0	0.0	0	0	0.0	0
Harrington	0	0:00:00	0	0	0.0	0.0	0.0	0	0	0.0	0
Team totals	5	1152:00:00	198	420	46.3	95.7	47.1	43	95	45.3	99

Table 18.2 Game Results, Last Five Games

Date	Home	Away	Result	Score
3/5/2007	Charlotte	Utah	Loss	95-120
3/7/2007	Charlotte	Phoenix	Loss	106-115
3/10/2007	Charlotte	Memphis	Loss	107-115
3/12/2007	Charlotte	Orlando	Win	119-108
3/14/2007	Charlotte	Sacramento	Win	111-108

At this point, we walk through the opponent's actual plays. The numbers of plays vary from team to team. However, the average is 8 to 10 plays, including side out-of-bounds and baseline out-of-bounds plays. We have determined these to be the opponent's most frequently run plays or its most important plays. We demonstrate how to cover these plays and, at times, provide alternative coverages in case we need to employ a backup plan. Again, we value input from the players, knowing that along with contribution comes ownership. We review the tendencies of our opponent regarding presses, traps, and defensive schemes it might use to cover our important

FTA	FT%	O-R per game	D-R per game	Reb per game	Ast per game	PF per game	Stl per game	TO per game	Blk per game	Pts per game
38	78.9	3.2	5.6	8.8	3.4	3.6	1.6	2.4	1.0	22.4
25	80.0	1.2	1.8	3.0	6.0	2.4	1.4	2.2	0.4	17.2
8	62.5	1.3	5.0	6.3	2.0	4.3	1.3	0.7	0.3	15.7
14	92.9	0.2	2.0	2.2	1.4	1.8	0.8	1.4	0.0	12.4
10	90.0	1.0	1.8	2.8	4.0	2.2	1.4	0.8	0.2	11.2
3	100.0	0.6	1.4	2.0	1.2	2.4	0.4	1.6	0.0	8.8
10	80.0	0.5	1.8	2.3	5.0	2.5	1.3	0.5	0.0	7.0
8	50.0	2.0	5.4	7.4	1.2	3.6	0.8	1.4	1.2	6.8
2	100.0	0.0	1.0	1.0	0.0	1.3	0.0	0.7	0.0	6.7
6	50.0	0.8	1.6	2.4	1.0	3.4	0.2	0.8	0.2	6.6
0	0.0	1.0	0.0	1.0	0.0	2.0	0.0	1.0	0.0	4.0
7	28.6	0.5	0.5	1.0	0.0	1.0	0.0	0.0	0.0	3.0
0	0.0	0.0	0.3	0.3	3.3	1.0	0.3	1.0	0.0	2.0
0	0.0	0.0	0.0	0.0	0.0	0.0	0.0	0.0	0.0	0.0
0	0.0	0.0	0.0	0.0	0.0	0.0	0.0	0.0	0.0	0.0
131	75.6	12.3	28.2	40.5	28.5	31.5	9.5	14.5	3.3	123.8

plays. At times we also walk through parts of our offense to refine our execution or apply subtle changes to existing plays.

We conclude the morning session with shooting drills and free throws. The shooting drills are geared toward shots taken out of our play sets. In most cases we split the team into bigs and smalls and work on each end of the floor. This game-day practice, or shoot-around as it's referred to, is usually held on the actual game court; thus, you are limited to two baskets. We find this routine to be an efficient way to shoot the most number of shots in the least amount of time. After a prescribed number of free throws, we then adjourn. Coaches remain afterward and assist any players who want additional work; rookies and veterans alike often take advantage of this opportunity.

We then reconvene in the early evening and begin the pregame ritual. The coaches arrive at the arena between 4:30 and 5:00 p.m., and players begin to arrive around 5:00 p.m. The early arrivals consist of mostly younger players and rookies. However, some of the veterans opt for extra court time as well. Prior to any work on the floor, players check into the training room for ankle taping, treatment, or other training needs. Coaches are also available for last-minute individual film sessions. A common practice is to sit down with players and view briefly an individual edit of their defensive matchup for that night. At this point in the process, we try to keep it simple but remain focused.

With 45 minutes remaining before game time, all the players are in the locker room.

Andrew D. Bernstein/NBAE/Getty Images Sport

Just prior to tip-off and during time-outs in the course of a game, it's best to keep communication with players about tactics and plays as specific and concise as possible.

board is consistent with our basic defense, with some areas specific to this particular opponent. Based on our opposition, pick-and-rolls and the low post are areas that can change on a nightly basis. If we face a Steve Nash in pick-and-rolls or a Tim Duncan in the low post, we must be willing to customize our basic coverages or we could be in for a long night. We might decide to trap all pick-and-rolls with Nash or double team Duncan as soon as he catches the ball. Generally, our coverages remain consistent unless particular players warrant special attention. We will have a series of plays on the board that illustrate the opponent's basic offense. Once again, we talk briefly about each play and how to defend it. There are statistical categories on the board that are addressed; for example, three-point shooting capabilities and free-throw accuracy. If a particular player shoots a remarkably low percentage from the free-throw line, it is strongly noted. After any additional questions are answered and a few words of wisdom, the players move onto the court with approximately 20 minutes to warm up.

Since 5:30, a full-game copy of our last game versus our opponent has been running on the big screen for those who choose to watch. At this time players begin to look over the whiteboard, which has been made visible over the last few minutes. Because of the open access of the NBA locker room to the press and other credentialed people, the strategic notes on the board have remained covered until the 45-minute mark, when the doors are closed to outsiders. Shortly thereafter, our team meeting begins. The meeting starts with an additional 10- to 15-minute film edit, as described earlier. We then go through the basic points of our game plan and highlight the opposition's strengths and weaknesses while reiterating particular coverages of our morning walk-through.

Next, we turn our attention to the whiteboard. Most of the information on the

At some point before both coaching staffs go onto the floor, the official scorekeeper informs each locker room of the starters as designated by each team. Ninety percent of the time, this is a predictable event. However, if there's a surprise in the lineup, our staff will confer and decide on any defensive matchup changes.

Once the game has started we rely on our detailed preparation. With the exception of a few instances, we have rehearsed in some fashion all defensive schemes, anticipated matchups, and possible backup options. Because of our preparation, we're capable of making adjustments during time-outs, at quarter breaks, or, when necessary, on the fly.

At halftime, the staff converses briefly while the players have an opportunity to take care of any personal needs, speak to the trainer, and so on. The 14-minute break is brief, so our coaches' meeting and the address to the team must be short as well. Based on observations of the first half, we discuss any changes or adjustments with the team and then confer individually with players as necessary. We have usually taken notes on a form such as that shown in figure 18.3.

Immediately after the game, coaches meet for a few minutes to discuss any quick postgame thoughts and then assemble with the team for postgame comments. The following day at practice, the depth of our postgame analysis depends on the upcoming schedule. We might spend a few minutes or a few hours with the team analyzing our past performance. Yet one thing is certain—however long we dwell on yesterday's game, preparation for the next game is looming.

HALFTIME ADJUSTMENTS   vs. CHARLOTTE 3-16-07

PATIENCE vs CHARLOTTE'S ZONE   ACTIVATE hands - increase DEFLECTIONS
  -ATTACK GAPS, better ball movement   Provide quicker help vs Felton's
                                                          Dribble penetration

DEFENSE   __KEY PLAYS__   OFFENSE

P/ROLLS w/ FELTON - CONTAIN   P/ROLL'S were EFFECTIVE -

dribble, NO SPLITS!   keep good SPACING

ISOLATIONS w/ WALLACE -   HURT THEM INSIDE - READY

WEAKSIDE help WAS SLOW-ANTICIPATE!   FOR quicker 2X's -
                                          READ & RESPOND

SINGLE-DOUBLE w/ CARROLL - better CLOSE-OUTS

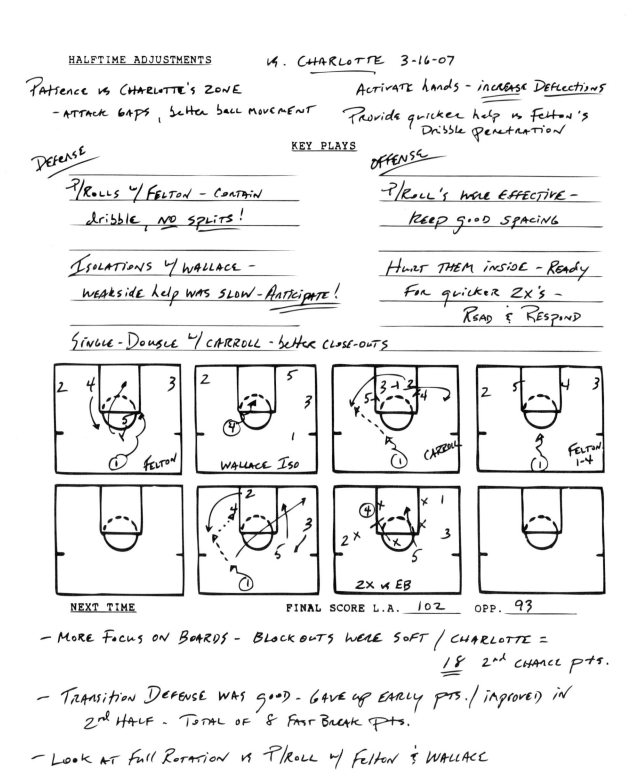

NEXT TIME   FINAL SCORE L.A. _102_   OPP. _93_

- MORE FOCUS ON BOARDS - BLOCK OUTS WERE SOFT / CHARLOTTE =
                                        18 2nd CHANCE pts.

- TRANSITION DEFENSE WAS GOOD - GAVE UP EARLY pts. / improved IN
      2nd HALF - TOTAL OF 8 FAST BREAK pts.

- LOOK AT FULL ROTATION vs P/ROLL w/ FELTON & WALLACE

Figure 18.3   Halftime adjustment form.

298

chapter 19

Player Development

Kevin Eastman

In today's game scouting is so sophisticated that an opponent will know your offense almost as well as your own team does. So, what happens when a play breaks down? Do you have players with the skill level necessary to beat the defense and get your team a basket? This is a common scenario that happens to all teams at all levels. The key question becomes: Have you prepared your players for those important possessions of the game, both on the technical and the motivational side?

A proper program for developing your players will get you through some trying situations, but having a quality skill-development program in place is not enough. You must have players who are willing to understand that their game is not a finished product and that there's still room for improvement. Even with a team full of players who understand they need to keep working, you'll still have to find ways to motivate and teach them on a daily basis. Anyone can work on his skills on a given day, but true development comes in two ways: knowing what to work on and consistently working day in and day out.

Coaches and players must have a shared responsibility. Players must understand that improvement is a process that doesn't happen overnight. They must comprehend the "theory of two"—that it takes a coach *two minutes* to explain a fundamental, it takes a player *two weeks* of daily practice on that fundamental to become somewhat comfort-able with it, and it takes *two months* before the player can call the fundamental his own and use it effectively in a game. So, yes, improvement is a process that takes time.

The coach needs to understand that he has to "bring it" every day as well. It's very important that the coach be into the skill work each day. Players respond much better to coaches who are enthusiastic, filled with energy, and convey a true interest in their improvement. Simply put, players like coaches who sweat with them.

MAKING THOROUGH PREPARATIONS

A coach has the responsibility to thoroughly study the game and his team. Just as players are required to work hard, so too must the coach. When creating your players' development program, you have several considerations on a variety of issues and situations, ranging from the number of shots your players take in practice to creating drills that best address the needs of the team.

Study your practice sessions: How many shots does your best player get (excluding shooting drills)? Tape your practices and count the number of shots your players get. I have found that it's a lot less than it should be; shooting is a skill, and skills require repetition.

Educate your players on how many shots they get during pick-up games in the off-season. I've found that in an average game to 7 points, each player gets an average of 3.2 shots per game. Each game takes about 15 minutes to complete, so extrapolated out, this gives each player 12.8 shots in an hour. This is not enough.

Develop a system of "bullet basketball" in which you have two or three quick teaching points to give each player on a particular fundamental. Keep them to just two or three so players will remember them. Here's an example.

When working on shooting, ask the player to always make sure that

- he is ready on the catch, with knees bent, hands up, and feet ready;
- he has "perfect feet," using the same exact footwork on every shot; and
- he has a perfect follow-through and maintains it until the ball gets to the rim.

Establish areas of importance for each position. Your big men should know what's expected of them, as should your perimeter players. Every player should have a required set of skills important to his position; then you must create drills that properly teach and train those skills.

Educate your players on the importance of giving themselves totally to the game. Many of today's players are not familiar enough with these three concepts:

- *Hard work.* This should be a given and is the price of admission for playing the game and improving a player's skills.
- *Competitiveness.* This is an attitude that won't let him give in. He might not win, but he should do everything he can to be successful.
- *Commitment.* Being committed is an everyday attitude. Players must commit not only to developing their skills but also to contributing to the success of the team and to taking care of themselves via diet, strength and conditioning, treatment and rehabilitation, and team

Great veteran players like Kevin Garnett are a joy to coach because they keep pushing themselves and seeking additional insights from the coaching staff to take their games to an even higher level. They also serve as great models for younger, less developed players.

success. Commitment is a year-round dedication to doing everything in their power to improve themselves and the team.

CREATING A BUY-IN FROM YOUR PLAYERS

Motivating today's players is difficult. All coaches must come up with ways to encourage their players to buy into the system. Players will much more likely buy in if they

Keys to a Quality Player-Development Program

Practice at a rate equal to or faster than that which will occur in a game. Players must practice skills at game speed, or even faster in some instances (for example, doing two-ball drills or using a toss-back device).

Understand that improvement is a three-step process:

- Proper conditioning *allows*
- effective practice, *which leads to*
- improved skills.

To improve their skills, players must practice effectively, and to practice effectively, they must be in shape. So the foundation of skill development is conditioning. Eliminate the "workout killers"—fatigue and boredom. Gradually condition your players and create a variety of drills that work on the same fundamental to avoid monotony.

Have a written workout plan each day. Know what it is your players want to accomplish. Work on these three areas every day: conditioning, dribbling and ball handling, and shooting.

Chart progress—players need to see that they're improving. They might make 12 shots on Monday and improve to 16 made shots on Thursday. They need to see a record of this improvement so that they're encouraged to keep up the hard work.

believe that what you want is what's best for their game. Here are five ways to promote players to buy into your system:

1. Thoroughly study the game. Your players should have no doubt that you know the game inside and out. Knowledge leads to respect.

2. Thoroughly study your system. Show your players that you know what it takes for them to improve within your system.

3. Catch them doing something right. If your players know that you believe in them, they'll be more likely to give their best effort.

4. Understand that it's not only what you know but what you bring to the workouts that will create a buy-in. Bring your energy, your enthusiasm, your work ethic, and your interest in the players—let them see this and feel this.

5. Tell players the truth. They might not like it, but they need to know where they stand and how they're doing. Tell them verbally, show them on video, and back up what you say with statistics. Communicate in a way that tells them you have their best interests in mind.

INCORPORATING WORKOUT MUSTS

Players must know what they need to consider when putting together their workouts. Along with the standard aspects of the game that they should always be working on (shooting, dribbling, conditioning, strength training, and so on), they should also include the following:

- Weak-hand development. Better opponents will make players use their weak hand, so all players need to be as effective as possible with either hand.

- Footwork and balance. They should focus on being balanced on every shot and every move. Footwork should be as efficient as it can be.

- Playing through contact. Players must be able to make a play, a move, and even a shot while the defender is applying contact. Use workout partners to give your players a true feel for real-game contact.

- Contesting shots. As much as coaches want players to take open shots, almost every shooter will have a defender coming at him and putting a hand up to contest the shot. Practice under game conditions and, again, tell workout partners to be aggressive with their defense.

SHOOTING: EVERY PLAYER'S FAVORITE WORKOUT

No matter what level of basketball you're involved in, your players will always want to practice shooting the ball. Shooting is by far the single-most practiced skill in the game. But it's up to coaches to make sure players are making the best use of their time while working on their shot. Here are seven keys to a quality shooting workout:

1. Incorporate catch-and-shoot shots (spot-ups).
2. Incorporate cut-catch-and-shoot shots (shots off the cut).
3. Incorporate shots off the dribble.
4. Focus on perfect form during shooting drills (perfect feet, perfect follow-though, and so on).
5. Contest all shots (get a hand in the face of the shooter).
6. Take game shots from game spots at game speed.
7. Chart makes and misses (players need to see their improvement).

COVERING THE BASICS

The majority of skill-development programs are geared toward offensive skills. While it is important to have a variety of drills in your coaching repertoire, it's imperative that you have some basic teaching points that are applicable to any drill you put your players through. Let's look at some key points to consider for each drill you use with your players.

Remember that basketball is a game of precision. Attend to every small detail. For example, if you involve picks in your shoot-ing drill, your players need to come off the screens tight, shoulder to shoulder. If they come wider, a defender will get through the pick. Again, if a player is beating his defender on a jab step, it is important that he go right past the defender in a straight line and not cut around him.

Use a "pound dribble" on any drill that requires dribbling. A pound dribble is a hard dribble that's pounded or pumped onto the floor. The harder and quicker the dribble, the more the ball is in the hand, and the more the ball is in the hand, the more the player can do with it.

Play the game low to high. Basketball is a game of centimeters and tenths of seconds. With players now so much quicker and longer than in the past, today's game should be played low to high—that is, every player should be down in a stance and ready for the next play. When shooting, they should have their knees bent and feet ready upon receiving the pass; once they have the ball, they move immediately into their shot, with no wasted time. They must be down and ready on the catch.

Keep in mind that basketball is a "shoulders game." To maximize quickness, explosion, and leverage, players must be aware of their shoulders: When using a screen, the cutter's shoulders should be below the level of the screeners' shoulders so that he's down and ready as he cuts off the screen. In the post, the offensive player wants his shoulders to be lower than his defender's for leverage and explosion; simply put, the lower player usually has the advantage. Think "shoulders–hips" when going by a defender. Get shoulders down to the level of the defender's hips.

Use feet first, ball second on all offensive moves. Both in the post and at the perimeter, the feet can give the offensive player the advantage. Get the footwork done first and then put the ball on the floor. When going by a defender on a jab-step move, get the foot past the defender's foot and then put the ball down. Use feet to gain advantage; use the ball to attain separation. Tell players, "It's a physical hand and forearm fight to get open (especially at the post), but it's a foot fight to score."

Find your feet on all shots. A critical part of any shot is the footwork. Often the quality of the footwork determines the quality of the shot. The shooter's feet should be the exact same on every shot, be it a spot-up shot; a shot off the cut; or a shot off the dribble. Tell shooters to "point 10 toes at the rim." Feet should always be squared up.

STUDYING THE GAME

Today's game has evolved to the point that players are much bigger, stronger, and quicker than they used to be. Not only are players more athletic, but they're also specializing at an earlier age than ever. Combined, these two facts mean it takes more than just what a player does on the court and in the weight room to become the player he wants to be. The most successful basketball players in the game have an incredible hunger to improve. They look

Layne Murdoch/NBAE/Getty Images Sport

Improvement in players who already possess abundant physical skills isn't always so apparent, but the great ones like Chris Paul keep adding to their knowledge, technique, and leadership skills to make not only themselves, but also their teams, better.

for every possible advantage they can find over their competition.

Watching games can be beneficial, but you have to watch actively, staying alert and focused. Study players to see what they do that makes them who they are. Consider the best thing to do on particular plays. When watching film of their own games, players need to be honest in their assessments of what they do well and what they need to improve on.

Along with games, have players watch video on whatever area they're trying to improve. Any time a new drill or a new teaching point can be found, it's well worth the cost. Players already know what they know; now they have to find out what they don't know. They should also read articles and talk to other players. A lot can be learned from reading what other players do, what they say, and how they think. Observe how good players develop their workouts: How long do they last? How many shots are taken per day? What dribbling drills do they do?

DEVELOPING CONSISTENCY AND MOTIVATION

Any coach prefers a self-motivated player over one who has to be pushed every second of every day. What must be understood is that even the great ones have down days, and that's when the coach steps in. Coaches can't take a day off from motivation. Motivation comes in many ways, including in your actions and what's in your locker room.

A coach has many eyes on him each day, including, of course, the eyes of his players. They are watching how you act, what you say, and what appears to be important to you. And whether they know it or not, they are in fact in a constant state of evaluation. This being the case, a good coach will take advantage of the influence he can exert.

When it comes to motivating your players, don't underestimate the benefit of the obvious. Sometimes something seems so obvious or self-evident that you don't think twice about it, but someone else might see it and think about it 100 times. For instance, consider the posters you put on the locker room walls. They're just posters, right? Well, not necessarily. A simple message at just the right time can make a world of difference to a player. I remember posters from my locker room. One read, "If your mother, father, teacher, or preacher saw what you did today, would you be proud?" Another said, "If an NBA coach saw you work out today, what would he think?" What posters might you post to influence your players? In what other small ways can you make a big difference?

In all your dealings with your players, be enthusiastic. You've heard it so many times, but it really works. Don't act bored when working with your players. If they sense you're just there to throw them passes during drills, they won't be fully engaged, either. Show your passion for the game and for teaching them the game; your passion should show in your eyes, in your voice, and in the way you move.

Improvement is a process that takes time, and not everyone is patient. Coaches know better than most people the importance of consistently working, and they must educate players on the importance of effective practicing day in and day out. The age of the player will dictate the number of practices per week, as well as the length of each workout. But some players, particularly young players who have been told time and again that they are gifted, don't fully appreciate the idea that no matter what their skill level, there's always room for improvement, and that improvement takes time. If you're a coach, always ask yourself what you can do to open a player's mind to improvement. For 10 different players, you might get 10 different answers.

Always be looking for ideas and opportunities for creating new drills. When you

Coaches involved in drills with players should approach the tasks with the same high level of enthusiasm and effort that we expect of the athletes.

watch games and observe your players' moves, look for things you could use in a drill. Being creative in your drills is important; keeping workouts fresh is crucial because today's players get bored more easily. Create fresh drills to mix in with the standard ones. Look for a variety of ways to work on the same fundamental.

Finally, cultivate relationships with your players that involve trust and mutual respect. You can't motivate anyone without trust. If players feel they can't trust you and if they think you don't have their

improvement in mind, your workouts won't be effective.

DRILLS FOR DEVELOPMENT

The drills in this section are meant both for use with your players and to stimulate your thinking to create drills of your own. You'll notice that three of the drills require chairs. The chairs have balls on them that players pick up before they shoot. We've found this helps players focus better and gets them down low as they come into their shots.

Warm-Up Drills

Circle Pass

Five players line up outside the three-point arc. Player A has a ball. Three other players are inside the three-point arc, including a corresponding player A, who's under the basket with a ball. Players B and D are at his left and right side. The drill starts when A inside the arc passes to B on his right, while A outside the arc passes to B on his right. The two As then sprint to exchange positions, and the drill continues (figure 19.1).

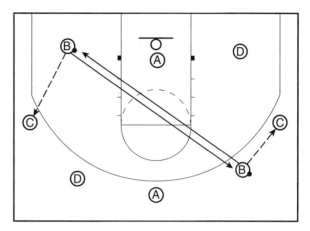

Figure 19.2 The circle pass drill: Players B pass to players C and then sprint to exchange positions with the player opposite them.

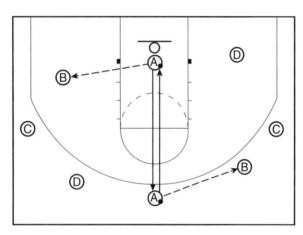

Figure 19.1 The circle pass drill: The A players pass to the B players (and so on) and then sprint to exchange positions.

The drill progresses with each player passing the ball to his right and then sprinting to exchange positions with his opposite player: B with B (figure 19.2), C with C, and D with D. Run the drill for a set number of passes or for a set amount of time.

Reverse, Replace, and Drive

Form a line of players on the left wing of the half-court, each with a ball. One player is in the middle of the half-court, and one is at the wing. The first player in line passes the ball to the player in the middle of the court, follows the pass, and replaces the player in the middle, who passes the ball to the wing and replaces the wing, who drives to the basket (figure 19.3). The drill continues for a set number of shots or for a set time and is then run on the opposite side.

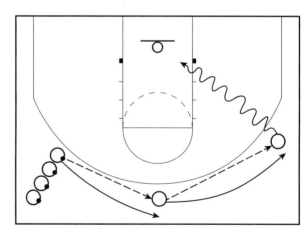

Figure 19.3 Reverse, replace, and drive drill.

Reverse, Replace, and Shoot

This drill is the same as the one just described, but now the player who receives the ball on the wing takes a jump shot. If these are warm-up drills, players take care of every detail of each fundamental involved in the drill, while the coach corrects every mistake.

Basic Drills

Over and Under

Two coaches each have a ball. One is outside the baseline; the other is in the central lane of the half-court. Two rebounders are in the lane. Two players—player 1 in the corner and player 2 on the wing—sprint and exchange positions, receive the ball from the coaches, and take a jump shot (figure 19.4). They repeat the routine for a set number of shots or for a set amount of time. Then they repeat the routine on the other side of the floor. The players work on their jump shots, simulating game situations.

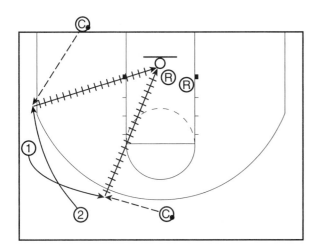

Figure 19.4 Over-and-under drill.

Flex

One coach with two balls stands in the middle of the half-court. One player is set up on the low-post spot. The player fakes a

cut into the lane and then comes high at the elbow, receives the ball from the coach, and shoots (figure 19.5). He then cuts into the lane and repeats the movement to receive the ball and shoot from the other elbow. Run the drill for a set number of shots or for a set time. Focus on precision of all details, from the fake of the cut to the jump shot.

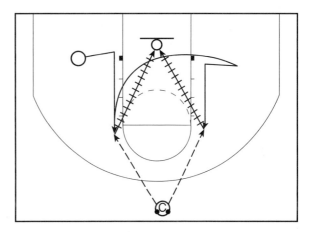

Figure 19.5 Flex drill.

Pin Down

The drill is similar to the one just described, but here the player starts outside the lane and can shoot from either inside or outside the three-point arc. Players simulate cutting off a pin-down screen, receiving the pass, and shooting (figure 19.6).

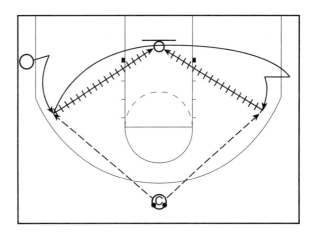

Figure 19.6 Pin-down drill.

Quick Square-Ups

A coach with the ball is outside the three-point arc, at the half-court line. A player is inside the arc, facing the coach. The coach passes the ball to the player, and, while the ball is in the air, yells "Right!" or "Left!" If the coach yells "Right!" the player pivots, squares up on his right foot, and shoots (figure 19.7). Run the drill for a set number of shots or for a set time. While pivoting and squaring up, the player stays low and then brings the ball up on the side between the shoulder and the chin (right for a righty, left for a lefty). The wrists of the shooting hand are bent back.

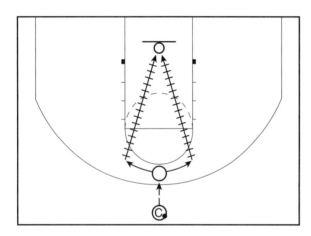

Figure 19.7   Quick square-ups drill.

Quick Square-Ups and Crossovers

The drill is similar to the one just described, but here the player, after squaring up, fakes a shot, makes a crossover dribble, and pulls up for a jump shot. Run the drill for a set number of shots or for a set time. Watch for players failing to make a true shot fake. During the crossover dribble, make sure the players sweep the ball quickly below the knees and make a lateral "pound" dribble so that the ball comes back up quickly to their hands.

Run the Line

A coach is under the basket with a ball; a player is at the left elbow. The coach passes the ball to the player, who takes a jump shot and then sprints to the other elbow (figure 19.8), repeating the routine for a set number of shots or for a set amount of time.

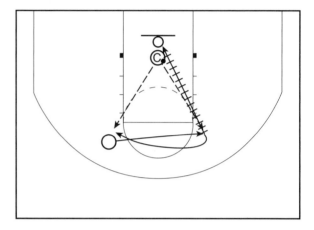

Figure 19.8   Run the line drill.

Chair Drills

Intensity Layup

Two chairs are set at the elbows, with one ball on each chair. A rebounder is under the basket. A player begins in the middle of the floor. The player cuts outside the chair on the right side, picks up the ball, and makes a layup. He then cuts out of the lane and around the other chair, picks up the ball, and makes a layup on the left side (figure 19.9). The goal is to make four layups in 15 seconds. The rebounder puts the balls back on the chairs.

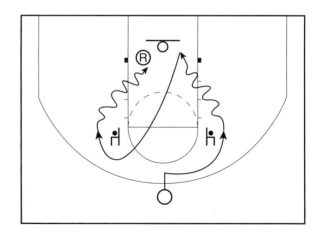

Figure 19.9   Intensity layup drill.

Elbow Jump Shot

This drill is the same as the one just described, but here the player fakes to go to the left side, then cuts to the right side of the chair, picks up the ball, squares up, and takes a jump shot (figure 19.10); he then continues the movement on the other side. Run the drill for a set number of shots or for a set time.

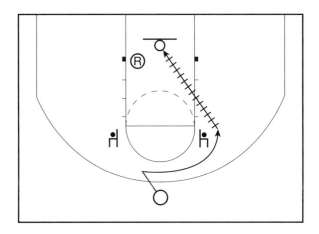

Figure 19.10   Elbow jump shot drill.

Reverse Elbow Pick-Up

The set is the same as just described, but here the player cuts to the right side of the chair, going past the chair, then stops, reverse pivots, comes off the other side of the chair, picks up the ball, and shoots (figure 19.11). He then continues the drill on the left side. Run the drill for a set number of shots or for a set time.

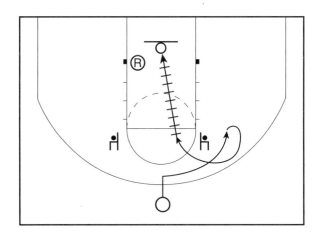

Figure 19.11   Reverse elbow pick-up drill.

Four Chairs

Two chairs are set up just inside the three-point arc near the baseline and two more just outside of the two elbows, with a ball on each chair and one rebounder in the lane. A player is set up at the low post. He starts to cut to chair 1, picks up the ball, squares to the basket, and shoots (figure 19.12a). He then repeats the routine at chair 2, chair 3 (figure 19.12b), and finally chair 4.

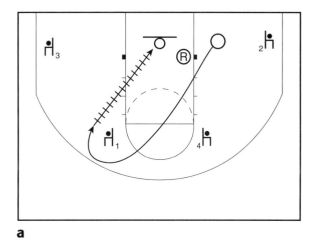

a

b

Figure 19.12   Four chairs drill.

Pin Down, Pull Up

Set up one chair (with a ball) on the wing and in the central lane of the half-court. Place a rebounder in the lane. A player is at the low-post position. He fakes to cut inside, then sprints to the chair on the wing spot, picks up the ball, squares up, and takes a jump shot; he then sprints to the midcourt line, touches the line with one foot, and sprints to the other chair, picks up the ball, squares up, and shoots another jumper (figure 19.13). Run the drill for a set number of shots or for a set time.

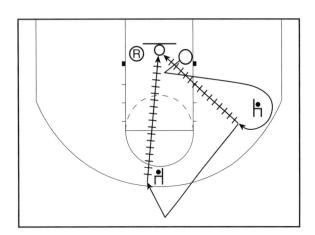

Figure 19.13 Pin-down, pull-up drill.

Dribble Intos

Three chairs are set up to form a tight tri-angle at the free-throw line; one reounder is in the lane. The player with the ball is outside the three-point arc; he dribbles fast into the chairs, makes a two-count stop under control, pulls up, and shoots a jump shot (figure 19.14). The drill can be run on either side of the half-court.

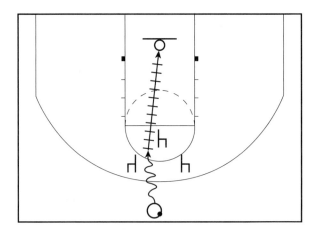

Figure 19.14 Dribble intos drill.

Cut Intos

Three chairs are set up just outside the left elbow. A coach stands outside the three-point arc with the ball. A rebounder is in the lane, with a player set opposite. The player fakes a cut to the basket and then cuts into the chairs, receives the ball from the coach, makes a two-count stop, and takes a jump shot (figure 19.15). He makes five shots and then repeats the routine on the other side of the court.

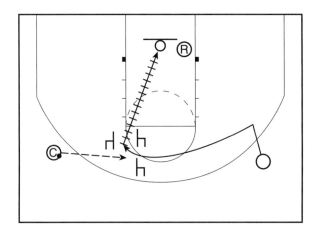

Figure 19.15 Cut intos drill.

Figure-8 Shooting

One chair is set up outside the right elbow and another near the baseline, inside the three-point arc. A ball is on each chair. A rebounder is in the lane. A player starts between the two chairs outside the three-point arc, cuts around the baseline chair, picks up the ball, squares up, and takes a jump shot (figure 19.16). He then loops over this chair, sprints to the other chair, picks up the ball, squares up, and takes another jumper. He continues this figure-8 movement for a set number of shots or for a set time before repeating the drill on the other side of the floor.

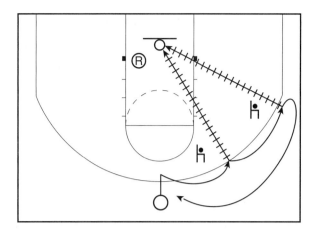

Figure 19.17   Flare screen shooting drill.

One-on-One Drills

One-on-One Baseline Touch (Perimeter Players)

Players 1 and 2 set up at the middle of the free-throw line; a coach is behind them with the ball. The coach yells "Go!" and the two players sprint to the baseline, touch it with one foot, and cut out to the wing area. The first player who gets out receives the ball and plays one on one against the other player until a basket is scored or the defender gets the ball (figure 19.18).

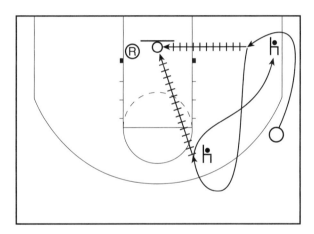

Figure 19.16   Figure-8 shooting drill.

Flare Screen Shooting

Set up two chairs on the right side of the court near the three-point arc, with one ball on each chair. A rebounder is in the lane. A player starts from the central lane of the half-court, cuts off an imaginary flare screen, picks up the ball, squares up, and takes a jump shot at the first chair. He then sprints to the other chair and shoots again (figure 19.17). He continues to repeat this movement for a set number of shots or for a set time before repeating the drill on the other side of the floor.

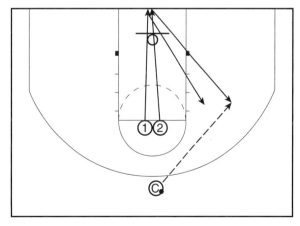

Figure 19.18   One-on-one baseline touch drill for perimeter players.

One-on-One Baseline Touch (Bigs)

Set up a chair in the middle of the lane with a ball on it. Two big men stand at the free-throw line (figure 19.19). The drill is the same as the one just described but this time run inside the lane.

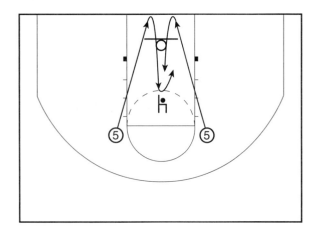

Figure 19.19 One-on-one baseline touch drill for the bigs.

One-on-One Half-Court Attack

Set up two chairs a few feet away from the midcourt line. One player with a ball stands on the corner near the baseline and the sideline, while a defender is near the lane. When the coach yells "Go!" the offensive player dribbles hard, curls around the chair in front of him, and attacks the rim. The defender runs around the other chair and tries to beat the offensive player to the inside spot. They play one on one until the offensive player scores a basket or the defender gets the ball (figure 19.20).

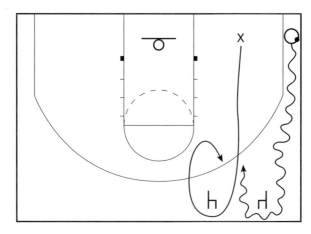

Figure 19.20 One-on-one half-court attack drill.

FINAL POINTS

The ball is in your court. As coaches, we must always remember that it's not about us—it's about the players. No matter what level of play you coach, your mission is the same: to help your players reach the top of their potential. Very few will become the next Kobe Bryant or LeBron James, but we want them to be able to say they received from their coaches all the technical and mental support they required as they worked toward being the best players they could be.

There are few things in life more satisfying for a coach than to see your players do something they felt they could never do—and then realize that you had a lot to do with it. That's just one of the many experiences that makes the coaching profession so rewarding.

chapter 20

Player and Coach Motivation

Scott Skiles and John Bach

Basketball is so much more than Xs and Os, flex offense, and matchup defense. It's also a mental game, a motivational game. The examples of the power of the mind in basketball are many. Think of the injured Willis Reed hobbling onto the court, willing himself to spur the Knicks to the 1970 NBA title. Recall an ill and weakened Michael Jordan's amazing 38-point performance in game 5 of the 1997 NBA finals that brought the Bulls to the doorstep of another championship. Remember a seemingly disheartened Dallas club overcoming a 24-point second-half deficit to edge Toronto in overtime in 2006. Such examples are numerous at every level of the game.

Of course, a negative psychological force can be just as damaging as a positive one can be inspiring. Prolonged shooting slumps, discord among coaches and players, injuries, and a host of other setbacks that we all experience in our careers can wreak havoc on an individual's psyche and prove disastrous for team spirit.

In this chapter we'll share our thoughts on player and coach motivation, as well as stories that highlight the importance of the mental side of basketball. By the time you've finished this section, you'll appreciate that the psychological aspects of the game are equally important as the techniques, tactics, and strategies.

MOTIVATING A TEAM

Self-motivation is expected, especially among professionals. After all, we were all apparently driven enough to excel at some aspect of the game, be it playing or coaching, or else we wouldn't be here. At our level, players and coaches should never suffer from a shortage of drive to compete and do their best.

Team motivation is another matter. Generating and maintaining team-wide motivation involves promoting enthusiasm and energy throughout your roster. This can be difficult, especially when a team is going through hard times, and many a coach has hung up his hat because he could no longer motivate his team to come together to play their best. A fellow coach once shared this advice: "If the game of basketball and the players in it excite you, then by all means, coach. But if it fails to excite you, do not coach." The coach has a responsibility to infuse in the team a love for the game. Your players should sense your excitement for the game from the first day on the court through the final game of the season. If along the way you lose your passion for the game, you also lose your team.

Strive to establish a rapport with your team as a whole as well as individual relationships with each player. One of our team's goals is to be excited by the work and the opportunity to contribute to the efforts of our squad. If we love our work, we will do our best, and day-to-day operations won't feel like work. The best teams achieve this viewpoint and apply themselves accordingly.

CULTIVATING A GAME OF HABITS

A team's excitement for the game and playing together cannot be faked or forced; it must come naturally from the heart. High achievement in basketball requires good habits and behaviors that players maintain after practice sessions. Such behaviors are often not in place initially—unless a player comes from a program whose coaches taught and exercised good habits. Good technical and social habits need to be established, as we'll discuss here.

Technical Habits

Walk into the locker room and on the blackboard write the word "Habit." Say to your players something like this: "You see this five-letter word? A habit is something that you repeat so often that it becomes automatic for you. You don't have to think about it. It becomes a part of your game, a part of your life. Notice that if I erase the H, 'a bit' remains. If I erase the A, we still have 'bit.' If I erase the B, 'it' is still with us. The point is that habits remain with you long after you have first established them—that's why they must be good habits. Because bad habits can stick with you just as long."

A basketball team must develop good habits—routines that allow them to establish and then maintain such fundamentals as footwork, passing, rebounding, and so on. Executing the fundamentals of the game automatically, habitually, or without having to think about them turns a group

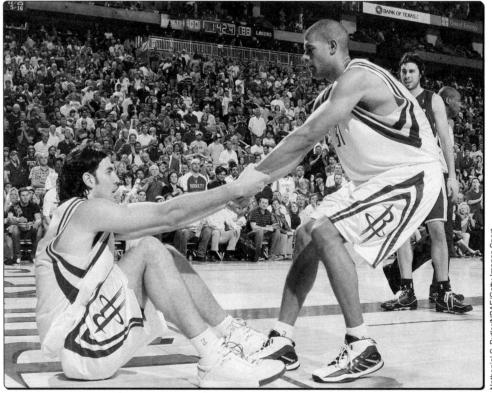

His combination of hustle, conduct, unselfishness, sportsmanship, and performance makes Shane Battier a tremendous asset to his team and the league.

of talented individuals into a winning team. A team doesn't win without good, solid practice habits. The fundamentals of our game are becoming a lost art as more and more players rely more on jumping and strength skills than on the basics of the game. But basketball is a game of finesse and forever will be, no matter how big and strong players become. Basketball is about a soft and accurate jump shot, a perfectly timed cut to the hoop, a precise pass kicked out to an open teammate just as he arrives at the three-point line. Our game is a game of details that must be practiced every day until they become habits. Such practice requires motivation. We believe one of the best ways to motivate players in practice is through competitive drills that work the fundamentals until they become habits, until they flow naturally from all players during a game. If you're a coach, you know what we're talking about. Those practices that begin so ugly, eventually, through continuous repetitions in drills, result in perfectly timed screens set at precisely the right angle, free throws and jumpers shot with delicate rotation, and would-be rebounders consistently and methodically blocked out from the basket. Over time, those once-ugly practices bring beauty to the basketball court.

Social Habits

In basketball or any team sport, one of the most important social habits is to be on time. Punctuality shows respect for teammates and the coaching staff. Require your players to arrive on time, focused and ready to practice. The practice can't be a good one if you start late. Starting late disrupts your carefully planned schedule and upsets the dynamics of the team.

Lack of punctuality can be a sign of other discipline problems. Don't let it happen. Maintain discipline. An undisciplined team might win some games here and there, but consistent success requires order, control, and restraint. Don't open the door to bad habits by letting your star player come late to practice. Next thing you know, he'll want to end early. Run your practices on time, with drills that lead into one another and start and end when you want them to. Orderly transitions from one phase of the practice to the next help develop discipline and good habits on the basketball court.

RUNNING DEMANDING PRACTICES

If you're a coach, you know that practice time is more important than game time. Practice is when you build your team. Good coaches don't accept mediocrity or bad habits, and they often address them immediately. When a coach says, "This is the third turnover. We can't go on making turnovers. Everyone get in line—we'll run a set of sprints." This makes players take notice, more notice than they would if the problem was just mentioned to them. Use running wisely in practices. A physical act like running, aside from being good for conditioning, can also bring a team together. Running your players might trigger them to think about the problem. They might decide, "The coach is right. We are making too many errors." So in that way, your team starts improving. If you had let them off easy, they would have learned nothing. The result of demanding practices is that a team comes together, and, coming together, they begin respecting themselves, the opponents, and the people around them.

Some coaches present a team motto every day in the locker room, and then during practice ask a player to recite the motto of the day. If the player doesn't know it, the whole team runs. Some coaches don't punish the player who didn't know the motto but instead have him stand next to them while everybody else runs. There are all kinds of ways to motivate. Figure out what works best for your team and don't let go of it. Be relentlessly demanding in practice, and your team will thank you later.

Randy Belice/NBAE/Getty Images Sport

Orchestrating hardworking, efficient, productive, and enthusiastic practice sessions will keep players attentive and motivated throughout the entire session.

LEARNING FROM GREAT MOTIVATORS

Look at examples of coaches who are great motivators. A coach who loves the game and exudes intensity in his verbal and body language is usually good at motivating players.

Phil Jackson is a great motivator. If his team did not speak on defense for one or two days, he called a "day of silence"—nobody was allowed to speak during drills. You can imagine the effect this had on the team. His players would wonder why, but he did not explain the reason—he expected them to understand why. Jackson is a coach who wants his players to grow; he doesn't jump on their backs every time-out or during every stop in practice because he's convinced that his players will never develop if he must constantly make every decision for them. In many time-outs he would ask his players, "What do you think will work?" He

threw the question out to the entire team, not just to his star players.

Another technique Jackson employed was to turn out the lights when the team was passing the ball very poorly. They practiced in the dark. There was enough light that they could see, but the players became very attentive at passing. He did not tell them why he turned the lights out; they figured it out on their own. He used some unusual methods, but always with a well-planned, clear objective because he knew what he wanted from his players—for them to grow as a team, not just as individuals.

TAILORING MOTIVATION TO THE PLAYERS

Coaches can read all the books they want to on motivation, but motivation must be part of you. As a coach, you always need to be asking yourself what motivates you. Can you express it? Can you show it? Can you bring it out of you? If you are lackluster on the court and in your daily operations with the team, burned down by the schedule or your team's standings, you can imagine the effect this will have on your team. It's easy to be motivational when you're winning, but even during the worst of times, you must find creative ways to motivate your players, ideas that suit the situation—sometimes a short practice, sometimes a longer practice, sometimes a team meeting in which players can air their dirty laundry, and sometimes very little talking or even no talking at all. Sometimes you need to try something unorthodox to jolt your team out of the doldrums or to give them a sense of a fresh start—even if you're in the midst of a losing season.

In any case, and at any level of the game, you need to take care of your players, recognizing that some players need a day off, others need attention, some need you to walk over and put an arm around them and say, "Good job." The great coaches in the NBA do that. They know they're dealing with people who are susceptible to the same feelings as anyone else. The pressure of playing in the spotlight can get to some players and affect how they play their game. Be sympathetic. One of the challenges of coaching is knowing when to be tough and when to be soft. Don't take the attitude that your players are grown men and don't need to be coddled. Often it's not coddling they need but simple respect and understanding.

I can tell you that the differences in NBA teams are not just the talent, but the people who have excitement, who submit themselves to the team, and ask themselves, "What can I do for the team?" Obviously, you can't direct your attention only to the team's top players. For instance, if role players don't accept their roles or aren't happy in them, it's your job to show them what they can do for the team and convince them of the value in doing it. You can motivate some players by encouraging them or giving them the opportunity to play, but sometimes you need to do more. You need to talk honestly, give them confidence in their role on the team. Let them know they contribute. You might say something like, "You'll be our backup center. You might not get the playing time you want or receive enough balls, but your role is important to our team. A team has to have a backup center."

Vince Lombardi, a legend in football but also a very good basketball coach, once said, "There are players on the team who do not have the experience and the responsibility of others, so I spend my time with the players who really need me." This illustrates a clear lesson: You need to give credit to the obscure players so they can feel big and important; they'll repay you through the effort they give in practice and during games.

ENFORCING RULES

Al Attles, who won an NBA title with Golden State, had a terrific view of the psyches of NBA players. He came from the playgrounds and the streets himself, and he also played in the NBA, so he knew how to deal with the problems of the players. There were very few things that were important to him and a lot of others that were not important, such as smaller details or minor rules. He used to say, "I have a few rules, not a 40-page rules handbook. I believe in having a few rules and absolutely living with these few rules, which must be punctuality, respect for the teammates and the coaching staff, accepting the responsibility that each player has in the team, and few others." He always had wonderful relationships with his teams.

Maybe you're a coach like Attles, who doesn't need a lot of rules, but you do need to enforce the rules that you have. You made the rules because you believe in them—so enforce them. If players don't follow the rules, you need to address that. You might fine your players, sit them out for a game or more, or require them to buy breakfast for their teammates, depending on your level of play and the severity of their infraction.

KEEPING REACTIONS UNDER CONTROL

Coaching requires a cool head. You don't want to overreact. You don't have to have a solution for everything, but you have to really see to observe, and you have to stay cool. You need to learn not to respond to everything. For instance, sometimes responding quickly to a loss can be detrimental to the team. Many coaches walk off the court at the end of a game, whether they have won or lost, played well or played poorly, and they say as few words as possible: "We'll see you tomorrow at practice, and we'll talk then." Be careful in showing your emotions after a game, especially when you're down on yourself or angry, because

Reading each player's mood and the situation and responding correctly will make player–coach interactions more positive on and off the court.

you run the risk of saying something that can negatively affect the team for days or even weeks to come. We recommend that coaches say very little after a game. Save it for the next day at practice.

A coach must be many people and do many things. He must be able to respect and adapt to different players' personalities. Some players like a pat on the back; others don't want to be touched. A coach needs to be flexible in his behavior and maintain balance for his team and for himself. If you've coached for at least a few seasons, you've probably learned about the role of balance in leadership—giving the team more of yourself without becoming exhausted and worrying too much.

We want to touch briefly on the subject of the coach–referee relationship. A referee might make some bad calls in a game, but a coach must always remember that the number of the referee's mistakes is far less than that of his players. The coach–referee relationship should be one of mutual respect. Don't be a bully. A team is a reflection of you as a coach, and while there's a time to stand and dispute a call or to discuss a situation of importance to your team, you can't constantly argue with the referees if you want your players to respect them. You must be in control and set an example for your players.

WORKING WITH ASSISTANT COACHES

Each member of the staff should bring different experiences and different perspectives. Look for assistant coaches who will be more than yes men. You want them to be loyal, but you also want them to make you think. Phil Jackson listens to every assistant coach, from the oldest to the youngest. During time-outs, he used to walk 20 feet away from the bench to give his assistants time to talk to the team. He constantly asked his assistants for input or advice on substitutions or what to do in certain situations. Then he made the final decision on what to do.

Eliot J. Schechter/Getty Images Sport

Noah Graham/NBAE/Getty Images Sport

Coaching staff interaction and respect are essential, not only during time-outs, but in every aspect of the job as well.

MOTIVATING DURING TIME-OUTS

Think of your time-outs not only as opportunities to share strategies or plays with your team but also as chances to motivate your players. Because time-outs are short, when it comes to instruction, you'll want to use few words to express a short and sharp message: "Go to the rebound. We need more rebounds. You've got to do better." Be terse and instructive without being negative or vitriolic. Now's not the time to be complicated. Players need to know what you want them to do and how you want them to do it. Keep it simple.

But along with clarifying your expectations for each player, take advantage of this short meeting to boost your players' confidence, to make them believe in themselves and their abilities to get the job done.

Remember that your players are likely tired, perhaps on an emotional verge. There might be 20,000 people or more watching. There's crowd noise, there's music, and there's unbelievable pressure. If you know your players as you should, you'll know what trigger to pull for each player to motivate him to block out all distractions and focus on his duties on the court.

In some cases, the coach might want to start the time-out away from the team. Phil Jackson would sometimes walk away from the bench to give players time to collect themselves and figure out what was going wrong on their own. You don't want to have the answer every time, or you'll have a team that totally depends on you and can't think for itself. Teams that look regularly to the bench for guidance tend to be weak teams. In some cases (though not always or even often), players have to help themselves.

They go out to the court, face their problems, and solve them.

All coaches I know motivate their players by subbing for them. Legendary coach Henry Iba once said, "There's one fundamental aspect of bench coaching that I use. I say to the player face to face, never behind his back, 'If you can't do the job, you'll be substituted.'" That sends a clear message; no one is going to dispute that the player who can do the job is the one who needs to be on the floor. When a player isn't working hard enough or is doing something fundamentally wrong, we have no problem pulling him out and telling him, "Sit down. Get yourself together. I'll give you a chance to go back in." Subbing is a stimulant for competitive players. They use it as self-motivation.

ACCEPTING THE BLAME

When a team wins, there's always enough credit for everyone. But when you lose, you as the head coach must take the blame. Don't ever explain a loss by saying, "My team did not play tonight." Instead say, "We were outplayed, and we're coming back on this floor tomorrow to do something about it." Step up for the team. Accept responsibility. Your players will reward you with loyalty and effort.

Members of the media are smart, and they love taking the opportunity to tell you everything that's wrong with you and your team. You need to accept this as part of the territory of being the head coach. Even when teams are surpassing all expectations, some people will find something to gripe about. You'll have to read it in the papers and hear it on the radio. And if you're losing, it never stops, and it comes from all directions. Think of coming to work each day knowing that you're going to hear from your boss, from the media, from the fans, and even from your friends, "What's wrong with your team? How are you going to turn it around?"

It's as if you haven't been asking yourself these questions every minute of every day. The amount of negative feedback you get when a team isn't meeting expectations, even while you recognize the progress being made by a group of players who are still learning to come together as a team (which takes time!), can be demoralizing for everyone involved. Look at these times as your opportunity to show people how strong you are. Instead of losing patience, smile, remain calm, and go about your business of making the team better. Don't let another loss tear you and your team apart. Take this attitude and share it with your players: "The game is over. Let's practice for tomorrow and work to avoid the mistakes we made today." Most teams are works in progress. It's very rare for a team to be clicking on all cylinders. When they are, of course you hear about it, and those are the teams that people notice and remember. But for every winning team or program, there's another team or program that's struggling, trying to get a little better each time out. There's no embarrassment in that.

FINAL POINTS

On these few pages we've shared with you some of the experiences during our coaching careers. We have coached some great players and been associated with great coaches, and we have always tried to learn something from them—not only from a technical perspective but from a motivational standpoint as well. Just like every team, every coach is a work in progress as he learns how to create and maintain good relationships.

If someone were to ask which is more important in basketball, the technical or the motivational, we would answer that it's about 50-50. Both are important at every level of the game, both in practice and during competition. We have seen many games won by teams with less talent but with greater motivation and mental toughness than their opponents.

In closing, we want to offer one last suggestion to coaches: Attend as many clinics as you want, watch practices and games to improve your basketball knowledge and to develop your own philosophy of play, but don't ever forget the human side of the game. Learning to understand your players psychologically so that you can recognize how to best motivate them on the court is as important to winning basketball as the Xs and Os. Basketball is a human game, played by people made of flesh and blood, and when we forget that and focus too much on the technical side of the game, we do our players a great disservice.

chapter 21

Modern Conditioning Methods

Rich Dalatri

There are many ways to train. If you're reading this book, however, I'll assume you're interested in my specialty—training specifically for basketball performance. To build a good base of strength and provide a solid foundation to build on, the work we recommend will start out high in volume and low in intensity. With weekly progress, we gradually lower the distance and increase the speed so that in the weeks just ahead of the competitive season, the training regimen is close to the competitive speed encountered on the court. All training should follow this principle.

Exercises progress from general movements over longer distances and time to more basketball-specific movements performed faster. In weight training, start with 10 to 15 repetitions with weights of 40 to 60 percent of maximum, and as the season nears, lower the reps and increase the weight being lifted. This basic principle might be adjusted depending on the strength level and experience of the player.

When working with someone just beginning a program, emphasize the basic movement skills of running, maneuvering, and lifting. In running, proper arm movement and stride length are especially important. In footwork and on-court movements, coordination is reflected in adjusting one's center of gravity effectively and starting and stopping properly. In weight training, lifts involving multiple muscle groups and total body movements are a good place to start.

HIGH-LEVEL COMPETITION CONDITIONING PROGRAM

The emphasis of this chapter is on players who play at a high level of competition. For these athletes, setting a good base is always a major part of the program. As I mentioned, they begin with longer, slower runs and with higher volume and less intensity in their lifting. The starting point is taken from their past performances in all areas. The starting point of any player's current program is higher than that of the last program he completed. The starting point of his next program will be higher than his current program.

We begin with warm-up and flexibility training and follow that with movement skill work and aerobic and anaerobic work. In running, we start with general running at slower interval times and longer distances. We progress to running with acceleration, stopping, and changing direction, and become more sport specific. Once we're sure the muscles are conditioned well enough, we add functional strength exercises, which are at a higher level of intensity and place more stress on the muscles.

Warm-Up

At the start of every good practice or workout is a good warm-up to prepare the body for the upcoming work. The warm-up raises the body's temperature from within

Nathaniel S. Butler/NBAE/Getty Images Sport

Not everyone can develop a physique like Dwight Howard's, but dedication and the proper conditioning plan will allow each player to achieve his athletic potential.

and increases blood flow to the working muscles. After a proper warm-up, the body can move more freely through all ranges of motions and movements. Your warm-up can be anything you choose, specific to basketball or otherwise, as long as you're working the muscles and joints you'll use in the workout.

We always do a basketball-type warm-up using the ball and movements we focus on in practice. An example of a warm-up drill we like to use is called X with the ball tossed ahead.

X With the Ball Tossed Ahead

A player starts in the corner of the court. He sprints to the free-throw line extended and closes out. He then slides on a diagonal to the pro-lane line and baseline. From there, he sprints to the elbow and then slides on a diagonal to the initial start corner. At this point, the coach (or the next player in line) tosses the ball ahead down the court, and he chases it down and dribbles to score a layup at the other end of the court (figure 21.1). From there, he repeats the routine to return to the original side of the court.

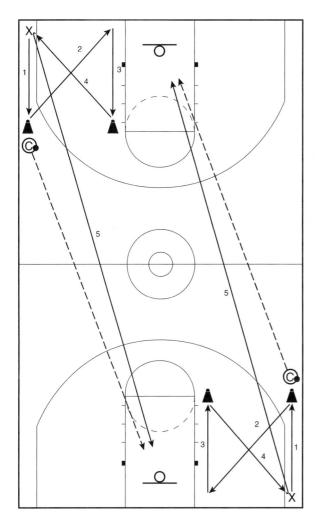

Figure 21.1 X with the ball tossed ahead drill.

Flexibility

Flexibility is a term used to define range of motion through a certain movement pattern. Flexibility helps all athletes in reducing risk of injury, both acute injury and that which occurs from overuse. Flexibility exercises are generally done as part of a warm-up routine. For athletes, flexibility workouts should be sport specific. Basketball players need to be able to move with ease in all directions and to change directions at top speed, so they require full-body flexibility with emphasis on the hips, back, and legs.

Movement Skills

When we think of movement in regard to basketball, we think of the first step—because no matter what you're doing, the first step puts you either ahead or behind.

Footwork exercises enhance foot-mind coordination and balance and make us more accustomed to moving our feet in all directions at a high rate of speed. These exercises are to be done at maximum speed for 6 to 10 seconds, before fatigue sets in and the body slows down. These exercises train the neuromuscular system to elicit a stronger, faster response.

We start with stationary exercises in which movements occur in only one plane, forward and backward or side to side. Use tape to make the lines on the court that you need for these drills.

Three-Line Drill

Refer to figure 21.2 for guidance on this drill. Players begin with both feet to one side of the lines. They put the inside foot in the first space, and then the second foot in the same space. Both feet go between each line, and the drill is completed when both feet are outside the third line. Player should not cross over and should move their feet as quickly as possible, going back and forth laterally.

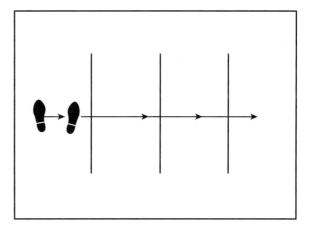

Figure 21.2 The three-line drill.

Line Slide With Change of Direction

See figure 21.3 for the configuration of this drill. Lines are straight and at 45 degrees. Players slide through the lines on the court, putting both feet in each space. At the 45-degree angle line, they pivot to turn around and face the opposite direction and continue without stopping. They should pick up the front foot as quickly as possible.

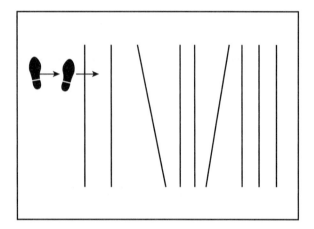

Figure 21.3 Line slide with change of direction drill.

Line Slide With Forward Step

Players slide through the lines, putting both feet in each space. When they come to a line that's in front of them, they step forward with both feet and then back into the square space, and continue without pausing to the rest of the lines (figure 21.4).

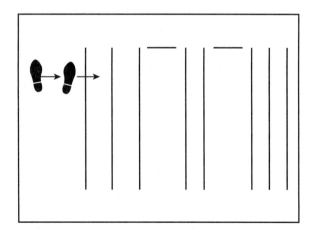

Figure 21.4 Line slide with forward step drill.

Now we can progress to movements in two or more planes and then to exercises in which players move through a predetermined sequence of movements, which in our case are movement patterns specific to basketball. These exercises can be done early in practice while the body is still fresh to ensure maximum speed of movement.

Through drills we can get the body accustomed to many of the situations we see in a game. Working on these movements with quality and intensity helps our neuromuscular system react and respond more easily in game situations. In the drills that follow we have mapped out movement patterns from basketball, taking them out of the game so we can work on them individually to improve them. We can then apply the improvements during play on the court. One example is help defense on the weak side.

Weak-Side Help

One player starts at the weak side of the basket. A player with a ball is on the other baseline, just inside the three-point line. When the player with the ball starts to dribble to the basket, the weak-side defender sprints to him, closes out, and forces him to make a decision. The offensive player now passes to another player or coach at the free-throw line. When the ball is swung to the top, the defender turns and sprints to close out on the coach or the player at the top. The offensive player now drives left or right, and the defender cuts off his penetration (figure 21.5).

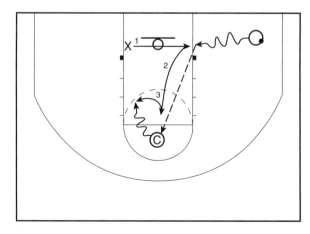

Figure 21.5 Weak-side help drill.

Aerobic and Anaerobic Work

To make the best use of their skills and play at the highest level, basketball players must be conditioned both anaerobically and aerobically. As mentioned earlier, we start our off-season with longer, slower distances in our workouts and week by week get shorter and faster, with specificity of movement also increased each week. As we near the competitive season, we are using the same muscles and energy systems in the same movements as we must use in our games.

Functional Strength

To gain functional strength for basketball, we choose exercises that replicate movements performed on the court but overload them for a certain number of repetitions. We then immediately follow with repetitions in an unloaded state, which replicates movements in basketball precisely. This method of overloading followed by unloading excites the neuromuscular system to a higher level.

In the overload segment, the muscles are put through movement that's more difficult than the normal task, so they must push harder and adapt to doing so. Then, during the unload, the muscles, after adapting to the overload, are preparing to push the same load they had pushed in the first few reps, but now without the overload, and as a consequence, they demonstrate a much greater force than they could generate during the previous reps. In fact, the force demonstrated now in the underload is greater than it would have been had the muscles not first experienced the overload.

The key to this type of training is to not fatigue the muscles too much with the loaded reps, so that when the muscles are unloaded, a strong and forceful repetition at higher speeds than the previous reps can be generated. Usually I use two to four loaded reps, followed by one to two unloaded. This is very high-quality work, and you don't want lactic acid buildup in the muscles to slow the actions down.

An example of this type of work as applied to basketball is to put a player under the basket with a medicine ball of 12 to 16 pounds (6 to 8 kg). The player with outstretched arms taps the backboard three to five times, jumping as fast and high as he can. After the last tap, the medicine ball is immediately replaced with a regular basketball, which is dunked or shot from under the basket as explosively as possible.

Another example is to put an elastic band around a player's waist. He starts at the elbow facing the basket with a ball. The player drives to the basket and dribbles against the resistance of the elastic, held by a teammate or a coach at the other end. He returns back to the start as quickly as possible and repeats this process twice. On the fourth repetition, the elastic is removed, and he drives to the basket at top speed and lays the ball in.

CONDITIONING WORKOUT

The conditioning workout load should depend on the level and expertise of your team. An experienced team can handle a longer, more difficult and taxing workout than a team that is at a low level.

Most of the conditioning we do is restricted to the confines of the basketball court. We use offensive, defensive, and transition situations to make up most of our conditioning drills. There are rare situations in which a circumstance, such as limited facilities at the basketball complex or a player's condition, such as a particular injury, requires us to work on a treadmill or a track or in a pool, but for the most part we condition on the court.

By conditioning on the court on which we play, we use the exact muscles in the exact speed and movements that we use for our sport. Even the smaller muscles of the legs and feet are worked by all the starting, stopping, and changing of directions that we do.

Also, by working on the court you eliminate the physical problems that can arise when a player trains on grass or on a track, such as shin splints, plantar fasciitis, and tendonitis.

By emphasizing skill work during conditioning, you bring a much more heightened level of concentration to the task. When a player starts to fatigue, he must really focus and push to complete the task at hand. At the same time, he is improving his conditioning. Mental toughness, which is a quality all coaches look for, is also developed in this kind of workout. The nature of the drills, combining skill with overloading the body past its comfort zone, measured by results of familiar aspects of the sport, is a way your players can see progress day to day.

Some conditioning drills we have used with success are a sprint, catch, and shoot drill and an offense-transition-defense sequence.

Sprint, Catch, and Shoot

This drill focuses on offensive skills. A player starts at the baseline. He sprints down the wing to a spot where he'll catch and shoot. After the shot, he turns and sprints to the other end and repeats. He then immediately sprints down the court to the wing, where he catches the ball, dribbles once or twice, and then pulls up and shoots. He does the same at the other end. The last sequence has the player sprinting, catching, and driving to the basket, where he either dunks or shoots a layup.

Offense-Transition-Defense Sequence

Here we try to simulate a game condition by using offensive and defensive movements and a transition in the same drill. The player starts at the baseline, sprints downcourt to receive a pass, and shoots from a random spot inside the three-point line. After the shot, he immediately sprints in transition to the other paint area, where he will do a defensive movement for 4 to 10 seconds. This movement can be as simple as lane slides or as complex as a help-and-recover defense. After this defensive movement, the player again sprints in transition to the other end, where he receives the ball and takes a shot with or without a dribble (figure 21.6).

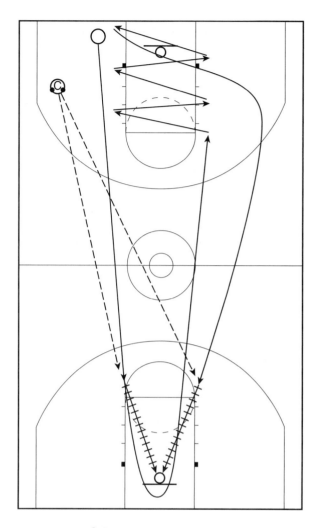

Figure 21.6   Offense-transition-defense sequence drill.

The offensive movements can be predetermined to replicate offensive moves in your offense, or they can just be random jump shots. The player continues this offense-transition-defense sequence for the prescribed amount of reps, usually four to six.

WEIGHT TRAINING

The last part of our program is weight training. When weight training with basketball players, we must keep in mind that we train with weights to help us in our sport. We are not weight lifters. We are basketball players lifting to become better basketball players. Too often I see coaches get way too carried away with weight lifting and actually hinder the performance of their players by making them less flexible and mobile or adding too much bulk without working to keep the players' movement and agility at a high level.

Your program must be balanced among its parts, and weight training should not be overemphasized. Basketball is predominately a sport of hips, back, and legs. Most movements—posting up, running, shooting, defending the post, rebounding, and maintaining a good stance—involve these parts. The upper body is always important for balance and is used to hold off opponents offensively and defensively, but for the most part, the rules of the game take a lot of upper body use away.

Strength Exercises

When we work the legs, we use a variety of exercises that we switch from workout to workout, including squats, step-ups, and split squats, which we'll describe here.

Squat

The player starts with feet in the same position he jumps from, with toes slightly pointed out. The bar rests on the shoulders at the base of the neck. The player's hands are close to the shoulders. Hands kept close will aid in keeping the shoulders, back, and chest out. Back is tight. From here, he lowers the body into a sitting position while always keeping the shoulders, back, and chest out, with the back tight. It's very important that he keep the heels on the ground and the knees in a position behind the feet. His shins should be in a vertical position. He rises back to the start position after a moment at the bottom position. He does not bounce at the bottom of the squat.

▶ *Coaching Point*

To help the player stay in a good power position with weight over his midfoot, he should widen his feet slightly and turn his toes a little more. To help keep his back straight, he can place a small disk under his heels or use a 2-×-4 piece of wood.

Step-Up

Holding dumbbells (or a bar on the shoulder), the player places one foot completely on a 24- to 30-inch (61-76 cm) box or a step. The other foot should be far enough back on the ground that he has to take a step similar to the length he takes when running. He keeps the back straight and the shoulders back on the way up and on the way down. He pushes off the back foot to start the motion and continues by pushing the body upward, driving the knee high as in a layup (figure 21.7). When up, he places the other foot on the box also. Then he descends by letting the leg go up through a full negative repetition, which means he must go down to the floor in complete control of the body.

▶ *Coaching Point*

To add difficulty to the lift in the down position, the player could start the movement by raising up on his toes on the back foot. From here he steps up. In doing this, he eliminates all momentum and intensifies the work of the front leg.

Figure 21.7 Step-up.

Split Squat

The player starts by holding dumbbells (or a bar on the shoulders). For balance, he places one foot ahead of the other in a slightly staggered position, not in a straight line. The front foot is placed far enough ahead so that in the down position, the heel remains down and the knee stays behind the foot, with the shin in a vertical position. The back foot is placed on a 12-inch (30 cm) box with the leg slightly bent (figure 21.8). When descending, hips are pushed forward and the back leg is kept as straight as possible. He'll go down to a 90-degree angle with the front leg, then push back up to the starting position. The movement is done slowly and under control.

▶ Coaching Point

If it bothers the player's back foot to have it on the top of the box, he can place it at the edge so the toes are off and the ball of the foot rests on the corner of the box. He must keep the shoulders back while descending to help him keep the back straight and the hips forward.

Figure 21.8 Split squat.

Strength Exercise Program Progression

We start the early weeks with higher reps with lower weights and, as the program progresses, move to heavier weights with fewer repetitions. A program might progress as shown in table 21.1.

When we have a good base of strength, we superset our leg work with an explosive speed type of movement. For example, we'll do a set of squats, immediately followed by a set of box jumps (in which we jump up to a box and step down).

When doing this sequence, we load the body and muscular system with an overload of weight and perform the movement. Immediately after putting the weight down, we do the same movement with no overload, and the body explodes and elicits a much more forceful contraction because it has prepared to push the overload again. We do this with the other lifts for the legs as well.

Explosive Exercises

The explosive movement can be anything that simulates the lift you just did with the weight. Explosiveness is a major component in basketball. We work on it in most facets of our program. In the weight room, we do Olympic lifts to improve in this area.

Following are a few of the lifts we do. These are all total body movements generated by a strong explosive push and extension of the legs, hips, and lower back (the areas identified earlier as the most important in basketball). These all use the fast-twitch muscle fiber, which is key in the development of speed and explosiveness.

Clean

The player starts with the bar above the knees, holding the bar with the hands just outside the knees. Feet are shoulder-width apart, and the back is straight; the chest is out and the arms fully extended. From this position, he pulls the bar by extending the

Table 21.1   Sample Strength Workout Progression

Week	Sets × Reps	Percentage	Explosive reps	Percentage
1	3x10	60%	3x6	60%
2	4x10	65%	4x6	65%
3	4x8	70%	4x5	70%
4	4x6	75%	4x4	75%
5	5x6	77.5%	5x4	80%
6	5x5	80%	5x3	85%
7	6x5	82.5%	6x3	87.5%
8	6x3	85-87.5%	3x3, 3x2	85%, 90%
9	8,6,4,2,2	60,70,85,90,95	6,4,3,2,2	60,70,80,90
10	8,6,4,2,2	60,70,85,90,95	6,4,3,2,2	60,70,80,90

back, hips, knees, and ankles simultaneously. The bar is pulled in a straight line close to the body. When the body is fully extended, he continues the pull with the arms and shoulders. At the last moment of the pull, before the bar starts to descend, he dips under the bar by bending the knees and hips. At this moment, he also flips the wrists and pushes the elbows forward. He catches the bar at his shoulders and stands erect with the lift completed (figures 21.9a and b).

Figure 21.9   Clean.

▶ *Coaching Point*

He should drop as fast as he pulls. When he finishes the pull, he must drop immediately because the bar will begin to descend, and the slower the drop, the harder it is to finish the lift.

Snatch

The start is the same as for the clean (see figure 21.9a) From this position, he extends the body by extending the back, hips, legs, and ankles. When the body is fully extended, he begins the pull with the arms and shoulders. He'll pull the elbows high with the bar moving in a straight line close to the body. At the height of the pull, he drops under the bar, catching it overhead with arms extended and locked at the elbows. The bar should be caught lightly behind the line of the shoulders in a line even with the back of the head.

▶ *Coaching Point*

To get a good starting grip, he should place the fingers together at the midpoint of the bar. He lays the arms along the bar, flat against it. Where his elbows touch is where he should grip the bar. As he becomes more experienced, he can widen the grip.

Push Press

The player takes the bar from the rack at shoulder height. He holds the bar above the shoulder. From this position, he bends the knees and hips slightly. Now he pushes with the legs to get the bar moving. The bar goes up overhead by continuing the push with the arms and shoulders. As the bar goes past the chin, he tucks the chin to the chest so to not look up and lean back. By doing this, he'll avoid putting too much pressure on the lower back. The leg bend is just enough to get the bar started and moving upward (figures 21.10a and b). The push must be enough, but not too much, so the upper body does not work.

Figure 21.10 Push press.

▸ *Coaching Point*

The player rests the bar on the front deltoids by keeping the elbows high. If the bar isn't touching the shoulders as he pushes up, the bar will probably go down and then upward, slowing the movement.

Clean and Press

The player starts the lift by doing a clean (see figure 21.9 on p. 331). With the weights now at the shoulders, he bends the knees slightly and drives the weight upward to an arm-extended position, using the coordinated push from his whole body. As he pushes upward, he keeps his head in a neutral position and does not look upward. (Looking upward causes his shoulders to go back and his back to arch backward.) He lowers the weight under control to the shoulders and then back to the thighs.

▸ *Coaching Point*

At the end of the clean he must be balanced and under control before starting the press portion of the lift. On the dip for the press, he pushes the butt backward slightly to keep the weight over the center of gravity.

Developing the Upper Body

To develop the upper body, we'll do traditional lifts such as the bench press, incline press, and shoulder press, as well as other assisted lifts, such as lat pull-downs, rows, and rear deltoid work. We also do medicine ball throws, pull-ups, and band work to supplement the program.

In the weight program it's important to emphasize all three parts of the lift on all repetitions (concentric: way up; isometric: holding; eccentric: way down). Technique should always be stressed before weight is lifted to reduce risk of injury. We use dumbbells as much as we use the regular barbell. We do unilateral one-arm and -leg movements as well as bilateral movements using either arms or legs at the same time. Remember to vary the stimulus to the neuromuscular system.

Core Development

Core development is a part of the strength program that can't be omitted. The core includes the abdominals and obliques, which make up a girdle of muscle that anchors the body through the moves we make in basketball. The core of every movement changes because of angles and forces involved, but we try to train in many planes and movements to better prepare our bodies for the rigors of the sport.

Core Stability Circuit

The core stability circuit is a series of exercises that strengthen the core of the body by constantly changing the base of the posture and the position of the limbs. The key is to keep the body aligned as long and straight as possible throughout the sequence of exercises. Through the constant change of position, the player changes the center of the posture and strengthens all the surrounding muscles. Here are some exercises to perform for improving the strength of the core of the body.

Core Exercise 1

Lie facedown on the floor with the body extended as long as possible. Lay the forearms on the floor, under the shoulders. Raise up and support the weight on the forearms and toes with the body as straight as possible. Keep the hips at or above body level, but don't let them drop down to cause an arch in the back. It's better to have the hips up in a bridge position (figure 21.11). Hold this position for 3 to 10 seconds, then lower the knees to the floor to rest.

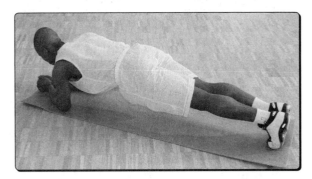

Figure 21.11 Core exercise 1.

Core Exercise 2

From the same starting position as in the previous exercise, raise one arm up and extend it to the side. After holding it out to the side for 3 to 5 seconds, extend the same arm forward and hold for another 3 to 5 seconds. Repeat with the other arm (figure 21.12). Keep the body level to the floor, not twisted to the side with the raised arm.

Figure 21.12   Core exercise 2.

Core Exercise 3

From the same starting position, raise one foot off the floor and hold it up with the leg straight for 3 to 5 seconds (figure 21.13). Repeat with the other leg. Keep the body level to the floor, not twisted to the side of the raised foot.

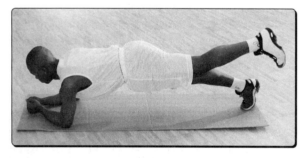

Figure 21.13   Core exercise 3.

Core Exercise 4

From the same starting position, raise one arm forward and the opposite foot off the floor. Hold for 3 to 5 seconds and then do the opposite side (figure 21.14). Try to keep the body as long and straight as possible. Don't allow the hips to drop below the level of the body. It's better to keep the hips slightly arched up.

Figure 21.14   Core exercise 4.

Core Exercise 5

Lie on the floor on one side with legs straight, one on top of the other, and the upper body leaning on the elbow. Place the elbow under the shoulder to give a strong base and protect the shoulder. From this position, raise hips off the floor and hold the body in a straight position, resting on the elbow and the side of the foot. Hold this position for 3 to 5 seconds, and then raise the upper leg about 6 to 12 inches (15-30 cm) and back three times (figures 21.15a and b). Repeat the two movements on the other side.

Figure 21.15   Core exercise 5.

Pilates Abdominal Circuit

Pilates is a form of conditioning that uses a stick or a machine called a reformer. Based on the research of Joseph Pilates, a German self-defense instructor who immigrated to the United States in the late 1920s, Pilates training is a way to accomplish much of our necessary core development. Each movement incorporates the player's whole body in synchronicity instead of concentrating on one precise muscle group. Although the core is the central part of each movement, the player is working it in conjunction with the rest of his body, as he would on the court.

Here we'll show only five of the several examples of Pilates exercises, which can be performed with or without the reformer machine. Perform 6 to 10 repetitions of each exercise.

Pilates Exercise 1

The player lies on his back with one leg up straight and the other one down. He holds the stick overhead, keeping arms straight. He raises the upper body and the arms; when the arms come up, he changes legs, and when the arms and upper body come down, he changes legs again (figure 21.16). Then he repeats the movement.

Figure 21.16   Pilates exercise 1.

Pilates Exercise 2

The player lies on his back with one knee bent to the chest and the other one straight and holds the stick overhead, keeping his arms straight. He raises the upper body and the arms, and when the arms come up, he pulls the other knee to the chest and extends the bent leg (figure 21.17). He then repeats in a continuous fashion. The legs are in a bicycle pumping motion.

Figure 21.17   Pilates exercise 2.

Pilates Exercise 3

The player lies on his back with legs 45 degrees from the floor and open. He holds the stick overhead, keeping arms straight. He raises the upper body; as the arms come up, he closes the legs; as the arms go down, he opens the legs (figure 21.18). He repeats in a continuous fashion.

Figure 21.18   Pilates exercise 3.

Pilates Exercise 4

The player lies on his back with legs 45 degrees from the floor with a basketball between the ankles. He holds the stick overhead, keeping arms straight. The legs remain in the same position, while the arms, always straight, come up and down (figure 21.19). He then repeats in a continuous fashion.

Figure 21.19   Pilates exercise 4.

Pilates Exercise 5

The exercise starts as the previous one, but now as the arms come up, the legs also raise about six inches (15 cm), and, as the arms come down, the legs lower to the starting position (figure 21.20). Repeat in a continuous fashion.

Figure 21.20   Pilates exercise 5.

PROGRAM DESIGN

When designing your program, map out each day, week, and month. Each part of the program must fit with the others. When setting up your program, first evaluate the level of each player. You can't go day by day without a real picture of where you want to be at the end of your workout period or, for that matter, how to get there. To map out the workouts is called periodization. You set up a workout schedule that contains heavy days, light days, and days off to recuperate. Varying the intensity and volume of your workouts is a must.

You can't do the same workouts day after day and expect to see long-range improvements. You would improve initially, as anyone would who starts a program, but after a period of time, you would level off and become stagnant, bored, and in many cases overfatigued. The initial development you saw won't increase, and in some cases performance becomes worse. The body needs a variety of stimuli to develop. Your neuromuscular system develops much better with stimuli from a variety of exercises at different intensities and volumes.

For example, in the off-season we use a four-day-per-week workout schedule: Monday, Tuesday, Thursday, and Friday. The total work of the week is broken down into four days of work, with a different workout each day. The work represents 100 percent of the work to be done for the week—we just do it over four days. The days are broken down as follows regarding the volume of work done on a particular day:

Monday: 32 percent
Tuesday: 22 percent
Thursday: 27 percent
Friday: 19 percent

As you see, we have heavy days, lighter days, and days off on Wednesday, Saturday, and Sunday. The body can't respond to a heavy workout every day. You need to back off or rest the day after a heavy workout if you plan to continue over time.

The body begins to recuperate on the lighter days (Tuesdays and Fridays) but is still being developed at a lesser intensity or volume. We follow the principle of periodization in most aspects of our workout (conditioning, weight training, movement drills, footwork drills, and functional strength).

FINAL POINTS

You want to use a sound strength and conditioning program that includes the following characteristics:

- Training drills and activities specific and functional for basketball

- Level of training that matches the physical maturity of players
- A variety of workouts and exercises
- Progression from longer and slower to shorter and faster
- High reps at lower intensity progressing to fewer reps at higher intensity
- Emphasis on speed and explosiveness
- Periodization of workouts
- Balance among all parts of the program

Conditioning is a major factor in a team's success over a long season. Implemented as described in this chapter, a training program is a big advantage for any basketball player or team.

Index

Note: The italicized *f* and *t* following page numbers refer to figures and tables, respectively.